COMMUNITY LIBRARY
3 2301 00105347 3
D1614049
3-10

# *Rods & Wings*

Bo Bennett

For Bob Marriott

I thank you for your help in my research for this story. I hope it reminds you of Alaska, the Great Lodge & the good times we shared.

Bo B[illegible]

# *Rods & Wings*

## A History of the Fishing Lodge Business in Bristol Bay, Alaska

Bo Bennett

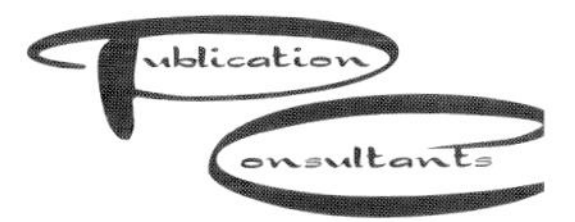


*PO Box 221974 Anchorage, Alaska 99522-1974*

ISBN 1-888125-62-4

Library of Congress Catalog Card Number: 99-067477


—First Edition—



Manufactured in the United States of America.

# Dedication

When I was about 10 years old, I didn't think my father was very smart. One day he said, "Son, there are a lot more horses' asses out there than there are horses." I can still remember trying to figure that one out. How could it be? I thought it must be a joke, but I really didn't understand. It wasn't too many years later that I discovered how smart my dad really was. Hell, he was a true prophet.

This book is dedicated to my father, Griffith W. (Red) Bennett, who loved hunting, fishing and flying. He took the time to teach me about the outdoors and gave me the direction to a life of adventure he could not follow. I learned way too late in my life how important my dad really was.

My father always wanted to go to Alaska. Although he was killed when I was sixteen, I still wish I could put him in one of Katmai Air's turbine-powered Cessna-207 floatplants and fly him to the places about which he always dreamed.

Rods and Wings is for all fathers, their daughters, and their sons.

*Griffith W. (Red) Bennett with a nice Washington State king salmon. Circa 1952—Bo Bennett Collection*

# *Alaska*

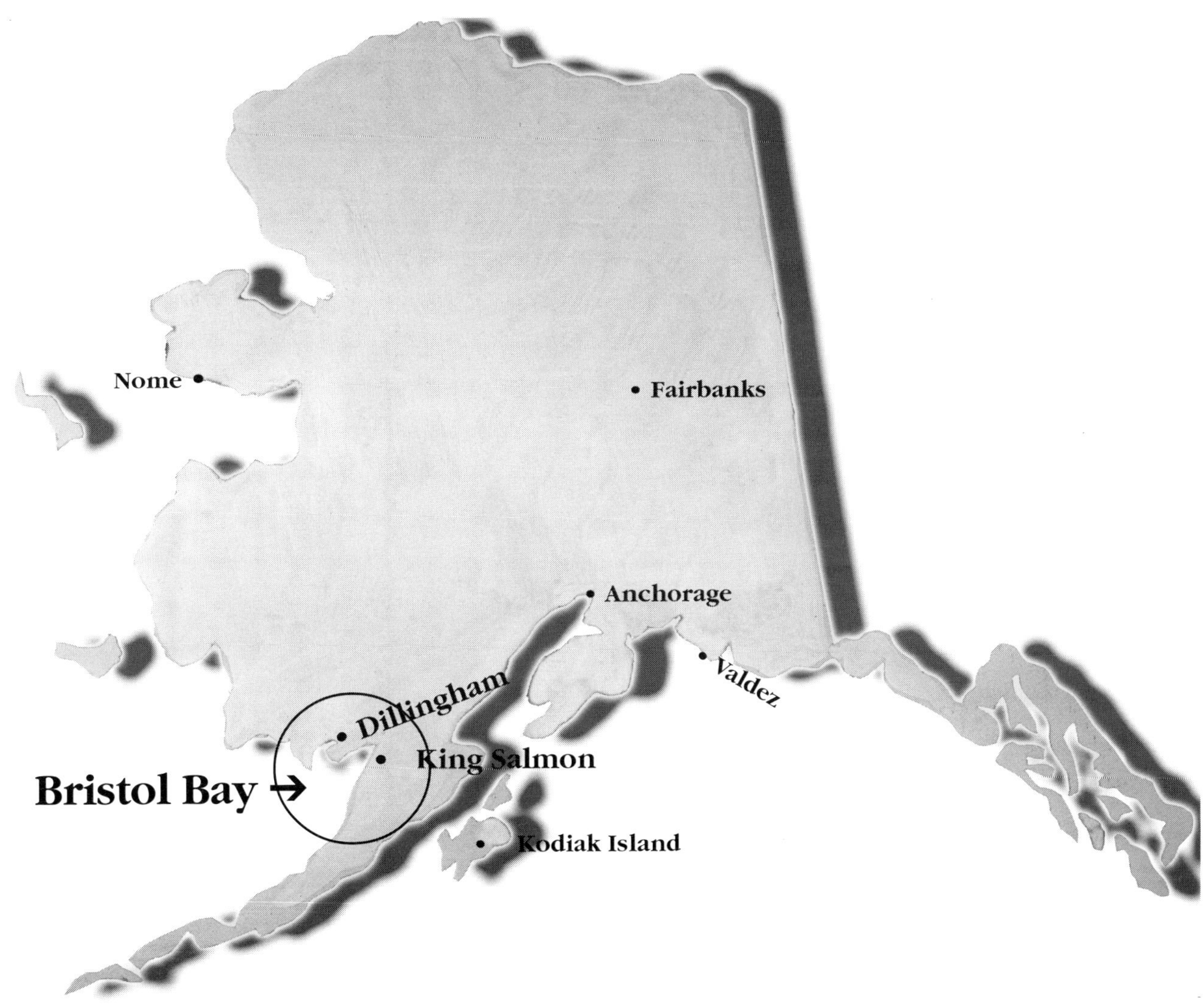


*Despite the fact that Alaska has a huge land area and contrary to public perception, fishing is not fabulous throughout the state. The Bristol Bay region is the world's best freshwater fishing—bar none.*

# Acknowledgments

This book is the culmination of more than six years of research and personal tribulation. While I had no concept of the monumental task I had undertaken when I started this project, pride would not let me quit, no matter how frustrated I became with computers and myself.

There is no way I can thank all those who helped develop my knowledge of the fishing industry and the great fishing lodges in Bristol Bay, but I can thank those who contributed directly to this work.

To: Judy Abbott, Steve Abel, Patty Able, Melissa Ackerman, Jim Albert, Gary Anderson, Dick Armstrong, Maurice Bertini, Dennis Branham, Chris and Linda Branham, Mike Branham, Gary Borger, Jim Broady, Trey Combs, Tim Cudney, Robert Curtis, Bob Cusack, Mike Cusack, Bob DeVito, Kirk Gay, Ted and Mary Gerken, Harry Gualco, Terry and Wendy Gunn, Daniel Gutierrez, Jay Hammond, Hugh Hartley, Van Hartley, Ron Hayes, Gayle Curtis-Hind, Jack and Sue Holman, Lefty Kreh, Ray Loesche, Bill Martin, Kip Minnery, Kay Mitsuyoshi, Jim Murphy, Deb Odom, Brian OKeefe, Lorane Owsichek, Al Perryman, Jerry Pippen, Walton Powell, Ed Rice, Tony Sarp, Ed Seiler, Dave Shuster, Hank Maves Skandura, Bill Sims, Dr. Tom Smith, Karl Storath, Charlie Summerville, Fred Walatka, Lani Waller, Doris Walker Porter, Dennis Woods, NPS historian John Branson, NPS historian Frank Norris, and artist Alan Robinson. I thank you—your help was greatly appreciated.

Gary Borger, in many ways my mentor, thank you for your kind words of encouragement and for providing the foreword to this book.

Bob Robb, who never let me waver from my task and who provided editing suggestions on a regular basis–thanks Bob, I owe you one!

Marianne Petersen, thanks for your dedication to detail.

Sonny Petersen, a great friend as well as an employer, thank you for all your help. One day we'll have the Louis XIII.

Mr. Raymond I. Petersen, whose demand for accuracy kept me questioning and whose patience was severely challenged by my questions—Ray, I'm proud to have met you. I'm proud to have worked for you, and even more proud to have worked with you.

# Table of Contents

# Foreword

Dawn comes early to a summer day in Alaska, but when it does arrive, I've already been up for an hour casting for silver salmon in the pool below camp. The fish are moving, their bow waves just visible in the shallows at the tail of the pool. The bright fly swings across the currents, its speed controlled by the frequent mends I'm adding to the line. And then just as the drill becomes monotonous, a salmon seizes the fly and dashes away, jarring me out of my self-imposed stupor. It's a bright fish, fresh from the sea, and I marvel at its strength. Released, it showers me with icy water—an appropriate baptism for this first-time angler to the large and desolate country of Alaska.

It's a lovely stream, this. One whose very appearance gladdens the heart of the fly-fisher. Not overpowering in its midcurrents, this wilderness stream has long, deep pools with plenty of holding water for trout and salmon. The bottom is a marvel of small and medium-sized gravels, perfect for the wading angler who is sometimes made careless by the urgency of reaching a good holding lie. Its cold waters strengthen the fishes and they fight as if possessed.

But though I fish these early morning hours and greet each new take with joy, my mind is distracted. For last night, my first in camp, as the moon crawled over the spruce trees to the east, I heard the hunting call of wolves. The flesh on my arms tingled and my scalp grew tight at the primal sound—this was their world that I had come to share in, and they had called to me. To that part that still understands the way of the hunter and the hunted. To that part that had come here to rediscover itself, and in their nighttime discourse, they made my trip complete before it began. For no matter what the remainder of the week should hold in terms of fishing, I will always remember this river as the place where the voice of wolves welcomed me by name.

What can I say, I'm overpowered, awestruck, beaten back, and not a little afraid of what lies before me. Roaring out of a jagged chasm of rock, this mighty Alaskan river crashes into an underwater shelf of bedrock, foaming and boiling upward in pressure waves four to six feet high. But in the dancing currents at the downstream lee of that shelf should be big rainbows. My fly is there now, searching in the hydraulic cushion close over the bottom. The take is unmistakable; the rod tip jerks down hard and the fish is immediately away and running.

It took me ten minutes of careful, adventuresome wading to get to this spot, and I dare not try to chase the fish. I'll have to stand my ground and depend upon the 150 yards of backing on the reel. As the spool continues to spin, I glance down; there are only a few turns of line left; I can see the metal of the spool's arbor. The final tug almost dislodges me from my precarious perch on the bedrock slab, and I can feel the now-free line swing down the currents.

As I reel the line back onto the spool, I wonder, "How big was it?" I've landed plenty of fish over ten pounds, and this one seemed much bigger. What was it? Though I'm here for rainbows, it may have been a big silver salmon. I'll never know. But neither will I ever forget. Not the mighty pull of the river, the coldness of its water, the texture of the tundra, the throb of the fish's take, the panicky yet somehow thrilling hypnotic feel as the backing came to the bitter end, The loss has sharpened my senses, and this moment will forever burn bright. This day, on this river, with its smells and sights and sounds will always be remembered, not for the many fish won, but for the one that got away.

The river comes from the hills strong and swift. It is met by low country that rises only a few feet above the Bering Sea and which offers no valleys to guide the water. Searching now this way and now that, the river loses its unity; here it becomes a river of a thousand tongues. And it is here in the braided currents that we've chosen to fish.

Wind, fresh in from the sea, pushes the rain against our faces and under the edges of a loose jacket hood; clouds rake across the land. But though the weather is harsh, the river has kept its promise and yields its fishes with arm-tiring frequency. Fingers made stiff by wind and rain fumble with the reel handle or drop a fly. No one complains. We are warm and dry, well fed, and doing what we have dreamed of.

On this day that speaks more of duck marshes than trout waters, we find the leopard rainbows native to the Far North. They're holding along the edges of gravel bars where the river slides over at a smooth, quick pace. A fluorescent-red egg fly possesses them. They come one after the other to the steel and yarn sham. Then, with an almost tireless strength, they twist the water about themselves, forcing the angler to struggle as much as they.

Here, in this wild place, surrounded by the indifferent elements, we are each caught up in thoughts about the river. At first as thin as the wind and as distant as our cares, it calls to us in plaintive tones. Then, as we strain to hear, it grows and crowds against our senses. It weaves a net around our hearts and minds as it sings to us. Sings to us as it has to men since time began. Like the ancient sirens of Ulysses, it calls to each in a different way, as if it knows our minds, as if it were a river of a thousand tongues.

We will take this song with us when we leave. To re-live these days we will only have to pause and look at the pale evening sky or smell the cleanness of the air after a storm. The river has found our heart of hearts.

Some day, I've promised myself, I'll come back. And after a shore lunch of salmon, I'll lie on a bar of river-sorted pebbles and look up at the clouds as they march in from their birthing place over an icy sea. I'll close my eyes and feel on my cheek the touch of the weak Arctic sun. I'll smell of the land; the pure, sweet air scented with the fragrance of willows and the musk of tundra. I'll open my hearing and dwell on the sounds; the raucous noise of quarrelsome gulls, the rasp of wind over the stones, the haunting pipe of the curlew. And then, as I drift into that quiet place just before sleep comes, I'll hear again the siren song of this river of a thousand tongues.

Alaska is a land that holds you once you've known it. Though perhaps misplaced on a busy day when the pressures of work hold all else at bay, it is never far from one's true self. In those quiet hours reading on the hearth or dressing next year's flies at the bench, it surges into being and crowds out all other thoughts, or perhaps augments grand memories of other lands and adventure. There is no place quite like the place we call Alaska.

Bo Bennett is part of my image of this vast land. He's a very skilled floatplane pilot who has ferried Jason and me into places where the only other footprints we saw were those with claws. As manager of Kulik Lodge (the first purely sportfishing lodge in Alaska) he has hosted us before a roaring fire with fine cuisine and sumptuous port. As a recounter of tales large and small, he has entertained and delighted us with knowledge of the fish, the animals, the land, the people, and the lodges of Alaska. He's the perfect host for a book on this larger-than-life and sometimes frontier land of the midnight sun.

He's spent time to pan the streams of history for the true gold of who done what when. As a result, *Rods & Wings* is a fun, witty, and accurate read of Bristol Bay's sportfishing, aviation, and political history. It will startle you in both its depth and breadth. If you've fished the waters of this land, you'll recognize your favorite places and read with interest how they evolved. If you've not sampled the piscine wares that Alaska offers, then you'll recognize those places you'd like to make your favorites. And in the process, you'll learn much about the whittling away at wild until a visit there becomes just another week away from home where hectic is the required pace and the fish are no more in numbers.

Read this book carefully; though it may seem like a bit of the frontier in places, look between the lines and under the words. It will entertain you, and I hope, provoke you to thought. It will make you salivate over fishing, and I hope, cry for what once was. But whatever emotions and thoughts it instills, it will change you. It will leave you with a truer, more realistic picture of the past and future potential of this incredible land.

*Gary Borger*

# Chapter 1
# Introduction

"It's hard to go full circle when you start with a triangle."
*Bo Bennett*

I'm in the fantasy business. Most adult men would gladly surrender some of their hard-earned riches and a pound or two of flesh just to get my job. In many ways they have a point. Mine may seem like the job of a lifetime, but this collection of wisdom isn't the place to point out the major downside of my work, the difficulty of maintaining a family life. Let's just say that so far I've had five wives, but none could comprehend, accept, or tolerate my priorities and lifestyle. I freely admit that the lodge family is my family. The guiding and outfitting business is my life. I learned to accept this style of existence (and the related drawbacks) many years ago during a brief but enlightening moment of reflection which, I'm sure, was caused by the consumption of way too much cheap whiskey. It may seem strange, but that day I suddenly realized that to succeed in the world, I needed to make myself happy. I just couldn't fit into the mold of someone else's expectations. I guess you could say I made that decision during the drinking phase of my life. Since then, I have cured my drinking problem; now I only drink when I'm alone or with someone else.

I know that a career in the stock market might have been more financially rewarding, but I don't really care. I thoroughly enjoy the chase. I call a fact a fact. I don't see many shades of gray, only black and white. I shoot to kill, and I play to win.

During Alaska's winter months, I travel extensively throughout our country and the world. I talk to hundreds of people about fishing in Alaska, specifically about the Angler's Paradise lodges at Kulik and Grosvenor. I tell them about the fish, the lodges, the scenic grandeur, and then help them imagine their wildest fishing dreams. During the Bristol Bay fishing season, June through early October, I help make their fantasies come true. I fly, I fish, and I enjoy hunting, although for the past few years my quarry has been fishing clients rather than trophy animals. Although being a pilot does have its ups and downs, I've had the opportunity to travel worldwide, meet some of the rich and famous, and most importantly, fish nearly all of the fabled waters. After all, someone has to do this job.

In my wanderings two truths seem paramount and are directly connected. The first undeniable truth is that the most productive freshwater fishing area in the world is that region of southwestern Alaska known as the Bristol Bay watershed. The area is huge and has a history rich with many characters and stories. I work and play in Bristol Bay by choice, not by necessity. Former Alaska fishing fanatic, prolific outdoor writer, and now Chilean lodge owner, Jim Repine, describes Bristol Bay better than most in his book, *Jim Repine's Alaska Fishing Adventures*:

> *It's the freshwater angling in a vast expanse of rivers, lakes, and streams called the Bristol Bay—Iliamna—Wood River—Tikchik Lake systems that make this the world's most famous and sought after freshwater sportfishing experience. Here you are talking about an expanse of territory encompassing as many square miles as New England. There are virtually no roads and the only practical way in is by floatplant ... . You see, in all the world this is the last place remaining where the quality of North American sportfishing is still close to the way it used to be....*

*The way it used to be.* I believe that to be an intriguing, even romantic notion. The thought of being the first to ever cast into an unknown body of water is bewitching, almost awe-inspiring for today's angler. Very few ever get the chance, especially since fishing has become so popular. I've had that distinction and honor only once in my lifetime of fishing, and that was in the 1980s. I was fortunate enough to be hired as a pilot-guide at a lodge in South America. I flew one of the few float-equipped airplanes in southern South America, and the only one in Chile. Upon my arrival at the lodge, the man who signed my paychecks told me that I had a mere twenty-one days to learn the area before the first clients arrived. For the next three weeks, local fishing guide Arturo Retlich and I put more than fifty flight hours on a float-equipped Cessna 206 with the goal of finding exceptional fishing destinations. We burned a lot of gas, tried a myriad of promising pools, and even caught some fish. Because of a total lack of floatplanes in the area and the difficulty and distance encountered in walking or horseback riding into most of the lakes and rivers in the Chilean Andes, I'm absolutely positive that Arturo and I fished where no other human had previously cast. Indeed, some of the lakes and rivers I tried didn't appear on the most up-to-date maps. Every night I studied those less than accurate government charts and planned each fishing day with meticulous detail. Some places were great, some were not; but I never found fishing to match the quality and quantity of Alaska's Bristol Bay region.

While I know the earliest Alaska sport fishermen carefully planned their fishing ventures, I am convinced that the immense size of Alaska coupled with its less than predictable weather contributed more to the discovery of the great fishing hot spots than all the planning and peering at questionable maps. It's happened to me more than once. I've discovered some excellent fishing because of bad flying weather. I start the day with a super destination in mind, only to find miserable weather trying to get there. As the weather worsens, the smart pilot quickly substitutes an alternate fishing destination while he waits for improved flying conditions. Sometimes the weather changes so fast that an immediate landing is the only option. In those rare cases, you land, have some coffee and hope there is some place to cast. Occasionally, Lady Luck smiles and you look like an expert.

I remember a Kodiak Island flight I made years ago. I was scheduled to fly three guys to Olga Bay. They had booked a guided bear hunt with the famous guides, Bill Pinnell and Morris Tolifson. When they arrived at the Kodiak Western Airlines office, they had a huge mound of gear that included an excellent supply of fly-fishing equipment. I loaded 734TQ, an amphib C-206, then checked the weather reports. I learned that the weather had been steadily deteriorating along the eastern side of the island. Just before departure, I checked with the chief pilot, Frank Humphreys. He looked over the recent weather and pilot reports and suggested that I fly down the west side and cut across the island at Frazier Lake. Frank had plenty of flying experience on Kodiak Island and I trusted his judgement. I took on a little extra fuel, loaded the hunters, and turned west after lumbering down the runway and easing into the sky.

Although it was raining when we left, the weather was fine for Kodiak. Conditions worsened by the time I reached Connecticut Creek at the top end of Frazier Lake. Low clouds and drizzle dropped the visibility below two miles. I circled the creek and thought about landing, then decided to go on. I knew that if I could get to the outlet river, I'd make it to Olga Bay. The going got really tough by the middle of the long, narrow lake. I told my passengers that we were getting close to Olga Bay, but I wasn't sure if we were going to get past the end of the lake. What I didn't tell them was that I was already preparing to land short of our goal. I reduced my speed to about 80 mph and dropped 20 degrees of flaps. I flew low and slow down the lake keeping the shoreline off my left wing. The worse it got, the lower I flew. My passengers breathed a sigh of relief when I finally eased the airplane onto the fog-shrouded lake. Following the shoreline, I taxied about a mile down the lake to the outlet river in order to find a suitable place to park the float-equipped Cessna-206 out of the big rocks that lined the shore. After I had the airplane secured on one of the few sandy beaches along the entire lake, I told the guys that there was a Fish and Wildlife cabin with a radio not too far away. Rather than just sit in the airplane, I suggested that they break out their rods and fish until the fog lifted. I told them I'd walk to the cabin to let the Kodiak Western dispatcher know we were sitting tight, and hopefully get some new weather information. I really didn't expect them to catch anything, but at least they'd have something to do. It was a great-looking spot, but I had never seen anyone fishing there before.

I was gone about thirty minutes. By the time I got back to the airplane the fog was starting to lift, and my passengers were thrilled. They had five of the nicest rainbows I'd seen taken on Kodiak Island. After I inquired as to where they caught the fish, they all pointed to the deep pool in front of the airplane. Although we reloaded their gear and headed toward Olga Bay, I had the impression that they wanted to stay a little longer. I wasted little time in getting back to that same place myself. Fishing was fantastic. Exploring and trying to find new places takes time and there are no guarantees. Only once in a while do the fishing gods smile favorably.

*John Walatka with a beautiful rainbow just above the "rock-hole" at Talarik Creek. One of the most famous streams in Bristol Bay, Talarik Creek will always remain available to fishermen thanks to recent efforts by the State of Alaska and the Nature Conservancy. Circa 1965—Ray Petersen Collection*

Bristol Bay is the land of millions of spawning salmon; indeed, the world's largest runs. According to Alaska Department of Fish and Game statistics, the Kvichak and Naknek Rivers alone attract more than 19.3 million sockeye salmon annually. Being in Bristol Bay means wading the shallow, clear rivers and streams with beautiful gravel bottoms. This is the place where your less-than perfect-casts are watched by elegant bald eagles and a gallery of coastal brown bears. Bristol Bay is the land of floatplanes and breathtaking scenery. Giant, vibrant rainbows can be followed, and where the beautiful arches touch the water, you won't find a pot of gold but something more precious to the angler. Bristol Bay is the best place in the world to fish for large rainbow trout. When trout anglers dream, they conjure up visions of Bristol Bay.

The second of the undeniable truths learned during my career of wandering is that sportfishing in Bristol Bay developed because of the rainbow trout. I believe the rainbow is the ultimate freshwater sport fish. *Alaskan Fishing Adventures* author Jim Repine shows his admiration for the rainbow:

*The most popular freshwater sport fish in all the world is, without challenge, the rainbow. This gorgeous high-jump artist has been introduced and is treasured on nearly every continent, and sure epitomizes the highest quality of angling experience; but only a century or so ago this rose-striped trout was found only in the western United States from California north to about mid-way up into the then Russian territory of Alaska. Now they have found their way around the world because in my strongly biased opinion, they are the most beautiful and spirited fish that swim....*

*The last place on earth where a large, wild population of really huge rainbows exists is in Southcentral and western Alaska. Mind you, I'm not talking about steelhead, the rainbows that go to sea and return to their native freshwater streams to spawn. I'm referring here to fish that never taste salt nor travel very far from their home.*

Russell Annabel sums up my feelings about Bristol Bay and fishing for rainbows in his book, *Hunting and Fishing in Alaska*. In his chapter called "In The Rainbow Kingdom," he lends credence to the majesty of one of Alaska's most famous and popular streams. Remember that as you read this description, it was written in 1948, prior to the establishment of any fishing lodges:

*So now we moved downstream a few yards and cast out into the foot of the pool. A rising trout made a ring on the quiet water thirty feet out, and Tex promptly dropped a silver doctor on that spot. Nothing happened. He cast again over the place, letting the fly float down with the slow current. Something that looked like a chunk of dark driftwood slanted up from the bottom behind the fly. There was a dimple on the water; then the silver doctor vanished, and Tex's reel purred as several yards of line ran off. Tex hit the fish, and abruptly the pool exploded. The fish was a rainbow and there were about three feet of it. That's merely an estimate, though, for we never laid hands on the noble creature. He blasted himself high out of the water, and when he came down he fell on the leader and smacked it with his great fluke. That was that. Tex reeled in and gazed thoughtfully at the broken gut. After a*

*This 15 pound, 11 ounce Talarik Creek rainbow was taken by International Sportsmen's Exposition's founder, Ed Rice, during a stay at Kulik Lodge in the late 1970s. Don Swanson Photo*

*moment he got out his kit and took from it his favorite combination of fresh-water tackle—a length of ten-pound test leader and a nameless oversized fly of his own manufacture that resembles nothing so much as a full-fed Malay fruit bat.*

*We were on the bank of Tularik Creek, a tributary to Lake Iliamna, two hundred and fifty miles southwest of Anchorage. Iliamna, which drains into Bristol Bay, is one hundred miles long and thirty-five miles wide and lies in the heart of what certainly is one of the finest of all rainbow fishing regions. Nobody knows how large the rainbows grow there. Anglers discovered the race of giants only about ten years ago and were just beginning to explore the many creeks, rivers and lakes on the watershed when the late war interrupted them. It is an established fact, however, that thirty-inchers are common, and that a number of thirty-six-inchers have been taken. The Indians and white trappers state, moreover, that rainbows measuring forty inches have been taken here in salmon nets. I have never seen one of these forty-inch trout, but once I did see, on the beach near an Indian fish camp, a rainbow tail that measured eleven inches across. Tex and I have spent a good deal of time arguing about the probable length and weight of that trout, and our estimates always scare us. It simply isn't possible that a rainbow could be so large.*

*We chose Tularik for our first evening's fishing because it is ideal for fly-casting and is one of the most beautiful stretches of water in Alaska. In the June dusk the glassy pools were ringed and dimpled by feeding fish as far as we could see. A slow wind moaned through the grass and the dark spruces, and all about us the huge snow-crowned peaks loomed, bright with the last of the day's sunlight. The creek chuckled and purred musically over its rocky bed. Tularik is the Tena word for Rainbow, and it is a most appropriate name for this lovely creek. Anglers who have fished from the Maori Pool to Oregon's Rogue River and northward to Alaska's trout waters will tell you that for its size Tularik probably is unequaled anywhere as a rainbow stream. I don't, myself, see how it could be improved.*

*Everywhere we looked under the plane's wings there were lakes and streams, and as you watched them slide past, you wanted to land and try them out. This is some of the greatest fish country we have left. It is vacation country. It is country every freshwater angler should visit.*

History reveals that sportfishing in Bristol Bay began with rainbow trout, followed later by grayling, arctic char, northern pike, lake trout, sheefish, and all the salmon species. Robert F. Griggs was the leader of five expeditions sponsored by the National Geographic Society to study the volcanic eruption near Mount Katmai in 1912. On their first excursion, Griggs and his party left Kodiak by boat and climbed into the Katmai region over what was left of Katmai Pass. This was an arduous undertaking, to say the least. The tremendous logistical difficulties encountered in their trekking make me understand why they didn't take a plethora of fishing equipment. As far as I can tell, these scientists were the first to sport fish the region. Although no specific fishing location references are given, I'm quite certain they fished many of the places we fish today including Margot Creek and the Brooks River. This short but highly important description of fishing in the Katmai country comes from the book, *The*

*Valley of Ten Thousand Smokes*, published by the National Geographical Society in 1922. This is the first written record of sportfishing in Bristol Bay.

> *The fishing in these lakes and rivers makes the region an angler's paradise. Their waters are alive with giant rainbow trout, with such voracious appetites that the angler never need cast more than once or twice before he has a strike that keeps him busy .... There is no occasion for the varied artificial flies often necessary to lure the sophisticated fish of civilized streams. Our bait, a piece of bacon rind, was snapped up so quickly as to make it appear that anything white would have served equally well. The only trouble our fishermen experienced came from the great size and weight of the fish. They were so big that they soon broke all our tackle. The average fish measured two feet, while the largest—caught by Wallace—was fully 32 inches from head to tail. Probably expert anglers who read this will simply recognize in the damage to our tackle a confession of incompetence in the art. The success of such novices gives ample evidence as to the quality of the sport that awaits the skill of the expert.*

Although all five species of the Pacific salmon were eventually targeted, I discovered that few sportsmen traveled to Bristol Bay specifically to catch salmon during the early years of lodge operation. I asked Ray Petersen to explain why he put his Angler's Paradise Lodges (Brooks, Kulik, Battle, and Grosvenor) where he did and not closer to the center of his flying business in Bethel. *Rainbows,* he replied, looking at me as if I had somehow lost my mind.

> *The sportsmen of the early years wanted to catch big rainbows. The great appeal of Bristol Bay was that we had those big rainbows not to be had in other areas of the world. We found the fishing was much better on the Katmai side of the Kvichak than over in the Tikchiks. We fished all the places enough to know. The char fishing was pretty good all over, but we wanted rainbows. We put the camps on the best rivers for rainbow trout. We looked for salmon spawning water that would draw the rainbows. We put the clients where the best fishing was at the time. Don't forget we had the whole damn country to choose from out there. The only place we couldn't put a lodge was at Kakhonak 'cause Bud [Branham] had a place over there. We didn't need to go that far. Hell, we had the best fishing for rainbows right in front of our camps!*

As a result of Ray's quest for the best rainbow fishing, he placed his camps on spawning water. Look closely at any map of the area south and east of the Kvichak River. At nearly every place with two lakes and a short salmon-spawning river connecting them, Ray put in a camp. This is the case at Brooks, Grosvenor, Battle and Kulik. When other lodges opened in subsequent years, those choice locations had already been selected. There is no doubt that the Angler's Paradise camps are in the best locations for the rainbow trout fishery.

I've been guiding and flying outdoor-oriented clients since 1975 in Canada, South America, Africa, and Alaska. I have worked for some of the most famous, as well as the most infamous, guides, lodges, and outfitters. Although outdoor clients worldwide express interest in their destinations, those traveling to Bristol Bay seem to ask more questions about lodge history than any others. Questions like who was the first to sport fish the Brooks River? Who built the cabin at Talarik Creek? Who pioneered the rainbow fishery on the Moraine River and king salmon fishing on the Alagnak River? How did the char get into the Kaguyak Crater? Who attended the first sport shows and when were the first films made? How was the fishing 50 years ago? When did all those lodges get started and who put them there?

At first, I responded to those questions with off-the-seat-of-my-pants comments that reflected my father's thoughts about horse anatomy. Interestingly enough though, the more information I acquired, the more questions developed in my own mind. I started asking those questions. Slowly, I began fitting all the pieces together. Being in the camps and lodges has given me a special opportunity to meet the players, see the places, and hear the stories. Believe me, I have heard some stories. Unfortunately, the more I learned, the more I realized I didn't know; but before I can actually address those specific questions and tell some of the stories that are printable, I need to take you back a few years and view Bristol Bay from my own first experience.

I flew to Alaska in August of 1966 to direct a big gymnastics clinic in Homer. I was chosen from a lengthy list of qualified gymnasts because I would work in exchange for hunting and fishing rather than cash. I was in Alaska for six weeks. At the end of the clinic, I was flown to the Bristol Bay region. I flew in a float airplane for the first time, had a great caribou hunt and caught some rainbows. Visibility was marginal on the return flight to Homer. We flew low over the most beautiful river I had ever seen. I kept looking at that river as we flew over Kulik Lake toward the mountains, but I didn't see the lodge buildings. I never forgot how much I wanted to fish that river.

I returned to Alaska a couple of years later with a commercial pilot's license and my own airplane. I was living in Kamloops, B.C. and had convinced one of my friends, Glenn Dreger, to accompany me on a 10-day Alaska hunt. I was flying a Maule M-4 Rocket, N5998M. After a great caribou hunt near Ugashik Lake, Glen and I loaded the airplane and headed for King Salmon. After fueling for Anchorage, I told Glenn that I wanted to stop at the river I'd described to him so many times before.

Unlike my previous glimpse of the Kulik River, this time the weather was great. The sky was clear and the wind was calm. My long wait to fish that river was almost over. Reducing power and dropping some flaps, I made two low circles over the river trying to spot some rainbows. The river was choked with sockeye salmon and we both knew the rainbows were waiting. Glenn and I were both getting excited. Before I lined up for the landing, he was trying to reach our rod tubes in the over stuffed cabin. I was concentrating on my pre-landing checklist when Glenn turned in his seat to look for his reel bag, and that's when he saw the buildings on the lakeshore. He was pointing to the right as he hollered, "What are those buildings over there?"

At the time I heard those words, I was on short final for the river mouth. A quick look was all it took. I added power for the go-around and yelled over the throaty roar of the big Franklin engine, "That's a lodge!" Disappointed beyond belief, I flew one more circle around the river and looked down at the most scenic lodge setting imaginable. Again my desires to fish that river were crushed. Somehow, someday, I just had to fish that river. I left the Kulik climbing northward. Later, I told Glenn why I decided not to land at the site of a fishing lodge. I knew it was private and we needed an invitation that only a few thousand dollars would bring. He nodded, knowing I had done the right thing. We could only dream.

In May of 1989, I went back to Kodiak to find a job after returning from Africa. When Dave Oberg asked me to fly his Uyak Air DHC-2 Beaver into Anchorage for completion of its annual inspection, I jumped at his offer. I had flown for Dave years before, but he'd already hired a pilot for the summer. Taking that Beaver to Anchorage would give me a chance to wander around Lake Hood to see if any lodges needed a pilot. After I made a few calls to let some lodge owners know I'd be in Anchorage, I fueled the airplane and headed north.

We had just pulled Dave's Beaver, N5354G, out of the water when one of Katmai Air's turbine-powered C-207s taxied in toward the Sea-Airmotive dock. When the pilot stepped out of the cockpit and onto the float, I recognized him to be Jeff Moody. I'd met him a few years before while I was flying at Jack Holman's No See Um Lodge.

*Hi, Bo. I haven't seen you since you had those girls out of their waders and fishing in their underwear over at Big River a couple years ago.*

Two mechanics standing nearby started paying more attention after Jeff's brief but colorful description. Jeff and I exchanged some small talk and then Jeff told me that his boss, Sonny Petersen, was looking for another pilot at Kulik Lodge. To make a short story even shorter, Sonny called later that evening. The following morning I headed back to Kodiak to get my fishing gear. A few days later I returned to Anchorage working for Katmai Air, pilot-guiding at Kulik Lodge. I was finally going to get my opportunity to fish the Kulik River. Although I didn't know it at the time, I was also going to learn the history of the Bristol Bay fishing lodge business from the man who was most influential in its creation, Mr. Raymond I. Petersen. I went to Kulik later that day and have returned every year since. It wasn't long after my arrival that I began wondering what it was like in the early days.

The earliest written word of sportfishing comes from Europe so long ago it's hardly worth considering. Lodges and inns catered to wealthy anglers in 15th-century Europe. As far as I can tell, one of the first fishing guide businesses in North America was operated out of a tavern in Philadelphia circa 1776. The first real North American fishing lodges began in upper New York State and off the east coast of Florida in the Bahamas during the early 1800s. Both had quite reasonable access. In Alaska, however, access was a major problem. Necessity forced the Alaskans to create the fly-out fishing lodge. This evolution seems natural when you consider the following statement by Merle Colby, an Alaska resident and author of *A Guide to Alaska*, published in 1941:

*Airplanes are very popular among anglers, since they permit a fishing party to leave town in the early morning, enjoy fishing in a lake or stream where perhaps no white man has ever fished before, and return the same evening.*

Colby continues with a comment that makes me wonder if he ever fished from an airplane, or at the very least, considered the physical ramifications to the pilot. I can guarantee that few of the pilots I know would consider straddling the propeller shaft anything but some form of punishment:

*Where the fishing grounds are so remote from civilization that there is no hunting lodge*

**FOR SPRING 1952**

**ALASKA!**

**HUNT GIANT KODIAK BEAR,** world's largest, take interesting movies and have some of the finest rainbow and other trout fishing in Alaska. We use a luxurious yacht to hunt the numerous bays, but also have fine camps in remote wilderness lake country. Take your wife along as a hunter or non-hunter. She'll enjoy every minute and be comfortable. Arrange **NOW** for one of our two week hunts in the Spring of 1952. Daily airplane service to Kodiak from any part of U.S.A. **WE FURNISH EVERYTHING.** For further information please write **AIR MAIL** or **WIRE**

**CHAS. MADSEN**

Guide & Outfitter, Box AG-905, Kodiak, Alaska

***BIG GAME HUNTING AND PHOTOGRAPHIC SAFARIS IN EAST AFRICA***

Safariland Ltd., is the oldest Safari Firm in East Africa. We have at your disposal modern and comfortable equipment, expert White Hunters and the wealth of nearly fifty years experience as Safari Organizers. Within four days of leaving New York you can be setting out into the heart of the African Game Country in our specially equipped safari trucks. Whether you wish to obtain good trophies or unique pictures we can arrange your trip with efficiency, courtesy, comfort and economy. Write to us for all details.

SAFARILAND LTD.

P.O. BOX 699, NAIROBI, KENYA, EAST AFRICA.

**ALASKA—and RAINY PASS LODGE means the world's finest in BIG GAME HUNTING AND SPORT FISHING.**

HUNT—Alaska Brown Bear (world's largest carnivore), Giant Moose, Stone Caribou, Dall Sheep, Grizzly and Black Bear. FISH—for Giant Rainbow, Salmon, Grayling, Dolly Varden. Trips by air only—all Guides are registered and pilots—strictly first-class equipment and lodges. Reservations only—references given and required. Now booking Spring Bear Hunting and Summer Sport Fishing. Write or wire,

RAINY PASS LODGE

Box 651 Anchorage, Alaska

**ALASKA**

**HUNT LARGE BROWN BEAR**

Alaska Peninsula in Spring

**MOOSE, CARIBOU, SHEEP, GRIZZLY BEAR**

Wood River Country in Fall

**CARL ANDERSON** **Lignite, Alaska**

Registered Guide & Outfitter

**ALASKA**

THE BEST IN BIG BROWN & GRIZZLY BEAR HUNTING, Spring or Fall. WHITE DALL SHEEP, CARIBOU, MOOSE. Every Hunt a Wilderness Expedition. 23 Years in the Big Game Fields of Alaska. Best of References.

LEE HANCOCK, Licensed Guide

Box 955 Anchorage, Alaska

*nearby, anglers sit on the pontoons of the plane and cast from there. To the pilot, as is fitting, is reserved the right to straddle the propeller shaft and fish from this honorable post.*

Before 1947, great transportation costs and the hardships endured just getting to Alaska necessitated that the earliest sport anglers be wealthy, powerful, and have a lot of time to spare. Continuing from *A Guide to Alaska*:

> *No regular scheduled passenger plane service was available in 1938 between the continental United States and Alaska. Three steamship companies provide transportation to Alaska from Seattle. A motor road to Alaska (the International Highway) already extends as far north as Hazelton, British Colombia, but will probably not be completed for some years to come. Living expenses for travelers, exclusive of transportation, range from $6 to $15 a day. In general, food is high, rooms are reasonable and travel is expensive. A typical round trip from Seattle to the Interior, taking about 19 days, costs about $250 for transportation and meals. Savings in money as well as in time may sometimes be made by air travel. Thus a trip requiring two weeks to make by water in summer or dog team in winter may frequently be made at no greater cost in four or five hours by plane.*

Fishing is no longer reserved for the wealthy. With today's ease in obtaining information and the growing use of the Internet, fishing information is only a mouse click away. Affordable air fares, lodge packages for nearly all budgets, and the great "catching" make Alaska one of the most popular fishing destinations on planet Earth. In the United States, only the state of Florida sells more nonresident fishing permits on a yearly basis, but when you factor in the seasonal nature of Alaska's fishing, even Florida has trouble matching the interest in the Great Land. Few other fishing destinations in the world have as many visiting anglers. More than 254,000 nonresident anglers plied Alaskan waters during 1998.

Considering those 254,000+ nonresidents who fished the 49th state, those who visited the remote lodges in Bristol Bay all had at least one similar experience. Not only did most of them board a commercial airliner to get to Alaska, but they also experienced flying in a float-equipped airplane. For many that come to Alaska to fish, airplanes make the experience both interesting and rewarding. Those who return often also learn that airplanes have become the backbone of the Bristol Bay lodges.

I believe that the entire angling world has changed because of the evolution of the Alaska-style fly-out fishing lodge. Improvements in angling equipment and technology have blossomed with the continued growth and popularity of the Bristol Bay fishing lodge community. Almost all of the movers and shakers of the sportfishing business, including nearly all of those self-declared fishing experts and gurus, have cut their teeth and sprouted their wings in Alaska. At the very least, most used the fishing boom in Alaska as a springboard for what little fame and fortune they have achieved in their other fishing ventures.

During the last five winter sport-show seasons, I spent considerable time in public libraries around the country perusing the more popular sporting magazines of the late 1940s and early 1950s. Compared with today's offerings, the obvious differences in price are noteworthy. As far as Alaska destinations are concerned, I found few advertisements for Alaska prior to the early 1950s. Although there were numerous other outdoor and adventure magazines published during the 1950s, *Outdoor Life* and *Field & Stream* were the major players. Several ads from Alaskans can be found on the opposite page.

In October 1986, the State of Alaska Historical Commission sponsored a symposium entitled *Fisheries in Alaska's Past*. Frank Norris, a noted Alaska historian and author, presented his paper *Sport Fishing in Early Alaska*. In his presentation, Mr. Norris clearly delineates the early history of the sportfishing business in Alaska:

> *Alaska's sport fishing industry (that is, the business of nonresidents coming to Alaska to fish came into its own during that two-decade period (prior to WW II), but its roots can be traced back a century or more. Four distinct traditions helped create Alaska sport fishing as we know it today: commercial fishing, tourism, fishing by residents and sport hunting. Sport fishing is an amalgam of the four traditions; it has drawn ideas from each as well as adopted patterns established in other states and territories. Sport fishermen came to Alaska as early as the 1860s. Some fished for food, others for enjoyment; both left notes of their experiences in magazines and journals. The first sport hunters came well before the Klondike excitement, but not until the gold rush period did many big game hunters decide to trek northward. Motivated by trophies and the lure of a long trek, sport hunters had little interest in fishing. They produced a spate of books and articles between 1890 and 1941, bearing such titles as "The Wilds Where Caribou Roam," "Hunting Big Game in Alaska," and "Bear Stalking on The Alaska Peninsula." Few authors, however, gave more than a passing glance to the fish they encountered. To them, catching fish in Alaska was simply too easy, and therefore, not worthy of sport.*
>
> *The sport fishing industry, like the tourist industry, was fairly localized, and there is little evidence that communities away from the sport fishing centers attracted many*

*nonresident anglers ... Appreciable numbers of fishermen from the United States started coming north in the early 1920s, and by the late thirties an industry catering to their needs was firmly established. Three factors appear to have been responsible for the industry's development: skillful marketing by Alaska boosters, the depleting opportunities for fishing elsewhere, and a transportation system that allowed easy access to many fishing spots. One of the first organizations to promote sport fishing was the Alaska Railroad. Its line was completed in July 1923, and soon afterward its management embarked on an extended campaign to "sell" Alaska. To attract fishermen, the railroad crowed about the advantages of the Kenai Peninsula's Russian River. By the early 1920s new roads and railroads had opened up many of Alaska's prime fishing areas, and sure enough, sport fishing enthusiasts began trickling northward. The Russian River-Kenai Lake rainbow fishery was particularly well known. Travelers into the region began their excursion at the Lawing railroad stop, where Nellie Lawing established a lodge in 1923.*

*This photo of a Star Airline fishing charter with a happy but unidentified angler was taken near Seversen's Roadhouse at Iliamna. Circa 1934—Ray Petersen Collection*

*Despite the improvements ushered in during the 1930s, some areas were not opened up to sport fishing. Near Lake Iliamna, for example, the Naknek Lake-Brooks River area was almost unknown before World War II. Although sport fishing mushroomed during the decades preceding World War II, few lodges resulted from the new influx. Nellie Lawing's resort, as has been noted, was the most visible. Fewer than a dozen sites existed elsewhere. Each was located along road or rail lines: each operated for brief periods during the 1920s.*

*In southeast Alaska, a major lodge was across from the Taku Glacier. Variously called the Twin Glacier Camp and Taku Lodge, it operated from 1923 to 1930 and from 1935 to 1942. Hot springs resorts also beckoned; Bell, Chena, Sitka and Tenakee Hot Springs all advertised the excellence of their fishing. Each resort, however, offered a number of other activities as well. The sport fishing industry, like the tourist industry, was fairly localized, and there is little evidence that communities away from the sport fishing centers attracted many nonresident anglers. Several hunting guides advertised fishing expeditions, and although some fishermen used guides, anglers were a minor part of the guide business. In the late twenties, a new era dawned when fishermen discovered the airplane. Pontoon flights revolutionized the sport...aircraft theoretically offered the angler access to any lake or cove in the territory. During the 1930s, however, most flights were limited to the Juneau, Ketchikan and Anchorage areas.*

Frank Norris was not the only one who studied the history of Bristol Bay. Fellow National Park Service historian John Branson filled me in on a few details of the early Alaskan hunting and fishing activities. He told me that Seversen's Roadhouse, originally built in 1913, was the first to host hunting clients in the Bristol Bay region. Records indicate that Seversen outfitted two prominent big game hunters in 1921.

*Ray Petersen shortly after his arrival in Alaska, 1934. Ray Petersen Colection*

Seversen outfitted the hunts, but the roadhouse certainly could not be considered a hunting lodge. In a later chapter you will learn that the first sport fishermen to come to Bristol Bay stayed at Seversen's Roadhouse in 1937, but hosting two fishermen does not qualify Seversen's home as a fishing lodge. Seversen's Roadhouse, like all the other roadhouses that grew up in Alaska with the increase in population and tourism, offered any and every activity they could sell, but they were essentially bed and breakfast establishments. There were not enough hunting and fishing clients to warrant full-time lodges as we know them today.

**Alaska**

300 miles of lakes and rivers. Fishing at its best

Rainbow—Spectacle Trout—Grayling
**and many others**

Let us book you a white whale hunt (a thrill of a lifetime)

licensed guide

Robert Rawls - Dillingham, Alaska

*An ad similar to this appeared in the January edition of* Field & Stream *in 1948.*

**Alaska - and Bud Branham's**

Rainy Pass Lodge

invite you to share ADVENTURE.

Now booking Spring Hunts for Alaska Brown Bear - World's Largest Carnivore. Summer fishing trips for Giant Rainbow - Grayling - Salmon. Exclusive - Personal Service - Safe. Dependable trips by air only. References gladly furnished

Wire or write

Bud Branham, Rainy Pass Lodge

**Box 651, Anchorage, Alaska**

*These Rainy Pass ads were found in* Field & Stream *beginning in 1952*

As interest in Alaska's hunting and fishing opportunities grew, more guides entered the business. While word of mouth helped spread their fame gradually, the more prosperous and eager guides started to pay for advertising, and their respective ads started to appear in major sporting publications. Hunting was not only popular, it dominated the guiding scene in Alaska. Hunting is what brought the majority of outdoor enthusiasts to Alaska. I found the following ads indicative of the guiding industry in early Alaska. As you review the advertisements (left), keep in mind that the hunt for the white whale was with a rifle—not a fly rod.

The evolution of the Alaska style sportfishing lodge and the resulting industry has taken time, and credit is due to the early guides and lodge pioneers such as Dennis Branham, Gren Collins, Don Horter, and Robert "Blackie" Rawls, Hans Seversen, and John Walatka. Others include Bob Curtis, Ward Gay, Bill Gurtler, Ron Hayes, Jay Hammond, Ray Loesche, Roger Maves, Bill Martin, and John Pearson. These men along with Bill Pinnell, Morris Tolifson, Red Clark, Lloyd Samsal, Ed Seiler, Bill Sims, and Bob Walker all helped acquaint the world with the splendor of Alaska's abundant fish and game.

When all is said and done, just two men stand tall at the beginning of the fishing lodge story. Although each faced unique circumstances and had different goals, both Bud Branham, the master hunting guide, and Ray Petersen, the airline tycoon, hosted fishing clients in permanent camps in the Bristol Bay watershed in 1950. Bud, who saw fishing as an extension of his hunting business, operated out of his hunting lodge at Rainy Pass. He knew well the guiding business and had an established client base of hunters. Bud built the first permanent lodge building in Bristol Bay at Kakhonak Falls during the summer of 1949; but according to his brother and partner, Dennis, he did not host any clients at that site until the summer of 1950. Bud used the fantastic fishing in Bristol Bay to augment his hunting business for a maximum of six weeks each year. Like most of the hunting guides that followed Bud's lead into the fishing lodge business in later years, Bud remained a professional hunter throughout his life.

Despite the fact that Bud Branham built the first building, I believe that the fishing lodge business that thrives in Alaska today is largely due to the commitment of Mr. Raymond I. Petersen. Ray first conceived the camp concept and then had the fortitude to modify his thoughts into a business. Add to this the fact that Ray didn't keep his success a secret, but rather encouraged others to follow his lead. Indeed, Ray did everything he could to encourage others to get into the business. Starting slowly at first, the number of lodges gradually swelled throughout Alaska. I believe that Ray Petersen was the guiding light to the development of the fishing lodge industry we have today. I'm not the only one who reached this conclusion. After Alaska State Senator Al Adams presented Ray's accomplishments to the Twentieth Alaska State Legislature, they officially declared Ray Petersen to be the **Father of Alaska's Sportfishing Lodges** on February 20, 1999. Ray Petersen and the Angler's Paradise Lodges that he developed are the beginning of the story in Bristol Bay.

Webster defines a lodge as:

*A small house, especially one for a servant, or one for use during a special season; as, a caretaker's lodge, a hunting lodge.*

For the purposes of this book, however, I'm going to use my own lodge definition which I crafted after consulting several of my more prestigious, eloquent, silver-tongued competitors, while imbibing numerous glasses of cheap red wine at the Villa Lounge in San Mateo, California. I'm sure Mr. Webster will be using it, too, after you call him and insist. He can use my definition for a small fee, just enough to buy a case or two of Kendall-Jackson's Grand Reserve Cabernet Sauvignon, rather than my customary screw-top brand.

An Alaskan Fishing Lodge according to Bo:

*A business run for profit from a fixed remote location, accessible only by airplane or boat, that provides lodging in a permanent structure, meals, and guided fishing. It must be promoted as a fishing lodge and fishing must be the major source of revenue. A lodge must have at least four guest beds, and must operate for at least twelve weeks a season. A lodge must also meet all guide registration and applicable licensing requirements established by state regulations.*

Now that I have alienated the hobbyists who are just trying for a tax-dodge, pissed off all those lodge folks with road access, offended the heirs of numerous hunting guides, and thoroughly annoyed all the guys offering float trips in tent camps, let's get to the story that is going to change your life, make you smile and excite you to the point that you can't wait to get out your checkbook to make a deposit on that trip of a lifetime. One thing for sure, you're not going to get any information in this book that isn't verified and certified. I can assure you that one of the facts I have always known but couldn't prove until this project is that there are lots of lying "sonsabitches" in Alaska. Having stated that, however, is Alaska any different than any other place when it comes to stretching the truth? Perhaps more than anything else, a lie is simply a variation of a truth. When you consider that Alaska is a land of variations, it's easier to accept the concept of stretching the truth.

Rather than make any comparisons to political figures and the concept of spin-

*The "Father of Alaska's Sportfishing Lodges" Ray Petersen with a Cessna T-50 Bamboo Bomber somewhere in Bristol Bay. Ray spent many hours fishing and flying the Katmai Country trying to locate the best locations for the Angler's Paradise Lodges. As a result of Ray's exhaustive search, his lodges at Battle, Brooks, Grosvenor, Kulik and Nonvianuk have offered clients the finest Bristol Bay fishing since 1950. Ray Petersen Collection*

# THE ALASKA LEGISLATURE

***HONORING***

***RAY PETERSEN***

***FATHER OF ALASKA'S SPORTFISHING LODGES***

The Twenty-first Alaska State Legislature is proud to recognize Ray Petersen as "the Father of the Alaska's Sportfishing Lodges".

In 1948, Alaska had no exclusive fishing lodges. As the founder of Ray Petersen Flying Service, Ray had many opportunities to visit the Katmai National Monument. (He started flying in Alaska in 1934.) Ray Petersen recognized the rich tourism potential that the region offered. He decided to combine his flourishing flying service, Northern Consolidated Airlines, with remote site fishing camps. In 1950, he built and opened five separate camps in the Katmai region of Bristol Bay, (Battle Camp, Nonvianuk Camp, Kulik Camp, Grosvenor Camp and Brooks Camp), all under the name of *Angler's Paradise Lodges*. He created a national marketing campaign promoting Western Alaska as a superb sportfishing destination. Ray's fishing camps were the first full-time fishing lodges in Alaska.

In subsequent years, Ray offered encouragement and support in developing other lodges in the Bristol Bay area. Today there are almost 80 sportfishing businesses in the Bristol Bay region and over 250 sport-fishing lodges statewide.

The Twenty-first Alaska State Legislature is proud to recognize Ray Petersen for his contributions to the development of sport fishing lodges as a viable entity in Alaskan tourism. They are delighted to proclaim him, "the Father of Alaska's Sportfishing Lodges", in recognition of his contributions.

Brian S. Porter
BRIAN PORTER
SPEAKER OF THE HOUSE

Drue Pearce
DRUE PEARCE
PRESIDENT OF THE SENATE

Date: February 24, 1999

Al Adams
AL ADAMS
PRIME SPONSOR

Cosponsors: Senators Pearce, Hoffman, Elton, Pete Kelly, Taylor, Tim Kelly, Halford, Green, Wilken, Mackie; Representatives Porter, Austerman, Berkowitz, Brice, Bunde,Cissna, Croft, Davis, Dyson, Green, Grussendorf, Halcro, Harris, Hudson, James, Joule, Kapsner, Kemplen, Kohring, Kott, Morgan, Mulder, Ogan, Phillips, Rokeberg, Sanders, Smalley, Williams doctoring, just let me say that Alaskans, even those nonresidents who only work in Alaska seasonally, are proud of the state and sometimes embellish the truth just a little for effect. Please consider the facts. Alaska is a massive state with a total land area of 586,400 square miles. Alaska is eighteen times bigger than the state of South Carolina, and 545 times the size of Rhode Island. It can truthfully be said that Alaska is twice the size of Texas with enough land left over to make twenty-five farms, each larger than the state of Delaware. I've also heard that after some Texans complained about those figures, Alaska's governor threatened to bring in the earth movers and flatten a few mountains and then divide the state into four new ones, making Texas number five.

*Jack Lemmon and his son Chris (on the left) with a fine Kulik rainbow. Ray Petersen Collection*

Alaska has more than 33,900 miles of ocean coastline, and that is more than the entire continental United States. With the exception of Vermont and Wyoming, Alaska has the smallest population. Alaska has few roads, and airplanes are used like taxicabs. After discussing the state with any ten first-time visitors, you will be told that Alaska is the coldest, hottest, driest, wettest, snowiest spot on the globe. Alaska farmers will tell you that their cabbages grow so large that it takes just five to make a dozen. In fact, cabbages weighing less than twenty-five pounds are usually sold as brussel sprouts. Are those lies or simply stories embellished just a little to emphasize the actual facts? Sometimes it takes an expert to decide.

Everything is big in Alaska, and this is even more important when it comes to fish and fishermen. I doubt that stretching the truth is unique to Alaska, but for some reason it just seems to happen more in the biggest state. I can also assure you that there are some instances where outright lies are told. As only one example, consider this. Jack Lemmon, the Oscar-winning actor, was a regular Kulik Lodge guest during the 1960s, '70s and '80s. I can't tell you how many times I was told "I fished with Jack," or "When I brought Jack to Alaska," or the best one, "When Jack Lemmon called me to ask where to go." More people made comments like that than fished the entire territory during those years. There just aren't enough guest beds in Bristol Bay to sleep all the guys who claim to be Jack's favorite fishing buddy.

It seems that whenever fishermen get together, stories about their Alaska fishing adventures are told that vastly exceed reality. Step into the halls of any major North American fishing show and you'll know what I mean. The enrichment factor does not belong to the clients alone; it permeates the minds of guides, pilots, and even some of the more colorful lodge owners. I know a few players who have told their enhanced versions so many times that they actually believe them. So many had the misplaced notion that they were the first to build, the first to explore, the first to catch, the first to pioneer, and the list goes on. Were these lies or exaggerations? Or were the players so misinformed that they actually didn't know that someone had done it before?

In a later chapter, I follow David Letterman's example and provide the list of ten important firsts in Bristol Bay that should both enlighten the casual reader and refresh the memory of a few of the players. Do all fishermen lie or are all liars fishermen? Others have pondered this lofty question. From *Three Men in a Boat* (1889) by British author Jerome K. Jerome:

> *Some people are under the impression that all that is required to make a good fisherman is the ability to tell lies easily and without blushing; but this is a mistake. Mere bald fabrication is useless. It is in the circumstantial detail, the embellishing touches of probability, the general air of scrupulous—almost pedantic—veracity, that the experienced angler is seen.*

Before we actually get to the lodges and the players, however, I believe a brief, yet somewhat enlightening smattering of Alaska's history is necessary. By reading the following chapter, you will get only a terse dissertation on geology, geography, and history. I believe it is important to learn about the Russians, the influence of commercial salmon fishing, gold, and Alaska's role in the history of flight. By doing so, I hope you will achieve an appreciation for Alaska's lodge pioneers and the difficulties they faced. Besides that, a little learning is good for the soul, or at least that is what the God-fearing types would have you believe. I personally disputed that fact with my fourth wife's preacher, but you'll have to read that story another time.

One reality to which I must confess is that I simply could not trace the entire history of each of Bristol Bay's great lodges, nor all the lodge players and their fantastic stories. To those lodges, players, and stories I have overlooked, I do apologize. I can only think of those immortal words spoken by my favorite TV character, Joe Friday, in nearly every episode of *Dragnet*: "Just the facts, ma'am, just the facts."

*The author with a client-caught char during the lodge season of 1983. Bo Bennett Collection*

I hope you enjoy my story of *Rods & Wings.*

# Chapter 2
# In the Beginning—40,000 B.C. to A.D. 1947

"Time flies when you're having a good time."
*Bo Bennett*

Alaska's history is a strange series of spurts, sputters, booms and busts. We've had more ups and downs than a new bride's pajamas. Today, the 49th state is considered to be a wilderness paradise with an endless source of raw materials. In the past, however, Alaska was regarded as a frozen wasteland continuously covered with ice and snow. Discovery of each new natural resource has been followed by a short period of prosperity and exploitation. In the beginning there were sea animal skins, then gold, salmon, logging, and most recently oil and tourism. After each resource was depleted, the territory's popularity plummeted until a new reason for prosperity was discovered. Boom and bust!

The earliest Alaskans migrated from Asia to North America some 40,000 years ago. According to accepted theory, the Ice Age caused a massive change in sea level. As the water dropped, a great land bridge rose from the sea that connected today's Siberia to that portion of North America known as Alaska. Centuries later, the climate changed again. The land bridge slowly disappeared under the rising sea.

No one really knows when, but the nomadic peoples from the Siberian side traveled eastward across the land bridge. They followed the animal herds that provided them with food and clothing. Researchers know these early nomadic travelers lived off the land and exploited the bounties of the sea. Catching, eating and preserving fish were vital to the survival of Alaska's earliest explorers.

The land bridge enabled numerous tribes to wander through Alaska. Most continued their travels southward. Some stayed in North America and others continued their sojourn toward Central and South America. Only five distinct ethnic groups remained in Alaska's vast wilderness. Rather than continuing south and east, the Athabascans, Aleuts, Inuit, Tlingits and Haidas ended their wandering ways and became Alaska's first permanent residents.

In the Bristol Bay region, the Ice Age ended about 12,000 years ago. As the glaciers inched their way back toward the mountains, the moving rivers of ice gouged and plowed huge depressions into the earth. These gigantic holes slowly filled with glacial melt water and rain. The moraine, a combination of dirt and gravel left by the retreating glaciers, dammed the rising water into enormous ponds which, over thousands of years, became the myriad of large lakes in the Bristol Bay drainage. So much for your lesson in anthropology and geology.

## The Russian Influence

Ivan Ivanovich (Vitus) Bering, a Danish navigator who left his homeland and joined the Imperial Russian Navy, made the first written record of the northern land. Bering sailed for the czar of Russia, Peter the Great. Despite the fact that neither Bering nor any of his sailors actually set foot on Alaskan soil during his voyage of 1728, Bering was the first explorer to report that America and Asia were separate continents.

Bering wasn't the only Russian interested in the landmass now called Alaska. Early explorers found strange and exotic forms of bark and driftwood along the coastline of Russian Kamchatka. This aroused their interest because there were few large trees to be found along their own beaches. Although the first exploratory voyages proved futile, curiosity intensified. Finding Alaska was difficult for the Russian boats due to the thick fog that often shrouded the Alaskan coastline. Many Russian explorers came close, but none produced any accurate mapping. Indeed, their earliest charts depicted Alaska as an island. Alaska was positively identified as part of the North American mainland by British explorer Captain Cook in the late 1770s.

In her book, *The Russian Population in Alaska and California*, author Svetlana G. Fedorova traces the history of the name Alaska:

> *Various unpublished reports and charts of Russian promyshlenniks (explorers) suggested the "wooded island" (Alakhshak) might be a cape; nevertheless, the government expedition of P.K. Krenitsyn and M.D. Levashov, (1764-1769), was sent to verify data showed "Aliaksa" as an island. The peninsula was first shown as the peninsula of "Alaska" on the chart compiled during the third voyage of the English explorer James Cook, who sailed the North Pacific in 1778-1779. On this map the islands Kad'iak, Shuiak and Marmot are joined with the peninsula, for Cook did not notice the strait (Shelikof Strait) which separated them from the mainland.*

I'm convinced that Captain Cook, like nearly all of his Russian predecessors, moved through the area during an extended period of nasty weather, including low visibility and thick coastal fog. Believe me, I've had difficulty identifying Shuyak and Marmot Island several times in similar weather. I had the advantage of being in an airplane and had accurate maps, too. Fedorova quotes Russian missionary I.E. Veniaminov and continues:

*The narrow part of northwestern America, protruding for several hundred versts (a verst is slightly longer than a kilometer) toward the southwest, is called Aliaska or Aliaksa, or in the Aleutian language Alakhskhak." Translated from the Aleutian, "A-la-as-ka" is "Great Land." At the end of the 18th century the Russians began to call not only the narrow peninsula "Aliaska," but the whole northwestern projection of the North American mainland. However, the name "Aliaska" as applied to the northwestern part of the North American mainland completely disappears from official documents after the formation of the Russian American Company in 1779 and is retained only as a geographical name for the narrow, saber-shaped peninsula, the name it bears to this day.*

Further comments on the origin of the name Alaska come from the *Dictionary of Alaska Place Names* by Donald J. Orth, Geological Survey Professional Paper of 1967.

*The name "Alaska" seems to have been gradually established by local use; vaguely applied at first to a supposed island, later found to be the Southwestern end of the Alaska Peninsula. The application of the name gradually developed from this beginning to include the whole area. The Russians officially designated it "Russian America" prior to the 1867 purchase by the United States. The name "Alaska" was proposed in 1867 for official acceptance by W. H. Seward, U.S. Secretary of State, the Honorable Charles Sumner, Senator and Chairman of the Committee on Foreign Relations, and by Maj. General W.H. Halleck, Commander of the Military Division of the Pacific. The name and its application to the State and the peninsula was well established in the late 1880s when W.H. Dall wrote: "This name, now applied to the whole of our territory, is a corruption, very far removed from the original word called by the natives Al-ak-shak or Al-ay-ek-sa. From Alayeksa the name became Alaksa, Alashka, Aliaska and finally Alaska."*

Thirteen years after his first successful Alaskan voyage, Bering commanded a pair of vessels into Alaskan waters. German botanist and physician Georg Steller became the official naturalist for Bering's historic mission. Steller was the first to describe the flora and fauna of the Russian New World. Among other creatures, he identified the Steller's jay, Steller's eider, the Steller's eagle and the rare Steller's white raven. Georg Steller also collected and classified numerous plant species previously unknown.

Bering's vessels sailed unhampered through Alaskan waters for months. Captain Commander Bering finally went ashore on an island near the present site of Cordova to become the first European to set foot in Alaska. Bering wanted to continue to explore the Alaska coastline but fear of rapidly approaching winter weather plagued his crewmen.

During the first of many violent storms, the two ships separated and lost visual contact. Both captains searched for each other. Bering and his crew experienced brutal weather and they feared the onslaught of even more severe storms. The weather wasn't Bering's only problem. Although he was unable to locate his second vessel, Bering knew that both ships were desperately short of fresh fruit and vegetables, and winter would exacerbate his problem.

Finally realizing that his pleading crew was right, Bering decided a little too late to try to return to Mother Russia. The weather worsened. In what was described as the storm from Hell, Bering's ship lost rudder control. Unable to steer and swept by fierce winds and massive currents, the *St. Peter* washed ashore at what is now Bering Island in present-day Russia.

Bering and his crew were stranded somewhere in the New World, but didn't know where. Survival became Bering's immediate order. The weaker men stayed aboard the beached and damaged vessel, while the healthier sailors went ashore and dug out fox dens, then covered them with driftwood and the rotted sails from the *St. Peter.* Their winter quarters were cold and damp, and provided little shelter from the bitter elements. Bering, near death, went ashore nine days after the ship foundered.

One of the major problems experienced by the sick, injured and weakening crew was the ferocity and cunning of the local fox population. According to Corey Ford's book, *Where the Sea Breaks Its Back*, the foxes had no fear of the men. They were so bold in fact, that no one was safe.

> *They preyed on the helpless and sick, tearing the clothes from them and chewing the leather soles of their boots. Even the well were molested. One night when a sailor on his knees wanted to urinate out of the door of the hut, a fox snapped at the exposed part and, in spite of his cries, did not soon want to let go. No one could relieve himself without a stick in his hand, and they immediately ate up the excrement as eagerly as pigs.*

Of the seventy-eight men aboard his ship, Vitus Bering, then nearly seventy years old, and thirty younger sailors died from scurvy during their forced stay on the barren island. Corey Ford reported that Bering had lost his will to live.

> *His bed was a little depression in the floor of his underground shelter, and the loose sand sifted between the uprights and trickled down the sides into the hollow. Bit by bit it covered his feet, then his legs and finally his thighs, until he lay half-buried like the hulk of the St. Peter. He died two hours before daylight on December eighth, and his body had to be exhumed in order to give him a decent burial.*

Lieutenant Alexei Ilich Chirikov, captain of Bering's second ship, the *St. Paul,* searched extensively for Bering and his crew. Chirikov sailed all the way to the present-day site of Sitka before he, too, turned toward Kamchatka. Fortunately for this crew, the captain avoided the murderous storms and returned the *St. Paul* to Mother Russia late that fall. Despite the hardships of their exploration, the survivors of these and other early voyages brought back lush furs and stories and tales about the vast fur seal and sea otter populations to be found in the new-world colony. Alaska's first boom was well under way.

Prior to Bering's fateful voyage, Gregor Shelikof, a merchant and fur trader, established the first permanent Russian settlement in Alaska at Three Saints Bay on Kodiak Island. Shelikof's vessels brought 192 explorers and trappers. These *promyshlenniks* also carried a good supply of firearms which gave the garrison great power over the indigenous people, and it wasn't long before the Russians enslaved them. After all, the promyshlenniks lived by the Russian proverb: *God is high and the czar is far away.*

The Russian fur traders wasted little time in overrunning the Aleutian Islands and quickly established five new settlements on Kodiak Island. These settlements had a population estimated at more than 2,600. Across Shelikof Strait along the Alaska

Peninsula, nearly 850 promyshlenniks, colonists, and Aleuts lived in Katmai Village. The local hunters routinely traveled between Katmai Village and Kodiak Island with their open canoes. This 20-mile stretch of open ocean is considered to be among the most treacherous waters in the world. Crossing the Shelikof Strait is a trick only the toughest of today's mariners would attempt in an open canoe.

Exaggerated tales of Alaska's fur trade brought greedy representatives from several other countries to the frigid waters. The Spanish, French and English each sent expeditions to the northern land. These visitors took many furs, but left neither settlers nor forts. They did, however, leave a few broken hearts and numerous single-parent families. With help from all the foreigners, the mixed-blood population was growing at a rapid pace.

At the height of Russian occupation, chaos reigned as bands of Russian hunters robbed and murdered each other for the spoils to be gained in the fur market. By the 1790s, Russia organized the Russian American Company to regulate the fur business and ease the violent competition in the New World. The Russian workers were expected to start families in America. This was a definite plan of the Russian American Company. Fedorova explains the policies in *The Russian Population in Alaska and California:*

> *(The Russian American Company) was interested in sending a male work force to the colony, as it was essential for the main branch of the economy (sea animal hunting and the fur trade).*
>
> *Sending women from Russia was unprofitable since from the very beginning there were broad plans to accustom the aboriginal population of America to Russian ways of life by means of mixed marriages.*

Fedorova quotes a letter from company leader Gregor Shelikof in Russia to Alexander Baranof, leader of the colonies in Russian America:

> *Try to marry the bachelor settlers now being sent to good American girls. I have sent you various articles of clothing as gifts for their brides and future wives, which you supply to each of them after marriage … . As for sending women from Russia, this is not as easy as it might seem, because no woman of good morals will go to America without a husband, and we cannot send deliberately those who are corrupt in the hope they will reform.*

Shelikof's letter sounded peaceful enough, although the actuality of the situation was far different. Seemingly without remorse, the Russians dominated local society. They intimidated the men and threatened bodily harm and even death to their women and children. The Russians demanded that the men hunt the sea animals and then assist with the skinning and preparations for shipment back to the Russian homeland. While the men did their bidding, the women were held captive in the Russian camps. They were forced to work for and service the promyshlenniks. The more the Aleuts rebelled, the more aggressive the Russians became. Despite the marriages and purported help from the Russian homeland, research indicates that the Aleuts were nearly annihilated during the peak of the Russian fur trade. Author Corey Ford describes the horrors endured by the Aleuts in *Where the Sea Breaks Its Back:*

> *Captives were knouted, blinded with hot irons, tied naked to stakes and castrated before the*

*assembled villagers. A favorite procedure was to line up the men of a settlement in single file, and fire a musket point-blank at the first man, while the promyshleniki made bets as to how many in the line would be killed. The best recorded score was nine, the bullet lodging in the ribs of the tenth man.*

By the early 1800s, at least one Russian started to realize the devastation caused by

*An early depiction of Alexander Baranof*

the continued sea animal harvest. Official shipping records indicate more than 1,232,300 sea otter and 72,000 seal pelts were sent to the Russian homeland. G.A. Sarychev delineates the demise of the sea otter in *Voyage of Discovery*.

*The most valuable fur is that of the sea otter, called by the hunters here and in Russia, "Morski Bobre." There are no more on the coast of Kamshatka: they are now very seldom seen on the Aleutian Islands; and of late, they have forsaken the Shumagin Islands; and I think, from the value of the skin having caused such devastation among them, and the pursuit after them being so keen, added to their situation between latitudes 45 and 60 degrees, that 15 years hence there will hardly be any more of the species.*

Sarychev could see it, but Alexander Andreievich Baranof would issue no stop to the hunt. His decision affected more than the hunters. Among Alexander's foremost critics were the Russian priests. They disliked Baranof because he begged, borrowed and stole his way to the top. Once there, he made no bones about being in charge. In *The History of Alaska*, Bancroft quotes a Russian priest who described Baranof.

*A man who became famous on account of his long residence among the savages, and still more so because he, while enlightening them, grew wild himself and sunk to a degree below the savage; a man who continually sat in his house hatching mischief.*

Vehement complaints by the clergy didn't faze Baranof. Although most of the priests disliked the New World leader, none was more outspoken than Father Juvenal. Bancroft quotes from the Father's personal diary as he described the holy service he held shortly after coming to the New World Russian colony at Kodiak.

*I could not help but marvel at Baranof, who stood there and listened and crossed himself, gave the responses at the proper time, and joined in the singing with the same hoarse voice with which he was shouting obscene songs the night before, when I saw him in the midst of a drunken carousal with a woman seated in his lap ... I dispensed with service in the afternoon because the traders were drunk again, and might have disturbed us and disgusted the natives.*

Wanting to be rid of the meddlesome ecclesiastic, Baranof ordered Father Juvenal to Old Iliamna Village, six miles up the Iliamna River. Arriving tired from this most difficult and lengthy journey, yet true to his cause, the Father promptly proclaimed to the villagers that their polygamous way of life was not acceptable to the church. Over time, his followers were to see their pathway to God through the lifestyle presented by the priest. Juvenal did a thorough job in converting most of the villagers. Some however, resented the change in their lifestyle and the constant preaching about immoral behavior that they deemed perfectly acceptable. The priest was on a roll right up to the time when, according to his own diary:

> *An Ilyamna damsel captured me by storm. With a trembling hand I write the sad occurrences of the past day and night. Much rather I would leave the disgraceful story untold, but I must overcome my own shame and mortification, and write it down as a warning to other missionaries who may come after me. In the middle of the night I awoke to find myself in the arms of a woman whose fiery embraces excited me to such an extent that I fell victim to lust, and a grievous sin was committed before I could extricate myself. As soon as I regained my senses, I drove the woman out, but I felt too guilty to be harsh with her. I have kept myself secluded today from everybody.*

The following day didn't go too well for the fornicating Father. Not only did he suffer from extreme humiliation, he also learned the wrath of the Natives was more than a few disgusted looks. He should have feared more than the loss of his integrity. The Natives found him in his quarters and beat him with ivory clubs, then stabbed him to death. It seems they didn't like their priests to "speak with forked tongue." Hypocrisy wasn't one of their favorite faults. Baranof wasn't too disturbed when he heard the news. According to the record, he simply made a note to remind himself to send for a less exuberant replacement. I should point out that although more than a few historians believe the diary notation to be a hoax written by Ivan Petroff, the fact remains that Father Juvenal died in the line of religious duty.

Once the harvesting around the Aleutian Islands and Kodiak started to wane and the fur colonies disappeared, Baranof moved his territorial capital from Kodiak to Novo Arkhangelsk (Sitka) in Southeast Alaska. This move expanded Alexander's power base. Similar to what he had done on Kodiak Island, Baranof moved a large force of Russian henchmen into the Southeast region. Only the Natives and the priests opposed his actions. Baranof forced the Tlingit Indians into his band of slaves. Using his strong-arm tactics, Baranof built an empire that stretched from Bristol Bay to northern California.

Because the Bristol Bay region didn't have the rich resources of coastal Alaska, the region didn't suffer under the iron fist of the Russians. Victor H. Calahane researched and wrote about the Katmai region of Bristol Bay in his book, *A Biological Survey of Katmai National Monument*:

> *Aboriginal existence was devoted largely to the process of survival hunting and fishing. It was marked by periods of famine and times of plenty and by raids and counter-raids of rival Aleut-Eskimo tribes. The coming of the Russians in the mid-eighteenth century may not have been as disastrous to these Katmai people as it was to the inhabitants of the*

*Aleutian Islands and other regions. Since Katmai had little or no natural wealth of gold and furs, it did not attract the attention of the rapacious Lords of Alaska.*

When a small trickle of adventurers, vagabonds, and derelicts finally began to arrive from the United States, four nations (France, Spain, Russia and Britain) had already profited from the wealth in Alaska. Spain and France were out of the area by the early 1800s, while the British were reduced to leasing only a few areas from the Russian land barons. It wasn't long before they, too, lost interest in the harsh land of the north.

The Russians found themselves financially overextended by the 1860s. This, of course, is the politically correct way of saying that the Russians were broke. Letters sent from the home office to Baranof in the New World indicated that shipping delays coupled with the declining profits in the fur industry were the reasons for their difficult circumstance. I believe, however, that the real financial headache for the soon-to-be communists was their expansive and expensive involvement in Napoleon's European wars.

Because of their financial difficulties, Russian diplomats made several overtures to the United States concerning the possible sale of Alaska. The American Civil War delayed all negotiations with the Russians. It was not until 1867 that William H. Seward, Secretary of State to President Andrew Johnson, signed a treaty to purchase Alaska for $7.2 million, which was less than two cents an acre. Soon after the deal was reported to the American public, protests erupted. Newspapers called it Seward's Icebox and Seward's Folly. On the Senate floor, the battle to ratify the treaty lasted six months before the sale was approved. One senator heatedly compared Alaska to a sucked orange as he thought nothing was left of the fur business. What the politician didn't know was that the use of guns would make the American efforts to harvest the sea animals even more successful.

On October 18, 1867, the formal transfer of Alaska took place on the parade grounds near Baranof's castle in Sitka. In the *History of Alaska*, Bancroft comments upon the acquisition of this fine piece of real estate.

*On the whole, the people of the United States have not paid an exorbitant price for the ground: trinkets and trickery, a little money. What we did not steal ourselves, we bought from those who did and bought it cheap.*

It is fairly clear that Bancroft, who was in Alaska during its transition from a Russian colony to an American territory, had some dislike for the crowd that swarmed north after the purchase.

*Within a few weeks after the American flag was raised over the fort at Sitka, flocked men in all conditions of life—speculators, politicians, office hunters, tradesmen, even laborers, loafers, harlots, gamblers, and diverse other classes of free white Europeans never seen in these parts before; for such is our superior civilization.*

As a direct result of the American purchase, there was another boom in the fur business. The Russian American Company was taken over by some equally greedy Americans who renamed it the Alaska Commercial Company. Alaska remained a lawless, unorganized territory for the next twenty years. From *Isolated Paradise* by Frank Norris:

*In the late 1880s, the fortunes of the Alaska Commercial Company began to drop because of a rapid decline in sea otter yields. The drop-off in the harvest was noted in many coastal areas. By 1890, the census agent visiting Katmai noted that "The number of skins brought home grows smaller and smaller every year." He made similar observations at Kukak and near Cape Douglas. Contributing to the otter's decimation was the killing by whites, who outfitted a "mosquito fleet" of 20-30 schooners and, quite illegally, hunted all summer long and well into the winter season as well. By the turn of the century, the sea otter trade had dwindled to economic insignificance. A more critical blow to the company as a whole came in 1890 when its Pribilof Islands fur seal harvesting contract was not renewed.*

Records indicate that first the U.S. Army and then the Navy had control of the territory. My guess is that many questionable and illegal activities weren't reported. Perhaps someone should have been paying closer attention. According to W. H. Dall's essay in *The Harriman Alaska Expedition, 1899*,

*Alaska was a country where no man could make a legal will, own a homestead or transfer it, or so much as cut wood for his fire without defying a Congressional prohibition; where polygamy, slavery and the lynching of witches prevailed with no legal authority to stay or punish criminals.*

Looking at it in retrospect, the Russians found Alaska and later sold it to the United States only after devastating her rich sea animal populations. Had the territory continued to be profitable, the Russians would still own it all.

## Commercial Salmon Fishing

Once purchased from the Russians, Alaska remained remote and inaccessible to all but a few hardy settlers, con men and derelicts. For all practical purposes, our most northern territory remained a dark and frozen mystery. Eventually its riches were discovered, uncovered, and stolen one industry at a time. First, it was whales, taken mostly in the southeast, the Bering Sea, and later from the Arctic Ocean. After whaling dwindled, the phenomenal salmon runs were targeted, tapped and exploited. The first salmon cannery opened in 1878 at Klawock on Prince of Wales Island. Land-based canneries were then established in Cook Inlet, the Aleutians and Kodiak Island in the 1880s. European fishermen and Chinese laborers were soon brought to the territory to provide labor. Both the whaling and commercial fishing industries helped start the steady trickle of seasonal workers into Alaska.

The commercial fishing industry is more than a volume in itself and space is limited. It is important to remember that the salmon runs in Alaska were (and are) the best in the world. From the onset of commercial salmon fishing, Bristol Bay has been the centerpiece of the industry. A. K. Larsen's *Fish & Ships*, published in 1959, gives some of the statistics.

*Bristol Bay's claim to fame rests on the very foundation that from the beginning of commercial salmon fishing in America, it has been the largest producer of red or sockeye salmon in the world. Yearly catch has reached as high as 24 million salmon and the yield to the salmon canneries as much as 30 million dollars. Small wonder that the name Bristol Bay has a magic sound in a fisherman's ear and is spoken with wonder and respect whenever fishermen get together. From the beginning of commercial fishing in Bristol Bay and for some sixty-odd years thereafter, the fishing was done with open boats, using sails and oars as propulsion, the use of motor boats having been prohibited by law. The reasons for this prohibition were not quite clear, it seemed. Some said that it was for the sake of conservation, as power boats would be so much more efficient than the sailboats. Others again insisted that motor boats were prohibited at the request of the canning companies, as motors cost big money, and had to be repaired and replaced when worn, whereas Squarehead, Finn and Italian fishermen could be thrown away when worn out, and replaced at no extra cost. Whatever the reason the law was there and had to be obeyed. The law prohibiting powerboats was changed, finally, and the fishing season of 1951 brought the first power boats to the Bay.*

To give some idea of the rapid growth and financial significance of the commercial fishing business, from the opening of the first salmon cannery in 1878, the number of processing plants in Alaska climbed to 156 in 1929. Between 1933 and 1960, about 100 shore-based packing plants were in operation. In Bristol Bay there were 51 canneries. The first of these was built on the Nushagak River in 1884. By 1950, however, 36 of Bristol Bay's original 51 shore-based canneries were abandoned, moved to another site, or destroyed by fire.

Throughout Alaska and particularly in Bristol Bay, the seasonal nature of the commercial salmon industry dictated hardship. The opening of each cannery was a monumental task. All the materials, new fishing boats, fishing crews, nets, cannery workers and their food had to get to Alaska. According to one report, the journey to the fishing grounds in Bristol Bay was dangerous at best. The fishermen became the working crew of the large sailing ships that departed from Washington and Oregon for Alaska during the late winter months. Voyages of forty to sixty days were not uncommon. The ships bound for Bristol Bay faced the dangerous waters of the Gulf of Alaska, then Unimak Pass and the Bering Sea. Laden with their cargo of gear, food and Chinese laborers, the sailors tried to avoid drifting ice packs and the treacherous coastal weather that sank many vessels.

The fishermen tended to be rather cosmopolitan. Italians, Finns, Norwegians, Swedes, as well as a few Germans, Danes and Americans plied the waters. What work the Americans and Europeans didn't want to do, the foulest of duties, was assigned to the Chinese labor gangs brought in by the fish processors.

*The actual canning work was done by the "China Gang," under the command of the China Boss. In due time the Iron Chink replaced the Chinese fish-cleaning gang, and Filipino laborers took the place of the Chinese cannery worker.*

No monetary references could be extracted, but I read several comments that indicated the Chinese laborers didn't expect much for their efforts. All they wanted was the promise that in the event of their deaths, their bones would be returned to the old country so they could be buried with their ancestors. Although politically incorrect today, the advertisement on the following page appeared in West Coast newspapers during the early 1900s.

The growth of the salmon fishing industry was monumental in Alaska. The conditions were difficult at best for the fishermen. During my research, I found the *Articles of Agreement and Wage Scale for the Season of 1907 between the Various Alaska Salmon Packers and the Alaska Fishermen's Union.* Some 3,000 fishermen thought it was a good deal and signed the contract:

> *They agree to give their whole time and energy to the business and interests of said company, and to work day or night (Sundays and Holidays not excepted), according to the lawful orders of Captain, Superintendent, or whoever may be in charge for the Company, and for the compensation provided. While preparing to fish or after fishing has closed, the men shall not be required to work on Sunday as a rule, and if they be required to work any time on Sunday, such time shall be given back to them during the week. All gillnet fishermen in the Bering Sea are to receive fifty dollars (50.00) as run money. In addition to this, each gillnet fisherman shall receive five cents (5¢) for each King Salmon weighing over 15 pounds, one and one half cents ($1\frac{1}{2}$¢) for each Red or Cobo Salmon; one cent (1¢) for each Chum or Dog Salmon; one half cent ($\frac{1}{2}$¢) for each Pink Salmon caught and delivered to the company. The company is not compelled to take any Dog or Pink Salmon, but if received they are paid for at the above rates.*

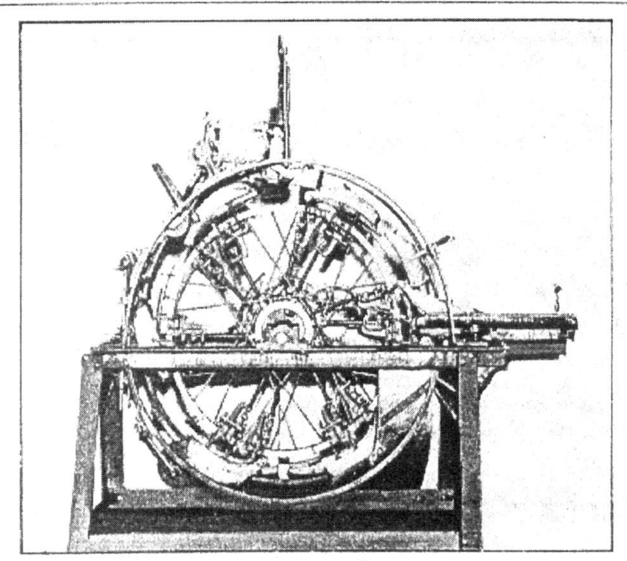


*This advertisement appeared in the early 1900s. One machine cleaned and cut 60 salmon per minute replacing 15 Chinese workers.*

Today, Bristol Bay commercial salmon fishing is a closely monitored industry. In earlier years, however, little was known of the salmon runs. Substantial scientific research was conducted on the fish in Bristol Bay. Both the salmon fry heading to the ocean and the adult salmon returning to spawn were the targets of early study. Perhaps Bristol Bay's most controversial salmon propagation project, however, was the work that led to the creation of the fish ladder on the Brooks River.

During a 1920 mission to Brooks Falls, a four-man fisheries research team came to the conclusion that they might help improve the sockeye salmon run if they modified the shape of the waterfall. Frank Norris describes their assistance to Mother Nature in *Isolated Paradise*:

*In early June of 1920, a four-man party headed by A. T. Looff of the College of Fisheries, University of Washington, began its Naknek Lake investigations. The crew found Kidawik Creek (Brooks River) to be an ideal salmon stream with fine spawning bottom .... They camped at its mouth and then ascended to a waterfall from 5 to 8 feet high, over which it would be impossible for fish to ascend during low water stage. In an attempt to improve its spawning possibilities, the crew proceeded to modify the falls. They had no power, but felt that a cut could be made with steel bars, etc. "We therefore secured several stone cutting gads, a steel bar, top maul, hammer and pick, and, after diverting the flow of water near the top left or north side of the stream, a cut was made 10 feet in width, sloping back about 15 feet, through which a fish could easily pass." A crew returned the following year and used dynamite to widen the slot.*

*Originally chipped out by hand on the north side of the falls, the fish ladder at the south end of Brooks Falls was constructed by Fish and Wildlife Service personnel between 1948-1950. Victor H. Calahane took this photo in August 1954. NPS Photo Collection, neg. 12,049*

*In 1936, biologists showed renewed interest in the Brooks Lake area. They noticed that the Brooks Falls was not a block to red salmon under normal conditions. During seasons of low water, however, they observed that many salmon died unspawned below the falls, presumably because of injury caused in attempting to negotiate them. Based on that overview, they made plans for blasting steps in the falls in the spring of 1937.*

Frank Norris notes that the previous work on the Brooks River fish ladder was continued in 1948 when another team of workers returned to the Brooks River to complete the job started in 1920.

*Materials went to Brooks Lake by air and to the falls by tractor and sled. Gravel and sand for concrete came from the beach at Brooks Lake. Four U.S. Fish and Wildlife employees—John Hurst, Mike Michel, Mike Wold, and Jerry O'Neil—blasted and hewed the ladder from solid rock to make it as natural-appearing as possible. Ten feet in width and at the south side of the falls, the ladder had seven pools, each 1 foot above the other. A headgate metered water into the topmost pool. The fisheries employees completed the ladder, except for the bottommost pool in 1949. The remaining portions were completed early the next summer, and the ladder opened on August 7, 1950.*

*Alfred C. Kuehl, Landscape Architect for the Region Four office of the NPS (National Park Service), first became aware of the fish construction in 1948. He visited the Brooks River as F&WS engineers were finalizing plans for the ladder. He came again in September 1949 during the midst of construction work. This time Herbert Maier, assistant director of Region Four, accompanied him. Neither protested the construction, either while visiting the site or after they returned to San Francisco. In late June 1950, Kuehl and George L. Collins, Chief of the Park Service's Alaska Recreation Survey, arrived at Katmai to find the fish ladder nearing completion. They made no protest at the time, but Collins was clearly perturbed at what he saw. After they returned to the regional headquarters, Collins let the regional director know his feelings:*

*I doubt that anyone in the Service paid much attention to the fact that the Fish and Wildlife Service has started a fish ladder at the falls on Brooks River. If there is a permit or understanding regarding that abortion whoever in the Service authorized it ought to be made to go to Katmai and tear it out single-handedly."*

*Scenes like this were common in the early 1950s. Fishing at the falls was great. The fish ladder can be seen to the left of the waterfall. Ray Petersen Collection*

Collins certainly represented the feelings of all those concerned at Brooks. Ray Petersen told me that the Fish and Wildlife Service (F&WS) seemed to develop the ladder overnight. This controversial act of the F&WS started a feud that is still alive. Control over the fisheries on the Brooks River has been in turmoil since the early 1920s. Norris chronicled the highlights:

*In 1871, the U.S. Fish Commission was established as an independent agency of the Federal government. In 1903 the commission was renamed the U.S. Bureau of Fisheries and placed in the newly established Department of Commerce and Labor. (The Bureau became part of the Department of Commerce when the department split in 1913.) In 1940, the Bureau of Fisheries merged with the U.S. Biological Survey, which had been in the Department of Agriculture, to become the U.S. Fish and Wildlife Service. The new agency was placed within the Department of the Interior. In 1956 the Fish and Wildlife Service was reorganized and two bureaus were created within it: the Bureau of Commercial Fisheries and the Bureau of Sport Fisheries and Wildlife. In 1970 the Bureau of Commercial Fisheries was renamed the National Marine Fisheries Service, and it became part of the new National Oceanic and Atmospheric Administration in the Department of Commerce.*

Alaska became a state in 1959 and promptly took over sport hunting and fishing management. With the exception of

Mount McKinley National Park, the Statehood Act specified that jurisdiction of sportfishing be transferred from the federal to state government. By 1961, state regulations were in effect in Bristol Bay, but conflicts with the National Park Service continued.

The commercial salmon-fishing industry was quite influential in Territorial affairs and remains one of the strongest lobbies at both the state and federal levels. Nothing stood in the way of the salmon industry. Not only did researchers and industry leaders tamper with Mother Nature, they also tried to eliminate all other creatures that considered salmon a part of their diet. In *Isolated Paradise, An Administrative History of Katmai Park*, Frank Norris declares:

> *The U.S. Bureau of Fisheries decided to undertake a predatory fish destruction program in the various major Bristol Bay tributaries. (At this time, salmon was the only fish desired by the local canneries. Therefore, any species that preyed on salmon was considered undesirable.) The bureau included a broad survey of fish populations as part of that survey, and studied the Naknek lake system as well as other drainages. Fisheries crews returned to Naknek and the Brooks River each year from 1920 to 1925. During that time they killed more than 13,000 sport fish, primarily rainbow trout, lake trout and Dolly Varden.*

Protecting the commercial fishing industry went to the very core of life in Alaska. Consider the bounty program that existed in Alaska until 1952. Every creature that ate salmon or salmon eggs was considered vermin and, indeed, the enemy. Victor H. Calahane, author of *A Biological Survey of Katmai National Monument* suggested:

> *The commercial salmon industry has long been seeking escape from its difficulties and has attempted to blame wildlife for the decline of the salmon catch. Among the numerous species "indicted" have been the bald eagle, gulls and terns, cormorants, herons, seals (especially the hair seal), sea lion, otter, and brown bear.*

The territorial government established a bounty program on all creatures that were deemed a threat to the salmon population. The bounty on eagles was removed in 1952, but the tradition persisted. According to Department of Interior records, the Alaska Legislature paid more than $100,000 for 100,000 bald eagles summarily dispatched in the name of helping the salmon population. To collect the bounty, hunters simply reported the number of eagles dispatched and submitted the feet for payment.

I was working as a pilot for Kodiak Western Alaska Airline during the winter of 1979. I remember flying into the Olga Bay Cannery, which was home to Bill Pinnell and Morris Tolifson. They were the most famous of all the brown bear hunting guides. Bill and Morris had been at Olga Bay since the 1930s, hunting the south end of Kodiak Island for bears and trying to carve out a living. It didn't matter how many times a pilot had been to Olga Bay, they simply referred to us as pilot.

Bill barked from one of the cabins at the old cannery. He wanted me to wait a few minutes. I held the amphibious float-equipped C-206 against the beach. Bill walked toward me and held out a box about the size of a case of beer.

> *Take this box to the Fish and Wildlife. They'll give you some money. Take the money to the liquor store and get me some Calvert's. I feel a whiskey front moving in.*

*No problem, Bill. I'll be here next scheduled mail day. What's in the box?*

Bill took the time to open the box for me. He was obviously proud of the contents. When he opened the box, I damned near passed out. There must have been eighty or ninety pairs of eagle feet in that box. I started to laugh and told Bill I'd buy him some Calvert's, but I would not take the box to town. By this time, Morris Tolifson, Bill's partner, was laughing out loud.

*Goddamned pilot, take the box!*

*Bill, if you only knew how much trouble we'd all be in, you'd know why I won't take that box.*

I didn't want to get him too mad. His age was showing as he took a few steps toward the cannery door and then turned back to me.

*I've been shooting those fish-eating bastards and collecting whiskey money since before you were born. I guess the Feds don't want me to drink anymore!*

I had the feeling Bill's tirade continued long after I was gone. On my next flight to Olga Bay, I took a few bottles of Calvert's to Bill. He reimbursed me with crisp dollar bills. I knew he'd rather have traded his eagle feet. Bill died a few years later. I'll bet he still had that special box.

The Dolly Varden bounty program was popular, too. According to a short article in the June 1936 issue of *Alaska Sportsman*, fishermen in the Egegik and Kanatak districts made as much as $2,000 each per year in extra income by harvesting Dolly Varden trout and turning in the tails. Each tail surrendered earned two and a half cents. These fishermen hoped to increase the run of red salmon in their fishing districts.

The bounty program continued with strong support from Alaskans. In 1939 the Territorial Legislature appropriated $165,000 for bounty fees on the wolf and coyote, $10,000 for eagles, and a whopping $60,000 for hair seals. Eagles, wolves, fish, coyotes, and seals weren't the only creatures to face the wrath of the commercial salmon business. Once the bounty was lifted on the eagle, the industry protectors tried to find a new target for their eradication campaign. Calahane continued:

*In the summer of 1953 commercial salmon fishermen on the Alaska Peninsula charged that beavers had become so numerous that they had seriously affected the rearing capacity of a number of streams tributary to Naknek Lake and Brooks Lake. The recommended remedy was reduction of the beaver population by trapping.*

I believe Calahane could see the errors in the argument because he ends his tirade by stating:

*It is unlikely that the beaver can be held accountable for any significant loss of reproductive capacity in the salmon resource.*

In the book *Hunting and Fishing in Alaska*, Russell Annabel, a true sportsman, takes a shot at what he considered the real culprits:

*This (bounty on Dolly Varden) began in 1929 when the Bureau of Fisheries, at the insistence of cannery owners, placed a bounty of two and a half cents per tail on the dolly. As a result, in one year, in the Bristol Bay district alone, twenty thousand dollars was paid out for trout tails. The avowed reason for the attempt to wipe out the dolly was that it eats salmon eggs (as all Pacific trout do in some degree), but the real reason was that bounty seining for the fish provided remunerative off-season employment for resident commercial salmon fishermen. So many fish were killed that for years dried trout tails were used as currency all along the western Alaska coast. It is well known you could collect on any kind of sport fish tail. Village postmasters, trading post proprietors, and local petty officials entrusted with the job of accepting the tails weren't at all particular what kind of tails you turned in. They took the tails of rainbows, grayling and steelhead as readily as dolly tails. Time and time again I watched the bounty fishermen seine the Iliamna creek mouths. I watched them pull the nets and chop the tails from thousands of living trout.*

*The weir on the Naknek River under construction. This photo shows how large some of the weirs had to be. Circa 1953—Jim Adams Photo*

The most visible signs of the salmon research were the weirs that appeared on many of the Bristol Bay rivers beginning in the early 1920s. Jim Adams worked in Bristol Bay from 1952 through 1960 as a federal research biologist. He explained that after Congress passed the White Act in June 1924, the fish had to be counted. The White Act established regulations to sustain and preserve the salmon populations. One regulation stated that the fishermen could catch only 50 percent of the salmon returning to spawn. To count the fish, Federal Fish and Wildlife departments constructed weirs on numerous rivers.

Mr. Webster tells me that a weir is basically a fence placed in a stream to catch or retain fish. Jim Adams told me that the weirs were put in place and assembled before the salmon runs started and then were removed after the runs ended. Part of the weir construction included building a trap door and placing a white panel on the bottom of the river below the trap door. The white panel made it easier to see the fish going through the gate. The earliest weirs were made from wood and held in place with large rocks and boulders. As technology increased, lighter materials such as aluminum were substituted. The upriver migration of salmon was held below the weir until the counters opened the door. As the fish rushed through the opening, each fish was counted. Jim told me that the counters would usually pull a blanket over both their heads and the trap door to reduce glare on the water to help their vision. He also told me that when the fish were really streaming through the trapdoor, they were often counted in multiples of 5 or 10. After years of counting and statistical analysis, the strengths of the various salmon runs became known and predictable. Commercial fishing was allowed only after the weir counts indicated that enough fish had passed through to ensure at least the 50 percent escapement level required by the White Act.

*The weir on the Brooks River. This view looks north, Brooks Lake is on the photo's left side. Circa 1953—Ray Petersen Collection*

In Western Alaska, weirs were established on many large rivers including the Naknek, Egegik, and Ugashik rivers. As more scientific information was obtained each year, other rivers were targeted for increased research. On some smaller rivers, such as the American Creek, the weirs were intermittently erected for specific research studies.

The Fish and Wildlife Service established a presence on the Brooks River in 1940 and constructed a fish weir and trap to count the salmon heading to the spawning waters. Each year from 1940 until 1967 the weir was installed on the upper end of the Brooks River. Ward Bower's *Alaska Fishery and Fur Seal Industries: 1940* states:

> *A new weir was established this year at the outlet of Brooks Lake, in the Naknek River system. The total escapement into the lake was 97,161 red, 11 king, and 8 pink salmon. Included in the foregoing is an estimated escapement of 1,450 red salmon which passed upstream in the three days prior to June 30, while the weir was being installed ... .The final count was on September 5, but the weir was not removed until September 15 as an attempt was made to check on the seaward migration of rainbow trout.*

Former research biologist Jim Adams indicated to me that he had some interesting assignments in Bristol Bay. He also told me that those involved in the research had serious concerns about their work. With a smile on his face, Jim said, *The strength of the salmon run was inversely proportional to the research effort,* meaning that their research may have done more harm than good.

Several accounts of tampering give some credence to Jim's words. According to Fish and Wildlife Service records from 1960 to 1965, researchers experimented with the salmon's sense of smell and sight in an attempt to determine how they found their way back to their birth streams. In another study, some salmon were severely hindered in their upstream movement into a particular creek to determine if they would choose another creek in which to spawn. They did not.

*Research biologist Paul Knapp with 35 grayling killed in the name of science. Jim Adams Photo*

Besides working on the weir and being involved in salmon research, Jim was an ardent fly-fisherman and on more than one occasion had to use his fishing skills in his work. During the summer of 1960 he was sent to the Ugashik Narrows to assist in a vast North American grayling study. Jim and his teammate, Paul Knapp, were sent to collect 35 grayling specimens. At the Narrows, they first constructed a large live trap, then fly-fished until they caught and collected their quota. Once hooked, each fish was carefully released into the trap. Jim told me that it was imperative that the fish remained alive.

Late in the afternoon, a Grumman Widgeon arrived with the necessary biological supplies to complete their work. The fish were systematically killed. Blood samples of each fish were taken, then placed in special vials which they carefully labeled. All the fish and blood samples were then flash-frozen with liquid nitrogen. They were put in special packages and sent to the University of British Columbia for further study. Jim told me that when the director of the study received the grayling from the Ugashik Narrows, he was impressed with their size. They were the largest found in their North American sampling.

Like most other industries, commercial salmon fishing improved due to research and advances in technology. The most significant change in Bristol Bay's salmon-fishing business, however, occurred in 1951 when the Secretary of the Interior, Oscar Chapman, announced a change in Bristol Bay's commercial fishing regulations. The long established prohibition against powerboats was finally lifted. According to news sources, the regulation was changed to protect the fishermen. Most of the cannery officials quietly opposed the change, but knew that progress could not be stopped. It's obvious to me that the men who ruled the commercial-salmon fishing industry had no plan to yield their power. Later you will learn that some of these same powerful men were among the first to enjoy fly-out fishing.

## Gold Fever

Although commercial fishing dominated Alaska's financial pages during the early years of American ownership, gold brought Alaska into the world's limelight. The mere mention of the word still creates dreams of wealth and a get-rich-quick frenzy. The promise of quick dollars and the adventure of the frontier became the most effective lure Alaska had ever seen. Not even the oil boom in the 1970s would compare.

Gold was discovered in the Gastineau Channel in southeast Alaska in 1880. The towns of Juneau and Douglas sprang up overnight, providing support for the productive Treadwell and Alaska-Juneau gold mines. Farther north, gold was discovered in the interior in 1893. Circle City grew out of the tundra from the discovery of gold near Birch Creek.

Three years later, the world's most colorful gold rush occurred in the Klondike region of Canada's Yukon Territory. The Klondike gold rush took place when the United States was suffering a severe recession. Caught up in the fever, thousands of men quit their jobs and sold their homes to finance a trip through Southeast Alaska toward the territorial boomtown of Skagway.

The number of miners who actually made a fortune was small, but the tales and legends that they spawned were huge. The Klondike stampede lasted from 1896 to 1899. It was followed by the Nome stampede of 1899-1902, and the Fairbanks rush soon afterward. The era of the gold rush earned Alaska the reputation of being the country's last frontier, and it was her most colorful moment in history.

The exploits of those who came to Alaska were exciting and gave other dreamers hope. There was gold to find and many tested their luck. From the tent cities at Skagway and Dyea almost 30,000 prospectors tackled the steep Chilkoot Trail to Lake Bennett. From there, they built rafts to float the rivers that led to the goldfields. It was a long and arduous journey wrought with many perils, not the least of which were con men eager to fleece the unwary.

Along with the miners, the gold rush also brought those eager to provide services to the gold fields. Along their way, the multitudes of get-rich-quick hopefuls faced the temptations brought by the houses of ill repute that lined the path to the gold fields. The gold mines those girls worked certainly weren't underground. The introductory statements by June Allen in her book, *Dolly's House*, describe Alaska's prostitution boom:

> *The prostitute was one of the first of the gentle sex to arrive in Alaska during the economic boom of the Gold Rush. Her presence was welcomed by the early-day sourdough, and tolerated by a mercantile generation of later, and easier, days. Wherever men stampeded (for gold, copper or to fleece those who dug for it) she followed. She practiced her trade near the diggings, dance halls, bawdyhouses or degrading cribs. Robert Service wrote about her. Lonely men adored her. But as the twentieth century aged and accelerated into a modern era, her profession as practiced in early days became obsolete. She left Alaska. Or she stayed to become the matriarch of an Alaskan family.*

While I cannot agree that the prostitute became obsolete in Alaska, she did become mired in regulation and law. Allen describes the end of an era in the North and the subsequent effect on one Alaska town:

*The girls considered themselves a part of the business community. Their sense of humor was evident in a flyer they had printed during the early years of World War II when the Coast Guard, with a base in Ketchikan, insisted that the brothels be closed in the interest of national security. An institution was ended.*

Numerous books and personal accounts described the perils and difficulty of traveling into the gold country. A few gold seekers even used Katmai Pass to get to Nome. Unfortunately for those who came late, the single most significant geological event in recorded history occurred on June 6, 1912, and all but eliminated this route. The volcanic eruption of Mt. Katmai became more important to Bristol Bay than gold ever was. Victor Calahane describes the events in his book, *A Biological Survey of Katmai National Monument*:

*As the beach sands at Nome were panned out, few travelers used the trail across Katmai Pass. Most of these were Natives en route to visit relatives and villages across the Aleutian Range, or trappers with furs to sell at some distant trading post. Then in June 1912, the centuries-old track through the wilderness was destroyed in a most spectacular debacle.*

*A week of increasingly severe earthquakes was the only prelude to an awesome series of events. Beginning June 6, and continuing for about 60 hours, the area around Mount Katmai was racked and convulsed by earth forces of tremendous magnitude. One effect of internal pressure was to blow enormous amounts of ash and pumice out of Novarupta, a relatively insignificant volcano located about six miles southwest of Katmai.*

*Almost simultaneously with the thunderous eruption of Novarupta, a series of glowing avalanches of sand mixed with hot gases burst out of numberless fissures in the head of the valley west of the Katmai Pass. Rushing down with incredible speed, these avalanches buried the floor of the valley, 3 to 6 miles wide and 15 miles long, to a depth of 700 feet. The body of tuff consolidated, but it was perforated by countless fissures through which steam and gases escaped from the hot mass. These millions of fumaroles later gave its name which became known throughout the world as the Valley of Ten Thousand Smokes.*

*More than 7 cubic miles of rock and pumice were spewed onto the surface or into the atmosphere. So much material was ejected from the conduits leading to Novarupta and nearby fissures that a giant cavity formed under Mount Katmai and the upper third of the mountain collapsed. Thus a crater, almost 3 miles across and 3,500 feet deep, was formed. A mass of andesite lava and cinders erupted on the caldera floor, forming a small cone. Eventually a lake accumulated, covering the cone beneath hundreds of feet of turquoise-blue water.*

The volcanic activity caused severe problems for local residents and nearby villages, yet didn't stop the interest in gold. Despite the fact that precious little gold was ever found in the Katmai region, hearty explorers scoured the area. Both Bill Hammersly and Ernie Pfaff had gold on their agendas during their days in the Katmai region. Mining wasn't their only forte;

they enriched the visits of many early fishing guests at Kulik Lodge.

Bill Hammersly staked a gold claim or two close to Nonvianuk Lake in the 1940s. Ed Seiler, an early lodge player, recently told me that Bill's claim was in the big, rocky canyon on American Creek. He also told me that the quantity and quality of the color wasn't good enough to make a commercial operation worthwhile. Bill didn't have any problems talking about his Alaskan gold mine, however. Once he started working with Ray Petersen and the Angler's Paradise Camps in the early 1950s, he earned more talking about his gold claims than he ever found in his pan.

Another character who searched the Bristol Bay area for gold and other minerals was Ernie Pfaff. Like Bill Hammersly, Ernie was a walker. He traveled and explored the area near Kulik Lake entirely on foot. He found enough mineral deposits near the Moraine River that Marathon Oil decided to test the feasibility of a mining project in the area. After an exploratory season, the Marathon executives determined it wasn't worth the effort to pursue Pfaff's claims. Their decision was economically great for Ernie, however. When the Marathon-Pfaff effort ended, Ernie had enough fuel, propane, and mining supplies to last him many years.

*John Walatka, Slippery Bill Jefford, Ernie Pfaff with his dog, Bozo, and Raphael Kuponak on the beach at Kulik Lodge. Circa 1965—Ray Petersen Collection*

As age slowed Ernie's pace, he sought out an occasional airplane ride to get closer to the areas he wanted to explore. Both Ed Seiler and Sonny Petersen flew Ernie into various lakes north of Kulik. Sonny told me that Ernie worked for meals and flying time, and eventually stored some of his exploration equipment at Kulik Lodge where guests enjoyed Ernie's stories. Ernie wasn't a purist when it came to his mining efforts. Sonny said that Ernie just wanted to strike it rich. He didn't care if it was gold, copper, or oil. Ed Seiler nodded in agreement.

Through a strange set of circumstances, Ed Seiler also filed a gold claim in the 1960s. It seems that while Ed was operating the Sky-Tel in King Salmon during the early 1950s, a geological engineer arrived late in the fall and needed a flight to explore a gold claim located in the mountains on Shelikof Strait. According to Ed, the engineer had researched the archives and had filed a claim on a site previously owned by some Russians from Kodiak Island. Since their deaths, no one had shown any interest in their claim. The geologist, however, knew something. He told Ed about the Russians and the improvements they'd made. He also told Ed about the rumors that surrounded the Russian's secret location, and how he hoped to locate the exact spot.

The weather was good when Ed made his first low pass. Ed dropped the geologist on the beach. The geologist made it clear that he did not want to be stuck at the site for any length of time. If Ed got word that a storm was coming, he wanted to be picked up before, not after. Ed returned to King Salmon and checked the weather. Naturally, there was a storm brewing. Early the next morning, he flew across the mountains again. The geologist scurried to get to the airplane. He was excited when he told Ed what he had found. He said he found the site, and vowed he'd return.

Once they got to King Salmon, the geologist took Ed aside and paid for the flight with several gold nuggets, which he said he'd found at the old mine site. Then he told Ed that if he didn't return within five years, Ed should file a claim on the site. With that, the geologist climbed aboard a Northern Consolidated flight and disappeared. Ed never saw him again.

Several years passed, but Ed never forgot the claim. Later he befriended another traveling geologist. Ed told him about the claim and invited him back to King Salmon. As soon as he was available, Ed took him to the remote location. The claim included a beautiful waterfall and Ed found the remnants of the Russian camp. Their old cabin had long since collapsed. Ed got excited when he told me:

*Every time my geologist pal pulled up his pan, we had color. There was gold there, lots of it.*

Several years went by. Ed filed on the former Russian claim in the early 1960s. On more than one occasion Ed planned to start a mining operation, but something always came up. By the summer of 1965, he was building Enchanted Lake Lodge and simply didn't have enough energy to devote to gold.

Unfortunately, by the time Ed had the opportunity, time, and energy to devote to his claim, the Katmai National Park boundaries had been expanded. Ed's claim, which contained more than enough gold to make it a viable commercial operation, ended up inside the new park borders. Government regulations, not time, prevented Ed from chasing his golden dreams.

## Railroad and Roadhouses

Thirty years after the purchase of Alaska, the Federal Government started to explore and map the Territory with the intention of establishing roads and railroads. Alfred Hulse Brooks came to Alaska armed with a great reputation for accuracy in his mapping. His work was so thorough that he was placed in charge of the U.S. Geological Survey. Today, Brooks Lake, the Brooks River, and the vast Brooks Range bear his name.

The government knew that gold was not the only source for potential growth in the northland. The creation of a railroad could only help. Shortly after 1900, Alaska's first railroad began limited service. The Alaska Central Railroad improved access in Alaska, especially along the Kenai Peninsula. Roadhouses sprang up along the railroad lines to fill the need for overnight facilities. Interest surged as new roads and several roadhouses emerged. Following closely were more settlers, governmental visitors, and a few sportsmen eager to explore the region.

The world changed rapidly during the early twentieth century and Alaska was no different. The U.S. Congress gave Alaska a non-voting delegate to Washington in 1906. Three years after gaining a delegate, Alaska submitted its first request for statehood. Congress denied that request, but it assisted in setting up a Territorial government. Alaska's Territorial Legislature met for the first time in Juneau in 1913.

During the 1920s, the first of several crude lodge-type facilities appeared. All of these roadhouses had a similar beginning. Each one was located near a road or railroad, and each operated for brief periods during the 1920s. They were the homes of their proprietors and offered whatever services they could sell. The Kenai Peninsula hunting resource and Kenai Lake fishery became well known by the efforts of the railroad and a few of the roadhouses. The railroad advertised the availability of sporting opportunities, and the roadhouse proprietors provided those activities.

Webster indicates that a roadhouse is an inn, a restaurant, or a nightclub located on a road outside a town or city. That wasn't necessarily the case in Alaska, however. The majority of the roadhouses evolved along the railroad corridors, others developed on winter sled trails. Still others developed in isolated locations to serve the increasing demand created by airplane travel.

Probably the most famous of the early lodges was Lawing's Roadhouse. Nellie Lawing was an Alaskan pioneer. She worked at various construction camps during the railroad building phase. She saw the need for clean and comfortable lodging for both the railroad workers and the tourists that were destined to follow. Nellie opened a roadhouse adjacent to the railroad tracks leading to the Kenai Peninsula. Over the years, she hosted a gauntlet of guests and dignitaries at her famous home. The walls of her inn were covered with big game trophies she personally collected. Working with her husband Billy, she encouraged hunting, fishing, and other forms of sporting activity. Nellie hosted many famous visitors including Archie and Kermit Roosevelt and the Duke and Duchess of Sutherland, and wrote about them in her book, *Alaska Nellie*.

> *Billy and I were kept busy caring for the many travelers during the tourist season which started June first and continued until September first. Besides the presidents, dukes, duchesses, counts, and countesses who came, there were generals, admirals, governors, authors, and one of Hollywood's most beautiful motion picture stars, the lovely Alice Calhoun, and her mother, staying at different times at our lodge, until the names on the register totaled over fifteen thousand guests.*

In Southeast Alaska, the most prominent early lodge was the Taku Lodge, established in 1923 by Juneau doctor Harry D. DeVighne. The lodge was noteworthy as it was reached only by boat. The first sleeping accommodations were tents, later followed by rustic cabins. In the article "History of Taku Lodge 1923-1963" which appeared in the *Juneau Herald* on July 7, 1966, Norman Banfield states:

*In the fall of 1930, Mrs. Eric L. Smith brought her son, Leigh Hickey Smith, to Alaska on her yacht "Stella Maris" for a hunting trip. She also brought along her nurse, Mary Joyce. They decided to buy Taku Lodge and develop it as another home for both summer and winter use.*

*At Serversen's Roadhouse. Standing from the left: George Seversen, Mary Seversen, the hostess Mrs. Hans Seversen or Mrs. Hans as she was called, and Edward Seversen. Sitting from the left: Anne, Alexan, and Martin Seversen. Circa 1925—Photo courtesy of Helena Seversen Moses*

Continued perusal of Banfield's article indicates that few, if any, visitors traveled to the Taku Lodge specifically to fish. At no time in their history did the Taku Lodge, Lawing's Roadhouse, or any other roadhouse meet my definition of a fishing lodge. Fishing just wasn't popular enough to sustain any full-time business operation in Alaska.

Situated on the largest lake in Alaska, the village of Iliamna was a strategic location for early explorers and government officials who traveled the Territory. As more and more airplanes flew through Lake Clark Pass, Iliamna became the place to stop when inclement weather held up progress. Because of its geographic location, Iliamna was a prime location for a roadhouse and the Iliamna Road house became the most famous in Bristol Bay. According to National Park Service historian John Branson, the Roadhouse was built about 1913 by Koggiung merchant Herman Gartelmann, and by Jack Kinney and Ed Ahola from Old Iliamna village. About 1917, Old Iliamna merchant Frederick Roehl purchased the roadhouse from Gartelmann. By 1921, Hans Seversen was using the facility. Previously, Hans had been a junior partner to Roehl at a small store in Nondalton. Roehl died in 1923 and the first written reference to Seversen's Roadhouse appeared. During the 1920s, Seversen's Roadhouse became the commercial and social hub of the Lake Clark-Iliamna country. Records indicate that Seversen hosted big game hunters as early as 1921 and outfitted more hunts in 1925-26. During the 1930s,

Seversen's Roadhouse became the air crossroads of Bristol Bay as aviation became the driving force for change in Southwest Alaska.

Hans Seversen entertained the first sport fishermen, Fred Hollander and Ray McDonald, in 1937. He hired Lake Clark sourdough Jack Hobson to guide these fishermen on the Newhalen River for giant rainbows. Seversen's assistant, Art Lee, ran the roadhouse until 1946, when Martin Seversen took over the operation and erected a new building. The roadhouse served as a summer youth camp from 1952 until it was sold by Mary Seversen Clark in 1956. After serving as a Bible camp and school, the new buyers modified the facility with the intent of making it a sportsman's lodge. A period of inactivity and a few seasons of general roadhouse operation followed. By 1969, the name Iliaska Lodge was used in advertisements.

I stayed at the site of Seversen's Roadhouse (Iliaska Lodge) in the fall of 1973. I was working for a private hunting club in Seattle and had come to Alaska to hunt caribou with Alex Russell, my former instrument flight instructor. We were in Alex's Super Cub heading west when the weather went to hell. Alex pointed the Cub toward Iliamna. I remember that Alex didn't land at the airfield, instead choosing to land on a village road closer to the roadhouse. After securing his airplane, we grabbed our sleeping bags and registered for the night.

I didn't realize it at the time, but Alex and I followed the pattern of many roadhouse guests since the 1920s. We didn't plan on staying; we were forced by the weather. The roadhouse accommodated our needs. As I recall, the roadhouse had a totally different atmosphere than a hotel. It was a warm and friendly place with not only stranded travelers, but also a couple of government types who had been there for more than a week. I guess the closest thing we have today is the Bed and Breakfast locations that are so popular. The hosts were inconspicuous and the food was good. We paid our bill the next morning and continued on our way. That was my first and only night in an Alaska roadhouse;

*Hans Seversen (1870-1939) Courtesy of Sonja Seversen Arduser*

but like most other roadhouse guests, I was glad it was there.

## The Fly Boys

Because fishing and flying have become so tightly interwoven in Alaska, no discussion of the fishing lodge industry can proceed without considering the history of Alaska's role in aviation and the impact airplanes had on the territory. Nearly 40 years after the Russians sold us Alaska, the Wright brothers captured the attention of the world with their first powered flight at Kittyhawk. Although their first flight on December 17, 1903 lasted only about nine seconds, Orville and Wilbur introduced the age of aviation.

The years following saw a frenzy of airplane activity. The early days of aviation were amazing to say the least. Airplane flight records were set and even more record attempts failed. The barnstorming era created both public excitement and interest in airplanes, yet a carnival atmosphere surrounded both the airplanes and their pilots. Only the most courageous members of the public considered flying, even though serious strides were made worldwide. These history-making flights eventually shaped an industry.

Alaska played a prominent role in early world exploration by aircraft. Considered a strategic location from the first, the earliest strategists and army air commanders used the northernmost territory to their fullest advantage.

The first international cross-country flight from New York to Nome was one of the more important early flights. This army-sponsored mission utilized American-built, two-man, open-cockpit, 400-horsepower training aircraft. The squadron commander was the soon-to-be-famous General Billy Mitchell, who advanced the theory that airplanes could bring all the nations of the world closer together. Since only 50 miles separated Alaska from Siberia, he noted that Alaska had great strategic importance. General Mitchell put his thoughts to the test and conceived this daring flight plan.

General Mitchell considered it vital that military leaders learn whether aircraft could fly safely to Alaska, and return. "Yesterday a month was required to reach the Yukon Territory. If our expedition is successful, it will prove that the Yukon is but 3 days distant, by airplane!" The reporters all shook their heads. They remembered that nine months earlier, in October 1919, the Air Service had sponsored the first transcontinental air race across the U.S. The race was completed in 42 hours' flying time, but nine pilots lost their lives along the way. Now eight brave men would attempt to span the 4,500-mile expanse between New York and Nome, much of it over rough and uncharted country … it would be a small miracle if all completed their mission without being injured or killed.

The four aircraft departed New York City from what is now Mitchell Field on July 15, 1920. Some 50 hours of flying time later, all four aircraft landed in Fairbanks. Only a few years earlier during the gold rush days, travel time to the goldfields near Fairbanks had been more like eighteen to twenty months from New York. People were excited. From the book, *New York to Nome-the First International Cross-country Flight*:

> *Imagine, some of the Fairbanks townspeople enthused, how much of interior Alaska could be opened up if a prospector or trapper could travel quickly deep into the wilderness and land safely in a moose pasture or along a sand bar. Think how much could be done if supplies could be dropped at regular intervals by air, and the gold or furs hauled out before winter closed in and the mercury dropped to the bottom of the tube. Obviously, the captain wrote later, he didn't have to "sell aviation to the Alaskans." The squadron had already proved the feasibility of airplane travel to and in Alaska. But these intrepid young airmen*

*could not foresee that as a result of their trailblazing, Alaska would come to depend on aviation and profit more from it than any other American state or territory.*

The first around-the-world flight was made in 1924 by the U.S. Army. Using four open-cockpit aircraft named the Seattle, Chicago, New Orleans and Boston, the U.S. army pilots and navigators flew more than 26,000 miles. They left Seattle in April 1924. Because there were so few runways, this record-setting flight was made in part with float-equipped aircraft. Congress backed this challenging mission by sending spare parts, including fourteen sets of floats, forty-two sets of landing gears, twenty-seven propellers, six spare engines and a couple of spare wings to various military bases along the route. Naturally, the parts left several months before the celebrated mission's departure.

The airplanes departed Seattle on floats and headed for Calcutta. Once they arrived in India, the airplanes had their floats removed and wheels installed for the flight to London. They returned to floats between London and the Atlantic coast of the United States, then again changed to wheels for the final segments across our country. Records and displays at the Smithsonian Air and Space Museum in Washington, D.C., indicate that the first major problem occurred in Alaska.

Between Seward and Dutch Harbor, the Seattle, piloted by Maj. Frederick L. Martin and Sgt. Alva Harvey, flew into an area of low ceilings and poor visibility. I have flown this route and can imagine some of the problems they experienced. The Seattle crashed into a mountainside near Chignik. The airplane was destroyed, but the pilots survived unharmed. They walked for ten days before stumbling into the salmon cannery at Port Mollar. Those pilots must have thought they had been killed and sent to hell considering the conditions they faced. The Boston, New Orleans, and Chicago pushed on while the support crew searched for the missing airplane and crew.

Over the Atlantic, engine problems forced the New Orleans into the rough ocean water. The airplane wasn't damaged in the landing but was completely destroyed during an attempt to put it on the deck of a passing ship. The Boston and the Chicago continued and completed the flight nearly 175 days after it started. The completion of this mission was a gigantic step in the development of the air industry.

Although the military missions were characterized by precision planning and dispatched with duty and discipline, it was the civilian pilots who brought excitement and intrigue to the fledgling air industry. Charles Lindbergh captured the world's attention when he completed the first solo flight from New York to Paris in 1927. His flight took 33 hours to complete. Lindbergh pioneered instrument flying and garnered worldwide admiration for his efforts. Slowly, the airplane started to become accepted as an alternative method of public transportation.

In 1931, Lindbergh and his wife, Anne, paved the way for overseas aircraft routes when they flew to Japan via Canada, Alaska, and Siberia. While in Alaskan territory they stopped in Nome, Pt. Barrow, and Shishmaref. That flight proved the feasibility of the great circle route. By 1933, the Lindberghs were working as advisors to Jaun Tripp at Pan American Airways. They continued their route exploration by flying a Lockheed Sirius to Europe via Greenland.

The first great threat to the airplane's emerging dominance in world air travel occurred in 1929. German designers who advocated gigantic dirigibles attempted to capture the hearts of future travelers and the expected lucrative market by sending the Graf Zeppelin on the first around-the-world commercial flight. The lighter-than-airship carried 20 passengers in a record-setting 21 days. Each passenger paid $2,500 to make the historic flight. Amenities included a full cocktail lounge complete with a grand piano. What those passengers didn't know was that the hydrogen gas that filled the lighter-than-air ships was extremely hazardous. A few years later, the airship Hindenburg burned in New Jersey. That incident dramatically ended the airships' threat to the airplane.

More than the airplanes, it was the pilots who made headlines and history. One of the most famous was Wiley Post. He was a barnstormer and a visionary of the aircraft industry. Post set a new around-the-world speed record of 115 hours, 36 minutes and 30 seconds in mid-July, 1933. For that, and several other record attempts, he flew a Lockheed Vega named the Winnie May. Despite the fact that Post was a record setter, aviation gained more notoriety from him through the publicity given to his friendship with Will Rogers, the famous newspaper columnist and Hollywood celebrity.

In 1935, Rogers hired Wiley Post to fly him to Alaska. He wanted to get some new material for his newspaper column. Specifically, he wanted to go to Alaska so he could interview Charlie Brower, a 50-year resident of the Territory. Charlie worked as a whaler and an ivory trader, and Rogers thought a story about this Alaskan might intrigue the readers of his weekly syndicated column.

*The ill-fated Orian only a few days prior to the famous crash of Post and Rogers. Ray Petersen Collection*

Knowing that he would need a good set of floats to complete his charter, Post ordered a new set for his Orion. He was still waiting for them to arrive when Will Rogers arrived prematurely. Post knew his famous columnist friend was anxious because he had a deadline to meet. Rogers's popularity prompted several local outfits to offer the use of their floats for the much-publicized flight. Feeling the pressure, Post made a fatal decision and installed a set of floats under his Orion that were designed for a much larger aircraft, making the Orion extremely nose-heavy. According to several accounts, Post was uncomfortable after the test flight, but decided that if Rogers sat far enough aft, he could make it work. Unfortunately for Post, and many pilots since, the I-can-make-it-work assumption is fine until, quoting my good friend and fishing lodge owner Jack Holman, Shit happens!

Although Rogers didn't say much about it, sitting in the back of the Orion wasn't to his liking. Records indicate that the flight went as expected until the famous duo departed Fairbanks and headed north. With no electronic guidance and getting short on fuel, Post was unsure of his position. Trying to find Barrow in bad weather was his second mistake. When he spotted some Eskimos along the shore of a large lake, Post landed to ask for directions to Barrow. Rather than wait for better weather as the Eskimo leader suggested, Post decided to push ahead. He knew that there were celebrations planned for their arrival, and Rogers was more anxious than ever. In my opinion, Post's final and fatal third mistake occurred when they climbed back aboard the airplane for departure. Rogers sat up front to help look for the landmarks described by the Eskimos. I believe Post was so concerned about his fuel condition and the dismal weather that he didn't consider his critical weight and balance configuration with Rogers in the front seat. Shortly after take-off, the engine quit! The nose-heavy Orion smashed into the water from about 50 feet. Wiley Post and his famous passenger were killed instantly.

News of the crash stunned the country. News agencies around the world clamored for photos of the victims. Due to Rogers's popularity, some saw the crash as a strong setback to civilian air travel. This event was so newsworthy that Noel Wien, Alaska's first commercial pilot, flew photos of the disaster from Alaska to Seattle. Ironically, Wien's flight with the crash photos proved to news agencies and their waiting audiences that the airplane was the best way to cover great distances quickly.

Despite rapid developments in airplane technology, public perception of commercial aviation endured a bumpy ride due to the loss of popular fliers such as Wiley Post, Amelia Earhart, and passengers such as Will Rogers. The public considered the early flyers larger than life, daring, adventurous, and a little crazy. Howard Hughes set a new around-the-world speed record of 3 days, 19 hours and 17 minutes in 1938. Even though this record was proof that the airplane was the future of rapid transportation, the public was still skeptical. The memories of the fatalities and the potential for personal disaster were on the minds of many.

While skepticism of personal air transportation persisted in the Lower 48, the airplane thrived in Alaska. Flying in horrid weather and with few technological improvements, the early Alaskan pilots had spirit and guts. They were the true pioneers of the airline industry as we know it today. One of those brave pioneers was Ray Petersen. Ray learned about airplanes during the golden age of aviation.

Born in York, Nebraska, on August 10, 1912, Ray got an early taste for travel. He grew up on a ranch in Wyoming and later moved to the Chicago area where he worked on a farm. He watched one day as a barnstormer flew overhead and landed in one of the cleared fields. The pilot climbed out of his aircraft and asked the farmer if he

*Ray Petersen shortly after his arrival in Alaska in 1934. Ray Petersen Collection*

could use his field as a landing strip so that he could practice a few landings and perhaps sell a few airplane rides. The farmer, Bill Harbecher, quietly sized up the barnstormer. Without wasting any time he pointed to his young employee, Ray, and said, "If you take the kid for a ride, yes!"

According to Ray, he didn't like the idea very much but was too embarrassed to say anything. Ray told me that his first airplane ride convinced him that airplanes were safe. Ray was the first passenger given a ride from that makeshift field. Talk about irony. Chicago's O'Hare International Airport now covers that same field the barnstormer used as a landing strip. Ray Petersen, who became one of Alaska's foremost pilots and one of the world's top airline executives, may have been the first passenger in the history of Chicago's mighty airport.

Ray arrived in Alaska in 1934, a stowaway on a ship out of Seattle. He found there were already 55 pilots flying Alaska's stormy skies, only 10 years after Noel Wien's first commercial passenger flight. Ray went to work for Star Air Service (the predecessor of Alaska Airlines) that September. He served the Lucky Shot mine north of Anchorage in addition to hauling supplies to a scattering of trappers and prospectors. Recalling his days with Star, Ray Petersen informed me that the owner of the Lucky Shot mine, William Dunkle, was an investor and major sponsor of Star Air Service. At the time Ray started flying for Star, Steve Mills was the senior pilot and the manager. Ray explained that part of his job was to service the mine, and to transport personnel and freight. On the return flights, he would bring in the fruit of the miner's efforts, gold bullion. Servicing the mine with timely airplane service was essential. Ray also suggested that despite the fact that the miners considered beer and tobacco essential, his manager's list included only essential food items outbound, and gold on the inbound flights.

Pilot Ray Petersen hadn't been an employee at Star very long when fog started to hinder the scheduled flights to the mine. Day after day, poor visibility kept the more senior pilots drinking coffee at the Star office. Steve Mills was anxious to get the mine flights completed. He also knew the miners were out of beer.

Mills was getting desperate. There hadn't been an airplane at the mine in 10 days. At his chief pilot's urging, and with the older and wiser pilot's pity, Ray finally said he'd try. He loaded the essential items, then added a healthy supply of beer. He took off, climbed through the fog, and made numerous circling approaches until he finally landed at the mine. Although he became a hero to the miners that day, Ray told Steve Mills that flying in such poor weather was a bad deal. Steve Mills remarked,

*Kid, I like a pilot with guts!*

On another fateful, yet foggy flight, the visibility was marginal at best. Like he had done a few times before, Ray pressed on and managed to make a landing at the mine. Rather than just fly back into the fog, he used the radio and called the Star manager to get new weather information. Steve Mills told Ray that the weather seemed to be breaking.

*"From this angle you can't see the dent I put in the tower," said Ray after he crashed his Curtis Robin into the top of the Merrill Field tower during heavy fog returning from the Lucky Shot mine in 1934. Ray Petersen Collection*

Armed with hope, Ray headed back toward Merrill Field. Arriving over Anchorage, he found no breaks in the thick fog. He circled lower and lower. Finally Ray started to see 5th Avenue through the foggy mist; at least he knew he was getting close to home. He flew above the road and headed toward Merrill Field. Ray forged on. His windshield was a sheet of ice, making forward visibility almost zero. He knew that he had to spot the Star hangar and land just to the left of the tower. As he touched down on what he thought was the runway, he spotted a man running to his left. Almost immediately Ray knew he had landed too far to the right. Things were going well right up to the moment when he spotted the tower. He tried to turn but it was too late. Ray slammed into the beacon tower, causing extensive damage to Star's Curtiss Robin. The airplane came to rest right in front of Star's hangar. Ray was just climbing out of the twisted airplane when Mr. Dunkle came out of the hangar and started yelling:

*Is this my airplane?*

*I don't know. All I know is that there is a star painted on it!*

Toni Schodde Petersen after a day of grayling fishing. Circa 1934—Ray Petersen Collection

A short while later, Ray walked into Steve Mills' downtown office and told him that he'd just wrapped the Robin around the beacon.

*Well Petersen, at least you put the airplane in front of the hangar. The other guys who crack 'em up leave 'em all over the territory. Then we've got to go and get the airplanes back. It's all in the game.*

*Well, it's not in my game, you just lost a fog pilot.*

I asked Ray about that flight and some of the others during his first flying job. He sat back in his office chair and looked me straight in the eye and said,

*I don't have an alibi. I shouldn't have been flying in that kind of weather. The compliments of the mine workers weren't enough. After fighting the fog for the winter, I reached a decision: If I'm going to get killed, I'm going to die flying for Petersen and not dear old Star Air Lines.*

The next week, Ray began flying for Marsh Airways based in Bethel. He also flew occasional trips to the platinum and iridium mine at Goodnews Bay. By the end of that summer, he had become a founding partner in Bethel Airways. A major break for Ray came in 1937 when he obtained an exclusive contract to fly for the platinum mine at Goodnews Bay. Consistent work allowed him to form the Bethel-based Ray Petersen Flying Service. For the next several years, Ray plied the skies from Anchorage to the Lower Yukon and Kuskokwim Deltas. It seems love started to sprout wings, too. Fellow aviator and Reeve Aleutian Airways founder, Bob Reeve, commented on Ray's love life in an article he wrote in 1975.

*Ray started carrying the torch for a fair charmer residing in Anchorage named Toni Schodde. As Ray puts it, "That was a pretty expensive courtship, flying 400 miles to Anchorage to spend Saturday night to hold my own, especially when things didn't look so good. Her mother took a dim view of all bush pilots in general." When the Civil Aeronautics Board certified new Alaskan air routes in 1940 they recognized these trips as "grandfather rights" over the route and awarded it to Petersen.*

*Ray Petersen at the controls of a Wright J-4 Travelair 4000 at Fairview, Alaska, 1934. Ray Petersen Collection*

Life was going well for Ray. The Goodnews Bay mine remained a consistent source of revenue. He earned both a good reputation and a little prosperity by hauling miners and company supplies in a timely manner. Ray moved to Anchorage just before the outbreak of World War II. Frank Norris describes the developments in his book, *Tourism in Katmai Country*:

*Once the war began, the planes owned by many Alaskan pilots were sometimes commandeered to haul military supplies. Ray Petersen flew primarily for civilian purposes. He flew packed fish out from the Bristol Bay canneries and continued to serve the mine at Goodnews Bay, which remained open because both platinum and iridium were classified as either critical or strategic minerals. As the war progressed, Petersen and others recognized that Alaska aviation was changing. Increased business, the introduc-*

*tion of scheduled service and improved navigation aids all demanded the purchase of larger aircraft, and only through consolidation could the capital be raised to acquire the necessary planes. In 1943, therefore, Petersen purchased the Bristol Bay Air Service, operated by Bert Ruoff, and the Jim Dodson Air Service, which served Ruby, Beaver, and adjacent points out of Fairbanks. Before those purchase agreements could be approved, however, Ray and several other airline companies decided to amalgamate. Included were the Ray Petersen Flying Service, owned by Raymond and Toni Petersen and Glen Dillard; Jim Dodson Air Service, owned by Jim and Mildred Dodson; Northern Airways, owned by Frank and Hazel Pollack and Terrence McDonald; Walatka Air Service, owned by John Walatka; and Northern Air Service, owned by Robert and William Miller. They entered into a corporate organization agreement on October 22, 1945; three months later, on January 30, 1946, the carriers formally applied to the Civil Aeronautics Board (CAB) to create Northern Consolidated Airlines (NCA). On May 8, 1947, the CAB approved Petersen's two airline purchases as well as the four-company consolidation. By that time, NCA had purchased several war surplus DC3s, its first large planes. Petersen, the major shareholder, was elected president of Northern Consolidated, a position he would hold for more than 22 years.*

Pan American Airways Announces

FLYING CLIPPER SERVICE BETWEEN ALASKA AND THE U. S.

**Twice-weekly service, started June 20 with giant 4-engined Clippers, brings all principal Alaskan and U. S. cities within quick reach of each other, opens new business and vacation opportunities.**

Alaska is now within hours of all major U. S. cities, as Flying Clipper Ships speed back and forth twice weekly between Seattle and Juneau, the final link between Pan American's Pacific Alaska Airways division and U. S. domestic airlines. From Seattle to Ketchikan is just 5 hours, but 2 hours more to Juneau, and proportionately fast service to White Horse, Fairbanks, Nome, Bethel and other Alaskan points.

This is great news for vacationists—whether going from or to the States. Spectacular, unspoiled Alaska, formerly visited only by the chosen few with plenty of time to spare, is now opened to the U. S. tourist within the limits of even a short vacation. Similarly, the swift Clipper Ship schedules will give the Alaskan resident more time to enjoy longer and more frequent visits in the States.

Great news, too, for business men! No longer need the time barrier hamper trade in both directions. More important than ever will be the Alaskan market, with 5 to 1 greater per capita buying power than the U. S. average.

For further details, consult your travel agent, any Pan American or Pacific Alaska Airways office, or write Pan American Airways System, Chrysler Bldg., N. Y. C.

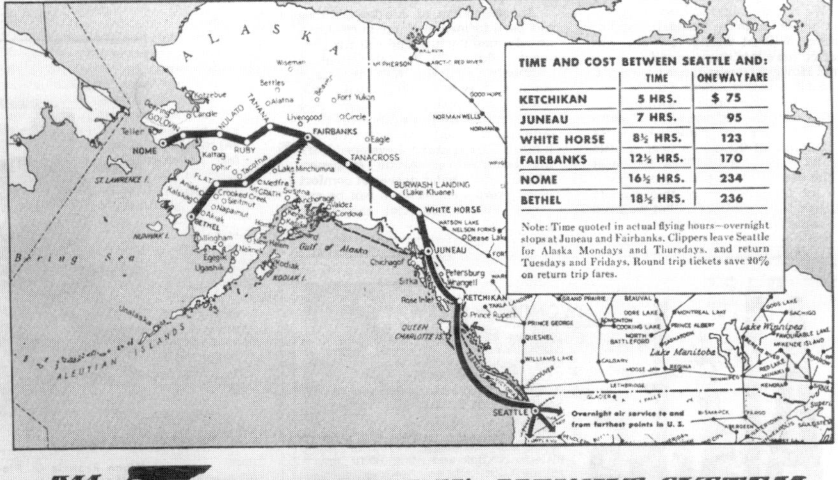

TIME AND COST BETWEEN SEATTLE AND:

| | TIME | ONE WAY FARE |
|---|---|---|
| KETCHIKAN | 5 HRS. | $ 75 |
| JUNEAU | 7 HRS. | 95 |
| WHITE HORSE | 8½ HRS. | 123 |
| FAIRBANKS | 12½ HRS. | 170 |
| NOME | 16½ HRS. | 234 |
| BETHEL | 18½ HRS. | 236 |

Note: Time quoted in actual flying hours—overnight stops at Juneau and Fairbanks. Clippers leave Seattle for Alaska Mondays and Thursdays, and return Tuesdays and Fridays. Round trip tickets save 20% on return trip fares.



*Pan American experimented with air service to Alaska in 1940. Similar ads appeared in many national publications. Ray Petersen Collection*

Public interest in airplanes boomed, especially in the northernmost territory. Alaskans accepted flying as the best way to move the mail and freight. Passengers were happy with the prompt service. When the Japanese bombed Pearl Harbor and followed with the invasion of the Aleutian Islands, both civilian and military flying became critical. Ray Petersen and other civilian pilots accepted contract work and continued to keep the territory supplied. The military leaders expanded several bases and built new ones to help stem the rising tide of the Japanese threat. The new bases became the jumping-off place for U.S. aircraft flown to Russia to aid the allied efforts. Flying was more than important in Alaska, it was critical.

Most pilots will tell you that flying in Alaska is unlike flying in other states because the territory is so big that it's almost like flying in a foreign country. In geography, if not in political reality, that's true. Certainly in terrain, vegetation, animal life, and population, Alaska has more in common with northern Canada and Siberia than with the continental United States, or "outside," as an Alaskan would say. Compared to the rest of the country, it has relatively few aids to navigation. We don't have huge metropolitan centers. At the outbreak of World War II, the total Alaskan population was less than 100,000. Juneau, the capital, boasted about 6,000 and five of the eight largest cities were in southeast Alaska. Anchorage, today Alaska's largest city, barely had 4,000 residents.

This enormous transformation was further reflected in the patterns of travel, especially by air. Before the war, the companies that called themselves airlines operated somewhat haphazardly, primarily because of severe weather conditions and the absence of good navigational aids. Flying conditions were so bad in Alaska that the Civil Aeronautics Board had difficulty in reconciling its regulations tailored for operations down south. Long periods of subzero temperatures, persistent fog, continuous rain, and driving wind were common flying partners in Alaska. These conditions often interrupted daily routes. Alaska airline companies found it difficult to maintain published schedules, which was a CAB requirement to maintain airline status. Eager to set the record straight for the northern fliers, the CAB sent some investigators to Alaska to clarify the rules one more time. Once they experienced Alaska's conditions, however, the desk-flying bureaucrats from Washington immediately granted special privileges to the Alaskan carriers, some of which continue today.

*Discovered but no one stopped. Ray was forced down on the Rhone River in his Curtis Robin. Ray carved out a huge SOS in the snow. Seeing that everyone was walking around and waving, several potential helpers took care of Ray's flying first, then planned his rescue. Ray and his passengers camped four nights on the frozen river. From the left are passengers Leonard Grau and Jerry Bishop, pilot Ray Petersen and Don Glass, the rescue pilot. Ray Petersen Collection*

## World War II and After

The United States experienced its only foreign invasion on home soil during World War II when the Japanese attacked and bombed Attu, Kiska, and Dutch Harbor on Unalaska Island. Unlike at Pearl Harbor, Japanese soldiers went ashore in the Aleutian Islands. Congress and military leaders really pushed the panic button and rushed to develop and protect the remainder of Alaska. Large military bases were built in Anchorage, Fairbanks, Sitka, Whittier, Seward, Kodiak, and Naknek. Thousands of military personnel were shipped north. Military strategists faced a huge problem. It was almost impossible to supply Alaska by air. They needed a land route.

The single most important project of the military build-up was the famous Alaska Highway. The allied command felt that Japan and Germany, united with Italy, looked all but unbeatable. The only countries with sufficient resources and war machines to confront the aggressors were the United States, Great Britain, and the Soviet Union. The U.S. and the Soviets had only one common border, the Bering Strait, which separates Alaska and Siberia. There was a need to supply military hardware to Russia and to protect America's northwest flank, neither of which could be accomplished by sea after Japan bombed Pearl Harbor in December 1941. An overland route, far enough inland to be out of range of the airplanes carried by Japanese aircraft carriers, was the only solution. The 1,520-mile road was a major engineering feat and became the only overland link between Alaska and the rest of the United States.

This massive project was led by the U.S. Army Corps of Engineers. Along with Canadian civil and military help, they conquered the formidable wilderness and built the road. The U.S. used seven regiments of men and a staggering amount of machinery to finish the project in record time. In eight months and twelve days, the soldiers felled trees, put down gravel and built pontoon bridges. They used tons of garbage, broken down vehicles, and anything else they could find in their attempts to create a stable roadbed across the boggy swamp and muskeg. The highway opened on November 20, 1942.

The road was built because of the war, but it was the residents of Alaska who benefited most from the construction. The highway stimulated another postwar boom, and increased development of Alaska's natural resources. This growth led to a new drive for statehood. Alaskans wanted full representation in Washington, D.C. In June 1958, Congress approved the Statehood Act and Alaskans quickly accepted. On January 3, 1959, President Eisenhower proclaimed Alaska to be the 49th state.

The impact of World War II had on aviation was monumental. The war necessitated training pilots and prompted airplane production. Creation of the Alaska Highway added airports. The military presence provided numerous high-ranking commanders, some of whom enjoyed sportfishing. These commanders used their rank to enjoy the world's best fishing. During the period immediately following the war, Naknek Air Force Base in Alaska and the air force base at Goose Bay, Labrador, were probably the most inspected military bases in existence. Goose Bay had Atlantic salmon and Naknek boasted the world's greatest fishing for big, wild rainbow trout. Along with a few commercial fishing tycoons and cannery managers, the military leaders were among the first of the nonresident visitors who spread the word about fishing in Alaska. Always a popular activity with residents, fishing was rapidly becoming financially important. To accommodate that interest, more was needed than the roadhouses of the past.

Lawing's Roadhouse near Seward, Taku Lodge near Juneau, Bell Island Resort near Ketchikan, Sitka and Tenakee Hot Springs, along with Birch Lake Cabins near

Fairbanks, Dwyers Inn near Chitna, and the Woodland Lodge near Talkeetna all offered fishing in their advertisements, but each had many other activities to lure tourists. There simply were no lodges or roadhouses that catered specifically to fishermen. Fishing was becoming more popular, but certainly not popular enough to sustain any full-time seasonal businesses. What fishing existed was conducted on a day-to-day, trip-by-trip basis. Prior to the war, hunting brought sportsmen, and some Alaska residents engaged in sportfishing for the table, but no lodges entertained fishing clients on a regular basis. Careful perusal of *Tewkesbury's Who's Who in Alaska and Tewkesbury's Alaska Business Index* reveals that no fishing lodges or sport fish guiding businesses were operational in 1947. Despite the lack of fishing lodges, fishing was a very popular activity. Fishing was so popular in the 1940s, in fact, that the government decided to make some money from the activity.

Once the government gets an idea that might generate some income or add a new level of bureaucracy, neither hell nor high water can stop the march of progress. Licensing of fishermen, both residents and nonresidents, was definitely planned for the Territory of Alaska.

Walton Powell, son of the famous fishing rod designer and builder, E.C. Powell, received Alaska's first nonresident fishing license. Like many young men of his time, he came to Alaska because of the war. His father started building fly rods in 1910 in Red Bluff, California. Born in 1915, Walton started working at the family factory at the tender age of seven. The factory flourished for almost 20 years before the war changed his life and his father's business. According to Walton, all sportfishing rod manufacturing ceased by governmental decree right after the bombing at Pearl Harbor. The government wanted the raw materials for the war effort. The war changed occupations for many people but not for Walton Powell. The government didn't need rod builders, but Walton was a well-qualified machinist.

The young Powell was drafted and sent to Seattle where he waited nearly a month for passage to Alaska. He traveled to Juneau aboard the Canadian Pacific's *Princess Nora*. Eventually he made his way to Excursion Inlet, where he served his military duty time.

Being around the saltwater bays and inlet streams gave Walton the opportunity to fish. He made numerous trips around Southeast Alaska conducting military business. He was able to explore and fish in many rivers during his travels. While traveling on military business, he befriended Frank DuFresne, head of Fish and Wildlife in Alaska. The two worked on several projects and eventually became good friends.

Walton learned about the plan to issue nonresident fishing licenses and asked his friend for the first one. Frank agreed and made arrangements for Walton to arrive at Fish and Wildlife's Juneau office early the next morning. As Frank had already signed the first three nonresident licenses, he called his secretary and gave instructions to issue Walton the first early the next morning. Later that same day, a ceremony was planned to issue the coveted first license to Ira Gabrielson, the Director of the U.S. Fish and Wildlife Service. He had traveled to Juneau only for the presentation. In one of those politically delicate moments, Frank DuFresne was able to pass the blame onto his secretary for making such a crucial mistake in issuing the first license. Begrudgingly, Mr. Gabrielson had to accept license #2. Privately, however, Mr. DuFresne expressed some displeasure with his federal director. He was glad that the license went to a fisherman and a friend. During my interview with Walton, I asked him if he ever heard from Ira Gabrielson about the license-issuing fiasco. Fellow lodge operator Jack Holman and I noticed a small grin developing on Walton's face. We sat and listened as Walton did a Paul Harvey and told us the rest of the story. He was obviously proud of the whole experience.

*Yes, I did hear from him, but he wasn't a fisherman; he was just a politician. I met Ira in Juneau a few days after I got the Number 1 license. Considering he had come all the way from Washington, D.C. just for the ceremony, I knew he might be a little mad considering his trip and all. We had a short but pleasant chat and then he expressed a little concern at the circumstances regarding the issuance of the license. I just looked at him and said, "Screw you!" I never heard another word about it.*

IN REPLY REFER TO

UNITED STATES
DEPARTMENT OF THE INTERIOR
FISH AND WILDLIFE SERVICE
ALASKA GAME COMMISSION

Juneau, Alaska

July 26, 1943

Mr. Welton E. Powell
Yuba City, California

Dear Walton:

As requested you will find enclosed Non-Resident Fishing License No. 1 --- the first ever to be issued by the Alaska Game Commission since Game Fish guardianship has been delegated to this Commission.

You are indeed fortunate to secure the first license. Dr. Ira N. Gabrielson, Director of the Fish and Wildlife Service, Washington, D. C., who is now in Juneau, was issued No. 2, while the Honorable Fredrick C. Walcott, President of the American Wildlife Institute and former Senator, received License No. 3.

Hope to see you on your return to Juneau from the commercial fishing venture.

Best of luck and yours for fine Powell rods,

LEO RHODE
Jr. Administrative Officer

*This letter presented courtesy of Walton Powell.*

The history of scheduled airline service to and from Alaska is much like the territory's history, boom and bust. Prior to World War II, sporadic flights occurred more at the whim of a pilot than on any scheduled basis. Eventually, Pan-American Airlines provided Clipper Service into the Territory. Pan-American's service operated between Seattle and Alaska twice a week. Because of the war, this service ended shortly after it started in 1940. Ray Petersen told me that the airplanes were used in the military effort. According to Ray, there was little, if any, civilian traffic during the war years.

Prior to their Clipper Service, Pan-Am, as well as a few other carriers, flew a circuitous route to Alaska. Airplanes left Seattle for Juneau, then to Whitehorse and into Fairbanks. After the war, there were numerous nonscheduled flights to and from Alaska. Ray Petersen's Northern Consolidated Airline entered into that market when Ray bought a surplus DC-3. These flights were sporadic, however, as Ray Petersen kept a wary eye on safety. Ray halted the nonscheduled operations at NCA once the major airlines such as Pan American, Western, and Northwest started scheduled service to Alaska. Ray told me:

> *It just wasn't worth the headache. I arranged interline agreements with all of them. Because Northern Consolidated was a scheduled carrier, the major airlines were eager to work with us.*

By 1947, Alaska had daily scheduled airline service from several cities in the Lower 48. What Alaska didn't have, however, was big civil airports in Anchorage and Fairbanks to receive the passengers, nor much of a tourism industry.

I'll bet that was the fastest you've ever covered 40,000 years. At least now you have the basic knowledge of the Territory, some of the major events and characters involved, as well as a little understanding of Alaska's role in commercial fishing and developing aviation. I thought the details presented might help you appreciate the stories to follow.

ALASKA GAME COMMISSION $2.50
JUNEAU, ALASKA
№ 1
NON-RESIDENT FISHING LICENSE

THIS IS TO CERTIFY that Walton E. Powell of Yuba City, California is hereby licensed to fish for game fish in Alaska during the open season of the year ending June 30, 19......, subject to the Alaska Game Law as amended, and regulations thereunder.

Description: Age, 27 years; height, 5 ft. 7 in.; weight, 150 lbs.; complexion, dark; color of eyes, brown; color of hair, brown; other distinguishing characteristics ..........

*(1) Citizen by *(a) birth, *(b) ~~naturalization~~.
*(2) ~~Foreign born with valid first-set first papers~~, .......... (Nationality)

Issued at Juneau, Alaska. Countersigned by [signature] Issuing Officer
Date July 26, 1943
[signature] (Signature of licensee—*must be signed before use*)

A. G. C. Form 87c * Strike out inappropriate wording.

*The first Alaska nonresident fishing license issued to Walton Powell on July 26, 1943, Juneau, Alaska. Courtesy of Walton Powell*

# Chapter 3
# The Party Begins—1948 - 1959

"Let us steer by the stars, and not by the lights of each passing ship."
*General Omar Bradley*

Before I actually get started with the players and the events leading to the opening of the first sportfishing lodges in Bristol Bay and Alaska, I thought I'd try to put your thoughts, at least, into 1948.

The postwar baby boom was in full swing in the United States. Globally speaking, the world was still in turmoil. Soviet forces in Germany set up a blockade in July to cut off rail and highway traffic between West Germany and Berlin. The famed airlift began later that month when American and British aircraft delivered food and supplies to more than 2 million people in West Berlin. The Republic of Korea came into existence in August, but the North Korean People's Democratic Republic denounced President Syngman Rhee and his regime. North Korea claimed dominion over all of Korea. Threats from the Russians and the Koreans prompted U.S. presidential adviser Bernard Baruch to coin the phrase *cold war.*

Meanwhile back in the USA, an energy crisis at the start of the year brought urgent requests for voluntary reductions in the use of gasoline, fuel oil, and natural gas. The United States became a major importer of oil by developing low-cost petroleum sources in Venezuela and the Middle East. In the world of American politics, Thomas E. Dewey of New York made his second run for president. Harry Truman won the election by a very close margin. The race was so close that the *Chicago Tribune* was totally embarrassed when their paper hit the streets with a front-page headline proclaiming Dewey the winner. A noteworthy candidate in the 1948 presidential campaign was Dixiecrat Strom Thurmond, one of today's

# Welcome to ALASKA

*The increasing thousands who head north for recreation each year will find in Alaska a country whose beauty is not exceeded elsewhere on earth.*

**ERNEST GRUENING**

**Governor of Alaska**

*Nowhere else is there so striking a juxtaposition of high mountains and sea, of virgin forests, of lofty waterfalls, of glaciers discharging their crystal cargoes into the salt water of the ocean. Nowhere else on the American continent is there such an abundance of wildlife. Nowhere else can even the most casual tourist have the opportunity to see the largest species of bear, largest species of moose, mountain sheep, mountain goat, and caribou. As for the fishing—our rainbow trout run as large as 36 inches and in many of our lakes and rivers every cast means a strike.*

*I have never known of anyone who came to Alaska as a tourist who was not thrilled by his experience and eager to return for a longer stay.*

*The greatest handicap at present to the development of a great tourist country is the lack of sufficient resort facilities for all those who would like to come. We welcome investors who desire to build lodges and tourist camps. We think there is a prosperous and enjoyable occupation for those who come north with that in view.*

ERNEST GRUENING,
*Governor of Alaska.*

*An invitation to investors to "build lodges and tourist camps" from the territorial governor appeared in the "Travel Agent" in 1950, during the height of Ray Petersen's advertising blitz. Ray told me it was merely coincidence, as he didn't get involved with Mr. Gruening until after statehood.*

senatorial legends. An Income Tax Reduction Act became law on April 2 despite President Truman's veto. Speaking from Spokane, Truman called the 80th Congress the worst we'd ever had.

On a more personal level, American consumers benefited from both war research and product development in 1948. Armour and Company introduced Dial soap as the world's first deodorant soap. This new product employed the bacteria-killing chemical hexachlorophene discovered during World War II. The Campbell Soup Company introduced V-8 cocktail juice that same year.

Speaking of food, there weren't the fast-food restaurants that we have today. The McDonald brothers, who opened the McDonald hamburger stand in Pasadena in 1940, turned their small business into a fast-food franchise opportunity in 1948. The Baskin-Robbins ice cream chain began its rapid growth as California entrepreneur Burton "Butch" Baskin merged his small business with the Snowbird Ice Cream Company of Glendale, California. Baseball Nut was an early flavor favorite.

By 1948, nearly one million American homes had television sets. The first sets featured small black and white screens encased in huge wooden cabinets. Compared with today's multitude of channels, programming was crude and limited. There were no television stars. The Ed Sullivan Show debuted in June with newspaper columnist Ed Sullivan as the master of ceremonies. Unknown comedians Dean Martin and Jerry Lewis headlined the first broadcast. Hopalong Cassidy, television's first western series, aired that year on the fledgling television network, NBC.

In Alaska, things were going well. Anchorage, the largest city, needed a new civilian airport.

## The First Lodge Players: Bud Branham and Ray Petersen

The flying business was good for Ray Petersen and his wife, Toni. Raising a family became important as their first child, Rose Marie, was born in Bethel in 1939. Ray moved his airline headquarters and his family residence to Anchorage in 1941. Their first son, Chuck, was born later that year. Family life and the aviation business kept the Petersen family busy.

By any standard, Ray's Northern Consolidated Airline was a dominant force in Alaska's aviation community by 1948, despite the fact that Anchorage didn't have a major civil airport. Like other local carriers, Ray's smaller airplanes used Merrill Field, but large aircraft such as the Douglas DC-4s that plied the skies between Alaska and the Lower 48 needed the long runway available only at Elmendorf Air Force Base. While civil use of the military runways was difficult at best for the domestic air carriers, the military leaders found it increasingly difficult to keep the facility at a state of heightened readiness. The military hierarchy was concerned about the Cold War that developed after the end of World War II. Russia was a potential military threat and Elmendorf was a primary base in our first line of defense.

One of our foremost military commanders, Lt. General Nathan Twining, was appointed commanding general of the Alaskan Department on October 1, 1947. Later that month he became commander-in-chief of the Alaska Air Command. Twining's military career was no less than brilliant. He was a highly decorated strategist who believed in air power. According to the December 1953 edition of *Current Biography*:

*Soon after the end of the war in Europe, General Twining returned to the United States for interim duty at Washington, and on July 24 he was appointed to succeed General Curtis E. LeMay as commanding general of the 20th Air Force based on the Mariana Islands in the Pacific. B-29 Superfortresses of Twining's command dropped the atomic bombs on Hiroshima and Nagasaki, and other 20th Air Force very heavy bombers made devastating incendiary and demolition attacks on the Tokyo area.*

Like many upper level military and political leaders of the day, the general was an eager angler. General Twining often cited fishing as one of his favorite pastimes and took every opportunity to fish. Once assigned to Alaska, the general made numerous inspection forays to the Naknek Air Base to check on the troops under his command. I imagine that on more than one occasion his surprise visits had more to do with fishing than with inspecting. I asked Admiral Thomas Moorer, retired chairman of the Joint Chiefs of Staff and Twining's contemporary war hero, if he ever had the opportunity to fish with General Twining. He told me he had fished with Twining for Atlantic salmon at Gander, Newfoundland. Admiral Moorer told me that Twining was a good fisherman. The Admiral led me to believe he would have liked to have fished with the general in Alaska, but Twining was air force, and he was a navy man. Unfortunately, the navy had little presence in Bristol Bay.

As the top military commander in Alaska, Twining proved instrumental during the campaign to obtain federal budget approval for the much-needed Anchorage International Airport. The general found it difficult to combine traffic on Alaska's biggest military facility with the ever-increasing civilian air traffic. He had to separate civilian and military traffic and facilities. To accomplish his goal, he joined forces with the Anchorage Chamber of Commerce. The chamber members applauded the general's support because of his many political associations in Washington.

Anchorage chamber member and New York Life agent Hugh Doherty was sent to the political enclaves in Washington to do the legwork for the Anchorage airport project. During the various committee meetings and lobbying efforts, Hugh met the politically powerful New York congressman Leonard Hall and New York State Magistrate Russell Sprague, a major GOP strategist. If Hall and Sprague could be persuaded that the airport project was worthy of funding, they had more than enough political clout to make it happen.

By the winter of 1948 the lobbying efforts of Doherty and General Twining had been noticed. Feeling the time was right to include an airport for Fairbanks in the funding bill, Alaska's federal delegate, Robert Bartlett, lobbied hard to secure funding for both airports. By the time the budget was announced, new civil airports at Anchorage and Fairbanks were approved and scheduled for construction. When the news hit Anchorage, everyone was elated, especially Doherty. Now all he had to do was to reward his political allies.

Doherty decided the best way to thank his political supporters for their assistance was to invite them to Alaska and roll out the red carpet. Like the best lobbyists, Doherty had sat through enough budget meetings and political parties to learn the likes and dislikes of his powerful friends. He'd certainly sipped enough cocktails with the political big shots to learn that both Congressman Hall and Judge Sprague were ardent fishermen. It didn't take Hugh too long to realize that a fishing trip to Alaska would be the best thank you Alaska could provide. He also knew he had the right man for the job. Doherty returned to Anchorage and promptly had a meeting with fellow chamber member and aviation committee chairman Ray Petersen.

Hugh Doherty could have chosen no one better than Ray Petersen to host the two dignitaries on a deluxe fishing trip. Hugh knew Ray liked fishing. Since his arrival in Alaska in 1934, Ray had fished as much as possible. Because of his long Alaska tenure, piloting skills, and fishing experience, Ray knew the best places to go. Besides that, Ray had an airline.

During their meeting, Hugh explained to Ray that both Hall and Sprague had heard the rumors about the fabulous trout fishing in Bristol Bay and were keen to try it. A prominent New York hunter and enthusiastic fisherman, Fred Hollander, had been to Alaska numerous times and his stories and exploits permeated the sacred Halls of Congress.

Ten years earlier, a story about Hollander's first fishing trip to Bristol Bay had been printed in *Alaska Sportsman* with photo support. This article about the rainbow trout fishing in remote Alaska documented the first sportsman's trip into Bristol Bay for the sole purpose of catching large rainbows.

*Fred Hollander and Ray E. McDonald were the first to travel to Bristol Bay to sport fish. Circa 1937—Courtesy Alaska Magazine*

From the article "Giants of the Newhalen," by Ray E. McDonald, *Alaska Sportsman*, September 1938:

*In the Newhalen River, the rainbow trout are prehistoric in size! From time to time for a number of years, this report had been brought from trappers, prospectors, and members of Government survey parties. But the statement had never been verified. That is, not until one day in the summer of 1935 when an airplane pilot brought three giant rainbow trout back from Iliamna to Anchorage. He opened up a burlap sack and dumped beauties 28 to 32 inches in length on the sidewalk at my feet...this was the first confirmation of stories I had heard and then and there I determined to some day fish the stream or streams from which these rainbows had been taken. I was particularly interested because I had fished every available stream known to contain trout in and around Anchorage. I talked to Fred Hollander about the giant fish. Fred, a New York big game hunter and enthusiastic fisherman has been visiting Alaska every summer for a number of years (often twice a year) so we decided that we were indeed duty-bound to fly to the land of "Prehistoric Trout" at the first opportunity. It was 1937 before Fred and I could make arrangements to go to the Newhalen together. Early in June Fred joined me at Anchorage and asked me to be his guest on the trip. I was delighted.*

*We reserved passage with Star Airline for June 4. We had two days in which to obtain the necessary equipment and pack. From the extensive fishing outfit Fred had brought from New York, he chose two fishing rods (a 12-foot salmon rod, used previously for Atlantic salmon fishing in New Brunswick, and a 6-ounce Hardy. Also, he added a quantity of fancy flies, some plugs, an assortment of spinners, a salmon gaff, a landing net and some imported leaders which had been at $5.25 each in England. My outfit included two 6-ounce rods, a Montague and an Edwards Special, but only 50 yards of 28-pound test line. My leaders, made by me and fashioned from Japanese gut, cost only 10 cents each. To play safe, I took fresh salmon eggs for bait.*

*We had 417 pounds more luggage than the weight (300 pounds) allowed by our tickets, although we tried not to take unnecessary baggage. The excess weight cost 24 cents a pound in addition to the $48 per passenger fare one-way. In the old days, the trip from Anchorage to Seversen's Roadhouse and trading post, on the shore of Iliamna Lake, would have meant either going by portage from Iliamna Bay across the precipitous Aleutian Range to Old Iliamna, which was rough and tiresome, requiring weeks of preparation beforehand, or one could have gone by boat down Cook Inlet and Shelikof Strait, around Alaska Peninsula through Unimak Pass, up Bristol Bay to Kvichak Bay, north up Kvichak River and across Iliamna Lake to Seversen's Roadhouse. Under those conditions, it is not surprising that no sportsmen ever had fished that district. Since the advent of planes, Hans Seversen's place has become the crossroads-of-the-air for planes between the Cook Inlet and Bristol Bay regions. It is a short ride and thrilling trip by air from Anchorage to Seversen's via the "back door" over the precipitous Aleutian Range, a distance of 236 miles.*

*Hans, whom I had met previously in Anchorage where he came occasionally to sell furs, helped unload the plane. He had one look at the amount of luggage deposited on the graveled beach before he asked, "What the hell you intend to do down here?" We told him we intended to fish for rainbow trout. "Well, I'm glad to have you boys with me," he said. "But, you are the first SPORTSMEN ever to come here solely for the purpose of catching these huge trout."*

The remainder of the article portrayed the fantastic fishing enjoyed by McDonald and Hollander, including a great description of fighting and landing several huge rainbow trout. This great story was accompanied by pictures of the big fish. This article provided enough details to whet the appetites of anglers Hall and Sprague. After all, they knew that in 1944 Bud Branham, a military Air-Sea Rescue pilot, had been assigned the unique duty of guiding the Commander-in-Chief, President Franklin D. Roosevelt, on an Alaskan fishing excursion. From Bud's book, *Sourdough and Swahili:*

*Providence, it seemed, had selected me as the personal guide of FDR. I was ordered to Hickam Field in Hawaii, and the Sacred Cow, the personal plane reserved for the President, was sent to Kodiak to pick me up. That was the first nonstop flight, as far as I know, from the Aleutians direct to Hawaii. Upon arrival, I learned that the U.S.S. Alaska, the President's flagship for this trip, had departed for Kodiak five hours earlier. After being on the ground for just a couple of hours at Hickam Field, we went back to Adak to meet the ship. At Adak, I was transferred to the USS Alaska. I met the President and most of his staff during a two-day voyage back to Kodiak with stops along the way. At Kodiak, I arranged for a picket boat (a small Navy personnel boat) to be transported to Buskin Lake, near the naval base, which held a great concentration of brook trout and a few browns and rainbows. There the President and I enjoyed a couple of days of marvelous fishing. Admiral Lebey, who was his personal physician and at least two Secret Service men who were over six feet tall and very brawny, always accompanied him. They carried Roosevelt everywhere, for his tragic affliction, poliomyelitis, had long ago left him unable to walk. Yet, he could cast 60 feet from a sitting position. He loved fly-fishing, and he was good at it.*

*Famed hunting guide Bud Branham with his brother, Dennis (far right), and an unidentified client at Kakhonak Falls. Circa 1950—Chris Branham*

*We chatted about all sorts of things, and one day he called me by my nickname, Bud, instead of Lieutenant. This greatly displeased*

*Admiral Lehey, but he couldn't say anything although his frown revealed his displeasure. The Secret Service men, on the other hand, seemed to get a kick out of it. Finally, the President asked me whether I had voted for him and when I told him I hadn't he smiled and said, "Could you tell me why not?" I said, "Surely, Mr. President. First of all, I'm not a Democrat. And second, Alaskans don't have a vote." He laughed at that and said, "I surely should have remembered that Alaska is still a territory. I hope that someday that will be remedied." In addition to fishing Buskin Lake, we fished off Juneau for a couple of afternoons. That surely must have been the first time in history when a battleship towed a fishing boat. Among my treasured possessions is a commendation that cites this incident.*

Judge Russell Sprague, Ray Petersen, Congressman Len Hall, and Bill Rudeman with a nice catch of fish near Aniak during the summer of 1948. Ray Petersen Collection

(Author's Note: With reference to Bud's comments on fishing, I spoke with Len Schwartz, Kodiak area fish biologist from the Alaska Department of Fish and Game about the fish at Buskin Lake. Len has been working as a fisheries biologist in Kodiak since 1976 and assured me there has never been a brown trout or a brook trout in Buskin Lake waters. He did tell me that the Dolly Varden are close relatives to both and that variations in the colors of the Buskin fish can sometimes fool even the most knowledgeable professional. Bud may also have been taking some poetic rights in naming the USS Alaska in his story, too. Perhaps he was keeping with the secrecy of the President's original mission. War records indicate that President Roosevelt was on a ship in the Gulf of Alaska with Bud in 1944, but research indicates it was not the USS Alaska.)

As president of Northern Consolidated Airline, Ray Petersen knew the political risk he would be taking escorting Sprague and Hall around Alaska. Congressman Leonard Hall was opposed to small airline subsidies and made no bones about his position. He had recently stated that he would cancel all the subsidies allocated to the smaller carriers. After all, the major airlines were opposed to the subsidy program and Hall was their man. Ray's airline needed the subsidy, yet he was happy at the prospect of increased business growth because of the new airport. Ray decided he'd risk the trip with Congressman Hall and Judge Sprague. After all, it was supposed to be a fishing trip, not a political campaign.

Over the next few weeks Ray, Hugh, and the rest of the Chamber of Commerce members made extensive plans. The group put together a detailed and extensive itinerary. Ray wanted Hugh Doherty to join the party because he knew the politicians personally. After completing all the plans, Ray and Hugh issued the formal invitations to Congressman Hall and Judge Sprague. Ray also invited his friend and recent fishing companion, Don Horter, to join them.

*New York magistrate Russell Sprague above the narrows on Coville Lake in 1948. Ray Petersen Collection*

Don Horter came to Alaska in 1946 and immediately became influential in Ray's thoughts about sportsmen, conservation, and fly-fishing. Ray admitted that before Don Horter's coaxing, he'd been strictly a salmon egg and spinner man. On several occasions the pair fished together in Bristol Bay. During these trips, Don extolled the virtues of fly-fishing as a sport and explained the concept of conservation. In addition to his extensive fishing knowledge, his considerable media background would make him a good addition to the trip Ray planned. Previously, Horter had worked as a public relations specialist for the fledgling television network, NBC.

The plans were set and the invitations accepted. The group would assemble in July 1948 shortly after the conclusion of the Republican National Convention. Hall and Sprague were supporters of presidential candidate Thomas E. Dewey. The Republicans, especially Sprague and Hall, were convinced that Dewey would defeat incumbent President Truman in the fall election and become President.

The trip to Alaska would not only be a good rest and reward for their hard work at the convention, it would also give these political powerhouses the opportunity to view the Anchorage airport project and the air transportation industry in rural Alaska.

The Anchorage Chamber of Commerce hosted a cocktail party honoring the Washington visitors shortly after they stepped from the airliner that brought them to Alaska. Immediately after Hugh Doherty introduced the politicians to Ray Petersen, Congressman Hall took Ray aside and took great pleasure in saying, "A lot of small airlines will die on the vine without the subsidies." He made it clear to Ray that no amount of fishing could be used to sway his political position. Ray didn't have much of a retort but thought that at least the Congressman spoke his mind.

With that ominous beginning, Congressman Len Hall, his secretary and aide Bill Rudeman, Hugh Doherty, Don Horter, Federal Judge Russ Sprague and Ray Petersen climbed aboard a Northern Consolidated Lockheed Electra and departed for western Alaska and the rich fishing grounds.

The trip was planned to last ten days. Ray decided to start the outing fishing for northern pike near the village of Aniak. Catching was better than expected. The politicians were able to take a little time to discuss the ramifications of living in remote Alaska with residents of the Kuskokwim region.

The group moved on to Platinum. Ray wanted the politicians to get a firsthand look at the problems encountered at an Alaskan mining operation. On their first day in Platinum, the grandson of the mine president, Andrew Olson, caught his hand in a meatgrinder. The young lad was severely injured. It was obvious that he needed to get to a hospital as soon as possible. The bureaucrats watched as the boy was given immediate first aid, then taken to Ray's airliner. They learned that the only way to get the boy to a hospital was by air and that the closest medical facilities were in Bethel, more than 150 miles away. Sprague and Hall hadn't realized that Alaska had so few roads and that airplanes were such a necessity.

Northern Consolidated captain Oscar Underhill left Ray and the political visitors at the mine as he departed on the medivac flight. Once airborne, the captain learned that the weather in Bethel was horrible, so he immediately turned toward Anchorage. Early the next morning, Captain Underhill returned to Platinum in a DC-3 with great news for the mining community. After he described the weather conditions that diverted his emergency flight to Anchorage, he reported that the prompt medivac had saved the boy's arm. The entire group felt relieved. Later that day, they departed the remote mine for Naknek Air Base.

As luck would have it, the worst storm that western Alaska had seen in twenty-five years occurred during the congressional visit. The politicians witnessed the devastation caused by that storm. Ray's five Republic Sea

Bees buzzed back and forth from all parts of Bristol Bay to the Naknek runway ferrying injured people and supplies. Again, Oscar Underhill was called upon to make medivac flights. In addition to the Northern Consolidated DC-3, several other large aircraft carried supplies and ferried the injured to Anchorage for treatment. The necessity for airplanes in the Alaska territory was obvious. Although this was a difficult time for local residents, Ray couldn't have written a better scenario for the politicians to observe.

Ray Petersen's decision to spend the final four days of the red-carpet trip fishing the great rivers in Bristol Bay was no accident. He'd fished Bristol Bay since 1942 and he knew it had the best sportfishing in the territory. He often took the managers of the large salmon canneries to the rivers and lakes in this area. As a fisherman, Ray frequented the Bristol Bay watershed whenever possible. It was the best place in Alaska to fish for big rainbow trout. Ray knew the best fishing rivers in the area; for sleeping and eating, however, the military offered a solution.

General Twining was advised of the fishing excursion planned by the Chamber of Commerce. He, too, had worked hard to get approval for the airport project and wanted his political friends to have a great trip. The general offered Ray Petersen and his guests the use of the military camp and facilities near Naknek Air Base, a military site established during the war. From *Tourism in Katmai Country:*

> *In 1941, the U.S. Army Air Corps established Naknek Air Base (which was renamed King Salmon Air Station in the 1950s). Construction and military personnel soon discovered that the nearby waters, because of their temperature and purity, offered superb sport fishing possibilities. Military authorities reacted by establishing two rest and recreation camps nearby. Rapids Camp (called Annex No. 1 by the Air Force) was located at the foot of the Naknek River Rapids, five miles southeast of the base, while Lake Camp (Annex No. 2) was located at the west end of Naknek Lake, seven miles to the east.*

Thanks to General Twining's interest in their success, Ray's fishermen were able to sleep and have morning and evening meals only 20 flying minutes from the greatest trout fishing in the world. Ray's Dillingham station manager, John Walatka, did the float flying during the Bristol Bay segment of the trip. Reputedly one of the best floatplane pilots to ever have flown in Alaska, John was another Alaska aviation pioneer who loved to fish. Ray felt that John would be a great asset during their stay at the military camp. With the help of Don Horter, John Walatka, and Ray Petersen, the politicians couldn't help but catch large rainbow trout. Although their stay was short in Bristol Bay, the entire group settled into the schedule with ease.

Every morning they climbed aboard a Northern Consolidated Norseman and flew to one of Ray's favorite rivers. After fishing all day, they would return to the Air Force camp where the military staff provided them with first-class meals. To ease the pain of all their hard fishing duties during the day, Ray supplied a bottle or two of fine Scotch whiskey. I was told that discussions about fishing, flying, and politics often lasted well into the night.

By the conclusion of the fishing trip, Ray felt confident that Alaska would benefit from the politicians' visit. He also knew that Alaska and her great fishing would again be discussed at the highest levels in the nation's capital. The whole group thoroughly enjoyed the experience and great friendships formed. Congressman Hall and Judge Sprague observed many things during their 10-day tour, only one of which was the usefulness of the airplane. They saw the need for improved airport facilities throughout the territory. It became obvious to Ray that Congressman Hall had a different perspective of small airline subsidies, too. During the farewell cocktail party and shortly before their return to Washington, Hall took Ray aside again.

*Mr. Petersen, I can assure you, one small Alaska airline will not wither on the vine.*

Not unlike Captain Kirk and Mr. Spock having a summary discussion at the conclusion of each episode of *Star Trek,* Ray Petersen and John Walatka had a meeting not too long after the politicians departed for Washington. During the course of the evening, Ray and John discussed the fishing trip and how it might have been better. During their discussion, Ray proposed building fishing camps on several rivers they had recently fished, including the Brooks and Kulik Rivers.

*I can't remember the exact moment or my exact words, but I do remember that was the first time I expressed my thoughts about having fishing camps aloud. John Walatka and I discussed the idea well into the night. Little did I know what I was getting into!*

John added fuel to Ray's thoughts. He stated the obvious advantages of having remote camps such as being able to fish early in the morning and late in the evening. He also pointed out that they could fish in bad weather but couldn't always fly. The more they talked, the more reasons they found to continue their discussion. Reality reared its ugly head when Ray brought up some crucial problems such as selecting the sites and building the camps. Then he focused on the major issue, the cost. Even a small camp would be expensive to build and maintain. The pair enjoyed a few more whiskies while they considered the possibilities. Ray decided to think about it for a while. He did. The more he thought, the more focused he became.

Ray's concept of having camps at his favorite fishing rivers was beginning to take shape by the start of 1949. He felt confident that his ideas were sound. First, he discussed the concept with General Twining. While in Washington on other business, he met and discussed his idea with Congressman Hall and some of his cronies.

At the urging of General Twining and with considerable encouragement and direction from his Washington-based political friends, Ray approached the National Park Service with his plans to establish fishing camps in the Katmai region. Among other reasons, Ray felt that establishing fishing camps would decrease the wanton disregard for conservation he and others had seen in the Katmai region. In *Tourism in Katmai Country,* Frank Norris outlines some of the events leading to the establishment of the first Katmai concession contract:

*During the late 1940s, NPS officials continued to receive reports from Fish and Wildlife Service officials about the degradation of area resources. Officially, hunting and trapping were prohibited within the monument. Fishing regulations specified that no more than ten fish could be caught per day and that the total catch be limited to twenty fish. The ugly reality, however, was that hunting and trapping violations were increasing, and the fish resource was being abused to the point where "poaching was rampant and the trout were caught with gobs of salmon eggs on giant Colorado spinners and hooks." By the summer of 1948, Fish and Wildlife Service representatives stationed at Brooks Lake noted quite definitely that the rainbow trout had decreased as the result of the popularity to airborne sportsmen.*

Long before Ray traveled to Washington to propose his plans, he had chosen the final locations for his camps. He had flown and fished the entire Bristol Bay watershed and picked what he considered the prime locations.

Based on his own experiences and with some direction from Don Horter and comments made during the congressional visit, Ray understood that his camps must provide the ultimate in fishing for rainbow trout. Although some interest was shown in other species, the rainbow was the king of Alaska's sport fish. The only places in Bristol Bay that were not considered in Ray's search for the best locations were Kakhonak Falls and the Naknek River. The area around Kakhonak Falls was eliminated from consideration because Bud Branham had started building a cabin at that location during the summer of 1949. The Naknek River was rejected because of the military base. The facilities were already well developed and the possibilities for improved public access were too great.

In searching out the best rainbow haunts, Ray looked for streams that remained clear and fishable during even the worst weather. Numerous Bristol Bay rivers, including the Copper River at the Southeast end of Lake Iliamna, were eliminated from his long list of possible locations because they had a tendency to get high and murky during prolonged rains. Ray also knew the need for spawning water. He looked for shallow rivers with gravel bottoms. He knew huge numbers of spawning salmon guaranteed great rainbow trout populations. Most importantly, however, the rivers had to be fishable for the average angler. Based on these criteria, Ray rated all the rivers for accessibility.

Ray was systematic in his approach to selecting the best places. After deciding the fishing was considerably better on the eastern or Katmai Monument side of Bristol Bay than on the Tikchik Lakes or western side, he concentrated his search in the Katmai region. From the vast number of possible fishing streams and camp locations, he narrowed his list to what he considered the five best fishing lodge sites in Bristol Bay.

Ray chose nearly every location on the eastern side of the Kvichak River that featured a short, salmon-spawning river between two clear lakes. When you look at a map of the area, it is easy to appreciate Ray's judgement in site selection. Specifically, the Brooks River is a short, gravel-bottomed river that drains Brooks Lake into Naknek Lake. The Battle River is a short, gravel-bottomed river that drains Battle Lake into Kukaklek Lake. A similar situation occurs on the very short river that flows between Coville Lake and Lower Savonoski (Grosvenor) Lake. The Kulik River is also a short, clear, gravel-bottomed river that drains Kulik Lake into Nonvianuk Lake. The only site Ray chose that didn't feature a short spawning stream between two lakes was Hammersly Camp, but even that is still a spawning river that drains a clear lake.

Author Frank Norris notes that Ray's plans were welcomed by the National Park Service because the agency had "locked up" the monument due to accessibility concerns. From Tourism in Katmai Country:

*Alaskan interests began to covet other monument resources. The NPS had allowed a company to harvest clams along the Pacific coast as an emergency food source. But in 1946, an application to carry on much the same uses was denied, and local residents howled in protest. In subsequent years came demands to extract pumice from the Kukak area, along the Pacific coast, and to allow hunting in the monument. One and all, it appeared, demanded that the monument be reduced or abolished. NPS officials reacted to the pressure by seeking methods by which visitation to the area could be encouraged while simultaneously protecting area resources. As official and recreational trips to Katmai increased, Petersen and others recognized the desirability of establishing base camps. General Twining, during a Washington visit in the winter of 1948 to '49, may have been the first to suggest such an idea. Other officials encouraged Petersen to go a step further and apply for a franchise for lodge operations in Katmai. They did so for several reasons: (1) Bad weather, which often caused flights to be delayed, made independent tent camping uncomfortable; (2) existing tent campers were interfering with operations at the Brooks Lake Fisheries Station; and (3) problems with littering and overfishing were arising on an increasing basis. NPS officials, for their part, recognized that a concession operation offered one of the most effective ways to combine increased visitation with park protection.*

*Petersen was initially unconvinced that such an operation would be economically viable, and he had additional doubts that a fishing camp was an appropriate or even legal adjunct to an airline operation. By the winter of 1949-1950, however, he was ready to consider the project, primarily because he believed tourists were a necessary adjunct to regional growth in southwest Alaska. Petersen, head of a cadre of NCA managers characterized as "young and desperately earnest empire builders," recognized that "tourists are the biggest thing that Alaska can develop," and further observed that "we are counting on them as our long-range, steady customers. We feel that people, more than goods, spell success for us."*

*On December 14, 1949, Petersen met with National Park Service and Bureau of Land Management officials in Washington and laid out his plans. His proposal called for the establishment of four small fishing camps. A camp "near Brooks Lake" and another near Lake Coville were planned on land located within Katmai National Monument. The two other proposed camps, at "Nanwhyanuke Lake" and Battle Lake, were on Bureau of Land Management land. Petersen had personally chosen the general locations for each camp, considering them the best fishing spots in the Katmai country. In order to create a suitable environment for his guests, Petersen had relatively modest plans for the camps. Petersen found a receptive audience.*

*The project being proposed was something new in the annals of the National Park Service. National parks had been dealing with concessionaires since the establishment of Yellowstone in 1872, and over the years had contracted with owners of hotels, gift shops, transportation companies, filling stations, and other businesses. By 1950, there were several hundred concessions active in the various NPS units. Some of those concessionaires operated airplanes in the parks. Never before, however, had the NPS leased a concession operation to a company whose primary business was the intercity transportation of passengers and freight. It was also the first time that the NPS had depended upon an airline as the primary means of access to one of its units. The arrangement worked because the camps were some of the least accessible facilities in the national park system.*

*Later on, at a spot I picked mentally long ago at the mouth of Kakhonak River, just below the waterfall of the same name, I started my own facility. Kakhonak Lodge was at first just a log cabin. In those days I used to base out of Rainy Pass Lodge for several good, virgin streams ran within half or three quarters of an hour's flying. One of my favorites was the Talachulitna. We explored the Tal from one end to the other, and we explored many other*

*Bud Branham and Ray Petersen on the ramp at Naknek. Circa 1947—Chris Branham Collection*

Ray Petersen's plan was clearly delineated by December of 1949. Only a few months earlier, Bud Branham had finished building a small cabin at Kakhonak Falls on Iliamna Lake. This cabin was the first of several buildings that eventually became Kakhonak Falls Lodge. Bud clearly points out that he didn't fish too much in Bristol Bay, choosing rivers closer to Rainy Pass during the early years. From *Sourdough and Swahili:*

*streams, including the Copper and the upper and lower Talarik.*

Dennis Branham, Bud's brother and partner, told me that the building of Kakhonak Lodge was really Bud's pet project.

*Bud had wanted to build at Kakhonak because he thought it was about the most beautiful place around, and the location offered good access to all the waters in Bristol Bay. One day in the spring of 1949, Bud loaded six sled dogs, building equipment and some supplies in the G-44 Widgeon and headed for Kakhonak. We worked hard on that project. Charlie Dennison had a sawmill at Tanilian Point. Charlie cut and milled the lumber. Bud flew most of the milled wood to the site in the Widgeon. We cut logs down the lake and rafted them back. By the time hunting season started, we had completed the cabin. Although we had the cabin basically finished in 1949, we hosted our first guests at Kakhonak Lodge in 1950.*

Although at first it was only one cabin, Kakhonak Falls Lodge was the first sportsmen's lodge building built in the Bristol Bay watershed. When I asked Dennis Branham if they hunted from Kakhonak too, he told me there were so few animals around there in the 1950s that they really couldn't.

*No, there weren't the populations of moose and caribou that are there now. We hunted out of Rainy Pass. Fishing, albeit only two couples at a time for a few weeks a year, was the only activity at Kakhonak. Bud did almost all the guiding and flying himself. I took care of the guests at Rainy Pass and only would take an airplane to Kakhonak if we had extra people. That didn't happen often. Once the place got a little bigger, I spent more time there.*

Evison - Int. 4481

DEPARTMENT OF THE INTERIOR

INFORMATION SERVICE

NATIONAL PARK SERVICE

For Release SUNDAY, APRIL 30, 1950

KATMAI NATIONAL MONUMENT, ALASKA, TO HAVE VISITOR ACCOMMODATIONS

Katmai National Monument, on the Alaska Peninsula, will provide visitor accommodations this summer for the first time since its establishment by President Woodrow Wilson in 1918, Secretary of the Interior Oscar L. Chapman announced today.

The National Park Service has just issued a 5-year permit to Northern Consolidated Airlines, Inc., of Anchorage and Fairbanks, Alaska, under which that company will operate two camps within the monument, with the main camp at the mouth of Brooks River, and will provide airplane transportation to them from Anchorage. In addition, the company will establish two camps on lands administered by the Bureau of Land Management.

Katmai is the largest of the national monuments administered by the Park Service and has many miles of frontage on Shelikof Straits. Lying west of Kodiak Island, it contains 2,697,590 acres of land and water. It has long been known to wilderness fishermen for its "big ones,"—rainbows, Dolly Varden, grayling, mackinaw and salmon; and the fishing is expected to be one of the principal attractions. Regulations generally applying to areas under National Park Service administration—which limit a day's catch to 10 fish and prohibit the possession of more than 20 fish at any time—will continue to apply to Katmai. Special regulations dealing with permissible types of lures are under consideration, Park Service officials said.

World attention was focussed on the area in 1912 when Mount Katmai, in a gigantic eruption, deposited volcanic ash over thousands of miles of land and water surrounding it. For many years, the area has been famed for its Valley of Ten Thousand Smokes, because of the many steaming fumaroles. However, these have almost completely disappeared.

Note to Editors:

Limited supplies of Katmai National Monument pictures are obtainable from the National Park Service, Washington 25, D. C.

*Ray Petersen Collection*

Ray Petersen was really in the thick of preparations by January 1950. Continuing again from Frank Norris's *Tourism in Katmai Country:*

*On January 21, 1950, Petersen formally wrote for permission to operate two camps in the monument for a two-year period. Citing the need to conserve park resources, as well as the need to recoup capital outlays, Petersen requested an exclusive concession. He gave additional details about his proposed camps. The base camp, which by now had been located at the mouth of the Brooks River, had increased in scope; it was to consist of framed tents, sufficient to house and feed twenty to thirty people. He also applied to operate another camp, to be "set up on the stream that connects Coville and Grosvenor lakes." Plans for an expanded camp system outside the monument were not forgotten. Petersen made arrangements for a meeting the following month in which he "would like to arrange for lease or purchase of three sites for the construction of camps." The fifth camp, although unspecified in his letter, was Kulik Camp, located on the north bank of Kulik River at the outflow of Kulik Lake.*

*On February 15, Assistant Secretary of the Interior William Warne approved most of what Petersen had requested, and the NPS issued a draft concession permit, in the form of a Special Use Permit, for the two camps in the monument. Petersen was pleased to find that the permit was valid until December 31, 1954, three years longer than he had proposed.*

On March 10, 1950, the first Katmai National Park concession permit was signed at the National Park Service regional office in San Francisco. Ray Petersen signed on behalf of Northern Consolidated Airlines, and Alfred C. Kuehl signed on behalf of Grant H. Pearson of the National Park Service. Once Ray signed the contract, he knew he had to spread the word and build the camps.

In what must be considered a planning masterpiece, Ray Petersen conceived and incorporated Alaska Consolidated Vacations on April 18, 1950. Along with Ray, J. L. McCarrey, Jr. (Ray's attorney) and Vernon L. Maxwell, another Northern Consolidated executive signed the original incorporation documents. Once those legal papers had been filed and accepted, Ray Petersen had little time to spread the word and even less time to build his camps.

## Spreading the Word

Before the camps could become a reality, Ray knew he had to get the word out to prospective clients in the Lower 48 and around the world. Shortly after the Hall-Sprague red-carpet fishing trip in 1948, Ray Petersen hired his friend and former NBC public relations specialist, Don Horter. Don's job was to design and create a marketing program for Ray's Northern Consolidated Airline and his future fishing camps, which became known as the Angler's Paradise Camps.

Ray Petersen worked with Don Horter and his public relations team at Northern Consolidated to create a two-phase public relations campaign that has never been equaled. Because national television programming was just beginning, Ray found an audience eager to publicize Alaska and the fishing trips he offered. The publicity campaign had to educate people about Alaska, as well as sell a product that had not been previously available to the average American, nor to the international fisherman.

You can now send your clients to ALASKA *with confirmed room and space* throughout their Alaskan trip on NORTHERN CONSOLIDATED TOURS.

— AND, WHAT'S MORE —

ONLY on NORTHERN CONSOLIDATED TOURS will your clients see and thrill to the REAL ALASKA . . . the entire intensely interesting and new Western Alaska, home of the Eskimos . . . the Arctic . . . Mt. McKinley . . . the land where pioneering is a daily chore.

Eskimos launching Oomiak at Nome.

Lake Eklutna near Anchorage

PLUS

KATMAI NATIONAL MONUMENT, open to the public for the first time, and *only* on NORTHERN CONSOLIDATED tours. Sell the famous and fantastic VALLEY of 10,000 SMOKES, the spuming volcanic beauty spot of KATMAI, the largest monument under the U. S. Flag.

With confirmation from N C A
Your clients see ALASKA the comfortable way.

All reservations must be confirmed by our Seattle office . . . 10% agent's commission paid promptly on all tours.

**Seven complete, thrilling, easy-to-sell Tours in Alaska are yours to sell . . . Sample tour costs to the Bering Sea and Katmai National Monument — from New York as low as $600. — from Seattle as low as $387.**

**Send today for brochures and worksheet.**

Salmon leaping falls on Brooks River (Katmai)

*Serving Western Alaska for fifteen years*

NORTHERN
Consolidated
AIRLINES, INC.
ALASKA

OFFICES: *Anchorage & Fairbanks*

**TOUR RESERVATIONS: 423 WHITE BUILDING, SEATTLE, WASHINGTON.**

*Reprinted from the "Travel Agent," March 10, 1950. Ray Petersen Collection*

Organizing such a media blitz would be nearly impossible today. Don Horter and Jim Chadwick, another Northern Consolidated media specialist, prepared this summary of their public relations campaign:

*The airline problem consisted of more than just selling, it necessarily had to be a combination of sales and education. We had to overcome the "Past" wherein stateside transportation companies and travel agents had been so badly burned that they shied away from Alaskan business. Progress can be noted through the list of interline and tour agreements with many stateside carriers and travel sales companies. By no means can we consider this campaign of "building confidence" completed, but we can look to the future with the knowledge that we will have the much-desired cooperation of the leaders of the travel industry.*

*Capitalizing on the adventurous attraction of the word "Alaska" … its tremendous news value and appeal … the airline has endeavored to make the most of its limited budget by supplying material and fostering connections with feature writers and columnists of leading metropolitan newspapers as well as of national publications. Through these interested airline friends we have had and will have highly prized outlets for spreading our informative and sales material. To attempt to cover such a circulation by paid advertising would have been prohibitive.*

AMERICAN EXPRESS NEWS BULLETIN

NEWS DIVISION - AMERICAN EXPRESS COMPANY
65 BROADWAY, NEW YORK

PHONE
WHITEHALL 4-2000

May 9, 1950

KATMAI MONUMENT
LISTED ON TOURS

New York.... Katmai National Monument, the largest monument under the administration of the National Park Service and this summer open to the general public for the first time since its establishment in 1912, has been listed on American Express 5 and 7-day Tours of Alaska, in cooperation with Northern Consolidated Airlines, Inc.

The 2,697,590 acres of the monument, warmed by the waters of the Japan Current, are widely known as a "Fisherman's Paradise" where Dolly Varden, Grayling, Trout and Mackinaw abound in numerous lakes and streams. The area also contains the now-extinct volcano, Mt. Katami, and the world-famed Valley of Ten Thousand Smokes. Modern and comfortable visitor accommodations are available at two camps, with the main one at the mouth of the Brooks River.

Views of majestic grandeur, visits to Eskimo villages and the sites of "Gold Rush" camps, with many unusual and picturesque sights, are included in the 5-7 day Alaska Tours.

*This 1950 news-flash to travel agents throughout the American Express travel system was well received and helped start the education of agents on the grandeur of Alaska travel. Ray Petersen Collection*

The first phase of the public relations and marketing blitz centered on creation of the press releases and notification to travel agents about the lodges. The advertisement (left page) and notice (above) demonstrate the well-conceived "Come to Alaska" program notification to travel agents.

Don and the rest of the public relations staff at NCA put together an extensive tour brochure during the final planning stages of the fishing camps. Reading through the *1950 Consolidated Vacations* brochure gives insight into the far-reaching program that Ray and his team created. This brochure went to print and was delivered to tour companies and travel agents around the world several months before any of the camps opened. From the 1950 brochure:

> *For the first time tourists can now see the real western Alaska—and you can plan your trip to this exceedingly interesting land with a guarantee of hotel and traveling accommodations. We stress this feature because until 1950 such space accommodations could not be confirmed—today, Northern Consolidated Airlines has eliminated such barriers by owning and operating the hotels and roadhouses (Alaskan vernacular for Inn).*
>
> *It is "Angler's Paradise" and now for the first time, comfortable camps border the best fishing stretches of this area and are your bases during your angling tour. Contrary to general stateside conditions, the best fishing is at the front door of your camp—less than 2 minutes away. It is indeed a rare cast which does not result in terrific action from a rainbow, Dolly Varden, grayling, mackinaw or salmon. Actually, we believe you will soon become fed up with fighting and landing the big babies.*

Reviewing the 1950 brochure, I found the tourism packages varied from 3 to 14 days in length and could be altered and modified by request. I'm positive that this brochure was put together after reflecting on the success experienced during the red-carpet fishing excursion planned and executed for Judge Sprague and Congressman Hall. The second phase of the campaign couldn't begin until the lodges actually opened for business. Don Horter's vast experience as a fisherman and his acquaintance with some of the top outdoor writers would prove very useful to Ray's lodge endeavor but only after the construction project was completed. Fishing options from the 1950 Consolidated Vacations brochure are shown on the opposite page.

## Building the Angler's Paradise Camps

One of the things I have come to appreciate about Ray Petersen has been his constant drive for excellence. Ray believes that if you want a job done well, hire a professional to do it. This attitude was particularly evident in his approach to setting up the Angler's Paradise Camps. A tremendous amount of work had to be completed in a short time to be ready for the guests already being sought. Choosing the right person for each phase of the project became Ray's primary task. Although he had many good NCA employees from which to choose, he wanted the best, even if that meant he had to do some serious recruiting.

For what he considered the time-critical job, Ray had to recruit. He gave the overall project of planning the camps and setting them up properly to Alaska's petticoat pilot, Vera Lieble. Ray knew Vera had the experience necessary for a project of this magnitude. He had known her for a long time and was impressed with her efforts in similar jobs overseeing the planning and construction of Bureau of Indian Affairs schools and hospitals. Perhaps more than for any other reason, however, Ray chose her because she was a pilot and Ray re-

### TOUR 6 RAINBOW TOUR

Departs from Anchorage daily

**1st DAY:** You leave Anchorage, winging your way down the beautiful Cook Inlet bordered for 150 miles by the Chugach Range rising to 10,000 feet and the Alaska Range capped by 12,500 foot Mt. Redoubt and the active volcano, Mt. Iliamna, over 100-mile Lake Iliamna to the Naknek Air Base where you transfer to amphibian airplane and after a 20-minute flight you land at Camp No. 1 at the mouth of Brooks River—located in the heart of the Katmai National Monument. You are assigned accommodations and arrangements will be made for your fishing license which costs $2.50. Excellent fishing spots are at your front door.

**2nd DAY**: The day is yours to enjoy the finest rainbow, Dolly Varden, mackinaw trout, and salmon fishing in the world on the beautiful Brooks River.

**3rd DAY**: You board the scheduled seaplane for Camp No. 2 at Coville Lake with a side trip flight (weather permitting) over the active volcano of the Valley of 10,000 Smokes.

**4th DAY:** After an exciting day of fishing at Camp No. 2, Coville, you move on up by plane to Camp No. 3 at Nonwhyenuk, where you fish the outlet to the large lake, an extremely exciting fishing stretch.

**5th DAY:** You catch the seaplane on its schedule to Battle River, Camp No. 4, nestled at the foot of snow-covered mountains where huge, deeply colored rainbows, grayling and mackinaws await you in the white waters of the river.

**6th DAY:** Another full day to battle the Rainbows—late afternoon departure for Naknek where you spend the night at the Sky-Tel—dreaming of the big ones that didn't get away.

**7th DAY**: Return to Anchorage for connection with Stateside plane, boat or train.

TOUR 6: Rainbow all-expense tour
From Anchorage................................$245.00 plus tax $14.75

### TOUR 7 GREAT NORTHERN PIKE TOUR

Departs from Anchorage or
Fairbanks daily except Sunday:

**1st & 2nd DAYS:** You fly from Anchorage over the pioneer dog team trail across the Susitna Valley, through Rainy Pass over the Alaska Range south of Mt. McKinley, to McGrath(short stopover with a tour of surrounding points of interest—continue on down the Kuskokwim River to Flat, site of the 1912 gold stampede where you land on the actual goldfield—then on to Aniak, dinner and overnight at Aniak Roadhouse (Inn). Evening fishing at Aniak and all the following day you can do battle with the pugnacious Great Northern Pike in the tributaries of the Kuskokwim and nearby lakes. Boat and guide arrangements will be made prior to your arrival.

**3rd DAY:** After a morning's fishing, you board the daily flight to Bethel and Platinum, and from this latter point you will catch the flight to the ghost mining camp at Snow Gulch on the Arolik River—renowned locally for its huge fighting rainbows, Dolly Varden Trout, and grayling. Both the fly-fisherman and bait caster will always remember the angler's paradise on the Arolik.

**4th DAY:** Rainbow, grayling and Dolly Varden fishing.

**5th DAY:** Rainbow, grayling and Dolly Varden fishing

**6th &7th DAYS:** You return to Aniak or Bethel where you enjoy an evening and morning's return engagement against the Great Northern Pike. In the afternoon you board the daily flight to McGrath and Anchorage or Fairbanks.

TOUR 7: Great Northern Pike all-expense tour
**From Anchorage or Fairbanks....$254.00**

**FOOTNOTE TO RAINBOW TOUR.** TWO-PERSON tent houses are available in limited numbers at the four Northern Consolidated Angling Camps for man-and-wife combination; otherwise, six-to eight-man capacity tent houses are used. All meals are served in separate mess tent house, and the camp cooks will gladly cook your fish.

spected pilots. Vera was thorough in her planning and he knew she was a stickler for details. He realized that precise planning for the camps was essential because everything had to be delivered by air, and mistakes would be extremely expensive.

After meeting with Ray Petersen and John Walatka to get their concept plan, Vera went to work. She knew that time was her enemy. Vera ordered the building equipment and materials, and quickly sought out the help of Anchorage resident Frank Irick who supplied the tents. She kept her deadline in mind as she ordered and procured the various building materials and had them pre-cut to blueprint dimensions. For the next few weeks she continued ordering and organizing materials and goods for the camps. She even designed special liners for the sleeping bags to be used by overnight guests. Finally, she accompanied the materials as they were delivered to the camps.

*A DC-3 on the ice at Kulik Lodge in 1997. Although the first landing was on Kulik Lake in 1950, this landing at Nonvianuk Lake brought in supplies during the spring of 1997. Gary Luper Photo*

Early in March, Ray's vision of fishing camps started to become a reality when a Northern Consolidated DC-3, certified for civil use, landed on the ice at Coville Lake with the first of several loads of pre-cut building materials, tents and supplies. The crew unloaded and stacked the cargo on the beach. The DC-3 crew made similar flights to Ray's building sites at the Brooks River, Battle Lake, Kulik Lake, and Nonvianuk Lake near the Hammersly homestead. Even though she had planned and outfitted each camp, Vera Lieble wasn't involved in the construction phase. Her job was finished once the building materials and camp furnishings had been delivered.

John Walatka had been involved in the fishing camp planning since Congressman Hall had visited in 1948. Because John knew the details, Ray Petersen selected him to oversee the building phase. John was one of Ray's longtime friends and one of the men who amalgamated with him to form Northern Consolidated Airline. Ray knew of John's love of fishing and his excellence in a floatplane was unparalleled. Ray also knew that John was one of those characters who would enrich the lives of future camp visitors.

John put together a crack team of workers. He selected Bob Gurtler, a longtime friend of Ray's, Dillingham resident John Pearson, whom he had known for many years, and NCA employee Slim Beck. Walatka also brought in two men from the village of Aniak, Raphael Kuponak and Nickenoff Evon, both of whom he knew to be great workers. These two men were among the most valued and respected employees the camps would ever have. In addition to this core group, John drafted other NCA employees and local residents to spend a day or two at the camps when extra hands were necessary.

By May 12, the lakes weren't completely clear of ice, but what ice remained wasn't a problem for water landings at the sites. Walatka radioed for the remainder of materials and the builders to arrive. These final cargo flights were made with NCA's Navy surplus PBY. Although the PBY was able to haul quite a load, it wasn't able to drive up the beach like the Grumman Widgeon, Goose, and Mallard. The PBY stopped in deep water and the materials had to be ferried to shore in rafts and boats. According to the article "Katmai Sportsmen's Heaven" from the *Anchorage Times,* June 7, 1950:

*The first thing off the plane was a rubber life raft, Vera Lieble relates. We piled it high with lumber and supplies and snaked it to the shore on a lifeline. Everything had to be flown in and then ferried to the shore.*

Walls went up and the frames took shape. Construction was underway at Coville Camp by March 12 and the camp was completely ready for guests on May 3.

*Carpenter Mr. Larson, Slim Beck, John Walatka, Chief Needahbeh, Don Horter and Hans Artur at Kulik in 1950. As only Hans and the carpenter aren't wearing hip boots, it is probably safe to say that fishing was the order of the day. Ray Petersen Collection*

Coville Camp (now Grosvenor Lodge) featured a 16-foot-square cookhouse at the south end of camp. Guest quarters included one large and four smaller guest tent-cabins. Coville Camp featured both a pump house for water and a root cellar for food storage.

Ray made Coville Camp the Petersen summer home. Ray's wife, Toni, gave birth to their third child, Susie, in May 1950 and moved to her new summer home shortly after the camp was finished.

With her new baby and her two other children, eleven-year-old Rosemarie, and nine-year-old Chuck, Toni took care of all the guests who came to Coville Camp. She was wife, mother, cook, maid, and entertainer for the next 31 fishing seasons. All four Petersen children (Sonny was born in 1952) grew up at the camp among efited from Vera Lieble's planning efforts. All the guests at the camps slept on cots in sleeping bags designed by Vera Lieble. She had the bags specially manufactured with removable liners for easy laundering. Employees and guests alike felt comfortable with and used the pots, pans, dinnerware and bath supplies she purchased.

*John Walatka, Ray Petersen, Pan American Airlines photographer Ace Williams, Toni Petersen, Rose Marie, Chuck Petersen and Fred Walatka in front of the cook house at Battle Camp shortly after the Battle Camp was completed in 1950. Ray Petersen Collection*

the guests and staff of the Angler's Paradise Camps.

Brooks was by far the largest of Ray's camps. The cookhouse was a whopping 32-by-16 feet, and there were nine guest tent-cabins. The majority of guest cabins were 9-by-9's, although several were larger. All the tent-cabins had wooden floors, windows, doors, and screen doors.

Brooks Camp, like all the others, ben-

According to all the reports, everything was first class. With an advertised capacity of 30 guests, Brooks Camp offered running water, shower baths, and a large root cellar to store food and supplies. During the first summer season, Doug Barnsley assumed the managerial duties at Brooks Camp. Vera and Vern St. Louis handled all the kitchen and camp chores.

Battle Lake Camp was erected on the

Battle River at the northern end of Battle Lake. Because Ray and John found the fishing at Battle absolutely fantastic during their exploratory trips, Battle Camp was expected to be second only to Brooks in popularity. Battle Camp was the second largest camp after initial construction. It featured a 16-foot-square mess hall and kitchen, two other 16-foot-square sleeping quarters, and five 9-foot-square sleeping quarters. Unfortunately, Ray Petersen and John Walatka, like many of their future guests, would learn that the Battle River fishery was (and is) more cyclic than in other rivers in the area. I'm not giving away any secrets to say that during most years the Battle River is difficult to fish and more fishing is done than catching. Periodically, however, the Battle turns on and is better than great. I think that Ray and John did their exploratory fishing during one of those hot years. Kulik's popularity increased once the guests realized that the Battle River wasn't consistent. Weather also played a significant role at Battle Camp. Like Kulik, Battle had major wind potential and getting guests to and from the camp in heavy wind situations was difficult at best.

*Vera St. Louis in the first kitchen at Brooks Camp. Ray Petersen Collection*

Considering the isolated locations of the camps, their construction was a monumental task. No matter how thorough the planning, various items and materials had to be requisitioned and procured. John continued to bring in materials and supported the building crews with one of the float-equipped NCA Norsemen. Nearly everything went according to plan until one night at Kulik when the wind started to blow.

In evaluating the locations for each of the camps, Ray and John had flown from Naknek many times searching for the best sites. They fished and had flown around each of the campsites often enough to be confident they had chosen the perfect location. They had to consider many aspects at each site. The primary objective was fishing, of course. They wanted the camps as close to the fishing as possible. People certainly didn't want to walk too far to get to the best fishing spots. Next in importance was a reasonable place to park airplanes and boats out of the weather. Site evaluation had to consider drinking water, septic considerations and soil stability. Finally, the view from the camp was considered. In evaluating the entire project, the only mistake made was the selection of the original site for the Kulik River Camp. Ray had chosen a spot on the north side of the river just above the beach on Kulik Lake. This site is one of the most scenic places in all Alaska. Unfortunately, it can also be one of the most windy in Bristol Bay. Ray told me that during their numerous flights to Kulik to check out the fishing, they usually parked the airplanes on Kulik Lake and fished the upper part of the river.

*You must remember that we just didn't go too far when the weather was questionable in those days. John and I fished and sought out the campsites in good weather. We wanted access to be easy. In those days we only fished the upper end of the Kulik River. We certainly didn't want to walk from the lower lake to the upper river when we wanted to fish. John and I were well aware of the potential for strong wind but never realized how damaging it could be. All things considered, the Kulik Lake selection was the logical setting for our fishing camp.*

*Brooks Camp complete and ready for guests in May, 1950. Ray Petersen Collection*

One evening before the Kulik Camp was completely finished, a strong east wind started to blow. The mountains at the headwaters of Kulik Lake tend to funnel the wind right down Kulik Lake and directly into the first Kulik Camp location. Those who rode out the early season storm faced hurricane-force winds in a camp that offered little, if any, protection. Kulik Camp was razed to the ground in a matter of minutes. Fortunately, none of the tents nor frames was completely destroyed. The neophyte lodge builders were fortunate that no airplanes were parked on Kulik Lake, or they, too, would have been destroyed. John Walatka flew into Kulik shortly after the strong winds calmed. After he surveyed the damage, the decision to relocate the camp was easy to make. Walatka had to fly a few circles around the river to help locate some of the important building pieces. John and the boys gathered up the supplies and rebuilt the camp where it stands today, on the shore of Nonvianuk Lake. As a result of the storm and subsequent rebuilding efforts, Kulik Camp was not ready for guests until mid-July.

Kulik Camp was identical to the Battle Lake facility in buildings except that it had four instead of five smaller guest tent-frame cabins. The root cellar at Kulik was also larger. John Walatka and his wife, Lillian, hosted all the guests at Kulik during the 1950 season.

Nonvianuk Camp, later referred to as Hammersly Camp, was the smallest of the five Angler's Paradise fishing camps. It had just one 16-foot-square tent cabin, which served as both the kitchen and dining facility. There were just two 9-foot-square tent cabins for guests at Nonvianuk. The big attraction at Nonvianuk Camp was the great fishing and, according to several personal accounts, Bill Hammersly.

One of Bristol Bay's longtime residents, Bill Hammersly built his home at the outlet of Nonvianuk Lake. A trapper and noted wildlife expert, Bill liked showing and teaching the visiting guests the best techniques for fishing and relished the opportunities to tell a few stories. Bill certainly had the background and personality to tell stories. He discovered gold in the American Creek valley but never developed his claims. Bill was a major attraction at the camp despite his occasional comments about the invasion of his privacy. In time, Bill was so much a part of the camp that he accepted Ray's offer to manage the Nonvianuk facility.

Early in the planning stage, Ray had estimated the expenses for building and outfitting all the camps at about $5,000. By the time he sorted out the various charges and bills, he realized that nearly $60,000 had been invested. Not being one to criticize others, Ray noted that he was the one who had demanded that the camps be set up properly.

## The First Seasons

With the help of his friend, fishing mentor, and employee, Don Horter, Ray invited prominent newspaper outdoor writers to Alaska and the fishing camps. He knew they'd report the results of their journeys to their respective readers. As a media man for NBC Television in New York, Don was well aware of the large audience garnered by Ray Camp, outdoor columnist of the *New York Times*. He had similar admiration and respect for Enos Bradner with the *Seattle Times,* and Uncle Joe Dearing with the *San Francisco Call-Bulletin*. These men, along with several other noted metropolitan newspaper columnists, headed Ray's list.

Ray's public relations team was correct in their belief that they could not have paid for the advertising generated by the articles that followed the visits of these famous writers. Over the years, most of the famous writers, and some that were not so famous, would come to the Angler's Paradise Camps.

The actual opening of the camps drew no great fanfare. Ray had an unknown product and fishing was a quiet recreation activity. Ray wanted everyone to be able to come to the lodges, not just wealthy tourists. To garner some extra revenue from both local residents and those who could get to the camps themselves, visitors were also able to stay and eat at the camps on a European plan where food and lodging prices were itemized and published. To entice the local fishermen, the fishing camps also operated on the American plan. They charged twenty-five dollars per day, including meals, throughout the first season.

The first of the publicity trips began on June 3, 1950. Ray and one of his Northern Consolidated public relations managers, Jim Chadwick, hosted local news broadcasters Fred Thomas of Anchorage radio station KENI, Roy Norquist of Anchorage station KFQD, and news reporter Cliff Cernick to a weekend of rainbow fishing at Brooks Camp. These men were among the very first fishing guests. NCA Chief pilot R. J. Stevenson flew the party from the Naknek Air Base to Brooks in the PBY, giving a nice valley tour in the process. The *Anchorage Times* reported in a June 7, 1950 article entitled *Katmai New Sportsmen's Heaven*:

> For the flight over the gaping crater of Katmai, filled with an emerald lake, Northern Consolidated uses the same PBY that makes the regular flight to the fishing camps. Chief Pilot R. J. Stevenson has no worries when he banks near the crater and the still smoking rumbling cones of nearby Mt. Mageik and Mt. Martin. "The mountains are all alike for flying," Stevenson says. "It's like flying in the Himalayas, where I used to fly over the Hump. Only on these trips, I get to do some fishing."

Shortly after the first publicity-generating weekend, Ray Petersen hosted outdoor writers Ray Camp and Enos Bradner. Joining them was the famous New York artist, Louis Hendersen. During the course of the first summer of fishing camp operations in Bristol Bay, a plethora of writers and public relations experts enjoyed Ray's tours. The writers and broadcasters submitted stories to their syndicated audiences. Those stories were just a little different from the tales written by today's legion of experts. Most of the early writers described the exploits of the guests rather than trying to embellish their own fishing fame.

> **URGES ALASKA EXHIBITS AT US SPORTSHOWS**
> by Lu Ausman
>
> "Alaska has everything, fishing, hunting, scenery and climate," said Chief Needahbeh in an enthusiastic commentary today on his fishing expedition in the Katmai area last week.
>
> Needahbeh is celebrating his 25th anniversary with the National Sportsmen's Shows, which annually attract hundreds of thousands of visitors in the largest cities of the United States.
>
> "I would like to see a good Alaska exhibit at the shows," Needahbeh said, "with skilled native craftsmen working on the fine cultural exhibits in evidence over the entire territory. With exhibits of game, scenic backgrounds, and movies of fishing and hunting available here, it would provide the biggest boom for Alaska's tourist industry in history."
>
> "You've got the real thing here—you don't have to fake it," Needahbeh enthused. He told how sportswriters in the States had claimed how salmon would not rise to flies, and that Alaska fish are not "gamey."
>
> "That's not true at all. Fish just like to choose their menu. I tried a number of different flies and found that the salmon would strike at streamers or dancing surface lures. And they do jump and put up a good fight."
>
> "You must start putting teeth into your conservation laws now," Needahbeh warned. "Fishing is lots of fun and there are many fish to be caught, but people become greedy and carry away more than is sporting or useful."
>
> Together with Don Horter, public relations man for Northern Consolidated Airline, Needahbeh is making movies of the sportsmen's areas. Plans call for two weeks more in the territory with a trip to the Kuskokwim for sheefishing. Needahbeh hopes to bring back specimens of the almost unknown fish for display in the sportsmen's shows. "I'm looking forward to another two weeks of fun up here, and I shall be ambassador for Alaska when I reach the States," he said.

With Ray's blessings, Don Horter initiated one of the most important invitations to the camps. Don invited the spokesman and announcer of the National Sportsmen's Shows, Chief Needahbeh, to Alaska and to the camps. The Chief was a Penobscot Indian from Maine who had worked for the National Sportsmen's Shows for 24 years. Like the best writers, he, too, had a great following. He also knew the sales market which, for obvious reasons, appealed to Ray Petersen. After all, Ray had some sixty thousand dollars to recoup. Toward that goal, Needahbeh suggested they produce a feature movie about the camps.

Needahbeh caught both salmon and trout while visiting the fishing camps. The Chief fished with many of the guests. During this trip, Don Horter and Chief Needahbeh shot the film for the Angler's Paradise 16mm movie. Later they worked together to edit and narrate the film.

The Chief spent nearly three weeks fishing and filming Alaska with Don and Ray. Fishing near Aniak, the Chief became one of the first to catch the heretofore unknown sheefish. The newspaper article on the opposite page appeared in the *Anchorage Times* on July 12, 1950, and provides one of the first references to conservation in Alaska. Chief Needahbeh was excited about the camps. He was excited about the fishing, and even more excited at the prospect of having the Angler's Paradise Lodges participate in his National Sportsmen's Shows. At the urging of nearly everyone, Ray accepted the Chief's invitation and agreed to participate in the big shows in New York, Detroit, Los Angeles, and Chicago.

*Chief Needahbeh with a pair of Battle Lake beauties. Ray Petersen Collection*

In February 1951, the Angler's Paradise Lodges became the first Alaska fishing business to exhibit in a major sport show. The Chief made several excellent booth suggestions, one of which was to have a continuous playing of the film Angler's Paradise. Naturally, Chief Needahbeh was the fishing "star" of the 16-minute film.

Ray boosted his booth appeal by having Alaska homesteader and gold miner, Bill Hammersly, attend the shows. Rufus Knox "Bill" Hammersly had lived in Alaska since 1926 and had worked as a trapper, prospector and hunting guide. By 1945, he had established a homestead at the outlet of Nonvianuk Lake. Tall and sporting a full, gray beard, Hammersly looked like an Alaskan. His life in the bush authenticated that image. Among other claims to fame, Hammersly had found gold in the American Creek valley, and had carved out an existence in the wilds of the Katmai country. Ray told me that:

*The first Angler's Paradise booth at a sport show in 1951. Although different than today's modern displays, the message was loud and clear. Ray Petersen Collection*

*Hammersly stole the show in every town. Bill was able to tell people about the great fishing like it was a story, and they loved it. Bill was also handsome, looked to the public like an Alaskan should look, and as a result, the women in the Lower 48 just couldn't leave him alone. He was a real ladies' man. He had more women lined up than he could count. It was the same thing in every city we toured.*

Ray went on and told me a story about one sophisticated young lady from New York who fell head over heels in love with Bill. She was so smitten, in fact, that she packed up and left her Madison Avenue penthouse and rushed to Alaska.

*I tried to talk her out of it, but she was definitely in love. I tried to tell her that her dog lived in a better place, but her eyes were glazed, so was her mind. She was definitely in love with the image Bill portrayed. Before I knew it, she arrived in Alaska. I showed her around in Anchorage and got her on the right airplane headed to King Salmon. Once she got there, she found out how different reality was from her imagination.*

Ed Seiler lived in King Salmon during the 1950s and often flew to Bill's place. Just like on Paul Harvey's *The Rest of the Story*, Ed told me a little more about Hammersly's big-city houseguest:

*John Walatka stopped by the King Salmon Skytel one day. He'd had a problem with one of the NCA floatplanes and asked me if I'd fly him and a couple parts up to Kulik. I agreed and we decided on a time to meet at the dock.*

*I had the airplane ready when John arrived with this really good-looking young lady. It was obvious she had never been too far from Park Avenue in her life. She was dressed to the nines with high heels and a gorgeous full-length red coat. John seemed amused when he told me this was the lady whom we'd all heard about from Ray Petersen. This was the woman who had fallen in love with Bill Hammersly. She had come to stay. John and I loaded her and a couple travel chests into my C-180 and headed for Nonvianuk Lake. During the flight, I was able to strike up a good conversation with her despite the noisy engine. She seemed really nice and had no idea what she faced. I felt a little sorry for her as we unloaded the airplane in front of Bill's cabin and prepared to leave. Bill seemed to be a little more grumpy than normal, too. I could tell by her expression that old Bill didn't tell her too much about her new home. John helped Bill with the trunks and I told the young lady that I flew back and forth quite often and if she ever wanted me to stop, she should leave me a signal. We decided that she would put her beautiful, bright red full-length coat on the top of the cabin. John and I left a few minutes later for Kulik.*

*After a few hours at Kulik helping John with the disabled Norseman, I headed back to King Salmon. Flying over Hammersly's cabin, I spotted the red coat. Recognizing the pre-arranged signal, I made one quick circle to announce my arrival and landed. Her stay didn't last long. I returned her to the real world.*

Both Ed Seiler and Ray Petersen told me they didn't think old Bill was too depressed that she left so soon.

Unlike Hammersly's love life, the Angler's Paradise Camps blossomed from attention. Coupled with the lore, lure and adventure of Alaska, Ray's campaign was successful. With former NBC media man Don Horter making the vital contacts, the public appeal of real sourdough Bill Hammersly, and an enthusiastic promoter like Chief Needahbeh, Ray couldn't help but find a receptive audience.

*Bill Hammersly in Ray Petersen's office prior to heading to the first sport shows in 1951. Ray Petersen Collection*

Capitalizing on the interest in fishing they had created the previous summer, syndicated columnists such as Ray Camp, Enos Bradner and Joe Dearing wrote stories highlighting the Angler's Paradise Camps. Later they promoted Ray's attendance at the National Sport shows. Articles appeared both before and after the shows. Radio stations clamored to have the Alaskans on the air at every opportunity. National network television programming was inaugurated in 1949, and despite the fact that only an estimated 5 million homes had a television in 1951, the TV producers sought out new and exciting material. Once they realized the interest in Alaska, they wanted all they could get on the adventures that Ray, his airline, and the Angler's Paradise fishing camps had to offer. From the Northern Consolidated Public Relations report:

*Bill Hammersly's cabin at the outlet of Nonvianuk Lake. I'm sure the young lady from Park Avenue expected something more up-town. Ray Petersen Collection*

*NCA personnel have spread the word of the tours, the angling, and the airline over all the major radio networks and local outlets as well as sectional networks, reaching a conservative estimate of 75,000,000 listeners (also only on a one-time basis). While listed below only once, a detailed catalogue of appearances and stations would show that various NCA personnel have been heard several times over the same networks and local stations. This work was carried out as an added appeal to agents as well as to associated carriers, creating interest and enthusiasm to handle and feature the sale of NCA tours ... it also generously fostered interline harmony ... A concentrated drive for such appearances was made in February, March and April, 1951, in conjunction with NCA's participation in Sportsmen's shows in the following metropolitan areas: New York, Chicago, Detroit and Los Angeles. Through radio, TV, and newspapers we endeavored to attract people to our booth at these shows where the motion picture, "Angler's Paradise," featuring both color and sound was continuously shown, and where NCA personnel were available to hand out informative illustrated literature and make reservations.*

TELEVISION:

*NCA personnel and its color and sound motion picture "Angler's Paradise" have appeared on numerous networks and local TV shows. On one show, "Truth or Consequences," a network show covering the entire TV country, NCA and Western Alaska were featured for two weeks ... Among feature shows in which NCA participated are: "The Don McNeil Show," "Sportsman Club on the Air," "Kukla, Fran and Ollie," and "Hemingway and the News." By using this media (free except in one case) NCA was able to attract the interest of prospective customers, but even more important, was able to whet the appetite of travel agents to sell NCA tours and Alaska. Stations and affiliates include:*

***New York***
*WOR-TV, NBC-TV, WPIX-TV, WCBS-TV, WABD, WATV*
***Boston***
*WBZ-TV, WNAC-TV*
***San Francisco***
*KRON-TV, KPIX-TV*
***Chicago***
*WENR-TV, WBKB-TV, WNBT-TV, ABC (Network TV),*
*NBC (Network TV)*
***Los Angeles***
*KNBT-TV, KFI-TV, KTLA (Network TV). ABC (Network TV),*
*CBS (Network TV)*
***Seattle***
*KING-TV*
***Dallas***
*WBAT-TV, WFAA-TV, KRLD-TV*
***Detroit***
*WWJ-TV, WJBK-TV, WXYZ-TV*

*Packed with action and with the narrator detailing the angling tours, the wonders of Katmai, costs, etc., NCA's 18-minute 16mm color and sound film, "Angler's Paradise," was shown hundreds of times to sportsmen's clubs, at lunches and meetings, on TV all over the country. Today requests for prints and showings far outnumber availability. It is interesting to note that at each of the four sportsmen shows in which NCA participated and showed the film at its booth, the management requested that the film not be shown continuously as it drew too large a*

*Hammersly stole the show. Bill enduring an NBC interview during the winter of 1951. Ray Petersen Collection*

*crowd, blocking the traffic to other exhibits. The "Angler's Paradise" film was shown over the local TV outlet in the following cities during the show called the "Sportsmen's Club" produced by David Newell: San Francisco, Dallas, Salt Lake City, Detroit, Pittsburgh, Buffalo, Louisville, Syracuse, Binghampton, New York, Johnstown, Seattle, Oklahoma City, Los Angeles, San Diego, Minneapolis, Washington D.C., Atlanta, Cleveland, Dayton and Columbus, Ohio, Cincinnati and St. Louis.*

*RADIO:*

***New York***
*WOR, NBC (Atlantic and South Network ABC (entire network).*

***Boston***
*WBZ, WBZ (regional New England Network), WEEL (CBS New England Network), WNBC (Yankee Network)*

***Detroit***
*WWJ, WJR, WXYZ*

***San Francisco***
*KCBS, KNBC, KGO, KLX ( Oakland)*

***Chicago***
WIND, NBC (Network), ABC (Network), CBS(Network)*)*, NBC (entire network), WNBC, CBS (entire network), WOR (MBS network), WABC

***Los Angeles***
*KECA, KLAC, ABC (Network), NBC (Coast Network)*

***Portland***
*KEX, KRO*

***Seattle***
*KING, KIRO*

*There were also radio appearances on radio stations in Cleveland, Ohio, Washington, D.C., San Antonio, Texas, and St. Paul, Minnesota.*

The writers did their part. Stories were written with bylines from Kulik, Brooks and Battle Lake. The story of the Katmai country was being written as it was being experienced. More importantly, eager fishermen were reading the stories all over the country and the world. Newspapers in all the major cities carried articles by reporters such as Camp, Bradner and Dearing. Each of them had a different angle and each was eager to relate his experiences to his equally receptive audiences. The stories described the great air service to Alaska, the fantastic scenery, and the unequalled fishing opportunities.

Circulation numbers and rating services during that first summer indicate more than 12 million people read the articles about the Angler's Paradise Lodges. When you combine the estimated 75 million TV and radio listeners during the winter of 1951 with the estimated 12 million readers of the articles that appeared in syndicated columns during the summers of 1950 and 1951, you get one hell of an audience in a short period of time. Ray's PR campaign had reached a whopping 87 million people, each one of them hearing about the great fishing at the Angler's Paradise Camps.

In conjunction with the first articles and sportshow visits, the Shakespeare Company of Kalamazoo, Michigan, got into the act. One of the largest manufacturers of rods, reels, lines, and baits in the United States, the company had been in business since shortly after the turn of the century.

At the urging of both NCA and Northwest Airline, officials with the Shakespeare Company traveled to Ray's camps to try their equipment on the Alaska fish during the season of 1951. These officials included Henry Shakespeare, vice-president and general manager and C.W. "Opie" Davis, vice-president of sales and marketing. Their group also included *Field &*

# Flying FOR FISHING

## IN KATMAI NATIONAL MONUMENT, ALASKA

Henry Shakespeare took particular delight in fly fishing for Grayling. Here's one of these Alaskan beauties (right) on the end of his line—in sparkling, crystal-clear water.

John Cook (left), advertising and sales promotion manager of Northwest Airlines, fell in love with both the fishing and Shakespeare spinning tackle, including this Wonderod and the new Shakespeare Spinning Reel.

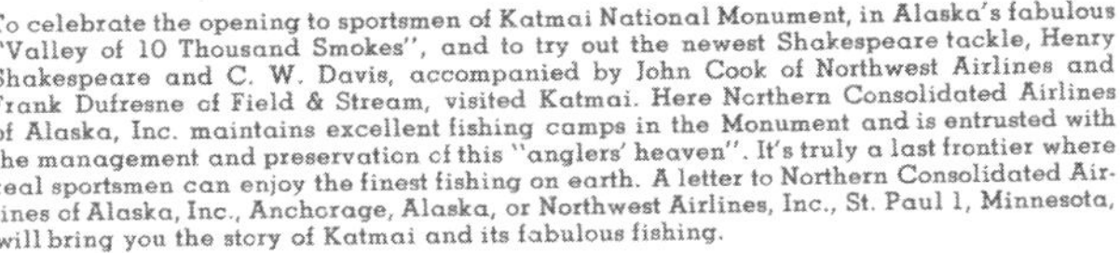

To celebrate the opening to sportsmen of Katmai National Monument, in Alaska's fabulous "Valley of 10 Thousand Smokes", and to try out the newest Shakespeare tackle, Henry Shakespeare and C. W. Davis, accompanied by John Cook of Northwest Airlines and Frank Dufresne of Field & Stream, visited Katmai. Here Northern Consolidated Airlines of Alaska, Inc. maintains excellent fishing camps in the Monument and is entrusted with the management and preservation of this "anglers' heaven". It's truly a last frontier where real sportsmen can enjoy the finest fishing on earth. A letter to Northern Consolidated Airlines of Alaska, Inc., Anchorage, Alaska, or Northwest Airlines, Inc., St. Paul 1, Minnesota, will bring you the story of Katmai and its fabulous fishing.

Arriving at Anchorage, Alaska, via Northwest Airlines from Seattle—Frank Dufresne of "Field & Stream"; C. W. "Opie" Davis and Henry Shakespeare of the Shakespeare Company.

The fascinated anglers watch one of Alaska's many wonders—"floating rocks", pumice stones of volcanic origin that actually float! The Katmai area is strewn with them.

Northern Consolidated Airlines amphibious planes (below) whisk your Alaskan fishing party from one incredible fishing site to another even more wonderful!



A scene that leaves Alaskan visitors spellbound is the sight of thousands and thousands of salmon fighting their way upstream to spawn.

Frank and "Opie" discovered a spot where Mackinaws struck on every cast! They caught and released them until their arms ached.

*Photographs: Don Horter for Northern Consolidated Airlines; John Cook for Northwest Airlines.*

38

*Reprinted from the Shakespeare Fine Fishing Tackle product catalog of 1952. Shakespeare was the first fishing equipment maker to feature an Alaskan destination and the first to build equipment specifically for Alaskan fishing. Courtesy of the Shakespeare Corporation*

*Stream's* Frank DuFresne. As you may recall, when head of the Alaska region of the Fish and Wildlife Service, Frank had slyly issued Walton Powell the first non-resident fishing license in Alaska.

Soon after the license fiasco, Frank retired from the Fish and Wildlife Service and accepted a writer's position with *Field & Stream*. It was no coincidence that DuFresne and the Shakespeare VIP's were there at the same time. Don Horter invited him specifically to cover the Shakespeare group.

*Frank DuFresne, Field & Stream, and Opie Davis, Shakespeare Company vice president, in front of an NCA Norseman in 1951. Ray Petersen Collection*

The 1952 Shakespeare catalogs extolled the merits of both the Angler's Paradise Camps and the great Alaskan fishing. Their catalog included numerous testimonials to their fantastic equipment. Shakespeare became the first company to design fishing equipment specifically for the conditions and fish found in Alaska. Shakespeare also became the first company to include and promote an Alaska fishing destination in its product catalog.

The lodge season of 1951 was better than that of 1950, and as each season opened and closed, more and more of the minor operational wrinkles at the Angler's Paradise Camps were eliminated. Knowledge of the fishery was accumulated. The same was true for Bud and Dennis Branham at their lodge facility at Kakhonak Falls. According to Dennis, Bud didn't have the extra cash to spend for massive advertising nor did he have a great public relations team headed by an expert like Don Horter. What he did have, however, was happy clients. Happy and satisfied clients sent their friends to hunt and fish. Like Ray experienced, numerous top gun writers hunted with Bud and they wrote articles about him and his business.

*We never had much money to spend on advertising. Bud did run ads in* Field & Stream *and a couple in* Outdoor Life, *but not many. We went outside and had parties, hosted by our clients, where we'd show movies and pictures and meet potential clients face-to-face. That was very effective. We certainly didn't have the money to go to any sport shows that seem to be so popular today.*

One day early in the 1950s, Ray Petersen happened to be at Brooks Lodge. He walked to the river and watched an obviously skilled fly caster working the river. Ray eased closer and watched as the man hooked, landed, and then killed a truly large rainbow. The fisherman was General Omar Bradley, a five-star general, and Chairman of the Joint Chiefs of Staff for President Eisenhower. As Ray got close enough for words, the general smiled excitedly; his hands were trembling more from excitement than from the cold water. Ray complimented him on both his fishing skills and the large fish. The general took great care in dealing with the fish.

*That's the largest rainbow I've ever caught. I wouldn't normally kill a fish but this is truly the best one I ever caught, and I'm going to have it mounted!*

*That is a great fish, General. I've got a little Scotch in my cabin. Would you care for a drink?*

*I sure would. I am just a little cold.*

*Your fishing outfit is well worn.*

*Yes, I'm sure it is. I'm pretty lucky. I have fished all over the world. I really enjoy fly-fishing.*

*General, how do you rate the Brooks River?*

Ray and the General made the short walk back to Ray's cabin.

*Mr. Petersen, without doubt, this is the best river I have ever fished.*

The two men enjoyed their drink of Scotch. Then Ray changed the subject.

*You know General, we have no idea how long the military presence will be required in Alaska. I can sure tell you that quite a few fish have been killed. The military presence at Naknek has taken its toll on all the fish and wildlife.*

Ray reported several instances of military pilots shooting moose, bears, and caribou from airplanes and helicopters. He told the general that boatloads of fish were taken from the Naknek River and, indeed, the Brooks River. He suggested that journalists visiting Brooks Camp observed the lack of control and wanton disregard for regulations and wrote stories that were critical of the military leadership. Then Ray related that Alaska Fish and Wildlife biologist Jim Adams, who had been assigned to the Bristol Bay area in 1952, often complained about the harassment of wildlife and the heavy toll on the fish population. Finally, Ray let the general know that the military had a bad reputation and deserved it.

*General Bradley, wouldn't it be great if future generations could fish this river and enjoy great fishing like you had today? I can assure you that won't happen unless some conservation measures are taken.*

General Omar Bradley didn't say much more. He and Ray finished their scotch. The General went back to the river and fished more, although he didn't kill another fish. Ray gathered his gear, walked to the river and joined his guest in casting. The two fished in silence, enjoying the fly-rodding for rainbows.

A few weeks later Ray was back at his desk in Anchorage running his airline. He received a call from the Commanding

General's office at Elmendorf AFB. The secretary to the commanding officer spoke:

> *Mr. Petersen, General Kepner would like you to work with him on developing a conservation plan for the Brooks River and surrounding areas.*

Although it was never stated as such, Ray's message did strike a chord with five-star General Bradley. The wheels of conservation started to roll. Ray's influence in conservation had clearly been established when, according to Frank Norris's *Tourism in Katmai Country:*

> *Petersen promised other conservation measures not specified in the permit. His exclusive permit allowed him to set specific regulations on the number of fish taken. He also insisted that the Brooks River be limited to fly-fishing.*

Even though Ray's conservation efforts appeared both in his concession contract and with the military, John Walatka, the overall camps director, had a major problem with the early conservation efforts. In addition to his camp piloting duties, John and his first wife, Lillian, took care of the guests who went to Kulik that first year. Both Lillian, who died of cancer, and John's second wife, Mildred, believed in the concept that happiness is a full box of fish. They felt that to be satisfied with their fishing trip, clients needed to show off the results. The ladies believed that taking fish home was a sure way that others would see the bounty and decide to come, too. With such pressure in the bedroom, John gave lip service to the catch-and-release concept, yet didn't enforce the unwritten policy.

The advertising efforts of the first lodge pioneers, Bud Branham and Ray Petersen, were doing well. After all, they had a common thread in their backgrounds; they were both pilots and both had worked for Star Airline after their arrival in Alaska, Bud as a dispatcher, Ray as a pilot. Not realizing it at the time nor working together in any way, these two men started to shape an industry. While the business Bud embraced was primarily hunting, he believed that fishing would surpass hunting in the years to come. Ray's forte was the airline business, and he knew that as more fishermen came to Alaska, his airline would prosper. During the first ten years of operation, Ray and Bud hosted the gauntlet of notables from kings to king-sized headaches and according to at least one employee's account, from jockeys to jackasses. Never underestimating the value of a personal referral, both pioneers made every effort to guarantee that each guest was treated like a king, even if only an average man. Both entrepreneurs knew that it would be the average sportsman who would make them successful; there just weren't enough kings to take any chances.

Both the Angler's Paradise Camps and Kakhonak Falls Lodge had more than a few operational changes from the time their first guests arrived in the summer of 1950. Besides the clients who paid to visit both Ray and Bud, there were also employees to add stories to the mix. Starting in 1956, there were also signs of new blood in the business.

## New Blood

The path to creating a fishing lodge was different for all the players, but perhaps none was more complicated and drawn out than the route followed by Bob and Doris Walker. Although they started down the trail in 1953, it wasn't until 1972 that the Walkers became full-time, bona fide fishing lodge proprietors.

Bob Walker felt the lure of Alaska late in the 1930s. It took him nearly two years to finally get all the puzzle pieces to fit. He had a great job at a paper production company. He finally convinced his boss to give him a year off to try the Great Land. If he didn't like it or couldn't make a living in Alaska, at least he would have a job if he returned to Minnesota. After selling his beloved Harley motorcycle to finance his adventure, Bob departed Rhinelander, Minnesota, for Anchorage in 1940. Doris, also from Rhinelander, joined him in Alaska a few months later.

Getting to Alaska in the early 1940s was much different than it is today. Doris's journey was similar to those described in chapter 1. Her trip took more than three weeks from the home she left in Rhinelander to her new one in Palmer, Alaska. She went by auto to Minneapolis where she boarded a train for Seattle. In Seattle, Doris had to wait for the SS Alaska and the voyage to Seward. She told me a little about that part of the trip:

> *Being on that ship was the worst experience of my life by far. We went out into the open water and the waves were huge. Everyone was seasick. It was a horrible trip for me.*

Bob and Doris were married in 1941 and moved from Palmer to Kenai in 1950. Bob built log homes and worked as a commercial fisherman. Early in 1953, Bob obtained his big game guiding credentials. He promptly accepted an offer from big game guide Gren Collins. Gren flew to Kenai to pick up Bob and Doris and took them and their gear to his Kvichak Club to work the summer and fall hunting seasons. Bob and Doris Walker found the Kvichak Club both fun and challenging.

Gren Collins came to Alaska in 1928 and decided that Alaska was the place to be. He finished his studies at the University of Washington and then returned to Alaska and became a game warden. He learned to fly from a Hollywood stunt pilot and in 1936 became the second flying game warden in Alaska Territorial history. Later he established Collins Airplane Service and Big Game Guide Service.

Late in the 1940s, Gren decided to start a limited membership club offering his hunting and fishing guide services exclusively to the joining members. Gren had little difficulty finding the eight original members. Knowing that some of the best fishing in western Alaska was in Bristol Bay, Gren chose the center of Bristol Bay at the outlet of Iliamna Lake to be the club's location. He took over Herman Sanvick's old Finnish Trading Post on the Kvichak River in 1949. He and his club members made a few internal structural changes and the Kvichak Club became reality. The Kvichak Club, often referred to as the Millionaire's Club, was not a fishing lodge in any sense of the word. Dorothy Collins told me:

> *Gren didn't want the problems associated with advertising and constantly finding new hunting and fishing clients. He wanted to do things differently than Bud Branham and some of the other big game guides he knew. He thought the club was a better idea.*

During the season of 1953, Doris cooked and Bob guided hunters and fishermen. When I asked Doris about the club she said:

*Most of the members came to hunt. Some of them came up in the summer to fish, too. Those who limited out hunting relaxed at the club and fished.*

Beyond the Kvichak River, Gren's favorite place to take his club members was the Copper River. At some time during late fall,

*Gren Collins at his camp in 1960. Ernie Renzel Photo*

Gren flew Bob Walker to the Copper with some club members. Doris told me that Bob fell in love with the river and the fantastic fishing. He couldn't get the thought of that river out of his mind. At the close of the season, Bob and Doris returned to Kenai, but Bob's heart stayed in Bristol Bay. Doris told me that quite often they would be sitting at home and Bob would point across the inlet toward Bristol Bay and tell her that they were going to have a fishing lodge.

Once the snow started flying, Bob rented a large shop building near their home and proceeded to build a 35-foot cabin cruiser. By late spring, the boat was done. Soon thereafter, the Walkers began a journey that would completely change their lives. Moving a family and all its possessions to a new home is difficult enough, but Bob planned to move his family to the Copper River where there was no community, no services, no schools, and no homes. Bob planned to build their home once they found the perfect setting.

The Walkers' grand adventure started with the loading of their entire household, four children, two adult and two baby goats, the family dog, all Bob's tools and a small diesel cat onto the scow *Skidunk* for the initial leg from Kenai to Seldovia. Bob followed in his cabin cruiser.

*We must have looked pretty funny, all our stuff piled up with kids and goats climbing all over the place,* Doris quipped.

Cook Inlet is notorious for bad weather and poor cruising conditions. Bob Walker was uneasy about Doris and his family traversing Cook Inlet in the heavily loaded scow. To calm his fears and in an effort to make their inlet crossing easier, Bob arranged for Doris and the children to board the larger and safer steamer, *Jimbo*. With Bob's cabin cruiser in tow, both the heavily laden scow and the steamer headed toward Iliamna Bay on the lower Cook Inlet. Their goal was Williamsport, where they planned to drive their belongings across the Iliamna Portage to Iliamna Lake.

What started out as an ancient Native trail connecting Old Iliamna Village and lower Cook Inlet, the Iliamna Portage now terminates at Pile Bay on Iliamna Lake. Historian John Branson filled me in on the details.

*The Alaska Road Commission made the first improvements to the trail in 1917 and the first vehicles made the crossing in the early 1930s. Before 1937, the road ended at Old Iliamna. In 1937, however, a bridge was built over the Iliamna River, and the roadway was extended to Pile Bay. Before the road, getting into the Bristol Bay watershed was an arduous task. It necessitated an airplane ride or a lengthy sea voyage down the Alaska Peninsula and then into the Bering Sea. Once in the Bering Sea, the difficulties prevailed. If Iliamna Lake was the final destination, the voyage also included a trip up the entire length of the Kvichak River. The road across the mountains from Williamsport to Iliamna Lake made it possible to take small vessels and equipment overland which provided a fantastic savings in time as well as in fuel.*

Arriving at the deepwater anchorage at Williamsport, Bob Walker and the crews of the two larger vessels started the laborious task of unloading their cargo onto the beach and then reloading it into a waiting truck and trailer. Doris told me it took about a week to drive back and forth across the mountains to get their household goods, all Bob's tools, the cat, the cabin cruiser, the kids and their pets over the precariously narrow roadway. To get his mound of equipment and home furnishings from the road terminus at Iliamna Lake to the Copper River, Bob contracted Iliamna barge operator Holly Foss to ferry his family and all their belongings down the lake to the Copper River. Doris said:

*Bob Walker making the logs fit at Iliamna. Circa 1957—Doris Walker Photo*

*Holly tried to get us to the Copper River. The water level was extremely low and we just couldn't get the barge close enough to get out. Bob and Holly searched and searched for a place where we could unload. They finally found a place in*

*Bidarka Bay across the lake from the Copper. Bob was disappointed, but not defeated.*

For the remainder of the summer, the Walker family stayed on their cabin cruiser and in tents on the beach while Bob built their cabin. Doris continued:

*It took most of the summer, but once finished, our cabin was warm and comfortable. I taught the kids that winter. No matter what challenge we faced nor the length of the delay, Bob never lost sight of his goal. He must have told me—next year, we'll make it to the Copper River next year—a thousand times.*

*Iliamna Roadhouse. Circa 1971—Bo Bennett Collection*

Once they were living in the area, Bob and Doris soon became acquainted with the ten or so full-time residents of present-day Iliamna. Over the next year, the locals finally convinced Bob and Doris to move to Iliamna and start their lodge operation there, not along the Copper River. Bob and Doris recognized that there was a need for a good roadhouse in the village. Within a year, they purchased a small house. Bob built two new cabins adjacent to their house. Immediately, they were in the roadhouse business. Their guests included various traveling governmental types and anyone else who needed a place to stay and a good meal in the Iliamna area. Iliamna was a good stop for pilots before entering Lake Clark Pass, notorious for its poor weather. Many pilots and their passengers were forced to wait it out in Iliamna.

By 1956, Bob completed his plans and started building the Iliamna Lodge. Doris told me that once they moved to Iliamna, and especially during the building of Iliamna Lodge, their lives were constantly in turmoil. Just as Seversen's Roadhouse had been in the past, Walker's Iliamna Lodge became the place to stay in Iliamna. More than once their kids had to sacrifice their beds and move to the attic to provide a bed for a needy traveler. Probably the Walker kids were the happiest of all when the lodge was finished.

Bob had done a fantastic job. When finished, the Iliamna Lodge slept about 40 people. Among other noteworthy features, the facility became well known for the beautiful rock bar. Bob and Doris operated the Iliamna lodge from 1956 until 1969. The lodge provided a full-time home for the Walkers. Although they didn't really want it, Bob and Doris took over the fuel-vending contract in Iliamna. The Walkers developed a good business and tried various things to increase their income. Bob started fishing with many of his guests. He fished the areas available by boat such as Talarik Creek and the Copper River. Bob Walker was not a pilot. He would arrange for one of the local pilots to fly guests to some other rivers if they wanted to do so. According to Doris, one thing Bob didn't ever do again, however, was guide hunting clients. Working for Gren Collins in 1953 convinced him that fishermen were fun, but hunters were just too much work.

Despite Bob's goal of having a fishing lodge, his Iliamna Lodge was a roadhouse and did not meet my definition of a fishing lodge. Throughout the years the lodge served as a safe haven for those caught in the treacherous Lake Clark Pass weather and as a base for various government types who traveled the state. Lots of those guests fished, and indeed by the end of their tenure, Bob and Doris had a great number of fishing clients. Bob's experience at Iliamna Lodge helped create the need for the non-fly-out fishing lodges to come. Bob's dream of having a real fishing lodge would come true in 1972.

## Early Players and Their Play

The guest registration books from the early days at the Angler's Paradise Lodges read like *Who's Who in America*. There were so many notable guests at the camps in the early years that it is difficult to delineate any realistic order of importance. For the purposes of this book, however, I believe the order of importance should dervive from those who brought the most changes to fishing lodge operation with their opinions and actions. Keeping that reference point in mind, perhaps the most influential early guest at Ray Petersen's fishing camps was Mr. Gordon Rupe.

Gordon Rupe was one of the first clients to arrive at Kulik Camp in 1950. He was an investment banker from Dallas and came to Kulik at the invitation of Tom Braniff of Braniff Airlines. An ardent and eager fisherman, Gordon became a regular visitor to the camps after his first journey to Alaska.

As Gordon became more acquainted with camp operation, he pushed both John Walatka and Ray Petersen for camp improvements and extra comforts. Each year Gordon brought more guests, and each time he came, he was more demanding.

Gordon Rupe was a prudent banking professional, a high financier, and he knew a good deal when he saw one. After careful observation of both Ray's airline and his fishing camps, Gordon agreed to finance the purchase of Ray's first F-27 with only one string attached. Gordon wanted Ray to assure him there would be flush toilets at Kulik before his next visit. Gordon told Ray that he planned to bring several lady guests during his next Alaska sojourn and felt that modern plumbing would be required for their complete comfort and dignity. Ray wholeheartedly agreed with his new bank-

*Mr. Gordon Rupe, perhaps the most influential Kulik guest in the early years. He was instrumental in bringing "flush toilets" to Kulik. It looks like he was adept at fishing, too. Circa 1953—Ray Petersen Collection*

ing partner and told Mr. Rupe that Kulik would be upgraded. Although not every cabin featured indoor facilities when the season started, enough were completed on Gordon's return to ensure both the gratitude of the lovely ladies and Gordon Rupe's continued financial support for Ray's future aircraft purchases.

Guests at the camps weren't the only people who created change. Dennis Woods was an employee at Kulik Camp during the 1953 season. John Walatka hired Dennis through family and friends in Minnesota. Once he arrived in Alaska and at the lodge, Dennis readily accepted any task. Among other jobs, he assisted in the logging operation that lasted several seasons. John gave Dennis the important job of selecting and cutting the large timbers that eventually became the logs for the main lodge building at Kulik. According to Dennis, he selected most of the trees from an area about five miles down the north side of Nonvianuk Lake, near the area that is now known as the Trapper's Cabin. Dennis told me that it was a long, time-consuming, and labor-intensive project.

First, the trees had to be selected and cut down. The trees needed to be both straight and have a consistent circumference. Once the trees had been chosen and then felled, Dennis had to prepare them for transport to the lake shore. The limbs had to be eliminated and the tops removed. Dennis cut down, topped, removed branches and then cut them to a manageable length. Dennis explained that often he would go down the lake alone and work all day with an ax and a chain saw getting the logs ready to move. Once he had enough timbers for a full boatload, he would tell John it was time for help. Depending on how many helpers were available at the time, the timbers were moved to the shore. Some were dragged and some were carried to the beach.

From the lakeshore the logs were loaded into one of the lodge boats. Because they were easier to load, Dennis preferred the longest skiffs available. After the five-mile boat ride, the logs were unloaded and stacked in a pile so that they could dry and cure before being milled.

Dennis Woods related a few stories about some of the rides he had while taking the log-laden boats back to Kulik. According to him, the worst part of the entire logging experience was the trip back to the lodge in the heavy boats. Dennis would head down

*Gordon Rupe's wife, Ruby, with a fantastic char. A pile of logs ready to be milled for the main lodge and other buildings is behind her to the left. The Kulik shop building is in the upper right corner over her shoulder. Circa 1958—Ray Petersen Collection*

the lake in the morning and return with a load of logs before dinner. Typically, the wind picks up in velocity later in the afternoon on all the big lakes of Bristol Bay, especially Nonvianuk Lake. The photograph of the heavily loaded boat (below) shows that strong winds and big waves created by gusty afternoon wind conditions might just be a problem.

Once the logs were loaded, Dennis certainly didn't want to face unloading the logs until they reached their final destination at the lodge. Dennis and the other boat drivers had to stay near the shore, keep their boats pointed toward Kulik, and hope for the best. Those who helped in the logging mission faced the perils of hard work and the possibility of swamping their boats in the wind and the big, cold waves with the exuberance and the bullet-proof valor of youth. What fun they must have had.

*"I was lucky to survive a couple of bad storms in that boat." After being cut, the logs were loaded by hand into the biggest skiffs available. Dennis Woods drove this load back to Kulik. It is easy to understand why building the main lodge took several seasons. Dennis Woods Photo*

No matter how hard the lodge crews worked at the camps, it was the guests who made the experience worthwhile for them. The staff gave the guests a trip of a lifetime and the guests gave the staff many good memories. Former Kulik employee Dennis Woods told me that one of the groups he remembered the most during the season of 1953 was headed by the famous hotel magnate, Conrad Hilton.

Baron Hilton and his colleagues had a great time at Kulik and caught lots of fish. One notable highlight for Baron Hilton was finding paint and a piece of plywood and making a personal Hilton Hotel sign for Ray Petersen and hanging it up on his cabin for all to see. Ray Petersen told me that the Hilton party was great. "There were eight of them in a 16-foot cabin and they loved it."

Another highlight in Dennis's memory was the day the Hilton group departed Kulik. According to Dennis:

*The Hilton group was scheduled to be picked*

*up by the Northern Consolidated PBY early in the morning. The Kulik weather was marginal and the radio call from King Salmon confirmed there would be a delay. I remember one of the lodge pilots offered to take them to King Salmon, but they wanted to travel together on the larger airplane and they decided rather than split up for the flight they would wait for the PBY. Well, as you might expect, by the time the PBY arrived the whole group was moving a little slower after consuming way too much "hundred-proof" coffee during their long wait for the airplane.*

*Once cut and delivered to Kulik, the logs were unloaded from the boats and stacked on the beach to cure. Dennis Woods Photo*

By the time the PBY got to Kulik, the wind was blowing about 40 knots out of the west. When the big amphibian flew over the lodge, Dennis was in the office. Captain Stevenson radioed in and told the lodge they'd need to bring the guests out to the airplane in a boat because he couldn't get the PBY close enough to the beach in the big waves and heavy wind. Captain Stevenson parked the big plane in the calmest water he could find and waited for the guests to arrive.

The senior guides and other employees decided that the conditions were so gruesome that they should try to take the baggage to the airplane before attempting to take passengers. Although he told me he didn't know how, Dennis was nominated to load up the bags in a boat and give it a try.

Dennis told me that the wind and waves created a miserable situation in which to operate a boat, especially alone. He not only had to deal with the boat, but he had to transfer the bags to the airplane without getting anything wet or damaged. With the help of the airplane's co-pilot, he finally got the bags loaded. Then he went back for the passengers.

Climbing into a PBY from a boat is difficult on flat water, let alone in gale force winds, in big waves, and with clients feeling great thanks to a little extra-spirited coffee. All the time Dennis was throwing the bags to the co-pilot and later helping the fishermen get into the PBY, the captain was standing on top of the wing yelling at the top of his lungs not to let his boat touch the airplane hull. Dennis summed it all up with, "We sure had a lot of fun that day!"

Another notable visitor visited the camps in 1953. Adlai Stevenson and his assistant and right-hand man, John Fell, journeyed north to the camps. Prior to

*The Kulik "Hilton Hotel." Baron Hilton (back to camera) and two of his cohorts with a couple great fish in 1953. Dennis Woods Photo*

coming to Alaska, he had both lost his 1952 presidential campaign and completed his last term in office as governor of Illinois.

Mr. Stevenson came to Alaska on a Democratic Party fundraiser but was determined to try a little fishing. While in Anchorage, he was constantly surrounded by eager Democrats. Ray told me that once the former governor reached the camps, he started to relax. Resting on the beach near Coville Camp one sunny afternoon, the former leading candidate of the Democratic Party told Ray:

*I'd like to spend a month here and get away from all those politicians.*

Ray explained that Adlai wasn't too adept with a fishing rod, and then made some comments about the two-time presidential election loser:

*The former governor was having all kinds of trouble hooking fish. It didn't seem to matter where we were or with whom he fished. He just couldn't catch a fish. He was getting anxious about the whole experience. Even though he was one of the best negotiators in the world, I could tell he wasn't too experienced in fishing matters.*

*I finally took him over to Coville Camp and had my son, Chuck, take him out in a boat*

*Guide Chuck Petersen (upper) and fishing guest Adlai Stevenson at Grosvenor Lodge. This group of fishermen (lower) was delivered to the beach at Big Ku sometime in the early 1950s. Unlike the amphibious Mallard and Goose, the PBY had to be parked in deep water. A raft or boat was needed to access the beach and airplane. Ray discovered early in the going that the PBY simply wasn't a good lodge airplane. Circa 1953—Ray Petersen Collection*

*right in front of the lodge. I don't want to say it was easier there, but once he started catching fish, he relaxed and really enjoyed himself.*

*One time Adlai went out a little too deep and the water went over the top of his waders. He had a perplexed look on his face as he walked back to shore, sat down on the beach and then raised his legs to get the water out. The result—he was more wet than when he started. Adlai Stevenson was a good sport and I enjoyed his company. He was a better politician than he was a fisherman.*

Beginning with the first guest in 1950, Ray and his staff at the Angler's Paradise Camps started to amass the knowledge of the fishery necessary to lodge operation. Each successive year, more was learned about the fish, the weather, the concept of customer service, and the quality of experience to be expected in Bristol Bay.

By 1955, the Angler's Paradise fishing brochure changed to reflect the popularity of Ray's camps. The tours became more specialized to fishing. As Ray and John had found good fishing for Northern pike close to the lodges, there were no more excursions to Aniak. The tours were longer and focused on the best that Bristol Bay had to offer.

To facilitate additional building at Kulik, it became necessary to add some machinery to the rapidly expanding lodge facility. A small Holt caterpillar-style tractor was flown to Kulik during the early spring of 1955. Due to its size, it was disassembled and loaded into a DC-3. Just like the first building supplies, the cat was flown to Kulik and landed on the hard, early spring ice. Once reassembled and put to work, this tractor supplied the power necessary to run the sawmill that came to Kulik in 1956. From the Northern Consolidated company magazine *Midnight Sun*, May 1956:

Six DC-3 loads of supplies have been flown in to the Angler's Paradise camps for the coming summer tourist season. Landings were made on the ice at both Kulik and Brooks Camp. Supplies at Kulik included a sawmill, lumber, gas and stove oil. All told, a total of 18,000 pounds went to Kulik. The 17,000 pounds at Brooks included a Pan Abode red cedar log building which will be used as living quarters for the camp manager, and serve as office and a camp store. The building will be 24 by 20 feet. The log lodge at Kulik will be finished this summer. Logs were cut and the foundation put in last fall.

John Walatka ordered a complete sawmill unit from Montgomery Ward's catalog. He had the mill assembly shipped to Alaska from stateside. The sawmill, like nearly everything else at Kulik, was flown to the lodge site from Anchorage. Using power from the caterpillar tractor motor, the sawmill cut lumber for Kulik and Nonvianuk Camps until it was removed in the early 1970s. The Holt cat cleared the first crude runway at Kulik. Although rough at first, it wasn't too long before the runway was being used for lodge support with small airplanes. According to government survey records, the Holt cat proved so useful that Kulik had a 2,000-foot runway by 1955.

Kulik Camp soon became the second largest of the Angler's Paradise Camps. In the summer of 1956, the camp consisted of three 16-by-16 tent cabins, four 9-by-9 tent cabins and a root cellar. The construction of the rough runway at Kulik really eased the growth process. Ray pushed camp development over the next several years. By early 1958, the camp became a 26-building complex, including eight log buildings and at least 13 tent frame cabins.

To give you just a slight time perspective on the 1950s and to stimulate you

## *All Aboard for Katmai!*

**"KATMAI!"** . . . **"ANGLER'S PARADISE"** . . . magic words to sportsmen rapidly discovering the best fishing on the North American Continent is a mere two hours beyond Anchorage, largest city in Alaska and known as the "air crossroads of the world."

Aboard Northern Consolidateds' DC-3 mainliner en route to the Katmai Camps the angler enjoys a breath-taking panorama of picturesque Cook Inlet . . . towering Alaskan Range peaks . . . Kenai Peninsula, "Alaska's Bread Basket" . . . and the still active volcanoes, Redoubt, Iliamna, and Augustine.

**KATMAI NATIONAL MONUMENT** and the Valley of 10,000 Smokes is located 250 miles southwest of Anchorage in the heart of Bristol Bay, the world's largest spawning ground of the Sockeye (red) Salmon.

**"ANGLER'S PARADISE"** is comprised of five comfortable wilderness camps, established and operated by Northern Consolidated Airlines for the sport fisherman . . . Brooks River Camp, Coville, Nonvianuk, Kulik and Battle Camps . . . all located on large crystal-clear lakes fed by easy-to-wade sparkling streams abounding with Alaskan rainbow, Arctic grayling, dolly varden, lake trout, salmon and pike.

**BROOKS RIVER**, one of the world's renowned fly streams offers an added attraction . . . spectacular Brooks Falls where the angler can battle the fighting sockeye salmon jumping the falls as they head upstream to spawn and die. This thrilling spectacle of hundreds of sockeyes leaping the falls makes this a photographers and anglers paradise alike.

Magnificent Katmai inspired 20th Century Fox to produce the first Alaskan cinemascope film . . . "FLYING TO FISH" . . . a full-color sport short featuring Katmai fishing and currently being shown in theaters throughout the United States and foreign countries.

## *Katmai Trout Tours*

**Operated by**

**NORTHERN CONSOLIDATED AIRLINES, INC.**

**ANCHORAGE, ALASKA**

**ALL-EXPENSE** TOURS ORIGINATE AT ANCHORAGE INTERNATIONAL AIRPORT AND INCLUDE BOARD AND ROOM, TRANSPORTATION AND TAXES . . . START YOUR KATMAI TOUR ANY DAY OF THE WEEK . . .

### KATMAI TROUT TOUR No. 1

7 Days and Nights

Seven exciting days of the best grayling, rainbow, salmon, lake trout and pike fishing in all of Alaska. Includes all transportation and camp facilities.

| | |
|---|---|
| One Person | $350 |
| Two or Three Persons | 325 each |
| Four or More Persons | 300 each |

### KATMAI TROUT TOUR No. 2

10 Days and Nights

This tour is substantially same as No. 1 but allows the sports fisherman 10 days for additional leisure to fish the more exciting streams and lakes in this world-famous Katmai area.

| | |
|---|---|
| One Person | $500 |
| Two or Three Persons | 450 each |
| Four or More Persons | 425 each |

### KATMAI TROUT TOUR No. 3

14 Days and Nights

This trip is the same as Nos. 1 and 2, except that it allows the fisherman two full weeks and takes him farther afield, allowing more time for additional side trips.

| | |
|---|---|
| One Person | $700 |
| Two or Three Persons | 600 each |
| Four or More Persons | 575 each |

### THREE-DAY KATMAI SPECIAL (One Camp)

All-expense from Anchorage . . . Campsite left open so anglers can be taken to "hottest fishing"—depending on season. **Per Person $175.**

### FIVE-DAY KATMAI SPECIAL (Two Camps)

Five unforgettable days of this famous Katmai fishing at two of the Angler's Paradise Camps. **Per Person $250.**

**Payment: A deposit of $50.00 is required at time of booking to protect reservations. Balance is payable 30 days prior to departure from Anchorage.**

### HUNTING IN THIS AREA

Licensed Guides and Big-Game hunts for Brown Bear, Moose, and Caribou arranged on minimum of 90 days' notice.

Finest duck, goose hunting on North American Continent is found just 125 miles from Brooks Camp. 30 days' notice.

PTARMIGAN AND SPRUCE HENS—These upland birds some seasons are very plentiful at both Kulik and Battle River. So if you are here in season, bring your shotgun.

***(Issued as an insert to "fishing and hunting" brochure)***

*From the 1955 Angler's Paradise brochure. Ray Petersen Collection*

Baby Boomers into a nostalgic mode, remember that in:

**1949**-Direct-dial long-distance service was introduced in the United States, but operators were needed for all international calls;

**1952**-The first hydrogen bomb was detonated and the Cold War expanded;

**1953**-Sir Edmund Hillary and Tenzing Norgay were the first to reach the summit of Mt. Everest. Jim Whittaker became the first

*John Walatka and one of the boys working the mobile sawmill. Circa 1956—Ward Wells Collection–Courtesy of the Anchorage Museum of History and Art*

*By late summer of 1956, the sawmill had been mounted permanently and the milling process was in full swing. Please note there is no shop in these photos.Ray Petersen Collection*

American to reach the summit in 1956;

**1955**-Walt Disney finalized his plans for a backyard playground for his grandchildren and finally opened Disneyland to the public in April. The *Mickey Mouse Club* featuring Annette, Cubby, Bobby, Karen, Charlene, and other Mouseketeers with host Jimmy Dodd aired on television in October that same year;

**1956**-Elvis Presley made his first national television appearance;

**1957**-The Russians shocked the U.S. scientific community by launching "Sputnik," the first

satellite. America responded promptly, finally putting a man on the moon in 1969;
**1958**-*West Side Story* opened on Broadway;
**1959**-Pantyhose, waist-high nylon hose requiring no garters, garterbelts, or corsets were introduced by Glen Raven Mills of North Carolina.

Besides watching the *Mickey Mouse Club* on television, one of the great pleasures I looked forward to in my youth was the daily arrival of mail and especially our *National Geographic Magazine*. I loved to look at all the exotic places and read about people all over the world. At that time, home was in Los Angeles and we had great home mail delivery service. I'm sure the anticipation was not as strong for me as for those who lived in rural areas. Rural areas have always had less reliable mail service and that is especially true in bush Alaska. People who lived in the bush just didn't have access to the highlights of the news. No TV, few friends to come over to visit and the only radio communication was business oriented. Airplanes brought the mail. Every time the mail did come, the hope of a new magazine and news of the world had to be astronomical. Imagine the excitement when Chuck, Rosemarie, Susie and Sonny Petersen, living at Coville Camp, were hoping to get their *National Geographic*, only to find the publisher, Gilbert Grosvenor, and his wife Elsie Bell, daughter of Alexander Graham Bell, bringing the latest issue to them personally. Such was the case for the Petersen kids in 1954. The Grosvenors came to see the lake named in Gilbert's honor.

*Kulik Lodge at the height of the 1957 season. Ray Petersen Collection*

The National Geographic Society had sent Robert Griggs on several missions to Alaska's Katmai region after the volcanic eruption of 1912. During his 1921 mission to map the Katmai country and examine the Valley of Ten Thousand Smokes, Griggs renamed the larger of the Savonoski Lakes to Grosvenor Lake in honor of the work and support of Gilbert Hovey Grosvenor, president of the National Geographical Society, and editor of their publication. This was a rare event and only one of a very few instances where a landmark was named for a living person. Grosvenor was both surprised and elated when he was informed of this honor. He vowed to travel north and see the lake that bore his name.

Gilbert and his wife were extremely pleased with their Katmai visit. Both Ray and Chuck told me that Grosvenor very quickly developed a daily schedule with the lake. He would make several trips to the shore of the lake, fill a glass with the clear cool water and make a toast to the lake which he proclaimed to have the finest drinking water in the entire world, and then proceed to drink it down. That water must have had a great effect on both Dr. Grosvenor and his National Geographic magazine. While Gilbert led the magazine, more articles appeared in the National Geographic about the Katmai region of Alaska than about any other geographic location in the world.

Camp life for the Petersen family and employees living at all the camps was well established by 1958. Chuck started guiding full-time at the ripe old age of 11. Rose Marie worked and watched both Susie and Sonny get older and bigger. I spoke with Rose Marie about her thoughts on growing up in the camps.

*Well, I was introduced to lots of people but it was hard for me to relate them to the outside world. We just fished and had a good time. After dad introduced me to General Omar Bradley, I know he was embarrassed when I asked, who's he?*

Keeping the perspective of youth in mind, another story that Rose Marie told me involved her friend, John Walatka's daughter Johanna. According to Rose Marie:

*Gilbert Grosvenor and his wife Elsie, daughter of Alexander Graham Bell, visited the Petersens at Coville Camp in 1954. Perhaps "Gilbert's water" is the reason that there were more articles printed in the National Geographic about the Katmai country than about any other single destination in the world during Gilbert's tenure as editor. Coville Camp was later renamed Grosvenor Camp. Today, it is called Grosvenor Lodge. Ray Petersen Collection*

*One time at Grosvenor we*

*had some guests who were really grumpy. All they wanted to do was play cards, drink and complain that there weren't any fish to catch. Johanna finally got mad at them and went out of the cabin, made a good cast and caught a nice fat rainbow. She unhooked the fish, promptly walked into their cabin and said, "I thought you said there weren't any fish around here. You guys can't catch fish like this one sitting in the cabin playing cards!"*

Johanna Walatka and Rose Marie Petersen grew up, played at work and worked at the camps during their teenage years. They had a lot of fun and were introduced to many wonderful people. They had a chance to influence the guests as well. John Greenbank was a guest at Brooks Camp in 1954. He was so impressed with the girls that he wrote a poem at the lodge in 1954. He published an anthology of his work, *Love & Stuff* in 1958 and included the poem (right) for the teenage daughters of Ray Petersen and John Walatka.

Another employee who helped shape both the lodges and the guests was Floyd "Slim" Beck. He helped build the first cabins and worked at all the camps as well as in King Salmon. Slim was the manager at Kulik during the 1958 and 1959 lodge seasons.

Susie Petersen was born just before the start of the 1950 season and grew up in the lodge environment. Like most kids, she liked adults who were fun to be around. Susie told me that she really liked Slim Beck because "he was fun and the kind of guy you could tease, and he'd tease you back." She also told me one of the more popular and well-known Slim Beck stories.

It seems that Slim was staying at one of the lodges late in the season. One day he went to the shop to start a generator. Starting the generator meant turning a hand crank to get the motor up to speed, adding a little spark and poof! Power. On this cold day, however, things didn't go quite as planned. When Slim cranked the motor, his hand slipped off the crank handle. The metal handle flew off the generator shaft and smashed into his face. The handle hit him so hard in the mouth that it knocked out his front teeth. Slim was known to be very calm and in control of every situation. Once the intense pain and severe bleeding became tolerable, Slim picked up an old moose horn he found by the shop. He took out his pocketknife, sat down and carved himself a new pair of front teeth. Once he had the moose horn substitute dental replacements looking just right, he inserted them into the gaping holes in his mouth, and went on with his work. People say that

### End of Summer
**To Johanna and Rose Marie**

*There has been magic in these days gone by;*
*Have you not felt it in the pink sunset glow,*
*In flash of Arctic tern wings, sweeping low:*
*Have you not heard it in the soft wind's sigh?*
*In this our too brief season, you and I*
*Have watched our friendship, as fireweed, grow;*
*In a mad, harsh world, it is but peace to know*
*This summer's memories will not, can not die.*

*Never again will there be such a year—*
*Such breathless joy in all we feel and see;*
*For this short time, we have been free from fear;*
*Have known contentment, hope, and ecstasy,*
*Dear girl, life's summer never really ends*
*So long as faith endures, and we are friends.*
*Brooks Camp, 1954*

necessity is the mother of invention and I'm guessing that Slim just wanted some teeth.

Nearly a year later an orthodontist arrived at Kulik. Quick to notice the irregular look of Slim's smile and detecting a botched job, he asked who did the interesting dental work. Slim proceeded to tell him the story. Without hesitation the good doctor replied, "I couldn't have done much better in my office!" The dentist agreed to do a professional job of replacing Slim's teeth in exchange for the hand-carved set he wanted to display.

*Slim Beck and his wife, Geneva, and their son Mike at Kulik in 1952. Slim was involved in building the camps and served as Kulik manager in 1958 and 1959. Dennis Woods Photo*

Slim Beck had another bad day in April of 1958. Ray's airline and fishing camp master plan included expanding the runway at Kulik. He wanted to make Kulik a scheduled stop between Anchorage and King Salmon. The small, rough airstrip at Kulik just wasn't good enough for anything but small bush airplanes. The runway had to be made larger. The small cat flown to Kulik in 1955 had been used to clear the original 2,000 feet, but was too small to do much more. Ray had to get bigger and more powerful earth-moving equipment into Kulik.

During the fall of 1958, Ray purchased a large scraper, a grader, an International tractor, and some other equipment at a surplus military sale in King Salmon. Ray's proposed schedule included driving the heavy machinery to Kulik during the winter, completing the expansion work on the runway and then returning the equipment to King Salmon to be resold the following spring. Great plan!

Slim Beck and Bob Gurtler were chosen to drive the equipment over the frozen tundra to Kulik. Longtime Northern Consolidated employee Bill Tolbert was working for Ray in King Salmon when Ray first bought the heavy equipment. He told me that when Johnny Walatka brought Slim Beck and the boys down to get the equipment, all they had was a little food and a lot of time. Bill claims he convinced John and Slim that the trip was bound to take more time than Ray had planned. Bill knew they needed to be better prepared.

On Bill's advice, they quickly built a cabin atop a flat trailer. Called a wannigan, the cabin had a stove and provided a place to eat and rest out of the weather.

The cat-train left King Salmon in early March and headed toward Kulik. Slim Beck and Bob Gurtler drove the machinery toward the Alagnak River in the straightest possible path. I'm not sure if you have ever watched a large caterpillar tractor go across frozen tundra, but I have. I'm sure that my virgin grandmother was faster in her wheelchair up a flight of greasy stairs than Slim could push that cat-train. Our turbine-powered C-207 floatplanes are fast. It takes about 24 minutes to get from Kulik to King Salmon in good weather and in a straight line. Slim and Bob had no trails to follow. John Walatka monitored their progress from above as he kept them supplied with food and other necessities when he could land nearby with one of NCA's ski-equipped airplanes. Once they reached the Alagnak River, Slim and Bob slowly made their way to Nonvianuk Camp at the outlet of Nonvianuk Lake. Once there, John flew down the lake, picked them up and took them to Kulik for a well-deserved rest.

*Susie Petersen and Floyd "Slim" Beck in the Kulik fish-house preparing dinner. Ray Petersen Collection*

With only 18 miles of frozen lake left to go, spirits were high. John returned his crew early the next morning. Slim and Bob made great time on the hard lake ice. To avoid the big pressure ridges they deliberately traveled quite near the shoreline. The spring winds hadn't blown all the snow from the lake ice, but what little snow they encountered didn't hamper their progress. The cat-train was past the halfway point when, without warning, the heavy TD-24 cat hit a soft spot, crashed through the ice and plunged to the bottom of the lake. Fortunately for Slim, the water was only about 7 feet deep and the huge machine didn't take him completely under. Traveling further back in the cat-train, Bob watched as the cat quickly disappeared.

There is no record of the total number of days the cat-train journey lasted, but the journal entries in the Kulik Lodge guest book caught my attention. John Walatka documented the ordeal beginning on April 3, 1958:

*Walatka, Raphael and Wassille Evan arrived today to start opening camp for Beck and Gurtler who are on the way up from King Salmon with TD-24 cat and Woolridge scraper and wannigan. Very cold, landed on ice in front of camp.*

*4-5-58: Picked up Bob Gurtler and Slim Beck at Hammersly's Camp on wheels and brought them to Kulik for a rest and groceries.*

*4-6-58: Gurtler and Beck dropped the cat in 7 feet of water 10 miles east of Hammersly's Camp. Big job ahead. Boys went to logging camp, Beck and Gurtler walked to camp and radioed for triple and double blocks.*

*4-7-58: Waiting for blocks, etc. preparing dead-men rigging and cutting ice.*

*4-8-58: Started moving cat to beach.*

*4-11-58: Got cat out and running.*

*4-14-58: Slim, Gurtler and Raphael reached camp with cat at 7 p.m.*

With the cat train's arrival, the Kulik runway expansion was completed. The first scheduled passenger service to an Alaska fishing lodge became a reality during the season of 1959 with the first landing of Northern Consolidated Airline's F-27 at Kulik Lodge.

The heavy equipment that Slim and the boys worked so hard to deliver, and that Ray planned to return to King Salmon and sell, still resides at Kulik. Although it hasn't moved for many years, Harry Wehrman, the maintenance guru at Kulik for the last 19 years, told me that with some hydraulic fluid, a few new parts, and a little loving care, he could make the heavy machinery operational once again.

*The heavy equipment that Slim Beck and Bob Gurtler drove across the frozen tundra in 1958 is still at Kulik. James W. Albert photo*

Since I became the manager at Kulik, the most frequently asked question has been, "How did the vehicles get here?" Other than the overland cat-train in 1958, nearly everything else at Kulik Lodge, including the current vehicles, arrived by air. The pictures on the previous page should give the reader an idea of the

*The Kulik bus (top) being loaded into a surplus military C-82 for the one way trip to Kulik. The Kulik bus (middle) meeting an F-27 on the Kulik runway. A Northern Consolidated F-27 (bottom) being loaded with the John Deer cat that serves a multitude of uses at the lodge today. Ray Petersen Collection*

usefulness of a large runway. There aren't many civil float airplanes that could haul such loads, and if they could, unloading would be a nightmare.

One of the first great guides at the Angler's Paradise Camps was David Shuster. Dave was one of those young men who had adventure on his mind. By the start of 1955, the 23-year-old had read all he could find on the Katmai country and the great fishing it offered those adventurous enough to give it a try. He decided to outfit himself and give Alaska and the Katmai region a thorough test. In 1955, he booked a trip and came as a client.

*Dave Shuster with a great fish. Circa 1959—Dave Shuster Collection*

From his home in New Jersey, Dave made his way to Anchorage and then onto a Northern Consolidated DC-3 bound for King Salmon. From King Salmon, he flew in a Cessna T-50 with pilot Johnny Walatka first to Brooks Camp and later to Grosvenor Camp where he met the Petersen family. A few days later, John Walatka flew him to Nonvianuk Camp where he met and befriended Bill Hammersly. Dave spent nearly a month in the land of Katmai. He was impressed and vowed to return. He also made a great impression on all those he met and with whom he fished.

As promised, Dave Shuster returned to Katmai early in May of 1959. When he arrived in King Salmon, he found that spring was late and Brooks Lodge wasn't quite open. Dave jumped on the first flight he could get to Nonvianuk Lake and the Hammersly Camp. Not finding Bill Hammersly, Dave camped there and waited for Brooks to open. He had a grand time and caught some great fish. When John Walatka offered, Dave readily accepted a ride to Grosvenor where he found the Petersen family hurrying to get ready for the season. Young guide Chuck Petersen used the occasion to hone his guiding skills with Dave a willing fisherman. A few days later, Dave arrived at Brooks Camp. He had already been in Alaska for two weeks.

Angler's Paradise Nonvianuk Camp manager, Bill Hammersly, had become quite ill and had gone to California for medical attention after the 1958 season. Uncertain of Bill's health, John Walatka hired a guy to manage the camp at Nonvianuk until Bill's return. John hated to admit it, but things weren't going well. After several complaints, John went to Nonvianuk and explained the job again.

A few days later, all of Katmai was shocked when word came that Bill Hammersly had died of cancer on June 28, 1959. Once John knew that Bill would not be returning, he flew to Nonvianuk Camp to discuss things with his temporary manager. Evidently John didn't like what he found. He promptly fired the chap and helped him pack his bags for the quick flight to King Salmon. Within an hour, John was at Brooks offering immediate employment to Dave Shuster. Dave told me John didn't give him a chance to say no. Within an hour he was back at Nonvianuk, and several hours later he greeted his first guests as camp manager.

*Chairman of the Civil Aeronautics Board, James R. Durfey (front left), Ray Petersen (front right) and two unidentified vacationers ready to go fishing at the Angler's Paradise Camps. Circa 1959—Ray Petersen Collection*

David Shuster worked first at Nonvianuk and later at Brooks, Grosvenor and Kulik. He guided for the Angler's Paradise Camps for the next several seasons. I asked him about the fishing in the late 1950s. He told me they chased the rainbows just as we do today but there wasn't very much interest in salmon. According to Dave:

> *The best part of the fishing and being in Katmai was the complete solitude. I was just a guide but I can remember sitting around at breakfast discussing where to go. We always had the rivers to ourselves. It was a rare day to see an airplane other than Johnny or one of the other NCA pilots. It was great to hear the evening radio checks and listen to the Branhams and old John discussing the fishing plans. They never fished the same places. Bud had his places and we had ours. It was a gentleman's arrangement. I loved it. We had a great time and the guests always had a great time. I sure remember having a lot of big shots around. It seems that every time Ray would arrive, another group, more influential than the last, would get off the plane. Ray told me once that no matter who they are, they all put their pants on one leg at a time. I remember one guest who seemed pretty important to Ray. We took him to the American and Ray wanted to be sure he had a great time. Ray did everything possible to ensure his trip was successful. When the guy finally left, I remember asking*

*Ray about his special guest. Ray, in his most articulate manner, told me that the angler was James R. Durfey, chairman of the Civil Aeronautics Board, from Washington DC. I just wondered who would be next!*

Late in the 1950s, Ray Petersen was not only entertaining clients and enjoying the lodge business, he was the iron fist that drove Northern Consolidated Airline to be the state's leading air carrier. Ray purchased and brought the first turbo-prop airplanes to the state of Alaska. His vision of scheduled service to the camps became a reality with the extension of the runway at Kulik and scheduling the F-27 to use it.

Ray explained that First Lady Mamie Eisenhower dedicated the first jet airplane, a Boeing 707, that went into service for American Airlines in 1957, but he and NCA had to settle for Pat Nixon, wife of Vice President Richard Nixon, to preside over the inauguration of their F-27 service. As you might expect, Alaska and Northern Consolidated rolled out the red carpet for the visiting dignitaries. The Nixons arrived in September 1958 for the big inauguration party. When I asked Ray to identify the man at the microphone in the photo above, he said:

*From the left: Mrs. McCarrey, Tricia, Julie, Vice President Nixon, Toni Petersen, Pat Nixon, Ray Petersen and J. L. McCarrey at the dedication of Ray's Northern Consolidated Airline's F-27 Service in September of 1958. Ray Petersen Collection*

*Why that's Judge McCarrey. No, I'm sorry. He*

*wasn't a judge when that was taken. He was still my attorney. Numerous times I had been in Washington DC and each time I visited my friend Congressman Len Hall. I kept asking the Congressman when the Feds would appoint a judge for Alaska. "Hell, we just can't get any of your Alaskan attorneys past the FBI investigation." I knew he was referring to the normal Alaska activities (prostitution and gambling were accepted in Alaska but not by the FBI) in evaluating a potential federal judge. I told the Congressman I was sure that my attorney, J. L. McCarrey, a Mormon, would pass the most rigorous of tests. I don't know if I was responsible or not, but shortly after the picture was taken, J. L. McCarrey became the first federal judge appointed in Alaska.*

## Fishing
## How Was It in the 1950s?

Turn back the clock to the early 1950s and put yourself at Kulik Lodge, then plan your fishing trip for the next few days. I know that a great number of today's fishing lodge clients would have no problem picking five or six of the most famous fishing holes, but which places would have been chosen nearly 50 years ago when only a few of the rivers were known, let alone famous?

Once arriving at your first fishing location, which fly patterns would you use? Considering that most of the popular patterns used in Alaska today had yet to be tied, what choices would you have had? What kind of rod would you choose? Perhaps you are beginning to see the problems in comparing the fishing of the 1950s to the 1970s or the 1990s. Today, anglers have the advantage of more than 50 seasons of lodge operations, fishing experience, advanced technology in equipment design, as well as dedicated and experienced fishing guides. Even though I know that fishing is better now than at any previous time in Bristol Bay, the fishermen of those early years sure caught fish.

**Times Fishing Editor Finds Alaska Waters Teeming With Salmon**

**By ENOS BRADNER**
**Wildlife Editor, The Times**

*(Enos Bradner, The Times' fishing and hunting editor, is making a flying trip around Alaska's best fishing spots. This is his first report of the conditions he has found.)*

BROOKS RIVER, Alaska, July 10.—Fishing here is so varied and spectacular as to be almost unbelievable.

Last night we fished ourselves into utter exhaustion. We had caught and released so many trout and salmon we lost count.

**It was the first time in a lifetime of angling we could not keep up with the fish. They hit so rapidly and fought so savagely that at frequent intervals we had to stagger to the bank to rest.**

ENOS BRADNER

The day started with gentle fly fishing on grayling that required expert casting and delicate touch on the line. It continued with the type of rainbow fishing that anglers drive across the continent to reach. And it climaxed with salmon fishing I doubt can be duplicated anywhere else.

**The sockeyes are surging up Brooks River by the thousand to collect in the waters below the falls, which they are leaping continuously. A fly cast into the boiling white waters directly below the falls brings a savage sock of these extraordinary salmon.**

Their fighting qualities are superb. They are as bright as ocean-fresh fish with a steel gray back and silver sides. They run with the speed and power of a steelhead. They leap and jump with abandon. When they head downstream, they are virtually impossible to stop. They break leaders and take flies no matter what tackle we use. Never have we seen any other salmon put up the fight these sockeyes did yesterday, and I am not excepting a cohoe or king.

*From the Seattle Times, July, 1951*

Certainly during the first few seasons, the clients and visitors who braved the elements and traveled to Alaska had no idea of the quality of the fishing, except that it was reputed to be outstanding. The expeditions led by writers such as Ray Camp, Joe Dearing and Enos Bradner bore testimony to the quality and quantity of the fishing available to anyone who dared to try. Ray Petersen's earliest brochures highlighted fishing throughout western Alaska. In addition to fishing the well-known species, Ray and his fishermen plied the waters north of Bristol Bay for sheefish. At that time, the sheefish was unknown to the average angler, and the wire services and newspaper audiences clamored for more information. During those early years, fishing reports from Alaska were newsworthy.

During the 1950 season, Angler's Paradise records indicate that only 138 guests visited Brooks Camp. By 1959, however, more than 1,082 guests arrived at Brooks. Compared to today's pressure, I'm sure fishing had little, if any, impact on the fish populations. Although strict limits were established by the Fish and Wildlife Service for the rivers, fishermen didn't worry too much about killing fish for the table, or for home.

I researched the rules and regulations during the early days to see what changes have been made over the past 50 years. Frank Norris chronicles both the changes in regulations and monitoring by the National Park Service in *Isolated Paradise:*

*Ray Petersen, who was an ardent fisherman as well as an airline executive, was an early advocate for the imposition of fishing regulations. He could see that distinct fishing groups flew into the Brooks River area: Alaskans, who were the "hardware and bait" fishermen, and the "stateside" anglers, who were the fly-fishing enthusiasts. Petersen knew that any regulation that might be established would have to favor one group over the other. Petersen observed that fly-fishermen outnumbered the "hardware and bait" fishermen; he therefore advocated that Brooks River be limited to fly-fishing. George B. Kelez, who headed the Fish and Wildlife Service's efforts at the*

# Alaska Shee-Fish

## Specimens in Dearing Series Donated to S. F. Institution

Two specimens of shee-fish, hooked in Alaskan waters, were described today at the California Academy of Sciences as "an exceedingly important contribution" to scientific knowledge.

The fish were those described in the series of articles by Uncle Joe Dearing just concluded in The Call-Bulletin.

### First of Kind

They were shipped to the academy in Golden Gate Park through the generosity of Thomas E. Green and E. D. Landels, who accompanied Dearing on the northern expedition.

Northern Consolidated Airlines co-operated to rush the specimens here.

W. I. Follett, curator of ichthyology at the academy, reported the fish have been prepared as specimens for scientific study.

"They are the first of their kind that we have ever received," he wrote, "and we regard them as an exceedingly important contribution."

### Dearing Backed

Follett described the specimens as including the head of a fish stated to have weighed 10 pounds and to have measured 37 inches, and an entire fish weighing 4½ pounds and measuring 24¼ inches.

Noting they had been reported in detail in Dearing's stories, he commented:

"I confirm your identification of both specimens.

"For well over a century, this fish has been called the 'Inconnu'—which is the equivalent of our word 'incognito'—but recently it has been 'officially' renamed the 'Shee-fish.'

"Ichthyologists now include it in the same species with a fish reported from certain rivers of northern Asia, although it represents a different subspecies.

"Under this interpretation, its scientific name is Stenodus leucichthys Mackenziei.

### Fish's History

"The first of these words means 'narrow tooth'; the second means 'whitefish,' to which the Shee-fish is closely related, and the third refers to the Mackenzie River of Canada, from where it was first made known to science, by Sir John Richardson, the British explorer, in 1823.

"Richardson incidentally, was the scientist who originally described the cut-throat trout."

Circumstances under which the Shee-fish, long a mystery to science, were caught by Dearing and his comrades were told in Dearing's Call-Bulletin series.

*July 25, 1951 Call-Bulletin. Ray Petersen Collection*

*Brooks Lake Laboratory, agreed.*

*Senior Park Service officials also expressed concern about over-fishing at the monument. They believed the Park Service needed to find some way to protect Katmai National Monument and to regulate the public's use of it. But they needed to establish a presence at the monument. NPS officials were aware that agency regulations prohibited airplane landings in the monument by all but official personnel; as a corollary to that regulation, they had the power to arrest anyone who landed a floatplane on Naknek or Brooks Lake. Superintendent Grant Pearson of Mount McKinley National Park, however, recognized that it was far more prudent to change the regulation than to prevent violation. In 1949, therefore, the monument was opened to summertime air traffic. In June of 1950, shortly after Northern Consolidated opened its first fishing camps in Katmai National Monument, the F&WS established its first monument-wide fishing regulations. The regulations stated that: The limit of catch per person per day shall not exceed two red salmon, and ten fish or ten pounds and one fish of any other species. Possession of more than one day's limit of fish by any one person at any one time is prohibited. On the Brooks River, tackle was restricted to two flies; elsewhere in the monument, tackle could consist of not more than two flies or not more than one plug, spoon, or spinner, to which may be attached not more than one treble hook.*

*Joe Phillips from Seattle with a great sheefish. Joe accompanied Enos Bradner and Joe Dearing during their 1951 fishing expedition to the Angler's Paradise Camps. Ray Petersen Collection*

*The first scientific look at the sport fishing potential of and assessment of sport fishing pressures in the area came in 1954. At the request of the NPS, John Greenbank of the F&WS did a sport fish survey of Katmai National Monument. Greenbank and assistant Ronald Lopp worked through the summer of 1954 and described monument waters, examined fish distribution and abundance, sampled fish populations, and conducted creel censuses in various locations. Overall, the survey found fish populations high and fishing pressure light. Most fishing within the Monument occurred in the Brooks River. Practically no fishing took place in Brooks Lake. Naknek Lake was fished only at the mouth of the Brooks River. A limited amount of fishing, probably not over 200 hours in the summer of 1954, took place at Lake Grosvenor in front of Coville Camp. Pike Lake, north of Brooks Lake, experienced about 50 hours of fly-in fishing. There was also fishing in the vicinity of the Air Force camps on Naknek River. Overall, the censuses recorded that during the summer there had been 843 fishing hours on Brooks River with a total of 906 fish, primarily rainbow trout, caught; 1794 fishing hours on Naknek River a total of 1279 fish, primarily rainbow trout, caught; and 128 fishing hours on Naknek Lake with a total of 98 fish, mostly red salmon and lake trout, caught.*

*California resident Ed Landels with a pair of great grayling. Circa 1951—Ray Petersen Collection*

*When the field survey was completed and the collected data were analyzed, Greenbank made several recommendations. He suggested that (1) the restriction of fishing in Brooks River to artificial flies be retained; (2) the prohibition against the use of two or more hooks or flies per line be rescinded; (3) the prohibition against fishing within 300 feet above Brooks Falls be abandoned; (4) the daily catch limit for sockeye salmon be two fish killed, with no limit on the number caught and released; (5) all size limits on fish be dropped; and (6) no fish of any species be artificially stocked in waters of the Monument, and no new species introduced. Greenbank further recommended that consideration be given to the development of lake trout and northern pike sport fishery, establishment of a perpetual catch reporting system for Brooks River, and continuation of field studies. He believed that is was particularly important to conduct a survey of the rainbow trout population of the Naknek River system.*

One of the major problems with fishing on the Brooks River has been the almost constant struggle between the National Park Service and the Fish and Wildlife Service. I guess you could call it a power struggle. Fortunately for fishermen, Ray Petersen and his concession staff mounted strong opposition to some of the suggested rules aimed at preserving the salmon. Naturally, Ray's concerns stemmed from his own angling experiences and his desire to provide quality fishing for his guests. From *Isolated Paradise*:

> *Once they had established a presence, the NPS recognized that the goals of NPS and F&WS management were often disparate, and NPS officials felt that they too ought to have a say in determining Monument fishing regulations. Clarence J. Rhode, Regional Director of the Fish and Wildlife Service in*

*An unidentified angler with six beautiful rainbows from the Brooks River. Circa 1950—Ray Petersen Collection*

*Alaska, visited Brooks Camp on July 12 (1950) in hopes of clarifying the agencies' fishery management responsibilities.*

*Another problem faced by both NPS and Fish and Wildlife Service officials was the over-fishing of salmon. During the late 1940s the trout population had suffered from over-fishing, but the problem was eliminated when the new fly-fishing regulations had been imposed. The regulations imposed for salmon were not particularly strict, and by 1951 officials agreed that the current salmon catch rate(up to 100 per hour at times(was harmful to the fishery.*

*various fishing camps, met with regional director Lawrence Merriam and fought against the agencies' proposal. Don Horter, who served as NCA's publicist, noted that national magazines and newspapers such as "Argosy," "Colliers," "Esquire," "The New York Times," and "Saturday Evening Post" were about to publish stories on Katmai's superlative fishing. Horter protested against any regulations that restricted angling at the base of Brooks Falls because "most of the fishermen come to the Monument in order to hook salmon at the base of Brooks Falls." The concessionaire was also disturbed about the proposal to limit catch and release. Horter*

*The fish-drying rack at Brooks taken in 1940 by Victor Calahane. The fish are red salmon, not rainbows! Courtesy NPS Photo Collection, Calahane neg. 357*

*After the close of the 1951 fishing season, Rhode wrote NPS Director Demaray and made some suggestions that, he hoped, would clear up the jurisdictional tug-of-war and restore a healthy salmon run back to the Brooks River. He urged the NPS to prohibit angling (for any species) within 300 feet below Brooks River falls and within 300 feet of the weir at the exit of Brooks Lake. By this time, the NPS had also suggested that the daily salmon catch be limited to two, including those caught and released.*

*Northern Consolidated, which operated the*

*said he had fished Brooks River for seven years and believed unlimited catch and release would not harm the fishery, and vowed that the two regulations would force NCA to abandon its Brooks Camp operation.*

*On Oct. 3, director Demaray responded to Rhode and readily accepted his suggestion regarding fishing at the weir. Because of NCA pressure, Demaray rejected any regulations concerning Brooks Falls. The director, however, held fast with the agency's suggestion that anglers be limited to a daily catch of no more than two red salmon, including fish hooked and released. Fisheries personnel believed that even "catch and release" weakened salmon and would diminish the fishery.*

*By late spring (1952), compromise regulations were finally agreed upon and were submitted to the Federal Register. The new catch limits were the same as those issued in 1950 except that they included the NPS-suggested limitation on catch-and-release fishing. Allowable types of lures were also modified; instead of allowing a treble hook to be attached to each artificial lure, not more than two single hooks were allowed. In addition, fishing was prohibited within 100 yards of the weir. Finally a compromise was reached in regards to fishing at Brooks River Falls. The two agency heads decided to prohibit fishing within 100 yards above the fish ladder and on the ladder itself. Fishing below the ladder, however, was not prohibited. Efforts to perfect fishing regulations for Katmai continued. In the summer of 1955, Dorr G. Yeager, Regional Chief of Interpretation of the NPS, visited Katmai and discussed angling regulations with F&WS personnel, including regional director Clarence Rhode. As a result, Yeager believed that it would "not be objectionable to permit the use of hardware with barbless hooks in a definite area." He thought the lower pool on Brooks River beside the fish rack on the east side of the river might be a suitable spot to test the relaxation of fly-fishing-only restrictions.*

*In 1956, the National Park Service responded to earlier suggestions by adopting new fishing regulations. Following John Greenbank's advice to remove the limits on the number of salmon which were hooked and released, the agency opened the lower 880 feet of Brooks River near its mouth to fishing with "plugs, spoons and spinners with not more than one barbless treble hook and not more than one attractor blade" as well as to artificial flies. Katmai fishermen, still comprising the vast majority of Monument visitors, welcomed the new relaxed regulations.*

*Fishing below the falls was great, and legal in the 1950s and 60s. In 1971, the State of Alaska prohibited fishing within fifty feet of the fish ladder which is visible to the upper right. Ray Petersen Collection*

*In 1959, Alaska became a state. The Statehood Act, among its other provisions, specified that Mount McKinley National Park was the only park unit where state fish and game regulations would not apply. As a result, control of sportfishing largely passed from the Federal Government (Department of the Interior) to the state government (Alaska Department of Fish and Game). By early 1961, state fishing regulations were in effect. Federal regulations also remained in effect. The two sets of regulations would seem, at first glance, to be confusing. They do not appear to have conflicted, however, and Katmai Park rangers appear to have had little difficulty in enforcing both sets of regulations. And so ended the jurisdictional battles between the F&WS and the NPS over the management and regulation of sport fishermen.*

*Ray Petersen had no shortage of willing models to pose for publicity pictures. Don Horter took this photo of his wife fishing at Brooks Falls prior to the construction of the bear-viewing platform which was installed more than a decade later. There were few, if any, bears at the falls until years later. Early anglers were able to fish without fear of bears or eager National Park Service enforcement types. Ray Petersen Collection*

The regulations established at the urging of Ray Petersen and other NCA and Angler's Paradise officials were clearly established with sportfishing in mind. Ray was able to accept the inclusion of "hardware" in the lower stretch of the river in exchange for no limit on catch and release throughout the river. Over the next years, while fishing became more popular, few regulatory changes occurred.

The first decade of fishing lodge operations closed with little notoriety, but with a strong sense of accomplishment for Ray Petersen. Not only did he prove that a full-time fishing lodge operation was possible; he made it successful as well. Although Ray could not see too far into the future through the cloud cover of everyday problems, the success experienced by his Angler's Paradise Camps would eventually become the biggest threat to his lodge's economic survival. The time of being the only fishing lodge operator would change drastically over the next 40 years.

The decade of the 1950s drew to a close with numerous significant events for the fishing lodge industry of the future. Ward Gay, aviator and hunting guide, purchased some property at Six-Mile Lake near Lake Clark, and Graham Mower purchased the hunting facility at Chelatna Lake. Ed Seiler, the hotel operator in King Salmon, had been flying clients out for a day's fishing for several years in his Stinson Station Wagon. Among other places, he routinely fished the Brooks River and the outlet of Grosvenor Lake. By 1959, Ed's plans included building a lodge. On the other side of the Kvichak, three men living in the village of Dillingham started to dream about sportfishing. John Pearson hosted a few guests at a small fishing camp on the Wood River. Bill Gurtler, a commercial fisherman and Roger Maves, who had previously owned a lodge in Minnesota and was one of Ray's Northern Consolidated employees, started thinking that the fishing lodge business had been pretty good to Ray Petersen. In the years ahead, these and other men would bring new levels of competition to the sportfishing lodge business in Bristol Bay.

*Brooks guide Warren Tillman preparing a shore lunch along the Brooks River. Circa 1952—Ray Petersen Collection*

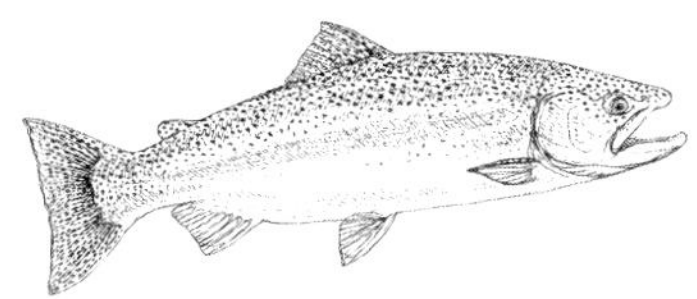

# Chapter 4
# The Decade of the 1960s

"We stand today on the edge of a new frontier—the frontier of the 1960s, a frontier of unknown opportunities and perils, a frontier of unfulfilled hopes and threats. The new frontier of which I speak is not a set of promises—it is a set of challenges."
*John F. Kennedy*

As years go, 1960 was great. Many of today's "baby-boomers" were approaching their teenage years, and their favorite music wasn't the choice of their parents. Chubby Checker made headlines with his new sound, "The Twist," and Roy Orbison hit the top of the charts with "Only the Lonely." In movie theatres around the country, Jack Lemmon starred in "The Apartment," and Alfred Hitchcock scared everyone with "Psycho." A new organization, OPEC (Organization of Petroleum Exporting Countries) formed and, if you can believe it, oil was only fourteen cents a barrel. A first-class postage stamp was still just four cents when John Kennedy won the big presidential election against Richard Nixon. Alaska, the nation's most northern state, was starting her second year of statehood.

The 1960 fishing lodge season started unlike any before in Bristol Bay. Two new fishing camps were eager for business. Ray Petersen's belief that more lodges would stimulate his airline business was about to be tested. Ray had operated the only full-time fishing camps for more than ten years without a major competitor. Bud Branham's hunting business was thriving, although each successive season he hosted more fishing clients. By the end of the decade, Bud Branham and Ray Petersen would no longer hold all the cards. The number of fishing lodges and camps would more than triple.

As they had done each year since developing their first travel brochure in 1950, Ray Petersen's public relations team put together another comprehensive and beautifully designed marketing brochure. Because one of their primary goals had been to promote tourism to and through Alaska, the brochure produced in 1960 continued that theme. Keeping the complete Alaska Adventure theme started a decade earlier, Ray advertised sightseeing flights around Mt. McKinley. The world-famous travel journalist, Lowell Thomas, called the flight around North America's tallest mountain, "an exciting experience that should not be missed by any visitor to our 49th state."

*Senator John F. Kennedy boards a Northern Consolidated flight to the bush in a whirlwind Alaskan campaign tour prior to the 1960 election. Ray Petersen Collection*

From the fishing segment of the brochure it is obvious that the knowledge gained during the previous ten years of camp operation manifested itself in the Trout Tours offered in 1960. Because so few previous guests had expressed interest in fishing for salmon, rainbows became the featured fish, and rainbow fishermen became the primary audience for the advertisements.

Prior to the 1960 season, Ray finalized a cooperative interline agreement with Northwest Airlines. This connection increased Ray's marketing potential, and eased travel difficulties for potential tourists. With the help of the huge marketing machine at Northwest, the Angler's Paradise Trout Tour Brochure went out to travel agents and tour companies in the United States and around the free world. The Northwest connection helped Ray promote Alaska, his airline, and his fishing camps.

In what would be considered suicide in today's seemingly greedy lodge market, Ray Petersen made a bold move. Inside his own fishing literature, he included a special brochure advertising two new fishing camps that he did not own or operate.

By including this special brochure with his own marketing materials, Ray clearly demonstrated his desire and determination to see an industry develop. I believe his interest in helping others follow him into the business unlocked the floodgate of progress that led to the thriving lodge business in Alaska today.

The idea for the special brochure developed late in the 1959 season, when two Dillingham residents presented Petersen with a plan. One of Ray's former employees, John Pearson and his friend, Bill Gurtler, traveled to Anchorage to meet with Ray and the Angler's Paradise Camps manager, John Walatka. During the meeting, both men confirmed their plans and outlined their ideas to start fishing lodges in Bristol Bay. I'm certain that Ray was pleased to learn that his concept of a lodge industry was finally gaining momentum. I'm also sure he was disappointed to learn that neither John Pearson nor Bill Gurtler had sufficient resources to both build and then promote their camps. When the meeting ended, Ray had agreed to provide some marketing assistance. Shortly thereafter, John Walatka and the talented marketing

## KATMAI TROUT TOURS

Air fares Seattle-Kulik round trip $216.00 plus Fed. Tax

Tours originate at Seattle-Tacoma Airport and include transportation from Seattle via Northwest Airlines or Pacific Northern Airlines to ANCHORAGE and Northern Consolidated Airlines to Kulik round trip. For guests scheduled to other camps than Kulik Lodge, or due to weather, the company will use King Salmon as the transfer point by Bushmaster float planes. Once all expense part of tour is started from Kulik or King Salmon, no refunds can be allowed.

### KATMAI TROUT TOUR NO. 1

7 Days and Nights

Seven exciting days of the best grayling, rainbow, salmon, lake trout, pike and arctic char fishing in all Alaska. Includes all transportation and camp facilities.

Per person . . . . . $455.00 plus Fed. Tax

### THREE DAY KATMAI SPECIAL

3 Days and Nights (one camp)

Three days of fishing, relaxing and for camera enthusiasts, wonderful pictures.

Per person . . . . . . $325.00 plus Fed. Tax

### ANCHORAGE-KATMAI TOURS

The above Tours are also available to visitors and residents in Anchorage at the following rates.

7 day tour, per person . . $330.00 plus Fed. Tax

3 day tour, per person . . 185.00 plus Fed. Tax

Additional time at the camps may be arranged when space is open.

Typical round trip fares to Seattle-Tacoma Airport

From:

| | |
|---|---|
| San Francisco | $ 68.60 |
| Los Angeles | 96.70 |
| San Diego | 108.20 |
| Denver | 114.40 |
| Salt Lake City | 82.10 |
| Portland | 16.30 |
| Miami | 269.80 |
| Atlanta | 234.30 |
| Las Vegas | 137.20 |
| Phoenix | 134.10 |
| New York | 213.00 |
| Chicago | 163.10 |
| Minneapolis | 153.50 |
| New Orleans | 254.70 |

To above must be added Federal Tax

For full information, see your travel agent, your airline office, or write—via air mail to expedite correspondence.

NORTHERN CONSOLIDATED AIRLINES, INC.

Box 6133

International Airport • Anchorage, Alaska

SEE THE

*The 1960 Trout Tours offered by Northern Consolidated Vacations. Ray Petersen secured interline agreements with many national air carriers. Check the prices from your nearest airport to Seattle on the chart above. Ray Petersen Collection*

## GENERAL INFORMATION

A $50 deposit is required with reservations. Final payment is requested thirty days prior to date of tour departure. Full refund will be made when cancellation is received 30 days prior to date tour begins. If cancellation is received less than 30 days prior to departure, deposit will not be refunded if accommodations cannot be resold.

**FISHING LICENSES** — may be purchased upon arrival in Dillingham. Special 10-day non-resident fishing license is $6.00.

**SEASON**—Opens June 1 and closes October 1.

**LEGAL CATCH**—The limit of catch per person per day shall be 10 fish of which not more than two shall exceed 20 inches. Possession of more than one day's limit of catch by any person at any one time is prohibited. Exception: the limit catch of salmon shall be two fish daily.

**NORTHERN CONSOLIDATED AIRLINES DOES NOT OWN OR OPERATE EITHER WOOD RIVER OR TIKCHIK LAKE CAMP, BUT ACTS ONLY AS BOOKING AGENT.** However, we do highly recommend the fishing at both of these camps.

FOR RESERVATIONS, or further details write or wire
**NORTHERN CONSOLIDATED AIRLINES, INC.**
Box 6133 • International Airport • Anchorage, Alaska
or
**SEE YOUR TRAVEL AGENT**

INTERNATIONAL AIRPORT, ANCHORAGE, ALASKA

*The cover and back page of the Special Brochure that accompanied the Angler's Paradise brochure in 1960. Ray Petersen Collection*

# Fish and Have Fun in the Angler's Paradise Area!

## WOOD RIVER LAKES TOUR

Wood River Trout Camp is owned and operated by John Pearson of Dillingham, Alaska, and will be opened to the general public for the first time in 1960. This is a truly virgin area—much like our own Katmai—with a magnificent chain of lakes, and miles of wonderful fishing rivers—amid beautiful forests and towering mountains. These lakes and rivers flow directly into Bristol Bay on the Bering Sea and are part of the finest Pacific salmon fishing area known to man.

You can follow your own personal preferences for fishing—fly fishing, spinning and casting just a few yards from camp—wonderful trolling on five large lakes. Streams and lakes abound with rainbow, Dolly Varden, Mackinaw and lake trout—also grayling, Arctic char, pike and Pacific salmon in season. Boats, motors, guides, tackle and other gear are available at Wood River Camp.

The camp is located 35 miles north of Dillingham on the Agulowalk River between Alegnagik and Nerka Lakes. It is served out of Dillingham by either bush aircraft or a car and boat combination. Northern Consolidated Airlines serves Dillingham daily (except Sunday) with its new F-27 Fairchild prop-jets. Flying time is one hour, thirty minutes from Anchorage. Mr. Pearson meets our flights every day at Dillingham to transport guests to Wood River Camp.

Wood River Lakes Tours originate at Seattle-Tacoma Airport and include transportation from Seattle to Wood River Camp (air fare Seattle-Dillingham $240.00 plus $9.36 tax). All expense portion of tour starts at Dillingham.

**7 DAYS AND NIGHTS**

**Per person** . . . . . . . . . . **$451.50**
**Plus tax** . . . . . . . . . . **13.36**

## TIKCHIK LAKES TOUR

Tikchik Lakes Camp is owned and operated by Bill Gurtler and located 65 miles north of Dillingham, Alaska, on Nuyakuk Lake, largest in the Tikchik area. The camp will be opened to the general public for the first time in 1960.

At the camp site is to be had some of the finest Arctic char and Mackinaw fishing that any angler could ask for. Within ten miles of camp is some of Alaska's best rainbow and grayling fishing. Northern pike fishing is excellent just a short distance from camp. Some of these babies are 50 inches long!

Present facilities consist of tent houses and a central dining area. A new lodge, now under construction, will be open for the beginning of the 1960 season. It's an excellent place to fish, have fun and relax in comfort.

Northern Consolidated Airlines provides transportation from Anchorage to Dillingham daily (except Sunday) in its new F-27 prop-jets. Transportation from Dillingham to Tikchik Camp is by bush plane.

Tikchik Lakes Tours originate at Seattle-Tacoma Airport and include transportation from Seattle to Tikchik Camp (air fare Seattle-Dillingham $240.00 plus $9.36 tax). All expense portion of tour starts at Dillingham.

**7 DAYS AND NIGHTS**

**Per person** . . . . . . . . . . **$596.00**
**Plus tax** . . . . . . . . . . **13.36**

*Ray Petersen encouraged lodge development. Ray agreed to help John Pearson and Bill Gurtler with their marketing. He included their lodge literature with his own. Ray Petersen Collection* staff at NCA produced the special brochure reproduced on pages 154 and 155.

## Wood River Trout Camp
### John Pearson

By the time John Pearson boarded the flight to Anchorage to meet with Ray late in the fall of 1959, he already had the attributes of a lodge owner. John Pearson really loved to fish, and he knew what a lodge was supposed to be; after all, he was one of the first men John Walatka had selected to help construct the first fishing camps in Bristol Bay. It may have been his love of fishing that Walatka used to persuade John Pearson to assist in the building of the Angler's Paradise Camps in the late spring of 1950. John Pearson was a carpenter by trade and jumped at the chance to work and to fish at Kulik. According to Ray Petersen:

*John Pearson was a good hand. He was a good carpenter and helped us quite a few times at the stations. He even installed the hardwood floor in our house in Anchorage.*

Several years after helping at Kulik, John Pearson started building again. This time, however, he was building for his future. John Pearson and his wife, Leta, had opened the Willowtree, a small bar and restaurant in Dillingham early in the 1950s. Several local residents told me that besides being a great bar, the Willowtree featured fantastic food. Leta did the cooking while John took care of all the bartending duties. Over the next few years, the Willowtree prospered. Unfortunately for the Pearsons, a series of fires wiped them out. Undaunted by the setbacks, each time a fire burned them out, John started again, and each time he put up another building, the popular restaurant and bar grew a little larger.

Along with his fire-induced building projects at the Willowtree, John built several small cabins along the Wood River, north of Dillingham. At first, he personally used these cabins for some hunting and trapping. One day, however, an idea came to John. Perhaps he remembered the camps at Brooks and Kulik, perhaps not. In any case, John decided to start a fishing camp. To attain his goal, he bought an old Tally-scow from one of the local canneries and spent the next few weeks converting it to "livable condition," then towed it up the Wood River to his nearest cabin site. With the modified barge in place, he had a "Spartan" place for guests to stay. Although he didn't advertise his camp until the following winter, John Pearson and his wife hosted a few revenue guests during the 1959 season. John Pearson's Wood River Trout Camp became the third lodge to open in Bristol Bay. The Pearsons' first revenue client, Dillingham resident Lars Nelson, made these comments:

*John was just getting started during the summer of 1959. He sure had some big ideas. He had numerous cabins in the area for hunting and trapping. He tore down one of his cabins and moved it up the river by boat. John had an old tally-scow that he converted into housing for his guests. I'm sure we were his first guests and it showed. John charged us $50 for the weekend. It was the fourth of July 1959, the summer before I got married. John took us to his camp by boat. I still remember there wasn't enough food. While we were there, all the guests helped with the cooking. More than anything else, I recall that fishing was pretty good, I was glad, too, because fish was all we had to eat.*

## The Lodge That Never Opened •Tikchik Lakes Camp•

### Bill Gurtler

According to knowledgeable sources, when John Walatka assembled a crack crew to build the Angler's Paradise Camps in the late spring of 1950, he tried to enlist the services of Bill Gurtler and his brother, Bob. The Gurtler brothers were hard-working young men from the Yukon River region. People were eager to hire one or both at every employment opportunity. As young adults, both Gurtler brothers earned their wages through commercial fishing. Those commercial fishing commitments kept Bill from working with Walatka, but he learned about the project from his brother who became a leader in the Angler's Paradise camp construction. By the mid-1950s, Bill continued commercial fishing while Bob eased into the airplane business. When Northern Consolidated Airline started scheduled service into Dillingham in 1955, Bob became Ray's station manager.

Despite his brother's success working with airplanes, Bill continued to spend his summer months commercial fishing. During the long months between fishing seasons, Bill occupied his time building several small cabins north of Dillingham. He built one of those cabins on the narrows between Tikchik and Nuyakuk Lakes. Slowly but steadily, Bill started to think of this small cabin as a fishing lodge site. Once the concept of starting a fishing lodge solidified in his mind, Bill started the process to obtain the land.

On October 10, 1959, the Anchorage office of the Bureau of Land Management received Bill Gurtler's location notice to obtain a Trade and Manufacturing site at Tikchik Narrows. Bill filed for four acres located on the peninsula between Nuyakuk and Tikchik lakes. In his application, Bill stated that the land was going to be used for a hunting and fishing lodge.

Bill Gurtler wasn't alone in his thoughts that a lodge was a good idea in the Wood River-Tikchik Lake region. He used one of his longtime friends, Bernard "Swede" Blanchard, as a sounding board. They discussed the idea of a fishing lodge whenever time permitted. Swede was another of Ray Petersen's Northern Consolidated employees who knew how popular the lodges were because he flew with John Walatka at the Angler's Paradise camps. Later, he had his own airplane and flying service.

After Bill Gurtler and John Pearson returned to Dillingham from their successful meeting at Northern Consolidated, Bill was more excited than ever, but he knew he had a lot of work to do to get ready. After seeing all the publicity for snow machines, the new way to travel over snow, Bill purchased a brand-new one. He decided a machine that could take him to his lakeshore site over the snow would be cheaper than an airplane and he could make several round-trips for the cost of one airplane ride. He also assumed the snow machine would be more dependable in bad weather.

The snow machine concept was new to Alaska when Bill took delivery of one of the first machines brought to Bristol Bay during the early spring of 1960. Personal accounts and newspaper articles indicated that the new machines were not as reliable as advertised. Unexpected difficulties with the newly designed drive system led to drive-belt failures on many machines, including Bill's. Several people told me that Bill was undaunted by the mechanical failures. Once he completed his initial tests and felt comfortable with his new machine,

Bill packed a huge load of equipment, including several new drive belts, and headed for his Tikchik Lake lodge site. Evidence indicates that he needed more drivebelts than he purchased. Miles before reaching his final destination, Bill's snow machine broke down for the last time.

Dick Armstrong, the founder of Armstrong Air, told me that Bill Gurtler was a popular man in Dillingham. When he was reported missing, many people helped in the search. Among others, Patrick Kohler, Walter Norden, Harry Shade, and Clyde Petersen assisted Dick Armstrong with flying duties. Dick spent nearly ten days flying search parties and searching himself for the long overdue Gurtler. He filled me in on a few details of the incident:

> *Snow machines were new and weren't too reliable. I don't know if the load was too heavy or what, but the thing quit. Bill was a wilderness survival instructor in the army and you couldn't ask for a better man in a critical situation, but I think his temper got in the way of his skills. I'm sure he was mad at the machine for breaking down. I'll bet he was frustrated as all hell when it kept stopping. I'm sure he finally got off the thing and kicked it a few times before he said "To hell with you," and walked off. He was alone except for a black lab puppy. Naturally, he wasn't wearing the proper clothing and didn't have much with him but a lightweight sleeping bag.*
>
> *Bill simply wasn't prepared for the bad early-spring weather. When the going got tough, the young dog left him and headed back toward the snow machine and a good trail. Some trappers found the dog not too far from the broken-down snow machine. Evidently, Bill crossed trapline trails but ignored them. If he had followed them he would have either found the trappers or one of their cabins. I guess Bill just wasn't thinking clearly by that time. He just wanted to get to his cabin. He walked toward Tikchik until exhaustion and the bitter cold got the best of him. We figured he tried to get some shelter under the limbs of a spruce tree, and that's why we never spotted him from the air. He only had that light sleeping bag and just couldn't get warm.*

Poor weather and heavy snow squalls covered Bill's trail and hampered the aerial search. Flying when he shouldn't have, Dick Armstrong pushed the bad weather trying to find his friend. The snows continued and all but eliminated any trace of the missing lodge developer. About nine days into the search, state rescue officials brought in a search dog from Anchorage. The dog, a sad-eyed bloodhound named Delilah, picked up Gurtler's scent at the abandoned snow machine. Able to follow the cold, snow-covered trail, Delilah and her trainers finally located Bill Gurtler under a low-hanging spruce tree. Partially covered by snow, he was still in his lightweight sleeping bag more than ten miles from Tikchik Lake. It was obvious to the professional rescue team that Bill had waited too long to try to start a fire. Once he stopped moving vigorously, his wet clothing froze against his body and hampered his movement. Darkness prevented him from finding much to burn. Without a warming fire, he had no way to dry his wet and frozen clothing, and more importantly, keep him alive. Only a few hours into the bitterly cold night, Bill's violent shivering had turned into a quiet sleep from which he never awoke. Although modern death records would list hypothermia as the cause, official records of the time specified exposure as the cause of death. For her work in the search, Delilah, the bloodhound, received honorary membership in the Alaska Department of Civil Defense at a ceremony held in her honor and reported by the Anchorage newspaper.

Bill Gurtler's death did not end the progress and development at Tikchik Lakes Camp, however. The ideas and plans that Bill discussed with Swede Blanchard lived on. Swede continued to mull the idea and eventually convinced two other men, Lawrence Glickman and Russell Roberts, that the concept of building a fishing lodge was sound and should be continued. Within a short time they formed a corporation, B.G.R., Inc., and made immediate plans to build a grandiose lodge. Before filing their land claim applications, they reputedly ordered all their building supplies, special plates, silverware, linen, light fixtures and other items necessary to open a lodge. A little more than one year after Bill Gurtler's accident, Swede Blanchard reapplied for the same parcel of land, which surprisingly was directly across the narrows from Bill's original cabin. Blanchard's filing on August 25, 1961, was accompanied by joint application for six adjoining acres by B.G.R., Inc., and a filing on an estimated two additional acres by Russell Roberts. From BLM Case File A-056802:

*The acting Land Officer Manager wrote to Bernard S. Blanchard on January 10, 1962, stating "As it was not the intent of the trade and manufacturing site shore space restriction to prohibit the development of land, such as you propose, and inasmuch as these three filings would have to stand on their own merits at the time when the application to purchase was made, it was decided that it would be best if all claims were relinquished and one filing made by B.G.R. Inc., under the Trade and Manufacturing Site Act, for the entire piece of land involved.*

Acting for his partners and representing B.G.R. Inc., Swede complied immediately.

*John Pearson's tin shed at Tikchik Narrows. Circa 1965—Robert Curtis Collection*

He cancelled the separate individual claims and filed a single claim consolidating all the land. From the time of the consolidated filing, however, problems started to mount for B.G.R., Inc.

*According to Sherman Berg (previous Area Manager, Bristol Bay Resource Area), Mr. Glickman was providing most of the capital for B.G.R., Inc. to build a high-class hunting and fishing lodge on the subject land. In the early 1960s, the materials for that lodge were in Anchorage awaiting shipment to Tikchik*

*Lake. Mr. Glickman died and, for some reason, the project was not completed.*

Even though the real reasons why the lodge project mentioned by Mr. Sherman was not completed remain unknown, I believe one major contributing factor was that Swede Blanchard's health failed and he was in no condition to start a business and build a lodge. Swede suffered from a terminal case of cancer. By the late winter of 1962, he was too ill to continue flying. Swede died later that fall, and any plans to continue the lodge project at Tikchik died with him. Although I could find no further information about Russell Roberts, I believe he was incapacitated in some way, too, because there were no guests and no further activity at Tikchik Lakes Camp until 1965.

Despite the tragedy suffered by Bill Gurtler, John Pearson charged ahead. When the 1960 season started, John was ready. Ray's airline delivered John's clients from Anchorage to Dillingham. Rather than cancel their trip, John agreed also to host those guests who had planned to go to Bill Gurtler's camp. Once the guests arrived at Wood River Trout Camp, they plied the local waters for rainbows, char, and grayling. They could not, however, catch lake trout.

During their early exploratory fishing excursions, both Bill Gurtler and John Pearson discovered that fishing for lake trout was no less than spectacular at Tikchik Narrows. Keeping this in mind, John Pearson raised a small tin shed directly across the Narrows from Bill Gurtler's log cabin. Pearson's tin shed was more like a storage facility than anything else. It was small, and because he didn't use it often, it wasn't well maintained. It was, however, an acceptable place for one or two clients to get out of the weather and eat lunch. Because it was not feasible to get a boat between Wood River Trout Camp and his tin shed at Tikchik without a healthy portage, when clients expressed an interest in lake trout, John used his radio and chartered floatplanes from Western Alaska Airline to shuffle the clients and equipment between the sites.

Unfortunately, I could not ascertain if John Pearson built the cabin before or after Bill Gurtler's accidental death. If the cabin was built before Bill's death, I believe it would be safe to assume that Bill may have helped in the construction. If built after, I believe that John just did not feel comfortable using Bill's cabin.

Over the next years, John slowly improved his camp. He added a plywood cabin that became a kitchen and dining room for his guests. He purchased a few boats and a moderate amount of fishing gear. The tally-scow that John had towed into position at Wood River Trout Camp lasted several seasons before the dark and damp floating bedrooms were destroyed. The waterlogged guest quarters were replaced by two extremely small, tin-covered cabins that had barely enough room for the bunk beds, let alone the clients and their gear. John quit using his small Tikchik cabin after the 1964 season, when Bob Curtis purchased all the assets of B.G.R., Inc.

As at the Willowtree, John's wife took care of all the cooking chores at Wood River Trout Camp. From the reviews Leta received at their Dillingham bar, I'm sure the guests ate very well after the shortages experienced during the test runs in 1959 were corrected. Although the less-than-luxurious conditions persisted and John never found time to build a major lodge facility at his Wood River Trout Camp, he hosted clients there through the fishing season of 1968.

## The Age of Competition

I've heard it said that competition brings out the best in people. I'm not sure if he was worried about competition from the new fishing camps or not, but at the same time that the "special brochures" were printed and distributed, John Walatka ordered three brand-new "jet-powered" boats for the Angler's Paradise Camps at Brooks, Grosvenor and Kulik. They were the first jet boats used at a fishing lodge in the Bristol Bay watershed.

The boats John purchased were made by Beuhler Turbocraft Boats and featured technology new to Alaska. The three boats were identical in every way. They were 16-feet long, had semi-V hulls and were powered by six-cylinder Ford inboard engines. The new technology, however, was in the drive mechanism. The boats did not have propellers; they had water-driven jet pumps designed specifically to operate in shallow water.

John Walatka had the boats shipped from the stateside factory directly to King Salmon. Expectations were high when the late-spring barge finally arrived at Naknek. As soon as he knew his new boats had been unloaded, John Walatka flew Grosvenor guide Dave Shuster and Kulik guide Wayne Carr into King Salmon. Former Brooks Camp manager Floyd "Slim" Beck assisted in the unloading process and had the boats in the water and ready to go when the other guides stepped out of the Northern Consolidated Cessna T-50. The boats made quite a splash with an audience of curious local fishermen as the soon-to-be deliverymen experimented with their new toys. After some basic handling experience on the Naknek River, they filled the fuel tanks and put some extra fuel containers aboard. Slim and Dave left the King Salmon dock and headed for Naknek Lake on the way to Brooks and Grosvenor. Wayne Carr watched his friends disappear up the river. He decided to wait for more favorable tide conditions before he departed the Naknek River for Kulik.

Once they reached the lodges, the guides raved about the capabilities of the new boats. They were fast and comfortable, albeit a little noisy. Although the new inboard-jet technology was great for some applications, Dave Shuster decided the boat was useless on American Creek. Dave told me he believed the boat was just too big and too fast to use on such a small river. As it turns out, the American wasn't the only place Dave had a problem with the new-style boats. Ray Petersen related a story about Dave and one of the new boats.

*The Chairman of the Civil Aeronautics Board, James Durfey, and several other high-ranking bureaucrats arrived in Anchorage to preside over some airline route hearings. They were meeting to decide the allocation of the Bristol Bay airline routes. I was lobbying a little and invited the group to stay at Grosvenor for a few days. Naturally, I wanted to impress them with both our airline service and our fishing camps. I wanted them to see firsthand that the camps were beneficial to the airline business.*

*Dave Shuster was our guide at Grosvenor and was still getting used to the Beuhler Turbocraft boat. He loaded my special guests into that boat one beautiful morning and took them fishing. About noon, the weather changed. The wind started to blow and the lake got rough.*

*Recognizing the situation, Dave made the guys stop fishing and headed for the lodge. He knew his new boat was fast, so he tried to race the storm. The closer he got to the camp, the bigger the waves became. Rather than reduce speed and ease his way back, Dave pushed the throttles forward. He smashed and crashed through the ever-building waves. He was traveling way too fast when he hit a big wave so hard that it split the hull. The boat started to take on water. Fortunately, by the time he realized he was sinking, he was so close to the camp that he just kept the power up and drove the boat onto the beach.*

*Sonny Petersen at the start of his guiding career. Ray Petersen Collection*

Facing a new age of competition, the Angler's Paradise Camps were steadily improved during the early 1960s. Keeping future guests in mind, building crews added a big bathhouse and new guest cabins at the Petersens' summer home, Grosvenor Camp. While most building and general camp changes occurred at Grosvenor and Brooks Camp, John Walatka refined the fishing program at Kulik. Speaking of fishing, Ray's youngest son, Sonny, started guiding clients at Grosvenor Lodge in 1963. Despite the fact that he wasn't old enough to officially go on the payroll, young Mr. Petersen earned the respect of all guests he guided.

I asked former Angler's Paradise guide, Dave Shuster, about the fishing at the Angler's Paradise Camps in the early 1960s. Dave and I compared notes about most of the rivers and particular "hot spots" of his day. Although I don't believe things have changed all that much, I was surprised at his comments about the Moraine River. Dave told me that Kulik had a tent camp on the Moraine River. The camp was on the biggest island in the lower part of the river.

*I used to guide at Grosvenor, and then John would fly me to Kulik when the Moraine fishing started to get good. From talking with a few guys who fished the Moraine recently, I think we did it differently in my time. The tent had a plywood floor and two metal sleeping cots. I had to cook my own meals, but occasionally the pilots would bring me some lodge leftovers when they brought over clients.*

Dave told me that he spent a total of three weeks living at the Moraine River camp in 1964. According to Dave, John never planned to have clients spend the night at the Moraine that season.

*It was just easier for them to have me stay there and be ready to guide every morning. I didn't have a radio so I didn't always know what was going on at Kulik, but when the fishing was good, everyone wanted to try the Moraine. John would bring me two clients in the morning and then pick them up in the afternoon. I think we had a big camp there just in case the weather got bad and the pilots couldn't get back.*

Then Dave related the story about one guest who spent three nights with him at the Moraine Camp during the 1964 season. He was Dave's only overnight guest.

*John flew in one morning and I could tell he wasn't too happy when he climbed out of the airplane. Normally, when the pilots brought me clients, they brought at least two. As John climbed out of the airplane, he announced in a loud voice that he wouldn't be back for a few days. He didn't offer any explanation as he unloaded just one fisherman, a small overnight bag and an unusually large box of food. John climbed back into the airplane, cranked up the engines and left before giving me a chance to ask what was going on. Well, I guided, cooked, baby-sat, and fished the guy 12 to 14 hours a day. He was some big shot, too. When he left, he gave me a five-dollar tip. I will never forget that!*

*I was happy when John finally came back to get the guy. I was surprised that he was there one night, let alone three. After he left, I figured he was probably being a total "pain in the ass" at Kulik, and Mildred insisted that John fly him anywhere to get him away from the other guests. As far as I know, he was the first guest to spend the night at our Moraine camp, and for sure the first ever to overnight on the Moraine River.*

Dave told me that he knew Ed Seiler had taken Kulik guests to the lower stretch of the Moraine River on a fly-out, but as far as he knew, no one else ever fished the river. He also told me that learning to negotiate the shallow stretches took some time. He had to learn because the big fish were too far up the river to walk. Dave described some of his experiences to me:

*I had a 14-foot skiff and a 25-horse outboard. I also had a small kicker just in case something happened to the big engine. I developed my own techniques for navigating the shallow water with a prop. I finally realized the best way was to put the outboard on the extreme left of the transom and put the clients on the same side so I could tilt the boat up and draw less water going across the shallow spots. John always insisted I take the props off the outboards when he took me back to Kulik. Although I never saw another fisherman up there, John figured there was no sense in leaving a perfectly good boat unattended.*

*I remember catching some large fish on the Moraine, but, as I recall, we caught all the biggest fish at Talarik Creek. I didn't get to go there too many times. Once the catching slowed down in the Moraine, I'd take the boat over to the Battle River. We had a boat at the Kukaklek outlet, too. When the fishing died off completely on the lower Moraine, we flew the whole camp back to Kulik. After that, Johnny*

*Dear Mother and Dad,*

*I am camped a mile up on Moraine Creek, a tributary of Kukaklek Lake. I left Brooks about 10 days ago for Kulik. I stayed only four or five days at Kulik before John sent me up here. We have a boat and motor here and another boat that John is getting a motor for. This creek is the last one left that has not seen a fisherman and you have to get far up it to fish. John and me only let people fish flies here and they can't kill any fish, except one to mount. All big rainbow trout in this creek. It is beautiful country here. I came here for good 3 days ago. Herman (Hermans) NCA bush pilot brought me in the C-180. After he left 3 days ago, the weather deteriorated. A violent wind storm has been blowing since and I guess the aircraft at Kulik are grounded.I have a comfortable camp on a choice spot on the river (an island). I made the whole camp by myself. I have a big wall-tent with a 2x4 frame with steel bunks and mattresses with room for 1 or 2 guests over-night. I have no idea how long I will be here, but I think when I go back to Kulik I will leave there shortly for home.*

*Dave*

*PS - Send me 8 feet of rainbow-colored rod-winding thread. It is in a dresser drawer in the attic in a tea cup in the top large drawer.*

*Dave Shuster chronicled his entire Alaska experience by writing letters to his parents. Dave wrote this letter on September 10, 1964.*

*Guide Dave Shuster (below) took this 1964 photo of the Angler's Paradise tent camp on the Moraine Creek. The angler is unknown. Dave Shuster Collection*

*would fly the guys to Cross Lake so they could fish Funnel Creek, which flows into the Moraine much higher than I could get with a boat. That was great, too, although I don't think we caught many fish bigger than 10 pounds, but you could catch five and six-pounders all day. The Moraine was prime duty, but my favorite was the American Creek. I really loved that river. I knew it better than any other place and that really makes a difference to a guide. I don't remember catching too many grayling in the Moraine, but the Battle was full of 'em. If a guy wanted to catch a grayling, we'd always go to Battle.*

It is noteworthy that during the 1950s and early 1960s none of the Angler's Paradise Camps were marketed as individual lodges. Each lodge was an integral part of an entire system. When a fishing tour was booked with the Northern Consolidated Vacations and Angler's Paradise, the actual lodge location was determined by the quality of fishing at the time of the trip.

At one time or another, each of the Angler's Paradise Camp locations offers "the best" fishing as the short Bristol Bay season moves from spring into fall. This was the rationale behind the pattern of opening each of the lodges based on the timing of the quality fishing. Brooks, Grosvenor and Nonvianuk Camps opened before Kulik and Battle. After all, Ray built the five camps to take advantage of the quality fishing at each location. Basing guests at the camp with the best fishing was an essential element of Ray's lodge concept. There just weren't enough visiting anglers during the 1950s and 60s to fill all the camps all the time.

It is also important to remember that because each lodge site featured great fishing, fly-outs were the exception, not the rule during the 1950s and 1960s. Neither Ray nor any of the early guests felt the necessity to fly out every day. During the 1960s however, the pattern started to change. As new rivers were explored and learned, more options were offered. By the mid-1960s, the Moraine River and Talarik Creek became regular fly-out destinations for guests at Kulik Lodge. The world was changing and so was the lodge business. At the close of the 1964 fishing season, there were just three lodge operations in Bristol Bay. By the start of the fishing season of 1965, that number would double.

## The Space Race and Bristol Bay

No matter how much the Alaskan fishing lodge industry was changing in the 1960s, it was absolutely nothing compared to the unprecedented scientific race-to-space between the United States and our Cold War enemy, the Soviet Union. Most Americans were shocked when the Russians beat us to the punch and launched "Sputnik," the first man-made satellite, on October 4, 1957. Trying to figure out why we were behind, I remember lots of political finger-pointing and a countrywide surge in school science programs. The Russians got our attention in a big way. Most Americans don't remember that the Russians launched their second satellite, "Sputnik II," a month later. Not to be outdone, we responded with our own satellite launch on January 31, 1958. The Russians maintained their lead when they launched the first manned spaceship on April 12, 1961, carrying Soviet cosmonaut Yuri Gagarin. We responded with our own man in space, Navy Commander Alan B. Shepard, on May 5, 1961. It was evident that the Russians seemed to be just one launch ahead until 1969 when we finally won the race and put men on the moon.

Walter Cronkite, broadcasting live to the entire world, chronicled the amazing sequence of events that led to our giant leap to the top:

*killed American astronauts Gus Grissom, Ed White and Roger Chaffee, there were serious doubts that we could beat the Russians to the moon. But tonight, only eighteen months after the tragedy of Apollo 1, the entire world watched in awe as Neil Armstrong and Buzz Aldrin landed on the moon.*

Summer 1965 THE MIDNIGHT SUN Page Three

## KATMAI IS OUT OF THIS WORLD

We have always maintained that the Katmai area was outstanding in its stark scenic beauty. Now we have on the best authority that it is 'out of this world.'

Late in June a party of 18 Astronauts, 12 geologists and a number of press representatives arrived to spend a week in the Valley of 10,000 Smokes. This area was selected by the National Aero-space Administration as a training and study ground which best simulated the conditions considered most likely to be encountered by a party landing on the Moon. It is quite possible that some of these very trainees will be the first men to make a trip to that nearby planet.

The geological members of the party were from the USGS, Division of Astro-geology which facility is located at Flagstaff, Arizona. The director and head geologist was Dr. A. H. Chidester.

The military lent their aid by furnishing helicopter lift between the Valley and Northern Consolidated's Brook's River Camp.

Airline employees interested in the AIRLINE SUN COUNTRY HOLIDAY should contact Elmer Ferrall, Committee Secretary, Phoenix Chamber of Commerce, 805 North Second Street, Phoenix, Arizona. This event is slated for October 21-24, and includes a special rate of $8.00 for two in the headquarters hotel.

NCA flight crew with NASA geologists on arrival Anchorage from Katmai National Monument. Astronauts were furnished Jetstar by NASA for their earthly transportation needs.

*This article appeared in the summer issue of the Northern Consolidated magazine, The Midnight Sun. On the opposite page is an article from the Fall issue of 1966. Ray Petersen Collection*

*Inspired by the late President Kennedy, in only seven years, America has risen to the challenge of what he called the most hazardous and dangerous and greatest adventure in which man has ever been involved. After trailing the Russians for years in the manned space program, and after that sudden and horrible fire on the launch pad during a routine test that*

**"Houston, We Have a Problem."** These words, spoken by Apollo 13 command module captain Jim Lovell, and then recreated and spoken on the big screen by Tom Hanks in Ron Howard's award-winning 1995 movie, "Apollo 13," gave the entire country a glimpse of how dangerous space exploration could be. I also found it very interesting to discover that three of the four actual Apollo 13 crew members, Fred Haise, Ken Mattingly, and J. L. Swigart, all stayed at Brooks Lodge and trained for their future lunar flight in the Valley of Ten Thousand Smokes.

Before the completion of the road to the Valley of Ten Thousand Smokes, the majority of guests at Brooks Lodge were fishermen. By 1965, however, many of the returning fishing guests opted to stay at Grosvenor and Kulik because there were so many "non-fishermen" visiting Brooks Camp. These developments clearly changed the marketing plan for the Angler's Paradise Lodges and the utilization of Brooks Camp. Tourists had new reasons to visit Brooks, including bus tours to the Valley; but few were as bizarre as the NASA groups that arrived at Brooks Camp in the mid-1960s.

Of all the important issues in our race-into-space program, training was the single most critical issue. Looking forward to lunar flights, NASA scientists searched the world for a suitable earth-based "lunar" training site.

It didn't take too long for the NASA staff to choose the unique landscape available in the Valley of Ten Thousand Smokes in the Katmai National Monument. The terrain provided a great opportunity to test both the astronauts and their geological sample

FALL 1966 THE MIDNIGHT SUN

**FUTURE SPACE TRAVELERS who visited the VALLEY OF TEN THOUSAND SMOKES for geological study include Astronauts (l. to r.) front row, Lt. Comdr. John Bull, Dr. Edward Gibson, Dr. Harrison Schmitt, Cmdr. Edgar Mitchell, and Lt. Paul Weitz; second row, (l. to r.), Capt. Stewart Roosa, Fred Haise, Lt. Bruce McCandless and Maj. Edward Givens, and Ray Zedekar, training office of the National Aeronautics and Space Administration. (Courtesy Anchorage Daily News)**

## Astronauts Train For Moon Landing

NCA Brooks Lodge in the Valley of Ten Thousand Smokes was headquarters again this year for a group of 24 future spacemen who have hopes of landing on the Moon. Last year the Valley was selected by the National Aerospace Administration as an area where conditions might be quite similar to those encountered by U.S. Spacemen when reaching the moon. Dr. Harrison Schmitt, a young geologist with the group, said the geological formations in Katmai are unique in that they are of recent formation. Mt. Katmai erupted in 1912, spewing lava over thousands of acres with ashes falling heavily in the Kodiak area.

Dr. A. H. Chidester, director and head geologist of the USGS, Division of Astrogeology, which facility is located at Flagstaff, Arizona, returned with the group again this year.

The future spacemen are from the Manned Space Craft Center at Houston, Texas.

Basing at Brooks Lodge, the group went into the Valley by helicopter; the remainder of the training exercise being on foot. The astronauts are hopeful of gaining an understanding of geological phenomena on the moon.

**THE MIDNIGHT SUN**

Published as an information service for the employees, customers and friends of Northern Consolidated Airlines.

gathering techniques. In 1965 and again in 1966, Brooks Camp became the base of operations for large groups of NASA scientists and future astronauts.

When I asked Angler's Paradise guide Dave Shuster about the NASA groups, he seemed proud to have been there and more proud to be involved with the astronauts. He explained some of their activities:

*Every morning, two big, twin-bladed military helicopters arrived from King Salmon. They landed right on the beach in front of the lodge. The engines never stopped as everyone climbed aboard. Once they were back in the air, they headed toward the Valley. Late in the afternoon, they'd land in the same place and everyone aboard would climb out and scramble to get out of the way. I don't remember any of them staying up in the Valley. I think there were about thirty-two scientists and astronauts that first year.*

*After dinner some of the NASA guys fished. A young Sonny Petersen and I handled all the evening guiding on the Brooks River. During the day, we had other guests to worry about, but I reserved my nights for the spacemen. Most of the astronauts seemed to enjoy fishing. After we quit fishing and nearly everyone else at the camp had gone to bed, the whole NASA entourage would meet at the lodge and have their meetings behind a big curtain they installed for privacy. I always wanted to ask what they were talking about in those clandestine sessions, but I never did.*

Lunar training at Brooks was not the only thing going on in the world during 1965. Some of you might remember that mini-skirts rocked the fashion world and Diet Pepsi swept the nation. Race riots in Watts and the assassination of Malcolm X added fuel to the racial fires. National and international anti-Vietnam War protests darkened the political scene while the Los Angeles Dodgers won the World Series. The major banks figured a new angle to increase their profits and issued their own credit cards, and the future fishermen of the world reaped the benefits when Sony introduced a small home video-recorder, the "Betamax." While the rest of the country listened to the Rolling Stones hit the top with "*Satisfaction*" and watched the Beatles twist and shout on American television, several Alaskans changed the future of sportfishing and the future lodge industry. Ed Seiler, Bob Curtis and Red Clark all started fishing lodge operations in Bristol Bay.

## Enchanted Lake Lodge
### Ed Seiler

Ed Seiler came to Alaska in 1944. He worked as a civil engineer for the Civil Aeronautics Administration, the predecessor of today's Federal Aviation Administration. Travel throughout the state was an important aspect of Ed's job. Because he was a fly-fishing enthusiast, Ed took every opportunity to cast a line. He tried all the popular rivers, streams, and lakes around Anchorage and was able to fish some of the more remote regions when he worked in the bush. On one of these business trips, he traveled to King Salmon and fished the Naknek River. While there, Ed heard stories about the country west of the Kvichak River. Early in the spring of 1947, Ed decided to explore the fishing potential in the Wood River Lakes region of Alaska, between the fifth lake and Dillingham, a distance of about 90 miles.

Ed explained that the lack of commercially made exploration equipment was a big problem in the late 1940s. Because this was an airplane excursion and weight was a factor, Ed needed an inflatable boat. Because he planned to travel through several large lakes and didn't want to row for hours, he hoped to use his outboard engine, a small 3/4-horse Neptune. He knew what he wanted but couldn't go to a big store and buy an inflatable boat with a transom. Ed searched the catalogs to no avail. He finally found a five-man survival raft in an old salvage yard. Once he had that, he built a tubular frame with a folding transom to accommodate his motor, possibly the first adaptation to add an engine to an inflatable craft. Ed felt confident that his equipment would function properly as he packed everything for a journey into the remote wilderness that he would not soon forget.

On June 1, 1948, Ed departed Anchorage for the Wood River Lakes chain. At Naknek Air Base (King Salmon), he transferred his 500 pounds of gear from the DC-3 to an NCA Seabee, piloted by Jerry Church, who had no information concerning possible ice conditions at the fifth lake. As Ed tells it:

> *A radio conversation with local bush pilot Bill Smith of Dillingham elicited the erroneous information that all the lakes were ice-free. Therefore, we confidently took off toward the Wood River chain. Sometime before we arrived there, it became evident that Bill Smith made a bad guess. The second, third, fourth, and fifth lakes were covered with ice. However, there was a little open water at the south end of the fifth lake. Jerry thought he could land. He made it clear that I had to decide if I wanted to be left there, as there was no room for a take-off with me and my gear once he landed. After looking the ice over from the air, it seemed fairly black and about ready to go out, so I told Jerry to set me down. Well, I camped at that spot until June 23, during which time the ice never did go out. My leave was running out and my food supplies were down to almost nothing. I decided to build a sled out of fir bows and haul the raft and all my gear about nine miles over the ice to the lake's outlet. I found the outlet wide open and from there on down to Dillingham, had no further problems with ice.*
>
> *Besides fish, my larder was enhanced with seagull eggs. I found superb fishing every place I stopped to fish. There were medium-sized rainbows at the heads of the rivers, and the char seemed to prefer the outlets. I found a very desirable lodge site on Aleknagik Lake opposite the outlet of the Agulowak River. It had a good stand of spruce for cabin logs and a promising potential for a small hydroelectric generating plant. It also had the advantage of barge transportation from tide water through the Wood River to lower construction costs.*

After terminating his Wood River excursion at Dillingham, Ed chartered NCA pilot, Elmer Nicholson, to fly him over to Coville Lake. From there, he used his trusty life raft to get him down through Grosvenor Lake, the Savonoski River, Naknek Lake, and the Naknek Rapids into King Salmon.

By the conclusion of this exploratory fishing trip, Ed had explored, fished, and discovered many things about the Bristol Bay region. Of one thing he was convinced: the sportfishing potential in western Alaska had no peer. During that trip, he made the decision to move to Bristol Bay just as soon as he figured out how to make a living there. Although he didn't know it at the time, he'd find his opportunity when he returned to his CAA office in Anchorage.

Early in 1949, Ray Petersen and Northern Consolidated Airlines negotiated a temporary airport real estate lease with the CAA for an indefinite period pending enabling legislation by Congress. The contract allowed them to open and operate a cafe and a hotel at the Naknek Airport. Shortly after the contract was signed, NCA employees converted a former military warehouse near the airport into a four-room hotel and café. They called it the Sky-Tel, and it was King Salmon's first hotel. The Sky-Tel was an important link in Ray's tourism campaign. According to Ray's 1950 brochure:

> *You can plan your trip with a guarantee of hotel and traveling accommodations. We stress this feature because until 1950 such space accommodations could not be confirmed today, Northern Consolidated Airline has eliminated such barriers by owning and operating hotels and roadhouses.*

Like most government bureaucracies, the Civil Aviation Administration held few secrets from employees. By the time Ray's airport lease was due for its first annual renewal, Ed Seiler had all the details. It didn't take Ed too long to research the Naknek airport lease proposal and decide to act. Wasting no time, Ed and a business associate, Ernie Weschenfelver, promptly put in their bid. Almost immediately, the CAA officials awarded the lease to Ed and his partner. With the contract in his hand, Ed retired from the CAA and moved his family to King Salmon.

*Ed Seiler's Stinson on the ice at Moose Pond. This was Ed's first remote cabin in Bristol Bay. Ed's dog, Fritz, is on the airplane's cowl. Circa 1960—Ed Seiler Photo*

Whether it was or not, the CAA's decision to award the contract to Ed Seiler was seen by NCA as an "insider" move. They certainly didn't expect another bidder, let alone a CAA employee. The information in their brochure immediately became obsolete. NCA personnel were annoyed to say the least. I asked Ray Petersen if he would comment on the CAA's controversial decision. According to Ray,

> *I was more disturbed about how the decision was made. It was obviously a political move by the CAA. Ed was a CAA guy. I didn't like to be "out-politicked." I don't recall talking directly to Ed Seiler about it at the time. Walatka may have said something, but I don't think I ever did. If you asked me that question in 1950, I might have had a few more things to say. Time has a way of easing the pain.*

Ed Seiler had these comments about the contract and his subsequent business venture in King Salmon.

> *Looking back on it now, it was the worst*

*decision I ever made. I had nothing but grief with that place. I can see why it might have looked like an insider move to NCA, but actually, there wasn't a shred of favoritism to it. A law passed by Congress in 1950 authorized the CAA to lease business sites at their various Air Navigation site withdrawals in Alaska. By law, this had to be done by competitive bidding, and the highest bids had to be accepted. We were simply the highest bidders. And since the bids were publicly opened at the same time, there were no opportunities for us to know the NCA bid beforehand. In fact, the CAA was a lot more chagrined about the outcome than NCA. One would only have to review the shabby treatment we received from the government on a number of issues regarding the operation of the Skytel to come to that conclusion. They did everything they could think of to put me out of business, in which they finally succeeded in 1965. Actually, I think NCA was nothing but lucky that they lost that contract. We took adequate care of their passengers and crews in every instance and they had none of the headaches involved in running such an operation in King Salmon. Believe me, there were many headaches. However, any animosity which might have existed between NCA and me ended and it wasn't long before we were mutually helpful friends.*

*I bought out Ernie after the first year. We moved in two more warehouse buildings from the base. We enlarged the place into an 8-room hotel, made a nice restaurant, a theatre, a general store and still had enough room for a small warehouse and space for our own living quarters. I think I wasted 15 years in King Salmon. While it was a step toward the lodge business, I don't think it was worth the time. I should have left King Salmon and started a lodge much sooner than I did.*

Although he was extremely busy at the Sky-Tel during his first years as a King Salmon resident, Ed fished and hunted as much as he could. Every now and then Ed would take someone fishing. As time went on, more and more of his hotel guests and other King Salmon visitors asked him for similar favors and even offered to pay. Feeling a need, Ed decided to build a cabin on a small lake he called Moose Pond. Situated near the American Creek Canyon, Moose Pond offered great hunting and fishing possibilities. Within a short time, he cleared a path from his new cabin to American Creek. Ed estimated that it was a little less than a two-mile walk to the American, one of the best fishing creeks in Bristol Bay. He hosted his first clients at Moose Pond in 1959 and continued to use it long after he built another hunting and fishing cabin at Talarik Creek in 1962.

When I asked Ed why he built a cabin at Talarik Creek, he looked at me with a big grin and said:

*The big fish, of course. I'd heard about Talarik from some Natives. They referred to it as the "creek with big fish," and that intrigued me. The first time I went there I had three guys who said they only wanted to fish virgin water. I was over in that direction and decided to take a look at Talarik. When I flew over the river, I spotted all these big fish. I told the guys that the fish I saw must be suckers or something else because they were so big and literally covered the bottom of the shallow creek, but we landed anyway. Immediately we started catching huge rainbows. I just couldn't believe it. I'd read some of the early stories about big rainbows but simply couldn't imagine that it could be that good. I don't think anyone knew much about Talarik except the Iliamna Natives. I never saw anyone else there for the first year or two. Since the weather can change quickly over there, I thought it would be a good place to have a cabin.*

*After filing on a five-acre recreational site, which later I failed to prove up on, I ordered a small Pan Abode cedar pre-fab cabin from Seattle. I had the cabin materials sent over the portage to Iliamna Lake and delivered right to the beach at Talarik. I had to fly up there and move all the pieces higher on the beach. The delivery crew left it where a storm might have washed the various parts and pieces away.*

*Ed Seiler, the first man hired to be a pilot-guide at a fishing lodge in Bristol Bay, with client Tudy Glover from Simsbury, Connecticut. This fine rainbow was taken just below the outlet of Gibralter Lake. Circa 1969—Ed Seiler Photo*

*I just barely finished the cabin before the winter weather set in. For some reason, we went "Outside" later that winter. On my return in early spring, I was on my way back to King Salmon and was flying somewhere near the mouth of Talarik Creek when I spotted something shiny on the ice. I thought it was a crashed airplane. I detoured to get a closer look and soon realized it was the aluminum-covered roof from my cabin. The vicious winter winds had blown the roof completely off the cabin and about 200 yards out on the lake ice. After checking it out, I continued to King Salmon. The following day I gathered up some tools and returned to Talarik. It didn't take me too long to dismantle the roof and then reinstall it.*

*My big mistake was following the assembly instructions provided with the cabin. The plans didn't call for securing the roof. I guess they didn't know how hard the wind blows in Bristol Bay, especially at Talarik Creek. Anyway, I cabled down the rebuilt roof and that ended the problem.*

Living in King Salmon, Ed had constant contact with both the activities of Northern Consolidated Airline and the Angler's Paradise Camps. He met John Walatka in King Salmon not long after taking over the Sky-Tel.

*After I picked up the mail, I stopped by Northern Consolidated's quonset hut at the airport to see my friend, Bill Tolbert. Bill was NCA's station manager at King Salmon. Bill was talking to John when I opened the door. Bill introduced me to him right away. I remember that John didn't smile as he made some "less than complimentary" comments. I knew he was annoyed because we had taken the Sky-Tel contract. I figured I wouldn't get along too well with Big John Walatka.*

Although the atmosphere of their first meeting remained cool, within a short time John and Ed became close friends. Ed was a regular visitor at both the Angler's Paradise Camps and the great fishing rivers in Bristol Bay. It wasn't long thereafter that Ed became more than an occasional visitor to the Angler's Paradise Lodges. Seeing and feeling a need, John Walatka started to make use of Ed's piloting skills and abilities.

The growing popularity and success of Northern Consolidated's sportfishing business by the late 1950s was giving John Walatka more flying than he could handle in some instances. Therefore, Ed Seiler was increasingly called upon to help on a charter basis to handle such chores as transporting employees and guests from King Salmon to the various lodges. On several occasions, he was asked to fly vulcanologists and National Geographic personnel for landing in the Valley of Ten Thousand Smokes using John's Super Cub on a rental basis. The flying he enjoyed the most, however, was flying and guiding on personalized all-day fishing trips.

On several occasions, John chartered Ed to be a fly-out pilot and fishing guide for Kulik guests. Before that, only Ray Petersen, John Walatka, and the Branham brothers did any pilot guiding. John Walatka's decision to use Ed as a pilot-guide in the late 1950s was a major step forward in the lodge industry. Ed Seiler became the first man hired by a Bristol Bay lodge specifically to be a pilot-guide.

Unlike the majority of pilot-guides in Bristol Bay today, Ed did not live at the lodge, nor did he work every day. Ed told me about some of his experiences working for Kulik as a charter pilot and guide:

*One time John set me up with a few guys who wanted a different kind of fishing experience than they were getting at Kulik. I decided to take them over to Talarik Creek. We caught several big rainbows, and I mean big rainbows. Before I took them back to Kulik, I told the fishermen not to tell anyone the name of the creek. Unfortunately, they took back one of those huge fish. Well, it wasn't long before the whole world knew about Talarik.*

*It was the same for all the Kulik clients I guided. Before I took them back to Kulik, I told them never to tell anyone where we fished, what we caught, or how we caught them. I tried to confuse the issue by giving phony names to most of the creeks. I know that at dinner, John always asked which creeks were fished during the day. He put in lots of time looking at maps trying to find creeks that didn't exist. Most of the time I did it more to get a rise out of John Walatka than anything else. I loved trying to fool him. There weren't too many places that he didn't know about, so I tried to keep him guessing.*

*When John needed help, he would stop in King Salmon and let me know. I guess the clients liked me because he never stopped asking me to help. I never looked at it as a job, only as a help to John and Ray. I guess that's why they helped me many times when I needed it.*

## Ed Named It "Enchanted Lake"

*One day I was flying close to Nonvianuk Lake when I spotted a large moose rack. I landed on a beautiful, small lake to inspect that rack. Maybe it was the right weather, or maybe it was the time of day and the light was right, I don't remember. I got out of the airplane and walked around a little. The lake made me think of a place in Maine, Enchanted Pond. I always liked that name. I knew the lake didn't have a name so I named it Enchanted Lake right then and there.*

*I got back in the airplane, flew to King Salmon and told my wife to get her coat because I was going to take her to Enchanted Lake. I flew her right back to that lake and then I told her that it would be the site of the lodge of my dreams. Josefina agreed. That was the first day I actually saw Enchanted Lake. I had flown over it many times before, but that day I appreciated it. Building a lodge there was something else, however.*

Ed proceeded to tell me the incredible story about building Enchanted Lake Lodge. Once he found the perfect location, Ed started planning. First he designed the lodge in his mind, and then he sketched it on paper. His previous cabin-building adventures were great learning experiences and a great preparation for what followed. The first step, however, was making a proper filing for a Trade and Manufacturing Site on 84 acres with the Bureau of Land Management.

Like his cabin at Talarik Creek, the new buildings were premanufactured in Seattle. He had the entire building package, along with extra equipment and all the furnishings, barged to Kodiak Island. As Ray Petersen had done in 1950, Ed planned to have the building materials delivered to Nonvianuk Lake during the winter. He arranged for Kodiak-based air-cargo pilot Bobby Sholton to land at Nonvianuk Lake early in the spring on the hard winter ice. Bobby planned to use his military surplus C-82 to deliver the huge pile of materials, including three complete Pan Abode cedar cabins with all their associated furnishings and fixtures. Unfortunately for Ed, the winter weather didn't cooperate. The ice surface was never thick enough for such a large airplane to land safely that winter. With his building materials already in Kodiak and no way to have them delivered directly to his building site, Ed had a big problem and not much time to find a solution. To solve his problem, Ed knew he had to go to his friend, the Angler's Paradise and Kulik manager, John Walatka, and ask for help.

*As soon as possible I found John Walatka. I invited him over for some coffee. After hinting around a little, I finally told him I was planning to build a lodge at Enchanted Lake, not too far from Kulik. I explained the dilemma caused by the mild winter weather and then asked if I could have my Pan Abode buildings and materials delivered to the Kulik runway, about ten miles from my lodge site.*

*I could tell by his reactions that I'd hit a nerve. After all, I was the one who got the Sky-Tel contract. It was one thing for me to fly-out a few Kulik guests and get an occasional favor or two in return, but to announce I was going to build a lodge so close to Kulik, and then ask to use their runway to put myself in business may have been a bit much! Anyway, I let him think it over for a while. A few days later he told me that I could use the runway. John's main concern was that the C-82 might damage the runway. My project would have to wait until all the frost had left the ground and the runway had a chance to harden.*

While he waited for the runway to dry out, Ed realized that he needed a way to move the building materials and furnishings from the lakeshore of Nonvianuk Lake all the way up the hill to his building site. Ed decided he needed a cat. Again, he called on John Walatka.

*John smiled when he sold me the old Holt Tera Track; the worn-out tractor first brought to*

*Kulik in 1955. It was a small cat about the size of a D-2 Caterpillar. I'd planned to drive it down the lake across the ice but that wasn't possible because the ice was rotten and there were clear spots. I had no choice but to drive the Holt around, through the trees and swamp to get it to Enchanted Lake.*

*When he sold it to me, old John told me it was mechanically sound, but I might have a problem with the tracks. I did, but I was still able to get it down the lake through the forest and the swamps. Once I had the tractor at Enchanted Lake, I had to come up with a plan to deliver my building materials down the lake, too. After all, I really hadn't planned to have the building supplies delivered to Kulik in the first place. I also knew that once they arrived, I'd need to get my materials off the Kulik strip as soon as possible.*

In the delay from early spring until the runway hardened, all of Ed's building materials sat outside, uncovered in the damp Kodiak weather. By the time the runway hardened and the skies improved enough for the flight to Kulik, the cedar logs were completely rain soaked.

When Ed ordered the building materials from the manufacturer, he paid extra to have the logs, etc, bundled in units weighing 200 pounds or less so that two men could handle them. Each bundle was to be clearly labeled for identification. By this time, however, they had soaked up so much of the incessant Kodiak rainfall, that they weighed about 400 pounds, way more than Bobby and his copilot could lift. The only solution to this was to cut the bands and heave ho. Once the airplanes arrived and the materials were unloaded and stacked on the Kulik runway, Ed ended up with thousands of logs, boards, beams, etc., for three lodge buildings all thrown together helter-skelter with no way of identifying where any one piece belonged in the final assembly. Ed told me that it took two men working the entire following summer to make order out of utter chaos before construction could begin. Then he continued the story and told me about getting his materials from the runway to Enchanted Lake.

*On the way to Enchanted Lake. Ed Seiler's Cessna 180 tied behind the raft full of building supplies. Ed had to buy a boat and motor from Kulik Lodge to pull the raft down the lake. According to Ed, this was a time-consuming project. Ed Seiler Photo*

*I'd done a lot of charter flying for the Fish and Wildlife Service in King Salmon and knew they had part of the solution to my problem. I flew to King Salmon and made a deal with one of the guys there to borrow their inflatable bridge pontoons. The pontoons had been in storage in their original packing crates since I didn't know when, and I knew they had no plans to use them. Those crates were huge, about 6-feet in every dimension, and weighed about 600 pounds apiece. The only way I could get them up to Nonvianuk Lake was to charter Bobby Sholton again to bring them from King Salmon to the Kulik airstrip. At the same time, he brought up my jeep station wagon, which also had to be taken to Enchanted Lake.*

*After the pontoons were delivered to Kulik and removed from the crates, I used a small 1500-watt portable generator and a vacuum cleaner to partially inflate the pontoons. I used a hand pump to finish the job, which took about one quarter day of hard pumping. As I remember it, the pontoons, when inflated, were each about 8 feet wide and 25 feet long. When tied together and decked with 8 by 10 foot floor beams and 2 by 6 foot roof ports, they made a flat top barge roughly 16 feet wide by 25 feet long. A full load was probably about 8,000 pounds. On the first trip, I had the help of two Anchorage high school boys for loading and unloading. On the subsequent seven trips, I did everything alone. I was a very trim hombre by the time that job was finished.*

*Once the first load was ready, I needed a boat to pull my raft down the lake. Again, John came to my rescue, but again with a price. John sold me a boat, a 35- horse outboard, and the gas I needed to run it. I tied my airplane to the raft and started out. The first load took about 10 hours, and I had seven more to make. What an affair. Well, once I got the load to Enchanted, I had to off-load the building materials onto the lakeshore and then take all the materials up to the building site with the Holt cat. Anyway, about two trips into the project the weather went to hell. I had no choice but to leave the raft tied up on the shore at Kulik and fly my airplane back to Enchanted Lake. A couple of days later the weather improved, and I got organized for another load. Once I got to Kulik, I found that the bears had ripped and gnawed big holes in both pontoons. Old Walatka knew it, too, and smiled again as he tried to sell me some old sealant. Instead, I chose to order and fly up from Seattle some special neoprene cement and patching material. Anyway, I finally got the materials delivered to the site and the buildings put up. I think every piece was*

*The first cabin at Enchanted Lake takes shape. Ed Seiler personally did all the construction with the help of one hired man, Hal Marchbanks, shown above. Ed Seiler Photo*

*loaded and unloaded seven times. That was a lot of monkey business. I know Big John was happy that it finally ended, although I'm sure he was eager to sell me something else. I was embarrassed as hell when I returned to the Fish and Wildlife Service office in King Salmon. I told them the whole story and they weren't too impressed. They decided that although my repairs worked, the bear-damaged pontoons were ruined and not repairable to their standard. I had to agree to give them $750 worth of charter flying to get off the hook, and that was a lot more than the pontoons were worth.*

Despite all the logistical difficulties encountered and the numerous times he handled the materials, Ed Seiler was ready for business and hosted his first fishing guests in 1965. Enchanted Lake Lodge became the first fishing lodge in Bristol Bay to compete directly with Ray Petersen's Angler's Paradise Lodges. Unfortunately for Ed, Enchanted Lake offered no fishing possibilities, and as a result, the guests had to be flown out each day. Enchanted Lake Lodge became the first full-time fly-out lodge in Bristol Bay. Ed handled all the pilot-guide duties, while his wife, Josefina, managed all the cooking and hostess responsibilities with the assistance of one hired couple. Because they wanted to emphasize personal service, Ed and Josefina hosted just four clients per week.

*The first cabin at Enchanted Lake nearing completion. Ed Seiler Photo*

Perhaps more than any other early Bristol Bay fisherman, Ed Seiler was interested in fish. Not only did he like fishing, Ed was the first and only person to be issued a permit to transplant and stock fish in Bristol Bay. I heard numerous stories about Ed's "fish planting" missions and listened as Dave Shuster gave me some details.

*I was guiding at Grosvenor in 1961. One time we didn't have any clients at the camp when Ed Seiler stopped in. It was early in the day and Ed asked me if I wanted to go fishing. I jumped at the chance to go and told him I'd be just a few minutes while I gathered up my rod and a few flies. Ed grinned at me and said, "Don't bother. I have all the equipment we'll need today." We climbed aboard his airplane. He flew up to Idavain Lake. Ed pulled out three old-style 20-gallon milk cans and a small-mesh seine net hidden in the tundra. We spent the next couple of hours netting the "golden" trout from Idavain Creek. Those Idavain fish are very colorful. Anyway, we carefully put each fish into a milk can full of the cool creek water to keep it alive. When we had about a hundred, we loaded the cans back into the airplane. It took a long time to get off the lake. Once we were in the air, Ed headed for a lake not far from Grosvenor Camp. We made sure all the fish were alive before we eased them into the water of their new home. That wasn't the only lake Ed stocked. I went with him quite a few times.*

Ed Seiler should be called the "Johnny Appleseed" of Katmai; only he planted fish, not apples. I had both Dave Shuster and Ed Seiler take my map and pinpoint all the places where fish were transplanted. You can be sure I check some of those populations regularly. Ed transplanted small char from Idavain Lake, king salmon fingerlings from the Naknek River and sockeye fry from Ugashik Narrows. Ed told me how he got started.

*It seems that every time I walked out on a dock in King Salmon I'd see hundreds of king fry around the pilings. I started thinking about taking them up to Moose Pond to see if I could get a run started, but I didn't have time to catch them. Well, some kids used to hang around the dock. I made a deal with a couple of them. If they'd catch the fish and keep them in a live-box on my dock, I'd pay them a penny a fish. This was a great deal. The kids were making money and I was flying kings all over the place, right up to the time old Walatka got involved.*

*One day when I came in to pick up the fingerlings, the box was empty. When I asked one of the kids what the problem was, he said, "that big man who is always smoking a cigar and who comes in here flying that twin-Cessna told us you were stinging the hell out of us. He says you should be paying us a dime apiece, and we should demand more money." I wasn't on the dock five minutes before I had a labor crisis. When the kids hit me up with the new price, I quit transplanting king fry and decided to try char from Idavain. I moved a few rod and reel-caught rainbows, too.*

*I had to find a way to get even with Big John. I did, too, but that's another story. The worst of it was, I could never get the satisfaction of telling John how I did it. He was big enough to beat the hell out of me coming and going.*

Probably the strangest of Ed's transplants happened more by accident than by design. One day Ed and Josefina had a load of char and were on their way to a "secret" creek on the Shelikof side of Katmai. To make a long story short, the weather deteriorated so much during the flight that Ed couldn't find the creek. Low clouds and building fog forced him to head back across the mountains. The wind was howling as he zigged and zagged around the clouds. Ed knew the fish had been in the milk cans too long. Rather than just let them die, he decided to release the fish at the first place he could land. Ed flew over the large lake inside the Kaguyak Crater, but the wind was so gusty that he was afraid to land. While barely keeping the airplane upright, Ed reduced speed and opened his window. He and

Josefina threw the fish out of the window one at a time to make an undignified landing in the lake after a drop of about 500 feet.

During his previous transplants, Ed checked each fish as it swam away. Ed knew the fish had little chance of surviving the fall from the airplane, but at least he didn't let them die in the milk cans. That was the only time Ed released fish into the Kaguyak Crater. Strange as it seems, they lived. Ed told me a little more:

*I landed in the crater many times to pick blueberries. The island in the lake is thick with berry bushes. Anyway, a couple years after I dropped the fish, I went to pick berries and saw some fish swirling. I guess they survived after all. I got out a rod, but couldn't catch one, as they were beyond casting distance.*

*A few days later, one of the Fish and Wildlife guys cornered me at the Post Office in King Salmon. He asked if I had planted any fish in that lake. I denied it, of course. He looked me right in the eye and called me a "lying son of a bitch." Then he told me he had been doing some survey work and had seen the fish from the air. I guess he was a better fisherman than I was because he landed and caught the hell out of 'em. I denied it again and excused myself. Actually, my permit was valid when I dropped the load there, but I still didn't want to tell them.*

Ray Loesche was one of the first lodge operators to regularly take clients into the Kaguyak Crater. I asked him why.

*I first landed in the crater in 1973. I thought the place was beautiful and unique. When the weather was good, we'd quit fishing and fly in there to have lunch. The clients loved it. The weather didn't always allow a landing, but when it did, everyone agreed that the place was fantastic. We found an active hot spring at the bottom of the southern snowfield. Some of my clients swam in the hot water near the shore. The farther out from shore you swam, the cooler the water. It was great.*

*Ed and Josefina Seiler at Enchanted Lake Lodge. Circa 1978—Ed Seiler Photo*

*I saw the small fish on one of my first trips into the crater. I knew they were char, and I knew they couldn't grow too big in that environment. Although I knew they were there, we never fished for them. I thought they should be left alone.*

When Ed first got the idea to stock a few places, he went right up to the Fish and Wildlife office in King Salmon and presented his plan.

*I guess they didn't give it much thought. They issued me a permit to stock. That's all it said. They didn't specify when, how many, or even what kind of fish. For me, stocking fish was like drinking booze, once I started, I didn't want to stop. I planted fish all over the place. One day they notified me that my permit had been canceled. They cited genetic conflicts as the reason. I told them that I thought they were the ones with bad genes. Once they told me, though, or at least as far as the government was concerned, I quit planting fish.*

To avoid the obvious public and governmental conflict, Ed kept his subsequent fish-transplanting missions rather quiet. When he had a permit, few knew. After it was revoked, fewer knew. Although I learned the real story about the Kaguyak fish many years ago, it always fascinated me to hear the various official explanations about the origin of the char in the volcano crater.

I'm sure I wasn't nearly as pleased as Ed when some years later he heard one of those official explanations given by someone who was "supposed to know," but didn't. Ed grinned when he told me more. Evidently he was at Brooks one day and found himself in a large group discussing the origin of Bristol Bay fish populations, and why there weren't fish in all of the lakes. Somehow, the topic switched to the char at Kaguyak. Not wanting to let the cat out of the bag, Ed feigned ignorance and then quickly asked a Ranger who happened to be standing nearby; "Do you know how the fish got into that lake?"

According to Ed, the omniscient, yet dedicated young government official made a sweeping gesture and a comment for all to hear:

*"Yes, I know about those fish. Obviously, seagulls ate some fertilized char eggs and 'shat them out' while flying over the lake. It happens once in a while." I damned near broke out laughing when he said that. Right away I knew I was off the hook. If I'd have been a little faster, I'd have added, "Once in a great while, you ignorant son of a bitch!"*

Keeping those "official" versions in mind, there is a great story about the introduction of parka squirrels at Brooks Camp, too, but from fear of litigation, I'd better tell you that one in person.

## The Branham Family Expands

Bud Branham and his brother, Dennis, operated Rainy Pass Lodge and slowly developed the lodge site that Bud started in 1949, Kakhonak Falls. By the early 1960s, both lodges were growing. At Rainy Pass, they remodeled and modernized the lodge, added a new kitchen and dining room as well as built separate quarters for the winter caretakers. At Kakhonak, the Branham brothers built a new lodge building complete with three twin-bedded rooms and three baths.

Bud's marriage ended shortly after the war. Although born in Alaska, Maxine just didn't want the kind of life that was developing. She worked for Alaska Airlines and wanted Bud to be an airline pilot. Bud didn't want to follow that path. After their divorce,

Bud stayed busy trying to make a living. He trapped and did whatever he could to return to a life in the wilderness. Slowly, his hunting business started to grow. The more it grew, the more time he spent "outside" showing films and recruiting new clients for both of his hunting and fishing lodges.

Late in the 1950s, Bud started to look for a place to spend the winter. After a long search, he ended up with a ranch in Utah. In 1959, Bud met a young man and his life changed forever. From Bud's book, *Sourdough and Swahili:*

*One day in the fall or winter of 1959, a man and his wife came to visit me at the ranch. The man's name was Dusty Rhodes, and he had been a client of mine a couple of times in Alaska. I had never met his wife. They had a youngster with them who was about eleven years old. His name was Michael Palmer-Wilson.*

*Dusty asked me if he could leave Mike with me for a few weeks while he and his wife made a trip to Mexico. It was apparent that they were having domestic difficulties and wanted to be away by themselves. I was glad to comply, for I was very much taken with the youngster. So, they went on their way.*

*Mike and I stayed together for three or four weeks. I found that he had been born in Tanzania, the son of a professional hunter I knew of, Clary Palmer-Wilson, and his mother's name was June. It was a broken home; June was married again, and so was Clary. Mike was the oldest of six youngsters. Dusty had become acquainted with Mike while hunting with Clary in Tanzania. He had agreed to bring the boy to the United States and to adopt and educate him. This came as a total surprise to me, since I had not had any close contact with Dusty Rhodes.*

*Mike was a bright youngster, very advanced for his age. We stayed together for three or four weeks, as I mentioned, and I made up my mind that if I could have a son, I would want him to be like this boy. Eventually, Dusty and his wife returned, picked up Mike and went on their way back to Cleveland. But I made Dusty promise me that if the adoption did not go through he would let me know so I could take over where he left off. Mike and I*

*Mike Branham (right) at the outlet of Kukaklik Lake. Circa 1970—Chris Branham Collection*

*Chris Branham (lower) took this Tanzania hippo for food at the young age of 14. Hunting at night, Chris had several close encounters before he dispatched this animal. According to Chris, the hippo provided nearly two months' worth of food. Chris Branham Collection*

*intuitively made a decision already, although it had not been put into so many words.*

*It took me three years to make the final arrangements to bring Mike back to this country. The Tanzania government had closed all white schools and destroyed all white records and we just couldn't get any information. I enlisted the aid of some political friends and finally, in the fall of 1963, we achieved success.*

Bud finally had a son. Mike fit in well, and when Bud traveled to Alaska to start the season at Rainy Pass Lodge, Mike was right there beside him. Mike worked as a packer and learned to fly. He spent the winters in school in Utah and the summers in the guiding business in Alaska. Bud couldn't have been more pleased with his new son. Things were going so well, in fact, that Bud asked Dennis to consider sponsoring Mike's brother, Chris, into the United States so that he, too, might get a good education. Chris gave me more details:

*Well, to sum it up in a nutshell, Dennis and Mildred invited me to come over from Africa to get educated. When I received their letter and invitation for sponsorship, I looked at it as a great opportunity because there wasn't much future for me in Tanzania. That was during the period of independence when many countries seized all the assets of white families and forced them to move out.*

*I met Bud Branham through my brother. Mike introduced us while he was on safari. Mike came to the United States much earlier than I did. He sent me pictures from Rainy Pass, and his picture was even in the client brochure. Bud sponsored Mike and then he asked Dennis to consider sponsoring me.*

*I left from Rhodesia (now Zimbabwe) and flew to Paris on South African Airways. That was a long flight. Due to political differences, South African Airways was not allowed to fly over the rest of Africa. We had to fly along the coast and cross over to the Canary Islands and get fuel, then go to Paris. From there I changed airplanes and then flew directly to Anchorage on SAS. I got here in June of 1966. As soon as I got to Anchorage, Dennis took me to their cabin at Finger Lakes, and then to Rainy Pass. I went to Kakhonak that summer, too.*

Later that fall, Chris enrolled at West High School in Anchorage. Because the administrators had not previously had any students from Africa, they had a little trouble placing Chris. It only took the school administration about three weeks to evaluate the records and decide he needed to be in college, not high school. Chris promptly enrolled in a local college program. He studied more than the general collegiate curriculum, too. During the fall of 1966 and the early winter of 1967, Chris earned his pilot's certificates and flew clients at Kakhonak during the following summer. Chris told me that his first pilot-guiding assignment was to the Copper River, near Kakhonak Falls Lodge.

Through their adopted fathers, both Mike and Chris became integral players in Alaska's hunting and fishing lodge business.

## Tikchik Narrows Lodge
### Bob Curtis

Bob Curtis entered the fishing lodge business in 1965 when he and his wife, Gayle, purchased the remnants of Bill Gurtler's Tikchik Lakes Camp business, B.G.R., Incorporated. Just like lodge operators John Pearson and Ed Seiler, Bob Curtis also collected some paychecks from Ray Petersen and Northern Consolidated Airline before he entered the fishing lodge business.

Already a pilot, Bob Curtis came to Alaska in 1947 after a distinguished military career. He grew up in Superior, Wisconsin and learned to fly at the tender age of 13, without his parents' knowledge. At the start of World War II, Bob Curtis was not old enough to enlist. Underage and with a strong desire to get into military action, Bob had to have his mother sign him into service. Only 17 years old, Bob entered the Air Force pilot training program and became their youngest pilot. Because his flying skills were already honed, the military leaders promptly placed Bob in a pilot seat, where he excelled in training. Among the airplanes he learned to fly were the B-17, B-19 and the big B-24 Liberator. During the war, Bob became a member of the 459th Bomber Group and flew 43 combat missions as captain on his own B-24, the "Qualified Quail."

After the war ended, Bob wanted to continue his flying career, but good airline jobs were hard to find. Rather than end his career in the sky, he took a job flying "crop-dusters" in Louisiana. The more he dusted, the more he knew there had to be something better. After more than a year of operating the spray airplanes, Bob decided to go north and try his luck. Like many before him, Bob dreamed about Alaska and the hunting and fishing it had to offer. Like many before him, Bob decided to follow his dreams.

Once Bob hit the ground in Alaska, he met Ray Petersen. Impressed with his military experience and his desire to stay airborne, Ray immediately offered Bob a job as a copilot on a DC-3 at Northern Consolidated Airline. Over the next several years, Bob continued his flying duties and served as the Northern Consolidated station manager in Nome. Using his flying skills he delivered mail along the Yukon and Kuskokwim rivers out of Bethel and developed a thorough geographic knowledge of the region. Later, Bob worked for Alaska Airlines where he flew mail and passengers before he plunged headfirst into the professional hunting business. The extensive

*Bob Curtis with his son Robert and a nice Tikchik fish. Circa 1967—Robert Curtis Collection*

mental "geographic" picture of the north country developed on his scheduled mail runs became a handy tool in Bob's endeavors in the professional hunting business.

Besides guiding for sheep, moose, caribou and brown bears, Bob was the first professional hunter in Alaska to offer guided polar bear hunts on the ice floes in northwest Alaska. Bob based those polar bear hunts out of Teller along Alaska's northern frontier. Feeling the need for a better base for all his hunting activities, Bob built a hunting lodge at Farewell Lake in 1957.

*The "plywood cabin" built by Bob Curtis at Tikchik Narrows Lodge. Robert Curtis Collection*

Bob and his wife, Gayle, ran hunters from their Farewell Lake Lodge location through 1969. Like Bud Branham before him, Bob Curtis realized that fishing was going to be the business of the future. A conversation overheard in a popular Anchorage café during the early spring of 1963 led Bob to his career in the Bristol Bay fishing lodge business.

Gayle (Curtis) Hind recently told me the whole story.

*Bob and I were sitting with several friends at one of Anchorage's landmark restaurants, Peggy's Café. We were due to leave for the Lower Peninsula on a spring bear hunt and we were relaxing and making some last-minute plans. We couldn't help but overhear the guys next to us talking about some kind of a fishing camp that was for sale. Curiosity got the better of Bob and he leaned over and asked them for some details. As I recall, Bob did a lot of research on the place and looked over a few maps. He planned to see the place as soon as we had time. Well, on the way back to Anchorage from another bear hunt the following spring, Bob and I flew our Super Cub to Dillingham. We landed at the Dillingham runway. Bob arranged to borrow a Super Cub on floats and we flew that Cub up to the lodge site and landed in the narrows between Tikchik and Nuyakuk Lake. After Bob looked around and studied the lay of the land, he decided right then and there that Tikchik Narrows was a perfect place to build a lodge. We returned the borrowed airplane, climbed back in our own Cub and headed back to Anchorage. Within a short time, we agreed to purchase B.G.R., Inc.*

According to BLM Case File A-056802:

Gayle W. Curtis, wife of pilot/guide Bob Curtis, subsequently purchased a controlling interest in B.G.R., Inc. The application to Purchase the T & M Site filed February 8, 1965, was signed "Gayle W. Curtis, President, B.G.R."

Once I read the remainder of the federal report, I called Gayle and asked what she purchased when she bought B.G.R., Inc. She said:

*As far as I can remember, we only bought the paper trail. B.G.R. applied for a manufacturing and trade site, and that was all there was. John Pearson's tin shed was on the property. Although we didn't have to, we paid him $1,500 for that pitiful shack. It was empty and useless to us, but we paid him anyway. We were told that the B.G.R. founders ordered plates, light fixtures, linen, and other essential items for the lodge they planned. I'm not sure if it stayed in California or was lost in shipping, but we never saw any of it. By the time we bought the place, Swede Blanchard (the B) was dead, Lawrence Glickman (the G) was dead, and Mr. Roberts (the R) evidently lost interest or for some other reason wasn't involved because I don't recall ever meeting or hearing from him. Actually, our attorney handled the sale for us.*

*Gayle Curtis on the porch at Tikchick Narrows Lodge with Orvie, reputed to be the best bear dog in the Bristol Bay area. Robert Curtis Collection*

When they arrived at the Tikchik site to start a summer season of building in late June of 1965, they discovered that Bill Gurtler had planned a lodge, but had made few improvements on the land. Gurtler had started the clearing process, but not in the areas Bob Curtis felt it necessary. Expecting a long delay before they could get building materials delivered to the site, Bob and Gayle faced hours of clearing before they were ready for construction. Because of high local costs and expecting a lack of availability in Bristol Bay, Bob ordered all the required lumber and building supplies from Seattle.

Once ordered, the entire load was barged to Dillingham. When the materials were finally off-loaded in the small Bristol Bay community, Bob contracted Northern Consolidated Airline to deliver the materials to the site. Bob knew that Ray Petersen had two Grumman Mallards that he had purchased and put into airline service in 1964. The Mallard was a huge amphibious airplane that could haul a big load to his water-bound site. Ray purchased the airplanes for use at his own lodges and Bob needed a big airplane. Bob Curtis had so much delivered, in fact, that Northern Consolidated pilot Oscar Underhill had to make 18 separate trips to Tikchik Narrows hauling the building materials. The entire process of clearing the land, preparing the site for building and unloading the 18 Mallard loads of materials took all summer, yet Bob and Gayle had time to complete one small cabin and still host guests at Tikchik Narrows Lodge. According to Gayle:

*By the time we left and went back to Farewell Lake in early August to run our hunters and hunting business, we finished our first plywood cabin and hosted our first guests at Tikchik. We had only two guests at Tikchik Narrows Lodge during the season of 1965, two doctors from New York. Actually, we tried to postpone their trip but they insisted on being our first clients at the new lodge. We were lucky, too, because our first guests arrived on the same day that we finished the plywood cabin. Bob and I had no choice but to stay in Pearson's old tin shed and let the doctors use the new cabin. I'd have to say the living conditions weren't too good for those guys. They had great fishing, but they never came back. I guess they didn't like the cabin we gave them.*

Bob and Gayle continued to operate Farewell Lake Lodge and the hunting business while their new venture, Tikchik Narrows Lodge, started to grow. And grow and get popular it did. Within a few years, Bob would quit professional hunting and would concentrate on his new fishing lodge horizons.

## Kvichak Lodge

### Red Clark

Red Clark was a resident of Naknek and a commercial fisherman during the early 1960s. After seeing and hearing about all the sportfishing business activity starting to grow in the area, Red decided that there was enough interest to warrant casting himself into a fishing lodge.

Red chose a site along the Kvichak River, near the outlet of Iliamna Lake, directly across the river from the Native village and runway at Igiugig. Red knew about the success that Gren Collins experienced at his private club headquarters on the Kvichak. The area was famous for big rainbows as well as for the fantastic runs of sockeye salmon that clogged the river as they headed for the spawning streams.

Once the ice cleared the river and before the start of the Bristol Bay commercial fishing season, Red used commercial fishing boats to haul the necessary lumber and supplies to his Kvichak site. He had the lodge ready for operation and hosted his first guests at the Kvichak Lodge in 1965. The majority of Red Clark's clients traveled to King Salmon via Northern Consolidated Airline. Once they arrived in King Salmon, nearly all of his guests were flown to the runway near the outlet of Iliamna Lake at the village of Igiugig. Red met all the clients at the runway and took them across the river by boat to his Kvichak Lodge.

The Kvichak Lodge was strictly a non-fly-out lodge. Because Red commercially fished in Bristol Bay during June and July, he opened his lodge after the close of the commercial season, just in time for the great early fall fishing. I checked numerous publications for advertisements for fishing lodges during the late 1960s. I reprinted an ad for the Kvichak Lodge and one from hunting guide Ray Loesche that ran in *Outdoor Life* in 1968. No other Alaska fishing lodge advertised in that publication. Like most other prominent hunting guides, Ray Loesche hosted fishing trips from his hunting camp at Ugashik Lake. Ray told me that he simply tried to find some additional revenue between hunting seasons, and never considered that he was in the fishing lodge business. Fishing would, however, become much more important to Ray Loesche in the early 1970s.

*An advertisement similar to this appeared in the January, 1968 edition of Outdoor Life and clearly indicates the late season fishing opportunities at the Kvichak Lodge. No other Alaska fishing lodge advertised in that publication. Hunting guide Ray Loesche's ad from the same publication is reproduced below.*

**Alaska Rainbow & Steelhead**

***Trophy Fish Our Specialty***

**Aug.—Rainbow, Silver Salmon & Grayling**
**Sept. 1 to Oct. 10—Steelhead, Rainbow and Grayling**

*Write Airmail or Wire for information and reservations*

**KVICHAK LODGE**
**Edward M. Clark**
**Box 37, Nahnek, Alaska 99633**

**ALASKA BIG GAME TROPHY HUNTS**

***FISHING*** ***PHOTOGRAPHY***

**August:** DALL SHEEP and CARIBOU in the Brooks Range, deep in the Arctic. Witness the caribou migration, excellent Sheep population, and enjoy some of the finest fishing in Alaska.

**September:** DALL SHEEP, MOOSE and CARIBOU in the Alaska Range, along with GRIZZLY commencing Sept. 15.

**October:** Largest MOOSE and CARIBOU in the World on the Alaska Peninsula. All moose in the 70 inch class, all caribou in the record book, along with fishing, Ptarmigan, Duck and Goose hunting.

1968 Polar Bear and Brown Bear filled, but available for 1969. Comfortable cabins in all areas hunted, excellent game areas, qualified guides and good equipment assure you a successful hunt. Check the Award sheets, my hunters have taken more top B&C awards in the past 5 years than any other guide in North America.

**FISH ALASKA AT IT'S BEST, WITH AIRCRAFT**

Customized fishing trips for Rainbow, Arctic Char, Arctic Greyling, Mackinaw Trout and Salmon throughout June and July. Small parties, personally conducted, with exclusive use of aircraft, excellent accommodations, good equipment, and the finest fishing areas in the State assure a never-to-be-forgotten trip. No extras, rates include all flying, room, board, guides, etc.

**RAY LOESCHE**
**Licensed Guide and Outfitter**
**Box 622, Fairbanks, Alaska 99701**

**Winter address:**
4615 No. 22nd St.
Phoenix, Ariz. 85016
(602)277-3177

## Solidifying Alaska's Skies

In early 1967, the rest of the nation watched the Green Bay Packers defeat the Kansas City Chiefs in the first Super Bowl, and moviegoers flocked to see *Bonnie and Clyde*. In Alaska, however, the news was more crucial to the flying public. Ray Petersen and Sigurd Wien, two of Alaska's foremost aviation pioneers, announced an airline merger, that would form Alaska's largest airline at the time.

The merger of Wien Alaska Airline and Northern Consolidated Airline was a sound financial move for both Ray Petersen and Sig Wien. Announced in 1967 but not approved by stockholders until 1968, the merger held great implications for the fledgling fishing lodge industry as well as for the aviation community.

Before the merger, Ray was highly involved in the day-to-day operations at his Angler's Paradise Camps in Bristol Bay. Once the merger was announced, however, time became a limiting factor for Ray and his involvement at the lodges. Frank Norris traced the events of the merger and the additional responsibilities assumed by Petersen in his book, *Tourism in Katmai Country*.

> *The stockholders of both airlines approved the merger on March 9, 1968. The merger, effective April 1, was formally that of Wien merging into Northern Consolidated Airline; therefore, the surviving corporation's name, for business purposes, remained Northern Consolidated Airlines, Inc. But the new airline's operating name was Wien Consolidated Airlines (WCA), Inc., and that was the new name so far as the public and the National Park Service were concerned. The new airline was headquartered in Anchorage, where NCA's base of operations had been. The firm operated a system in excess of 10,000 route miles, the largest home carrier in the state.*
>
> *Ray Petersen, who had remained as the president of NCA since its inception in 1945-46, was named chairman of the board of the new airline, and Sigurd Wien was named president. In 1969, the two officers switched positions in order to allow Wien to devote more time to his personal life. Five years later, Wien retired, and Petersen assumed the roles of president, chairman, and chief executive officer. The airline over which Petersen presided was known as Wien Consolidated Airlines from February 1968 until May 1973; its name was then changed to Wien Air Alaska, Inc. (WAA), out of respect for Noel Wien, the aviation pioneer.*

Despite the change in duties for Ray Petersen, the Angler's Paradise Lodges as well as the industry continued to grow and be successful

## Golden Horn Lodge

### Roger Maves

While Ray Petersen was involved in the big merger, Roger Maves' long wait to open a lodge finally ended. Roger Maves was a former Ray Petersen employee and a patient man. He was so patient, in fact, that it took him nearly 12 years to get from his Alaska fishing lodge dreams to hosting his first paying guests. To pursue his lodge goal, Roger and Henrietta (Hank) Maves moved from Minnesota to Dillingham, Alaska, in 1955.

I asked Hank about the circumstances of their move, and why they left a perfectly

PAGE 4 THE MIDNIGHT SUN SPRING 1967

**Ray Petersen, President & General Manager, Northern Consolidated Airlines, Inc.**

# PIONEER AIRLINES WILL LINK ROUTES

**Raymond I. Petersen,** president of **Northern Consolidated Airlines, Inc.,** and **Sigurd Wien,** president of **Wien Alaska Airlines, Inc.** made a joint announcement on the 15th of March that the two companies have agreed to combine into one.

The companies are presently headquartered at Anchorage and Fairbanks. Name of the new company will be announced shortly.

"When completed, the merger of the two pioneer Alaska airlines will form the largest of the Alaska based air carriers, and will initially have a net worth in excess of $7 million," Wien and Petersen said.

The merger will constitute a joining of two of the oldest commercial airlines in Alaska, whose operations predate the original Civil Aeronautics Act. They were formed many years ago by early pioneer bush pilots, who are now the presidents of the merging airlines.

Wien and Petersen said combining of the companies into a single operation will improve services rendered to the public by the two companies separately, using modern jet equipment now on order; and that such improvement, together with economics of operation, increased efficiency and increased traffic will better serve the State of Alaska, its communities and citizens.

They emphasized that the route systems of the carriers complement each other and that the integration of the continuous routes under one management "will make possible improved service for the betterment of the entire Alaska air transportation system."

Routes of the combined companies encompass substantially all of the vast area of Alaska and most of the important towns and cities. The route systems of the carriers extend from Juneau on the south, to Point Barrow, the northernmost point on the North American continent; and from White Horse, Yukon Territory on the East to Nunivak and St. Lawrence Islands, near the International Dateline in the Bering Sea on the west.

The system will operate out of the principal cities of Juneau, Anchorage, Fairbanks, Nome, Kotzebue, Bethel, Dillingham, King Salmon, and Point Barrow in the Arctic. It will serve more Alaska points than any other airline . . . over 150 communities . . . over more than 8,500 route miles and cover a territory of approxmiately 500,000 square miles.

The service territory includes the fisheries areas of southeastern Alaska, Cook Inlet and Bristol Bay, the Bering Sea communities, the entire north slope of Alaska to the Arctic Ocean, and the large systems of the Yukon and Kuskokwim River valleys.

The presidents announced that they anticipate no changes in staff, nor reductions in personnel. Wien presently has 289 employees, Northern Consolidated 165. Both work forces increase during the summer months.

**Sigurd Wien, President & General Manager, Wien Alaska Airlines, Inc.**

Details and terms of the transaction will be fully set forth in applications being filed with the Civil Aeronautics Board. The merger was approved by directors of the respective boards on the 18th of March. It is subject to approval by various other interests including the stockholders of each company and the Civil Aeronautics Board.

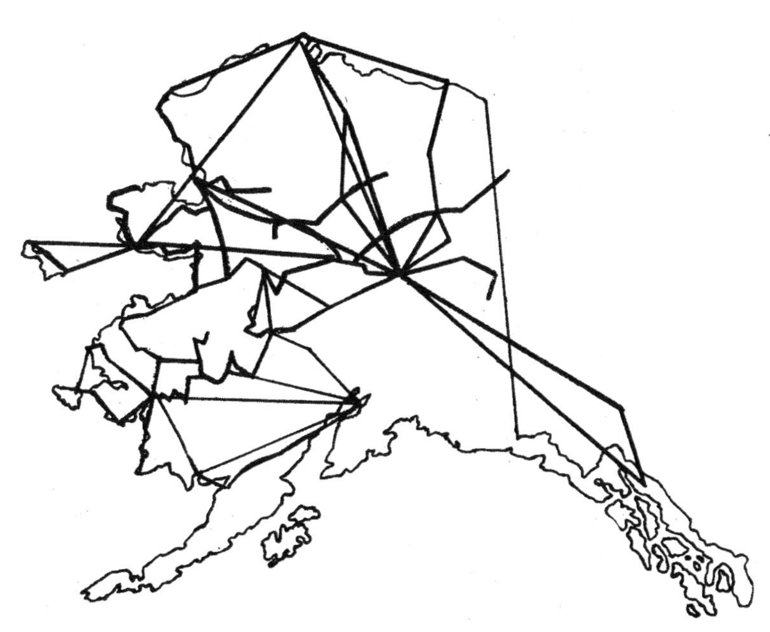

**Route map, showing Wien Alaska Airlines (dark line) and Northern Consolidated Airlines (light line).**

*Reprinted from the Midnight Sun, Spring 1967. Ray Petersen Collection*

good life in Minnesota for the wilds of Alaska. She explained:

*Well, Roger had a lodge business near Bimidji, Minnesota, before we were married. Unfortunately, gambling was the mainstay of his lodge, not fishing. When gambling was outlawed with the election of a less progressive government, fishing was popular, but Roger just couldn't make ends meet.*

*Roger looked for greener pastures and decided to return to Alaska. He had been in Alaska before and wasn't going to be happy until he went back. Earlier in his guiding career, he suffered a common fishing guide injury, a hook in the eye. I'm not sure how he did it, but Roger was able to get a medical waiver. With that, he was able to go back to flying and fixing airplanes.*

*Roger always had a good reputation as a worker. He knew some people in Alaska and he was able to arrange a flying job before we left Minnesota. He knew the flying business and he knew Alaska was where he wanted to be. He also knew he wanted to build a fishing lodge.*

When I asked Hank how she felt about coming to Alaska, she said:

*I really didn't think about it at all. I was newly married. As a young wife, I was excited about coming to Alaska; that's where my husband wanted to go.*

Shortly after arriving in Dillingham, Roger went to work flying and fixing airplanes. Sometime during the first few days in Dillingham, Roger met and befriended Bob Gurtler. During their first few weeks in the new community, Bob and the Maveses built a lasting friendship. Bob explained to the Maveses that he wanted to commercial fish with his brother, Bill, but had to find someone trustworthy and responsible to take over his job. Bob knew that his NCA job was important and knew he simply couldn't just "walk away." Over the next few weeks, Bob convinced one of the Maveses to take over his contract. It was Hank Maves, not her husband who finally became the Dillingham station manager for Northern Consolidated Airline. When I asked Hank about the turn of events, she related the story.

*There literally wasn't anyone else. Roger was too busy working on airplanes. Bob and Bill were commercial fishing. I was the only one that was left. I really wasn't sure of what I was getting into. Shortly after I agreed, Ray Petersen sent me over to King Salmon to study weather and learn the procedures at the station there. The next thing I knew, I was in charge of the station in Dillingham. I loved it. It was really a great job and I worked with wonderful people.*

Hank was the NCA station manager at Dillingham and a Ray Petersen employee until 1980. Roger was able to pursue his fishing lodge goal.

*The thoughts about having a fishing lodge never really left Roger's mind. He often thought of his lodge in Minnesota and he knew the success Ray was having with his Angler's Paradise camps. From his own experience, he knew how much he loved the lodge business. When Ray visited the station in Dillingham, he and Roger often discussed the fishing and the lodge business.*

In an effort to reach his fishing lodge goal, Roger Maves filed an application on

July 20, 1958 to lease or purchase five acres of land on Mikchalk Lake for use as a recreational site under the Small Tract Act offered through the Bureau of Land Management. Roger's dream of a fishing lodge was getting closer to reality. As you might guess, it was time-consuming and labor-intensive work, but Roger's efforts found success. By the fall of 1961, improvements at the site included a nice 12-by-14-foot cabin. While this was a great start, there still were no guests.

Roger and Hank added a partner in 1962. Dillingham resident Carl Nunn, like John Pearson, was in the bar business. He owned and operated the Sea-Inn bar. Carl realized that Roger's concept of a big lodge and the thought of getting into the fishing business was a great idea. With the knowledge of the success experienced by Ray Petersen and the recent start by John Pearson and Bill Gurtler, Carl eagerly became the Maveses' partner. Hank told me about the partnership.

> *Carl was in the bar business and Roger became one of his best patrons. I know they talked about fishing often. Carl was an experienced fisherman, too. I don't know if Roger convinced him to become a partner or if Carl convinced Roger to let him be a partner, but in any case, Carl became our partner in 1962. At first, we formed a partnership and then a corporation, called the Naves Lodges. It was somewhat crazy I guess, but we used the first letter of his last name and made it Naves instead of Maves.*

Hank told me they didn't want to invest too much money into the lodge facilities without having the title to the land, yet Carl and Roger continued to work at the site. While they waited for the land title, they added another Pan Abode cabin. Although Roger had filed for the land in 1958, nothing happened. Officials from the Anchorage office of the BLM finally told Roger that if he paid an independent surveyor to complete the work, they would get the title. To help defray the cost, Roger located several other people who were in the same predicament. Once he arrived, the surveyor completed work on numerous parcels in the Tikchik area on the same trip. After another short delay, the final paperwork appeared in the mail. The Maveses finally received their land patent during the winter of 1966.

Throughout the planning stage, Roger planned to buy and build a large Pan Abode lodge. They were popular in Alaska and not too difficult to assemble. After meeting Norman Rolf and seeing the beautiful log home he'd constructed just outside Dillingham, Roger and Carl Nunn decided to change their plan.

A carpenter by trade, Norman Rolf and his wife, Louise, arrived in Alaska from Wisconsin in 1958. Norman had been stationed in Alaska during the war and was eager to return. They moved to Dillingham and immediately started construction of their new home. During the building process, they became well known in the community. Among others, they met and befriended John Pearson, Roger Maves, and Carl Nunn.

Among other jobs the couple held in the Dillingham area, the Rolfs managed the Willowtree for John Pearson from 1960 through 1963. By late 1966, however, the Rolfs were looking for a business of their own. After a little market research and feeling a sense of adventure, they embarked on an attempt at wintertime commercial fishing on Nuyakuk Lake. Despite the fact that there were several silent investors involved in the project, the Rolfs were the only ones who planned to winter at the secluded lake site and fish through the ice for whitefish.

To get their plan to fruition, they purchased supplies, a big generator, and a cold storage plant. Rather than use a commercial air carrier to transport the supplies to Nuyakuk Lake, one of the investors decided to cut a few corners. He was a high-ranking National Guard officer. This gentleman used more cunning than sense. Under the guise of a military training flight, he ordered all the commercial fishing equipment loaded into a military C-123 that was rigged for landings on winter ice. Things were going well, right up to the time when that heavy and large military transport plane that just happened to be carrying all the Rolfs' winter supplies and the fishing equipment landed on the frozen stretches of Nuyakuk Lake. Before the crew was able to taxi completely off the ice, the heavy transport airplane broke through the ice and settled into the lake with only the wings holding it from completely submerging. That event completely ended the Rolfs' plan to commercial fish. Mrs. Rolf said:

> *I was looking forward to a little solitude in our winter fishing scheme at Nuyakuk Lake. Unfortunately, when the C-123 broke through the ice, all hell broke loose.*

In what must be considered a monumental effort to keep the "questionable" flight and subsequent difficulties quiet, an entire entourage of dedicated military personnel worked throughout the winter floating the airplane, dragging it over and through the ice to the shoreline, changing engines, and getting the airplane repaired and ready to fly. The airplane finally got back into the air on July 4, 1967. Shortly after that, the Rolf family headed back to Dillingham.

Lacking any other prospects, the Rolfs listened to a proposal offered by Roger Maves and Carl Nunn. In exchange for a place to live and a multi-year management contract, the Rolfs agreed to build a natural log lodge building at the Golden Horn Lodge. Within a few weeks, they were living at the lodge site. The Rolfs hosted the first guests at Golden Horn Lodge during the fishing season of 1967.

## Searching for the "Best" Lodge Airplane

Since the start of the Bristol Bay lodge business, owners, managers, and pilots alike have searched for the "best" airplane. A search, I might add, that continues to this day. Looking back a few years, Bud Branham started his lodge operation with the Grumman Widgeon. With the small flying boat, he could access water and landing fields alike. Ray Petersen fished Bristol Bay with the venerable Norseman and a huge military surplus PBY. Recognizing their shortcomings for lodge flying, Ray replaced the Norseman with the Cessna T-50, nicknamed the Bamboo Bomber, and later the PBY with the Grumman Mallard, then, the Pilatus Porter, the de Havilland Beaver, and the Cessna 180. In today's lodge environment with its heavy emphasis on fly-out fishing, the most common lodge airplanes are the float-equipped Cessna 206 and the de Havilland DHC-2 Beaver.

To the novice, I'm sure it seems like all small airplanes are the same. To the knowledgeable, however, the differences are huge. As an example, subtle differences in float size and propeller length can make substantial performance changes. Sorting out these differences took many years. Numerous aircraft types were flown at fishing lodges in Bristol Bay over the years, yet no airplanes were designed specifically for the lodge business. Instead, airplanes were modified and altered to fit new performance standards and the unique demands created by the lodge business and the individual pilots who operated the airplanes. Some of these airplanes were lodge efficient, some were not. Trying to sort out the history of lodge airplane development, I asked Ray Petersen to outline the process he used to replace the Norseman shortly after he started the Angler's Paradise Lodges.

*Northern Consolidated Noorduyn Norseman on one of the many great fishing lakes in the Bristol Bay watershed. Circa 1948—Ray Petersen Collection*

*Well, the Norseman just wasn't a good lodge airplane. It was hard to get into and it was under-powered. I developed a customized version of the Cessna T-50 because I was looking for an airplane, preferably a twin engine airplane, which could be used in the bush that would give me more capacity, speed, comfort, and safety for my passengers. I also wanted a multi-engine airplane so the bush pilots I hired would be better able to transition into the DC-3. I wanted to develop and promote my own pilots, and they needed a way to get multi-engine time.*

*We looked at an airplane that had the structural strength to get the full benefit of the 15 percent gross weight increase allowed under special regulation 422 which was promulgated for the state of Alaska. Therefore, we found that the only airplane that met that category and had the performance was the Cessna T-50. The objection to it was the 260-horsepower Jacob's engines. They just weren't worth a damn.*

*We checked further and heard that a charter company in Canada had both a Beech 18 and a Cessna T-50 on 8750 floats. John Walatka and I went to British Columbia to see for ourselves. The Fraser River operator told us that the Beach 18 wasn't worth a damn, but the T-50 was a good float airplane. John Walatka said that if a float airplane won't get on the step and take off with a 10-knot tail wind at gross weight, it was no good. So, we loaded the airplane right to gross weight and flew it. That twin Cessna did everything we wanted. As soon as we got back to the States, I bought seven surplus T-50s.*

*We figured the T-50 with Lycoming engines would be a better airplane. At the end of the war, many of those 300-horsepower Lycoming engines were available. They were used on the BT Bomber, a trainer-bomber built by Beechcraft. I bought six BT Bombers that were in storage in Tennessee, and planned to have them flown to Alaska. That's another story, but that's where I got those engines.*

*they couldn't do it. They didn't want to do anything with the surplus bombers. There were about 10,000 of them sitting in mothballs. Cessna wanted them all burned because if those airplanes were certified for civil use, it would raise hell with their new airplane market. I told Cessna that they didn't make an airplane that we could use in the bush. I explained to them that when they built an airplane we could use, I'd be in the market. Until then, I needed an interim airplane. Then I told them I'd seen a T-50 on floats in Canada and it was*

*This Travelair A-6000-A was delivered to Alaska by John Walatka in 1938. Ray Petersen delivered the first one to Alaska in 1935. Ray Petersen Collection*

*certified for civil use up there. With that, they finally admitted that they did have the engineering to put the airplane on floats.*

*The next thing was the floats. Well, there were no 8750s to be had anywhere. The McDonald Company built them in Canada on an Edo license, but there were surplus 6470 floats available. The 6470s were originally designed for the Norseman, but they were too small, and therefore, there were ten sets available for $1,000 a set. So I speculated, I bought them all.*

*Once I had the floats, I went to Cessna and said, "we'd like to see if you can put this airplane on floats." Of course, Cessna said*

*So I then went to Edo and told them that we'd like to put the T-50 on 6470 floats and asked if they could do the engineering. Fortunately, I ran into some old-timers at Edo. After we discussed the airplane, one of the engineers got intrigued with the idea. He said, "We can try. It will cost you $5,000 to see if we can do it. We want $1,000 down, and you may lose your money. We may find we cannot do it."*

Ray told the Edo manager he'd risk the money. The Edo engineering department went to work. Within a short time, they reported the 6470 float installation worked fine.

*We had to have an outfit in Iowa manufacture the flying wires, and somehow Edo came up with the struts. It cost me $500 per airplane for the struts and wires, $500 per airplane for the engineering and I paid $1,000 per set for the floats. I thought I'd made a great deal.*

*In the meantime, we bought the Canadian airplane with the 8750 floats and took it to Seattle to run the flight checks. John Walatka tested the airplane in Seattle at Lake Union. Once he knew what it could do, we applied for certification. We drew inspector Roy Petersen, a senior engineer who certificated the Stratocruiser for Boeing. Roy just happened to be an old-timer who flew in Minnesota with John Walatka. We felt pretty good about that. What we didn't know at that time was, however, that he'd already denied the first application to get civil certification for the Cessna T-50 a few years earlier.*

*The first thing Roy told us was that the damned airplane was no good. He admitted that he'd turned down the certification when it first came up. He said the thing wouldn't get off the water and the engines would burn up in a steep climb, but besides those critical items, he flunked it because it had an uncontrollable roll. Well, he hadn't been in one with Lycoming engines. The more time he spent with the airplane, the more enamored he became with it.*

It seems that after John Walatka demonstrated the airplane's capabilities, Roy's opinion changed significantly. It wasn't long before the former float pilot turned Federal Inspector declared the T-50 a great performer on floats and signed the appropriate paper work. The T-50 was approved and certificated on floats for civil use in the United States. Ray continued:

*After certification, we brought the airplanes up here. Harry Bowman was the son of an old friend of mine. Harry was an A&E (airframe and engine) mechanic and a half-assed engineer. The original control system on the T-50 wasn't worth a damn in cold weather because the long controls would freeze up. He engineered a beautiful cable control system that never gave us any trouble at all. Then we got that 15 percent increase in gross weight, so we wanted to get more passengers in. Well, it was originally a five-place airplane. We put in lounge type seats, three on the left side, four on the right side, plus one passenger in the cabin, which gave us a nine-place airplane, with two 300-horsepower Lycoming engines. Well, with more passengers, we needed to have a bigger cabin door. We engineered and modified the rear door so that we had a big double door.*

*By the time we were done with the modifications, we had quite an airplane. We figured that there would be a new airplane out in a few years, but we operated the T-50 for about seven. Because, for some reason or another, the Shorts Brothers, Cessna and de Havilland couldn't get their act together and get any airplanes built, we operated for a number of years with our own remanufactured airplane. As airplanes go, the T-50 was good. We had a real functioning airplane. It was one hell of a performer, too.*

*I remember one time, we were up at Battle Lake; the conditions were terrible for a floatplane, no wind and glassy water. There were nine of us. John and I were both big men, and we had seven of the biggest Texans you ever saw in your life. When we loaded everything and everyone into that airplane, I said "this airplane will never get off the water." It took a long time, but we finally made it. I often thought that if the engines even sneezed, we'd have had it. We were overloaded to beat hell. It was a special airplane on floats. We also got skis for it. Unlike some of the lodge airplanes used these days, our airplanes had to work all year, not just in the fishing season. We couldn't afford to have a limited-use airplane.*

*the engines to control the direction, and as a result, you were going like a bat out of hell when you got down to the end of the lake and had to turn around. If you hit a little bump in the ice, it would collapse the gear, but that was the only weakness of the T-50.*

Ray operated seven T-50s and had three extra sets of floats. When I asked him if the airplane served as a good transition trainer for the DC-3, he stated:

*Oh, hell, sure. It was a twin engine airplane*

*Ray Petersen's all-time favorite airplane N 1845Z, a Stinson Reliant. Ray Petersen Collection*

*In the winter, we operated the T-50s on skis, even though it was a retractable gear airplane. To operate it on the ice, we had to beef up the gear. We put on bigger wheels and stronger struts. The weakness of it was on skis, and the one thing we never got designed was some kind of speed break so you could control the speed during taxi operations, and it didn't have a steerable tail wheel. We just didn't do the engineering to improve it. That was fine, it was a wonderful ski airplane, there was just one thing wrong with it—when you got on glare ice with the thing and taxied downwind, it was uncontrollable. You had to boost*

*and that was a good by-product. We just needed an airplane of that capacity, and of course, that's how we got into the Mallard.*

*We were looking for an airplane with more capacity in the Twin Otter and Skyvan class. It was another deal where de Havilland, Shorts Brothers, Harlan and Cessna didn't have what we needed. After the Mallard, we started looking for a single-engine airplane that matched the capacity of my old Travel Air A-6000. The nearest airplane to that was the Pilatus Porter. So, we went over to Switzerland. When I looked at it, I realized that the airplane was built the way all airplanes should be. It was extremely well engineered and put together, so I bought one with the geared Lycoming engine. It was a swell airplane but the engine had a tendency to get out of dynamic balance, so it really wasn't worth a damn. So then, we put DeGaulle's revenge in it (Ray's name for the French turbine engine). That was a beautifully engineered system. The only thing wrong with it was that you had to have a beautiful engineer to run it; it just wasn't a good engine for the rough and tumble pilots we had flying our airplanes. Then we bought a couple Porters with PT-6s. Then we had something. Because it was such a STOL (short takeoff and landing) airplane, the thing would takeoff in twice its length, but it had two problems on floats. One was that it wouldn't weathercock in the wind because the nose stuck out so far. It was a bitch to handle in the wind. The other problem was that all the pilots were "stunt pilots" by nature, and of course, here you had an airplane that would perform like a helicopter. They weren't too sure it wasn't a helicopter, and they flew it like one.*

*Built for the airline business but modified and adapted to lodge work, the Twin-Cessna replaced the venerable Norseman and Travelair A-6000-A. Ray Petersen Collection*

While Ray Petersen spearheaded the state's biggest airline merger and the Rolfs were building the main lodge building at Golden Horn during the early spring of 1967, national newspapers featured stories about racial strife and the Vietnam War. Headlines about Ho Chi Minh and reports on the Tet offensive crowded the front pages of most major publications. Because Alaska was so far removed from mainstream America, however, news that wasn't reported had far greater implications for the lodge business. The unpublished report that John Walatka had failed a routine flight physical was more ominous to the lodge family than any newswire story.

During John's annual flight physical before the start of the lodge season of 1967, a routine but required EKG test revealed a disqualifying heart condition. Anchorage Dr. Asa Martin made John surrender his pilot medical certificate. John was grounded. Once the initial shock settled, he returned to Kulik and completed the season as a nonflying manager. John had no choice but to quickly qualify longtime friend and NCA pilot, Hugh Hartley, in the Mallard. John Walatka had to relinquish all his flying duties. For the remainder of the 1967 season, Hugh handled all of the manager's required flying throughout the Angler's Paradise lodge system. Hugh Hartley told me that even though John had lost his license, he didn't lose his spirit.

*Although John lost his medical, he didn't stop flying. I flew the right seat numerous times when John's managerial duties mandated a quick trip to King Salmon or Brooks. John was the backbone of the camps and he needed to be in lots of places at the same time. I know he hated to have another pilot fly him around. He figured that as long as I was in the airplane with him, it was acceptable.*

*Despite the fact that John had many duties at the camps, he always enjoyed fishing. He is shown here with a big Brooks River char landed only moments before. Ray Petersen Collection*

My research indicates, however, that he never flew any guests while he didn't have his medical.

John didn't like being grounded, and everyone knew it. From his office in Anchorage, Ray Petersen tried to "pull a few strings." As Ray described it, *We politicked it for a while.* Ray persuaded Dr. Martin to check with the famous Albuquerque airman medical specialist, Dr. Lovelace. Within a month, the good doctor evaluated the findings and found reasons for a change in the evaluation. He promptly notified Dr. Martin. After another short delay, John was relieved to receive written notification from the Anchorage doctor that he had acquiesced to the famous specialist. Dr. Martin reinstated Walatka's medical. The ink was hardly dry on the new certificate when John resumed his flying duties at the end of the season. John continued to fly at the lodges without incident until his heart problem reoccurred during the 1970 season.

## Time Marches On

By 1968, the steady growth in the number of fishermen visiting Alaska and Bristol Bay was beneficial to everyone. Alaska Department of Fish and Game records indicate that the number of nonresident fishing license sales more than doubled between 1964 and 1968, when a record 32,221 sport fishermen traveled to Alaska. Although it is impossible to determine from the state-issued information the number who fished at the Bristol Bay lodges, it is obvious from advertisements that appeared in national publications and newspaper articles that sportfishing was "on the move." The article on the opposite page appeared in the *Los Angeles Times* on July 5, 1968 and provides a reasonable description of the lodge situation to the west of the Kvichak.

Before the end of the decade, several interesting and newsworthy events occurred in Alaska and in the Bristol Bay lodge business. The face of Alaska's political future changed when Ted Stevens

# Alaska's Back Waters Opening to Angler
## By Lupi Saldana
## Times Outdoors Editor

**Anchorage**. Smoothly, like the stroke of an artist's brush, Bob Curtis lifted the four-place Helio Courier off Lake Hood and headed for one of Alaska's virgin fishing areas(the Tikchik chain of lakes. Curtis was flying C.H. (Woody) Jepsen and me to the Tikchiks for a preview of what's happening fishingwise. And what's happening there is happening throughout Alaska. Fishing, the state's sleeping recreational giant, is beginning to wake up.

"We haven't begun to scratch the potential of our fishing waters," said Curtis, a polished angler and one of the state's top hunting guides with 11,500 hours of bush flying to his credit.

In the entire Tikchik and Wood River systems, there are only two resorts under construction. This is like shooting a grizzly bear with a beebee gun—you're hardly scratching it.

The Tikchik area is 300 miles due west of here. On the flight, Curtis gave us the VIP treatment, taking us over and through one of the most scenic and spectacularly rugged pieces of real estate in the world—the Alaska Mountain Range. The range consists of a series of towering, jagged peaks seemingly held together by glaciers and generous amounts of snow. It includes 20,320-foot high Mt. McKinley, the tallest peak on the North American continent. The range houses lots of game. On one slope, Curtis pointed out about 200 sheep.

### Six Casts Produce Six Strikes

Beyond the Alaska peaks the terrain flattens out and becomes a vast wonderland of water. There are hundreds of lakes and streams of all sizes and shapes with lush growths of spruce, alder, and willow. Roaming the countryside are caribou, moose, brown, grizzly, and black bears. There are no deer.

At 10 p.m., 2 hours and 40 minutes after takeoff, Curtis splashed down on Tikchik Lake. He is building a resort on a finger which separates 15-mile long Tikchik from 30-mile long Nuyakuk Lake. He has a main lodge and four rustic cabins, but he plans to expand in the future.

Inasmuch as the sun never sets during the summer months, daylight is no problem. So Curtis instructed us to break out the fishing tackle for an immediate taste of fishing in the narrows directly in front of the lodge. Jepson and I went to work with light spinning rods and 6-pound test line. Using a chrome and red Hot Shot, I made six casts, had six strikes and landed two lake trout and two Arctic char weighing 6 to 10 pounds. Then we picked up fish on flies, using No. 4 and 6 maribou muddlers.

The next day was spent flying and fishing other waters in the Tikchik system. We also got a glimpse of some wildlife. As we stepped out of our cabin door, we ran right into three moose—two spikes and a cow. At Lake Kulik, we saw a large brown bear ambling along the shore. It bounded into the brush and disappeared as our plane approached.

### Grayling an Excellent Fighter

At No Name Creek, a small stream emptying into Kulik, we had terrific fishing for a combination of grayling, lake trout, and Dolly Varden.

This was my introduction to grayling, an excellent fighter with a pectoral fin like a sailfish. We had the best grayling fishing on Nuyakuk River, a large stream which flows out of Tikchik Lake. Many of the grayling weighed over 2 pounds. They hit lures and dark patterned flies in sizes 8 and 10. There are large rainbows in the river, but the best I could do was a 2-pounder.

Another guest, Chuck Mead, landed a 30-inch rainbow fishing in front of the cabins at Tikchik. His partner, Gerald Vollmer, hooked an 11-pound pike. Since practically all the fish are released, the barbs are removed from the hooks.

A second resort is being constructed on Mikchalk Lake by Roger and Henrietta Maves. They said it would be 85 percent complete next year. Construction is slow and difficult because all materials must be brought in by plane.

One area which is giving up good numbers of rainbows is Brooks Camp near King Salmon on the Alaska Peninsula. Actor Jack Lemmon's 14-year-old son, Chris, hit the jackpot, taking a 10-pound rainbow, a 10-pound sockeye, and an 8-pound lake trout.

This area, which figures to explode into a head-quarters for visiting fishermen in the future, is reached via Western Airlines to Anchorage and then King Salmon or Dillingham. The mileage from Los Angeles to Tikchik Lake via Dillingham is 2,900 miles.

was appointed to the United States Senate as reported in the *Anchorage Daily News*, December 25, 1998.

It was a quirky destiny that sent Stevens to Washington, given all the odds stacked against him back then.

First of all, Bartlett was a Democrat and Stevens a Republican legislator who had just been rejected by the voters in his second attempt to win a senate seat at the ballot box.

Until 1967, Alaska had a law that required governors to fill a vacant congressional seat with someone of the same party as the incumbent. But in 1967 Republicans controlled the legislature for the first time since statehood. All three members of Alaska's congressional delegation were Democrats. So the legislature threw out the old law. Should the occasion arise, they wanted Republican Gov. Hickel to be able to fill vacancies in Washington with Republicans.

The occasion arose just a year later, when Bartlett died unexpectedly of heart disease.

Hickel said that the Republican Party told him to choose between Elmer Rasmuson, who had just defeated Stevens in the Republican Senate primary, and aviation businessman Carl Brady.

"Elmer was my neighbor and Carl was my very good friend," Hickel said.

There was another choice, Hickel said. He could have appointed himself. But he had already agreed to leave his job as Alaska governor and become Secretary of the Interior for President Richard Nixon.

The Republican Party added some names to the list, including Stevens's. But he was still considered a nonstarter, except with Hickel.

"I had been through the battle on the statehood issue," Hickel said. "I saw how important seniority was in the Senate. I always thought Alaska, in order to really get on the scene with some strength, had to have a survivor in there. I looked way down the road. I wanted someone who would stay there a long time. I was really looking out for the good of the state way down the road."

Stevens "was a fighter," Hickel said. "I went on intuition and it worked out."

While Ted Stevens was getting organized in his new Senate office in Washington D.C., Bob Curtis made history in the Alaska lodge industry. In an unprecedented lodge facility acquisition scheme fueled by his tremendous success at Tikchik Narrows Lodge, Bob Curtis purchased Wood River Trout Camp from John Pearson prior to the 1969 fishing season. Promptly changing the name to Wood River Lodge, Bob Curtis booked a few guests into the lodge and made plans to build the big lodge building that John Pearson never had the time nor the money to complete.

Bob Curtis found himself entertaining guests at two lodges during the 1969 fishing season. Gayle told me that Bob commuted between the lodges and personally dealt with every client. Finding that an unacceptable way to do business, Bob hired a former hunting client and close friend, Gene Bird, to manage Wood River Lodge for the 1970 season.

## Rainbow River Lodge
### Lloyd Samsal

The Copper River, near Kakhonak, was one of the favorite "fishing holes" of Gren Collins as well as of early lodge operators John Walatka, Bud Branham, and Ed Seiler. The earliest lodge pilots took their clients to that river for nearly 18 years before anyone opened a lodge there. Bob Walker tried to build there, but high water stopped him late in the 1950s. Late in 1968, however, Lloyd Samsal, a guide and outfitter from Anchorage, started Rainbow River Lodge. When I asked him how he got into the fishing business, he explained that he knew other hunting guides were having success in the fishing lodge business, and, according to Lloyd, fishermen were easier to handle than hunters. When I asked him how and why he chose the location for his lodge, I could tell he'd been asked that question many times before. He explained:

*The Copper is a great river, but I knew working the large lakes with a floatplane could get pretty had. I wanted a place where I could land and take off every day, no matter what way and how hard the wind blew. I chose a small lake close to the Copper. More than one Fish and Game agent asked me why there? Other guides asked me why there? It seems like everyone asked why there, but only sensible pilots knew what I was doing. I still think it's the best location around.*

Once Lloyd finished giving me the story of starting the lodge, I asked if he had experienced any problems getting title to his land. He explained that he knew the property was on Native land but waited patiently for the final court determination. He told me that the Natives sold him the land after the December, 1971 settlement act. Lloyd said:

*I guess I had been there so long that the Natives didn't care. They never told me to leave. I never had any problems with anyone and just waited until they sold me the property. Compared to some of the stories I heard, I guess I was lucky!*

Across Iliamna Lake, Bob and Doris Walker sold their Iliamna Lake Lodge to local resident Dick Sjoden in May 1969. Because they did not plan to continue in the lodge business at the time, Bob agreed to sign a three-year non-compete clause as a condition of the sale. Little did they know that many of their former guests would ask them to return to the lodge business, and the small cabin that Bob built on the lower stretches of the Copper River in the mid-1960s would be expanded and become a full-fledged fishing lodge.

As the last fishing day in Bristol Bay ended and the lodges prepared for winter at the close of the decade, the ominous winds of change were in the air. Bud Branham and Ray Petersen had started the 1960s much like they ended the 1950s, operating their respective business operations without competition. By the end of the decade, however, Bob Curtis owned two lodge operations in the Wood River-Tikchik Lakes area, Red Clark had a lodge on the Kvichak River, Lloyd Samsal was getting started on the Copper River, Ed Seiler was going strong at Enchanted Lake and Roger Maves's dream came true at Golden Horn Lodge. Each lodge was different, yet the operations had many similarities. Although none of the players could see it at the time, an industry was starting to emerge.

Recently I asked Ray Petersen to relate his feelings when these fishing camps emerged and his lock on the lodge business ended. His reply was simple and direct.

*Well, you have to understand that I knew these men and their families very well. John Pearson helped us build Kulik, and Bill Gurtler's brother, Bob, was the first passenger I flew to Bristol Bay in 1935. Bill was a good hand, too. I don't recall if he worked for us or not, but he may have at one of the bush stations. He was a good man and a hard worker. So was Bob Curtis. He worked for me, too, before he went into big game hunting and then the fishing lodge business. Ed Seiler did some charter work and pilot guiding for us at Kulik before he started Enchanted Lake Lodge. Roger Maves worked for me, too. I encouraged everyone who wanted to try to get into the lodge business because I thought my airline would benefit. Hell, in those days I didn't look at any of them as competitors, I looked at them as customers.*

The developing industry, much like Alaska herself, was ready to accept the challenge of anyone and everyone who wanted to try. In the years to come, many more would make the attempt.

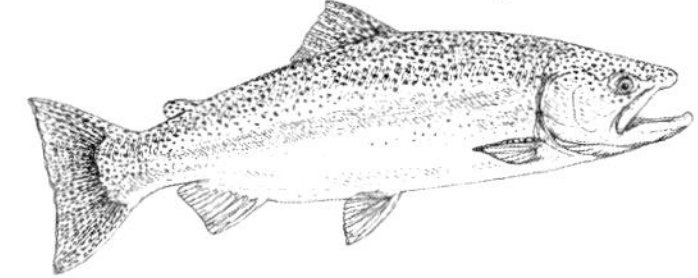

# Chapter 5
# The Decade of the 1970s

"It was you and me on a sea of booze, and then the boat sank."
*Jack Lemmon, "Days of Wine and Roses"*

Although the 1960 fishing season started the decade with two new fishing camps and expectations of continued success, the lodge season of 1970 started with the tragic loss of one of the industry's creators. Not even the tremendous land battles that would plague future lodge builders nor the infusion of many new and interesting lodge personalities could lift the shadow cast by the death of John Walatka on June 27, 1970. This loss affected all the established Bristol Bay lodges as well as those to come. Memories of John Walatka and the standards he set for the fishing lodge industry continue to this day.

From the initial red-carpet tour with the Washington bureaucrats to ordering the Kulik sawmill, John Walatka was like Ray Petersen's right arm during the establishment and building of the Angler's Paradise Lodges. Once they were opened, John Walatka was the on-site supervisor and operations manager. In many ways, John was Ray's working partner in the lodge business. He loved flying, fishing, and telling stories. Working and living between Brooks and Kulik, John amassed the astonishing record of 17 seasons as manager at Kulik Lodge and 20 seasons as the director of the Angler's Paradise Camps. Beyond his management and piloting skill, John brought to the camps the quality of a true sportsman.

John hired many young people to work in Alaska during his reign as camps manager. Those with whom I spoke portrayed John to be more of a teacher than an employer. John's nephew, Tommy Needham, journeyed to Alaska to work at the Angler's Paradise Camps in 1964 and continued his summer sojourns for the next six seasons until the burden of advanced studies altered his life. An older Dr. Needham arrived in Bristol Bay as a Kulik guest in 1996. Tommy made the following comments about his uncle and his philosophy:

*From building to guiding, flying, managing and courting the clients, my uncle, John "Big John," a true sportsman, abhorring those who were just fishing for meat, keeping everything they caught. He taught others, and me, arguing adamantly the sanctity of preservation of our country's natural resources, especially those of the lakes and rivers he cherished and loved so much. He was a strong advocate of barbless fly-fishing. He encouraged careful selection of a trophy fish*

*Big John Walatka and Ray Petersen at Kulik Lodge only weeks before John's death. Ray Petersen Collection*

*Walatka, was the primary workhorse of the camps. People returned for years because of their experiences with John. Our guests found a cherished home away from home, where the ideals and visions of men and women became a reality. The reality was an existence in beauty, humility in the eyes of nature, and for the sportsman catered to, a fantasy dream that lived.*

*By the time I got to Alaska in 1964, John was for mounting, as only one of the species would be allowed. This was not encouraged. It was accepted as a need for those from the Lower 48. Many wanted to have a trophy on their wall to remind them of the fantastic fishing. In some cases, it would be the only trip ever to a place like the Katmai area, creating memories he wanted to be sure to last a lifetime for those who were exposed to him and the area.*

From the very beginning of camp operation, John was responsible for client satisfaction. John's wife, Lillian, worked at his side at the camps until her health failed. She died of cancer during the winter of 1958. John wasted no time and remarried at the end of that year's lodge season. The marriage ceremony, which united John with Dillingham's Mildred Nicholson Oakley, was held at the Dillingham home of Roger and Hank Maves. Taking her position beside John, Mildred readily took to lodge life.

Of all the accolades and credits bestowed upon "Big John," those that reflect his piloting skills are the most common. Stories of John Walatka's piloting are famed, if not legendary. To this day, those who flew with him consider John to be the best floatplane pilot who ever turned a prop. According to Sonny Petersen, John Walatka didn't just sit in the airplane, he wore it like a glove. John was influential in Sonny's flying and early attitudes about airplanes. Ray Petersen made no bones about it either. He said that John was just about the best float driver there ever was. Ed Seiler, one of John's contemporaries, told me that there was never a doubt. John Walatka was just the best pilot any of them had ever seen or been lucky enough to ride with.

Although he lost his medical certificate in 1967 and had it restored before the start of the 1968 season, John didn't step away from his flying duties nor did he lose his "touch." Dave Shuster told me an incredible story about John's uncanny ability. According to Dave, he was with John in the Grumman G44-Mallard traveling between Brooks and King Salmon when John experienced every twin-engine pilot's nightmare, the double engine failure.

*Hugh Hartley in the Mallard. Circa 1973—Ray Petersen Collection*

*I was up in the front with John. We didn't have any passengers, and John told me he'd fly low once we hit the Naknek River so I could look for fish. Everything seemed normal to me. As we passed the lake, John dropped down over the river. I started looking for fish. I was concentrating on the river when all of a sudden things got real quiet–as first one engine quit and then the other. I heard a pop, a snap, and then the sickening sound of loud pounding from my own heart. Immediately I looked over at John. He bit down on his cigar a little harder as he looked for a safe place to land away from the big rocks and shallow water at the top of the river. He had a funny look on his face as he banked the big amphibious plane into position to land. John made a perfect landing and then coasted the airplane right to the beach. He eased out of the pilot seat as if he made landings like that every day. I don't know what caused the engines to quit, all I know is that it didn't seem to be a big deal to John. I loved to fly with him. John was the best!*

*John and Mildred in front of the Kulik office. Circa 1970*—Ray Petersen Collection

During the five years that I researched this book, I heard more stories about John Walatka than about any other personality in Bristol Bay. Most of the stories were true, although more often than not, the facts were misconstrued. Probably the most confusion of all centers around the circumstances and events following John's heart attack. To end the speculations and rumors, I conferred with longtime Northern Consolidated pilot Hugh Hartley to get the real story. Hugh gave me the following factual account:

*I never knew John had a serious problem with his heart. I knew he had trouble with his medical in 1967, but he didn't seem too concerned. If John had a big health problem, he never said anything about it to me. Anyway, during the 1970 season, John flew the Mallard on the schedule and I flew the Pilatus Porter. John's morning schedule began at Kulik. He'd fly to Grosvenor, Brooks, King Salmon and then go back to Kulik. After lunch, he'd do the flight again only in reverse order. On the day John had his attack, I had just landed the Porter at Brooks. Someone came running from the office and told me that Mildred had radioed from Kulik asking me to drop everything and get over there fast. I had no idea what was wrong, although I'd heard that John hadn't done the morning schedule. As soon as I unloaded the Brooks freight, I taxied out and headed for Kulik.*

*I couldn't get anyone on the radio, but I could see that the Mallard was still on the runway as I descended for landing. I taxied the Porter toward the beach in front of the lodge. Mildred was waiting for me as I climbed out of the Porter. She told me that John had had a heart attack and wanted me to fly them to Anchorage right away. I don't know if John had been loading the Mallard or not. He was in his cabin when I got there.*

*I don't remember who all helped, but I know there were many worried assistants. Quickly we loaded John into the bus and drove to the runway. Within minutes, we had him in the Mallard. Mildred strapped him down as I started and warmed up the big engines. I flew John and Mildred to Anchorage. I radioed ahead and there was an ambulance waiting for us when we taxied up to the NCA hangar. Once I had them unloaded and headed to the*

## John A. Walatka

Johnny Walatka was described by one of his closest friends as "kind of an old shoe—somebody you just felt comfortable with; no joiner just to get his name in the paper, but the kind of guy who simply inspired admiration and friendship." Walatka died Saturday of an apparent heart ailment at the age of 62, and a chapter of Alaska's great history of bush flying was closed when the life of this famed aviator, outdoorsman, and sportsman ended.

He had, says one of his associates, "a host of admirers–sportsmen from all over the world who actually came up to Alaska just to associate with John Walatka. He was the kind of man the Outsider likes to think of as a rugged he-man, bush pilot—a helluva advertisement for Alaska just by being a good Alaskan."

Walatka's home was in Turnagain, but his heart was in the Katmai and Bristol Bay country where for so many of his early years he was a pioneer pilot and in so many of his later years a fine camp supervisor at the Wien Consolidated operations–the sportsmen's paradise. Walatka, a member of the board of directors of Northern Consolidated and later with Wien Consolidated after its merger, had a rich background in flying in Alaska since the middle '30s. He was a partner in an air carrier operation in the Dillingham areas before the war, helped other now-legendary bush pilots develop Alaska's airport system during the crisis days of World War II, and formed his own air service after the war—one of which was merged with others to form Northern Consolidated in 1947.

Since 1950 his primary summer job was management of the Katmai camps for the airline, all the while maintaining an expertise in seaplane flying that left him with few peers. He was simply, his fellow pilots say, the best there was. But for all his skill as a pilot, and for all the fame of the service he provided to the people of Western Alaska, John Walatka perhaps will most be missed in these troubled times because of what he offered to young people fortunate enough to come in contact with him.

For many, many years, he had worked with youngsters at the camps and in the field. He was no permissive, weak hand that applied the rules of hard work and dedication to these young people. He was no soft and feeble tongue that verbally lashed at those who failed to produce to the level of which John Walatka knew they were capable. He was a tough but loving taskmaster to youths. And they responded to him, bloomed into strong and good men because of their association with him.

He was a credit to Alaska and to the profession he served. He was skilled to perfection within his field. He is a man whose friendship will not be forgotten by those who knew him. He was an Alaskan who earned a place in our history.

*hospital, I refueled and flew right back to Kulik. We had guests, and with both John and Mildred at the hospital, I had to be back at Kulik to run the camp. I'm not sure, but I don't think John made it through the night.*

It was ironic that Hugh Hartley flew the Mallard during the 1967 season after Dr. Asa Martin revoked John's medical certificate. John was reputed to be the best floatplane pilot in Alaska. Loss of his medical forced him to yield the controls of the airplane he loved to fly more than any other. By conducting Hugh's Mallard training and checkout, John Walatka guaranteed himself a quick medivac flight. Unfortunately, John Walatka made his final flight as a passenger in his favorite airplane, the Grumman Mallard. Ray Petersen told me that when Dr. Asa Martin learned of John's fate, the good doctor uttered a few comments about expert opinions that did not coincide with his own.

According to those who were there, the remainder of the season was uneventful, Hugh Hartley assumed the Mallard duties, and other Northern Consolidated pilots, including Pat Leonard, were brought in to fly the Porter. Hugh's son, Van Hartley, started working for the Angler's Paradise Camps during the 1970 season at Brooks Camp. Ray Petersen assumed Walatka's operational duties at the camps and his responsibilities in Bristol Bay. To keep the effect of John's absence at a minimum, Ray urged Mildred Walatka to assume the manager's position at Kulik. After all, she knew more about running the camp than anyone else. I spoke with many former lodge employees who were at the camps during the fateful season. The vast majority told me that everyone at the Angler's Paradise Camps pulled together and worked a little harder to make up for the loss of John. Because he had such a high profile in the lodge business, a reproduction of John Walatka's July 1, 1970, *Anchorage Times* obituary is presented on the preceding page.

During the winter before the lodge season of 1971, Ray Petersen realized that he could no longer run the camps and the newly merged airline effectively. As a result of that decision, Ray promoted his son, Chuck, to replace John Walatka as the overall manager of the Angler's Paradise operation. Mildred Walatka continued to serve as Kulik Lodge manager during the 1971 and 1972 fishing seasons. Ray also agreed to a lease proposal submitted by longtime Alaska resident and hunting guide, Ben White.

Because the fishing at Battle Camp had not been as consistent as at the other camps had been, fewer and fewer guests stayed there. In an effort to reduce the workload and increase the revenues, Ray thought it best to lease the camp to registered hunting guide Ben White. In the spring of 1971, Ben advertised his Battle River Wilderness Camp. Hunting and fishing were the featured activities at Battle. Ben hired young guide Mel Gillis to help him at the camp. Ben and Mel operated the camp for the next few years. The advertisements changed in 1976 and featured fishing as the primary activity. Ben continued to hold the lease through the remainder of the decade and into the early 1980s.

## Iliamna River Lodge
## Ron Hayes

One of the most prolific lodge builders in Alaska's hunting and fishing history has been Ron Hayes. From an extremely humble start in Alaska, Ron built at least four lodges and had a hand in several others.

*I first came to Alaska from Washington State in 1953. I came for the adventure. I drove the Alcan Highway in a 1947 Chevy pickup truck. I had lots of trouble. That road was awfully tough in those days. Anyway, about my third day in Anchorage I got a job as a mechanic. I wasn't a good mechanic, but there seemed to be lots of work. Jim Haagen, who now owns Northland Freight, gave me a try. He's still a good friend to this day.*

*Within two years of arriving in Alaska, I started flying. I bought an Aeronica Sedan and learned to fly in my own airplane. I wanted to get into the hunting business. I started working with and following guide Lee Holen. He was one of the best pilots I've ever seen. My airplane just wasn't good enough to use in the bush. One day I wrecked it trying to land in the wrong place. I went to Anchorage to get another airplane. In those days, a brand-new Super Cub was $5,700. I couldn't afford that much, so I had to settle for an almost new Cub for $5,000. In 1959, I built my first place in the Wrangell Mountains, Chelle Lake Lodge. I also built several other elaborate camps in that area. By the way, that's where I met my wife, Sharon. She came to Alaska to work for me at my hunting lodge.*

*By 1961, I started to hunt on the Alaska Peninsula. Jack Lee and I combined forces, pooled our money and had a contractor come in to build both our places. Wildman Lake Lodge started as one 12-by-12-foot cabin and we added on from there. Actually, Jack and I each paid for the materials, and then we took the contractor on a polar bear hunt. Everybody was happy.*

Late in 1969, Ron decided to start a fishing lodge in Bristol Bay. He partnered with Pile Bay resident Don Knighton and together they purchased a five-acre parcel of land along the Iliamna River, about four miles up the river from Iliamna Lake. According to Ron:

*Don's wife had an allotment and we purchased the property from her. Once we had the land secured, we ordered lathe-turned building logs from Kenai. During the late winter and early spring, Don and I borrowed a cat from someone at Pile Bay. We drove it across the lake and then cleared a 3,500-foot runway to enable Bobby Sholton to bring over our logs and other supplies in a C-82 cargo plane. During the time it took to get five full loads delivered to the ice-bound lake, things went fairly well.*

Unfortunately, Ron's luck had just about ended. As the last C-82 departed the icy runway, Ron Hayes circled overhead until the big airplane cleared the area, then Ron landed his Cessna 180 and parked in the same place where the big airplanes had unloaded their loads of building logs, plywood, and other construction materials. Once he climbed out of the airplane, Ron unloaded his cargo, then took an ax and proceeded to chop down a couple feet into the ice to put in an anchoring system so he could tie down the airplane. After he secured the airplane, he helped haul the building materials to the lodge site via snow machine.

No more than three days later, Ron went back to his airplane, did a quick pre-flight and then started up. He taxied to the opposite end of the runway. As he started to turn around, the airplane broke through the ice. It came to rest with the wings level with the rapidly deteriorating ice.

*Well, we went right back to the lodge site and had to haul most of our lumber back to the lake. Then we built a tripod and started to jack the airplane out of the icy lake. It took a while but we finally got it out. We had to send for a new prop, but that's about all the major damage that we had. I flew it out several days later. There was still plenty of ice, more than two feet, but it was honeycombed and rotten in that one spot. We worked hard and finished the lodge that season. It was a lot of work, too. We hosted our first fishing clients during the 1970 fishing season.*

Ron told me that in those days, they hosted fishing clients at Iliamna River Lodge in June, July, and early August. Then they'd move their base of operations to Wildman Lake Lodge where they conducted their fall big game hunts.

## The Great Alaska Lands Debacle

In reviewing the development of the fishing lodge business of the late 1960s and 1970s, complicated and controversial land use issues not only impacted the lives of Alaskans, they forever altered the availability of potential fishing lodge sites throughout Bristol Bay. The Alaska Native Claims Settlement Act (ANCSA), the Alaska National Interest Lands Conservation Act (ANILCA), the expansion of Katmai National Monument, and the preparation for the creation of Katmai National Park had staggering implications to say the least. Tightly connected to those highly debated congressional actions were the potentially restrictive "Wilderness" land designations created by the National Wilderness Preservation System and the National Wild and Scenic Rivers Act.

As a total and complete review of the governmental process would more than double the size of this volume, I thought it prudent to turn again to the work of National Park Service historian, Frank Norris. He chronicled the entire land issue debate in his lengthy volume, *Isolated Paradise.*

*The Alaska Native Claims Settlement Act (ANCSA) passed Congress and on December 18, 1971, President Richard Nixon signed it into law. The bill had been a long time coming. As early as 1966, Congress had begun to recognize that a bill "dealing with Alaska Natives' land problems" was needed. About that same time, the Secretary of the Interior, as if in agreement, ordered a large-scale land freeze. Bills intending to deal with Native concerns had little chance for passage at first, but the remarkable discovery of oil on Alaska's north slope, announced in March 1968, made the legislators realize that the Native land question had to be settled.*

*Over the next three years, the bill which became ANCSA, was debated with growing intensity. Its original purpose was to determine which lands should be allotted to Alaska's Natives, and how state land selections would be determined based on Native claims. It soon became apparent, however, that a third element (a national interest lands component) should be included as a provision within whatever bill emerged from the Congress.*

*What emerged from the process was a document which recognized the rights of Alaska Natives to 40,000,000 acres of land, and also paid them $925,500,000 for extinguishment of all previous aboriginal titles or claims to those titles. Most germane to Alaska's national parks units, section 17 (d) (2) of the act gave the Secretary of the Interior authority to withdraw up to 80,000,000 acres as so-called "national interest lands." These lands were to be managed as national parks, national forests, national wildlife refuges or as wild* *and scenic rivers. In addition, section 17 (d)(1) called for the withdrawal of other public interest lands in the state, asking the Secretary to "review the public lands in Alaska and determine whether any portion of these lands should be withdrawn to insure that the public interest is properly protected."*

*The act provided a series of timetables under which the withdrawals were to be made. The Secretary of the Interior was given just 90 days to withdraw lands under the so called "d-1" provision, and 9 months to withdraw lands under the "d-2" provision. Lands not withdrawn would become available for selection by the State of Alaska or for appropriation under the public land laws. Two years after the act, any lands withdrawn under the "d-2" provision that were not recommended as future parks, refuges, forests, or wild and scenic rivers would be released for other uses. The areas that were so recommended as parks or other reservations had to be created within seven years after the act's passage; otherwise, the lands would be released for other uses.*

*The National Park Service issued a draft wilderness study for Katmai National Monument in August 1971, the same month it issued a draft master plan. Public hearings for both were held that November. Soon after the mid-December passage of the Alaska Native Claims Settlement Act, it became evident that the monument was going to be enlarged. The act, in fact, mandated that a master plan be issued which encompassed proposed new monument boundaries. Wilderness, however, was not specifically addressed in ANCSA. Planners operating out of the Washington office prepared the master plan, while staffers at the Pacific Northwest Regional Office in Seattle prepared the final wilderness statement.*

The statewide land freeze, ANCSA, and ANILCA were extremely important to the development of the fishing lodge business. Although the earliest lodge developers Bud Branham, Ray Petersen, John Pearson, and Bill Gurtler, simply chose their sites with quality fishing in mind, those who came after had to contend with all the problems imposed by the land freeze and by extensive delays in title transfers. Ray Petersen, although he did not file paperwork for any property until 1955, had trouble in title transfer based on the implications of ANILCA and Monument expansion. Ed Seiler staked his Enchanted Lake property in 1964. Land claim difficulties plagued him for more than 15 years. Ed finally obtained title to his trade and manufacturing site in January 1981, only to find several restrictive covenants attached to his patent.

Gayle (Curtis) Hind explained that it took nearly 13 years for them to receive title to the property at Tikchik Narrows for which Bill Gurtler first applied in 1959. A quick review of Bureau of Land Management Case file A-056802 reveals some of the problems and frustrations experienced by Bob and Gayle Curtis. The previous chapter noted that after Gurtler's death, Swede Blanchard and two other gentlemen applied for the same land plus an additional 12 acres. After being notified by the BLM that the three claims should be condensed into one, B.G.R., Inc. complied, but no title was delivered. One major issue seemed to be the irregular shape of the land and the amount of shoreline it contained. Typical of government bureaucracy, if an item does not fit the exact description in the federal handbook, nothing happens while federal workers shuffle the papers until they're lost. From the "Background" section of the case file:

*Gayle W. Curtis, wife of pilot/guide Bob Curtis, subsequently purchased a controlling interest in B.G.R., Inc. The Application to Purchase the T & M Site filed February 8, 1965, was signed "Gayle W. Curtis, Pres. B.G.R."*

On July 25, 1966, the Chief of the Division of Engineering in the Washington D.C. Office wrote to the State Director in Alaska stating:

*Although the method for computing shore space for a claim of this shape is not covered in 43 C.F.R. 2024, it is our opinion that the shore space allowed this claimant exceeds the maximum allowance of 20 chains for a T & M Site.*

Correspondence between the attorney for the applicant, the BLM Washington Office, and the BLM State Office followed regarding the shore space problem. No solutions or recommendations were made. Continuing from the case file:

*B.G.R., Inc. filed a second Application to Purchase and Petition for Survey on February 27, 1967, signed "Gayle W. Curtis, President and sole stockholder." An October 27, 1966, letter from D. A. Burr, Attorney, confirms the fact that Mrs. Curtis was the sole stockholder in B.G.R. and mentions the 1966 construction of two new cabins on different locations within the T & M Site. Also mentioned was the intent to build a substantial lodge on the site. (The previous Application to Purchase filed February 8, 1965 was not rejected by the land office. Nothing in the case file tells what disposition was made of that application.)*

Despite prudent filings, no action occurred, yet the government sent three separate groups to the site to see the commercial activity. You would think that to see first-hand the commercial activity of a fishing lodge, the examiners would go there during the season. Not our government. They took the time, spent the money three separate times, and never did see the lodge in operation. No wonder Bob and Gayle were getting upset. Referring again to the case file:

*Three previous field examinations had been made by other BLM Land Examiners in 1965, in 1966 and in 1969. No commercial use of the land was actually observed during those examinations. The dates of examination did not coincide with the sportfishing season when the site could be expected to be occupied and in use.*

In an effort to stir the pot, Bob asked several clients to write the Government in support of his case for land title. In addition to those letters, Bob Curtis submitted his own statement to the BLM. It is obvious that by the time Bob crafted his formal statement, he was frustrated by the entire process.

*It has been my intention to improve these cabins so that they can be used with a greater degree of comfort; also it has been my plan to add other cabins on that part of the peninsula on a cabin rental basis for residents of Alaska who cannot afford our normal deluxe services. These residents of Alaska would be able to come in, furnish their own food, do their own cooking, and not have to go broke in the process for a fishing trip.*

*The main reason, in fact the only reason, this has not been done is that the Secretary of the Department of the Interior, who is the head of BLM in fact, if not in name, saw fit to put on a land freeze, which naturally would make any development of any property without complete title a seemingly chancy thing. I have had available at various times, loans from banks and individuals, where I easily could have made more permanent type dwellings on the north end of the peninsula. Had it not been for the interruption of normal handling of lands under the Homestead Act by the land freeze, all of this would not be the problem that it is now.*

In response to Bob's statement and the letters submitted on his behalf, the final examiner to handle the case flew to the site during the season and actually spoke with Bob and Gayle on August 3, 1971. The Bureau of Land Management office settled the claim in March of 1972. In determining the outcome, the examining officer, Jon A. Johnson, included these statements with his recommendation for approval:

*The applicant's argument is valid in part. BLM's inaction on the shore space question has kept the claim clouded with uncertainties regarding what portion of the claim could or would be approved.*

*Special instructions for surveying the subject T & M Site were prepared describing a dogleg survey line across the base of the peninsula as the applicant's original description specified. The survey instead ran a straight survey across the base of the peninsula. The intent of the "dog-leg" was to enable computation and assessment of shore space by the method prescribed in the CFR. Obviously, the specified method of shore space computation in the CFR is inappropriate for the subject land.*

*Continuing use and construction of additional improvements after Application to Purchase demonstrates the applicant's good faith. The high quality of the major improvements on the site represents a substantial investment by the applicant.*

*Additional administrative and resurvey costs would be incurred by the Government by approval of only a portion of the claim. Considerable time, effort, and money has already been expended in investigating and processing this case. I do not believe the accumulated information from investigation will support a successful Government contest to reduce the acreage of the claim. I recommend the application for the entire claim be approved.*

## Did Someone Say Dams?

One of the most fascinating, yet least known aspects of Bristol Bay discovered during my research was the possibility of the construction of hydroelectric power-generating plants (dams) on some of the most famous rainbow trout lakes and rivers. Interspersed with the literature and complex issues in the land debate, the possibility of dams loomed in the minds of some officials. During the early 1960s, the Bureau of Reclamation identified several potential sites. Included in their list was Grosvenor Lake dam with a potential 8,700 kilowatts; the American Creek dam expected to generate 14,300 kilowatts; and my favorite, the Nonvianuk Lake dam with an anticipated capacity of 27,000 kilowatts.

These famed lakes and rivers weren't the only places considered and charted for development. In what had to be a colossal proposal, the Federal Power Commission and the Alaska Power Administration stated in 1972 that the best location in Bristol Bay for a dam was the Naknek River, about six miles below the lake. On the positive side, the Commission argued that it could provide ample power to King Salmon and Naknek with a projected 108,000 kilowatts.

As far as the Government was concerned, the possibility of the dam seemed good. The NPS was not considering Naknek Lake for wilderness designation, and the dam site was outside the monument boundaries. Fortunately, someone considered the down side of the plan. Someone estimated that the level of Naknek Lake would climb to more than 116 feet, going up so far that it would flow into Brooks Lake, Grosvenor Lake, and Coville Lake. The resulting reservoir would eliminate forever the majority of salmon spawning water in the monument and eradicate the salmon runs in the Naknek River. It became obvious to the NPS that raising the lake to that level would cover all the visitor facilities already established.

It didn't take too long for the various power authorities to realize that they had major problems with each of the projected dam sites. By 1973, the Alaska Power Administration finally backed away from the Naknek project based on the adverse effects it would create. The Federal Power Commission agreed and abandoned their proposed dam site on Kukaklek Lake, then the Alaska Power Administration dropped the proposed Kulik Lake dam site. Fortunately, nothing came of the dam site selected in 1968 on the Alagnak River just below the confluence with the Nonvianuk River. What a colossal waste of time and money. Frank Norris, in *Isolated Paradise,* narrates the switch from potential dam sites to possible Wild and Scenic River designations for American Creek and the Alagnak River.

*The Federal Power Commission, in its 1975 survey, had identified Kukaklek Lake as a hydropower site. The Kukaklek project, which at the time was being considered part of the proposed Iliamna National Resources Range, was considered one of eleven "active potential sites" in the state that would be eliminated if the various park proposals were enacted. In addition, the Alaska Power Administration considered a Kulik Lake hydroelectric site.*

*Closely tied to questions of power development were those of the eligibility of certain streams to nomination in the federal wild and scenic rivers system. In 1968, Congress had passed the National Wild and Scenic Rivers Act and had designated the Bureau of Outdoor Recreation (BOR), in the Interior Department, to conduct the inventory and evaluation process for rivers throughout the country.*

*When the BOR made its initial Alaska survey, it tabbed two streams in the Katmai area–American Creek and the Alagnak River–as having Wild and Scenic River potential. All or a portion of both streams was situated in the area being considered as expansions to the existing monument. The entire length of the American Creek was considered; for the Alagnak River, the whole 64-mile length of the main stem was considered, along with the 11-mile Nonvianuk River, which originated in Nonvianuk Lake.*

*To gain additional data on the rivers, and to investigate their eligibility as laid out in the National Wild and Scenic Rivers Act, the BOR made an aerial reconnaissance of the area on October 3, 1972. The following spring, an interagency field team conducted the onsite inspections of both watercourses. Based on the data it had gathered, the BOR concluded that American Creek and the Alagnak River met the criteria for inclusion in the Wild and Scenic Rivers System. Both flowed through sufficiently primitive environments that they qualified as "wild" rivers within the system.*

The confusing and controversial lands issue added some new wrinkles for future lodge developers. At the very least, the uncertainty of land status and ownership created lengthy delays and interesting, if not stifling, obstacles to overcome. Some lodge builders had no choice but to obtain land that wasn't necessarily the best location for a fishing lodge, but was available at the time. Indeed, some lodges have limited, if any, home water.

Three new fishing lodges opened in Bristol Bay during the 1971 fishing season. Located near King Salmon, the Last Frontier Lodge faced almost insurmountable land problems and endured a lengthy court battle to get claim to the property before any building commenced. The other two, Bill Sims's Newhalen Lodge and Bob Walker's Copper River Lodge, had no land problems to overcome.

## The Last Frontier Lodge
## Dean and Dianne Paddock

Opening for the 1971 season, the Last Frontier Lodge was also the first Bristol Bay Lodge with road access to and from a major commercial airport. Located along the northern bank of the Naknek River below the outflow of Naknek Lake, the lodge could also be accessed by floatplane and by boat. Starting slowly at first, owner-operators Dean and Dianne Paddock proved to many that a sportfishing guide business didn't have to be completely remote to succeed. Although the Last Frontier Lodge did not meet my own strict definition of a fishing lodge, I believe that road access from King Salmon in the early 1970s was remote enough to qualify for inclusion in this book.

To get the ball rolling on their lodge project, Dianne Paddock filed a claim for a 4.95-acre site on January 4, 1968. Shortly thereafter, the Paddocks had their first load of lumber delivered to the building site. For reasons that will forever remain unclear, the Paddocks didn't start construction right away. Perhaps they were wary of building without title. Unfortunately for the Paddocks and their claim, a quick swipe of President Lyndon Johnson's pen on January 20, 1969, added 94,500 acres to Katmai National Monument. The Last Frontier Lodge site was immediately included in the Monument.

The Paddocks had to prove to the courts that they had improved their property before the day that President Johnson increased the size of the Monument. Receipts from their lumber purchase and the delivery manifests from their lumber order provided the proof. It is important to note that if the Paddocks had not been able to prove that they made improvements, the Federal Government would have assumed immediate control of the property. More than a year after their successful court battle ended, the Paddocks erected their first cabin. The lodge opened for the 1971 fishing season.

The Last Frontier Lodge served as the headquarters for clients fishing on the Naknek River and several out-camps. Among other places, the Paddocks operated remote camps on the Alagnak River and at the Ugashik Narrows. Their fishing business grew steadily and so did the Last Frontier Lodge. By the time Mrs. Paddock finally received the land patent in 1974, the lodge could easily accommodate six guests. Shortly after the 1974 fishing season ended, the Last Frontier Lodge closed and the Paddocks ceased all further lodge operations.

## Newhalen Lodge
## Bill Sims

Although Bill Sims didn't host his first fishing clients at Newhalen Lodge until 1971, he started flying and guiding hunting clients in 1959. As an 18-year-old, Bill had considerable outdoor work experience. While still attending high school in Seward, he worked summers commercial fishing with Denny Thompson. Fishing was good that year, too. Before his senior year, Bill earned enough to buy his first airplane, a 90-horsepower J-3 Cub on floats with skis. He owned an airplane before he owned a car. Denny Thompson, Bill's mentor and friend, took time from his professional hunting and commercial fishing duties to provide Bill's initial flight instruction. Bill practiced his lessons and flew whenever time permitted. He told me that he had more than one hundred hours of solo flight time before he even had a student flight certificate. To get one, he flew his airplane to Anchorage, landed at Merrill Field, parked his airplane in front of Wilbur's Flight School, and told the instructors that he needed a student license.

On his first professional hunt during the spring bear season of 1959, Bill flew a Super Cub and accompanied Denny Thompson down the Alaska Peninsula to the Sandy River, near Port Moller, where they hosted numerous clients. Although he admits he wasn't too interested in fishing, his attitude started to change:

*From our camp on the Sandy, I could see all these big fish in the river. I found an old rod and started fishing. I quickly learned that those big fish were steelhead. Although we never did weigh any of them, we caught some that were well in the 20-pound class. During the fall hunts, we caught the hell out of silvers, too.*

For the next few years, Denny Thompson continued to take his hunters to the Lower Peninsula. Bill flew, guided, and fished whenever possible. By 1960, Denny added late-season moose hunting to his schedule and moved those hunts farther north. Based out of Naknek, they hunted in the American Creek Valley and in the foothills adjacent to Nonvianuk and Kukaklek lakes. Bill told me that some of the hunters were able to sleep at Ed Seiler's Sky-Tel because there were no "same-day airborne" regulations in those days. By 1964, they had two camps at the head of Kulik Lake, about 18 miles from Ray Petersen's Kulik Lodge. They also established hunting camps adjacent to the Alagnak River. Denny Thompson was a popular and well-known hunting guide, and Bill Sims became an integral part of his business.

A telephone call during the winter of 1970 started the evolution of a fishing lodge. Bill told me the story:

*Red Murray, one of the vice presidents of First National Bank, called one night and said that he had a building that he had financed at Nondalton, near Lake Clark. He'd given the guy an extra year to see if he could make a go of it but hadn't seen any payments. He said he had to repossess the place. Then he said that he knew we hunted down there and wondered if we'd be interested in taking over the building for our hunting business. I believe the call came on Monday, and they were going to take it back the following Monday. We flew down there on Wednesday to take a look. Once there, we found out that the owner was from Cordova. His name was Thompson, too, but no relation to Denny. He built the place to be a store. He lived in a small area on one side and had a huge open area where he had his merchandise on the other. He already had the title to the property, so we didn't expect any land problems at all. The place looked good, except there was some water damage about eight inches up the walls. When he built the building, he didn't build it high enough. I guess he didn't think the lake would go that high.*

*At first, we decided the guy wanted too much money. We went back to Anchorage. After thinking about it a little, we offered to take over the payments and give the guy $5,000 for his trouble. I guess he realized he was going to lose it anyway, because he called a couple of days later and agreed to our offer. We bought the place early in the spring of 1970. I went out there before our hunters arrived and jacked up the whole building. I raised it a full 24 inches, put in walls, and made six client bedrooms in the area where the previous owner had his store. Denny and I used the building for our hunters during the spring and fall hunts. Once the state assigned exclusive areas, we used it even more because one of our areas was near Nonvianuk Lake and we had one up the Mulchatna River. Nondalton was a convenient location for us.*

*Once we had the lodge, I'd stay down there all summer. In 1971, I started to take out fishermen between hunting seasons. Denny wasn't interested in the sportfishing end of the business. At that time, I had a Super Cub and a PA-14 on floats. I only took two or three clients at a time because I was doing it myself. During those first few years, I had fishermen for about six to eight weeks. Later, I bought a C-185 and started to take more fishermen.*

In 1978, Bill bought Denny's share of the business, quit hunting professionally, and made fishing his only business.

## Copper River Lodge
## Bob and Doris Walker

By all accounts, 1969 was a great year for Bob and Doris Walker. In late May, they sold their Iliamna Lodge to local hunting guide Dick Sjoden. For the first time in more than 15 years, they had no responsibilities to keep them in Alaska. Doris told me that they really thought they were out of the lodging business for good. Consequently, they were more than happy to sign a three-year no-compete clause in the sales contract. After the sale, they left Alaska and vacationed outside. Although they had a great time and visited many friends and former guests, they both missed Alaska. Not only did the Walkers miss the lodge life, their guests missed them too. It didn't take the Walkers too long to decide to go back to Bristol Bay.

Doris and Bob's return to the Iliamna area wasn't nearly as hard on them as their first move nearly 23 years earlier. They had a place to go to. During the years at Iliamna Lodge, Bob had taken the time to build a cabin adjacent to the Copper River. Although it lacked some of the custom features of their last lodge, Bob's fishing lodge started to take shape.

Trying to honor their agreement with Dick Sjoden, Bob and Doris waited patiently for the 1972 season. Unfortunately, they were bombarded with requests from previous guests to take them fishing late in the season of 1971. Despite the fact that they used the majority of that season to improve the facilities and to publicize their future official opening, several clients arrived to fish with Bob and Doris. The Walkers' long wait to own a fishing lodge was finally over. Even though they did have some fishing clients at their Iliamna Lake Lodge, it was not a full-time fishing business. Eighteen years after Bob first guided fishermen on the Copper River, he hosted his first guests at his own fishing lodge.

### Bob Cusack and His "Barge on the Branch"

*Bob Cusack's barge moored on the Alagnak River. Circa 1973—Bob Cusack Photo*

Arriving in Naknek in 1970, Bob Cusack started hunting and fishing at every opportunity. Realizing that an airplane would dramatically improve his sporting capabilities, Bob found and bought a Super Cub. Then he asked King Salmon charter pilot and guide, Eddie King, to teach him to fly. Bob was excited when he met his instructor to start his flying career. His first lesson, however, nearly ended his life.

*I'd arranged to meet Eddie King after school one day to get in my first flight. When I got to the airport, he told me that his plans had changed. We'd use his airplane on my first lesson because he had to go on a short charter flight. He told me he'd show me a little about airplanes as the Cherokee he was flying and my airplane had similar systems. He gave me some basic instruction, then started the engine, taxied out, and took off.*

*We climbed to about 200 feet. All of a sudden, the damn engine quit. Eddie turned to land on the road but Hermie Herrmanns' car was in the way and he didn't see that we were in trouble. Eddie turned again to try to get to the riverbank. Unfortunately, there were some power lines in the way. We damn near stalled going over the wires. We were running out of speed in a hurry. Eddie pushed the nose down to try to get some speed. Nothing happened. The airplane dropped out of the sky and smashed down on a fence. Once the dust settled and we realized we weren't dead, we climbed out. We were lucky. The fence cut through the fuselage just behind the two front seats. The rifle Eddie carried in the back was cut right in half. It didn't take us long to get to the bar after that quick lesson on emergency procedures and short field landings. I'm sure we drank about a fifth of whiskey each and we weren't loaded. I never forgot that first flying lesson. Fortunately, that's the most excitement I ever had in an airplane.*

As you might expect, Bob Cusack continued his flying lessons. In fact, he told me he had a real flying lesson once his eyes cleared the following day. He also told me that the aftermath of the wreck was worse than the actual crash as far as some people were concerned.

*The worst part of the wreck was that old man Tibbetts was pissed off at Eddie because he didn't move the wrecked airplane and repair the damage right away. He left it where it dropped for more than a week, and we heard about it every day. The airplane was right in front of George Tibbett's house; it was the only thing he saw when he looked out his living room window. He was also annoyed because it was right on the edge of the Peninsula Airway's strip and George was a Pennair man.*

A curious set of circumstances enabled Bob to start a floating lodge operation on the Alagnak (Branch) River during the 1972 fishing season. Late in the fall of 1970, a major storm hit Bristol Bay. Many boats broke loose from their moorings and anchor lines. One of those was an old Tally-scow owned and operated by Alaska Packers. Crew-less and completely at the mercy of the wind and waves, it didn't take too long for the big barge to go under.

*The way it was in the mid-1970s. From the left: Geneva Meek, Bob Cusack with the king salmon, Tanina Meek and Lula Cusack at the barge. Circa 1973—Bob Cusack Photo*

A few days later, two local Native commercial fishermen spotted the barge during an extremely low tide. It had settled into the mud not too far from Naknek. Seeing no one else hurrying to rescue the boat, the Native fishermen decided to both salvage and claim the barge. They returned on the next tide with a vast array of equipment. Within two hours, they had the barge pumped dry and floating with the incoming tide. Believing the barge would draw a tidy sum, the tired twosome towed the barge back to Naknek where they proudly displayed their "new" vessel and proclaimed ownership from "salvage rights." Needless to say, the new owners and the original owners did not evaluate the "salvage claim" from the same perspective. According to Bob Cusack, the State Troopers had to get involved to stop the gunfight that nearly broke out during the ownership squabble.

*Rather than let the barge sink again while the court action continued, Jack Meyers and I pulled the barge out of the water at the Diamond O Cannery at South Naknek. We blocked it with several other big boats and waited. The court didn't accept the salvage claims and returned the barge to Alaska Packers. Not too long after the court case I spoke with Norm Rockness about the barge. He was the superintendent of the Alaska Packers plant in Naknek. Norm said he wasn't interested in doing the repairs, so I bought it for $4,000. The barge had four bedrooms and a nice kitchen. The bottom floor was ship style, but I built the upper deck. The Nakeen cannery was falling apart and the owners said that for five hundred dollars I could have all the wood I wanted. So Jim Rettig (my nephew) and I flew to the cannery and landed in that little tiny pond. We cut lumber all night. I hauled fourteen 13-foot floor joists per load and flew all day hauling the wood back to Naknek. That much flying sure helps a student pilot. Anyway, over the next few months, I fixed up the barge and then painted the whole thing. To get the barge up the Alagnak River, we tied a commercial fishing boat alongside and literally pushed it through Kvichak Bay and into the Alagnak. That worked a lot better than my first try at taking it back to Naknek after the season was over. Instead of waiting a couple of days for a commercial boat to come up the river to get the barge, I took all the outboards off my skiffs and attached them to the barge. I had eight 35-horsepower Johnson outboards strung across the back of the barge. It took four of us to work the motors. My sister-in-law yelled directions to us from the top deck. What a nightmare. Our directional control wasn't too good. We were lucky to make it down the river at all. I never did that again.*

Although not consistent with my own lodge definition, Bob Cusack started the first "mobile" lodge in Bristol Bay and gets the lion's share of credit for pioneering the great king salmon fishing in the Alagnak River. Longtime Bristol Bay hunting guide and the owner of Newhalen Lodge, Bill Sims, told me that he, too, fished the Branch for king salmon in the late 1960s and early 1970s. He told me that he met Bob Cusack when Bob was still teaching in Naknek. According to Bill, he watched Bob remodel his floating lodge and made suggestions to him about suitable mooring locations in the Alagnak. He also told me that Ray Loesche, another hunting guide who hosted fishermen between hunts, fished the Alagnak for king salmon.

I asked Bob to explain how he found the kings.

*Even though kings appeared in commercial nets, few people wanted to sport fish for the big salmon. As you might expect, we started fishing the Alagnak for rainbows. I fished there when I lived in Naknek in 1970 and 1971. I learned to land my Cub in the shallow river water. I fished the whole river. I never saw anyone on the river in those days. That's why I put the barge up the Alagnak, there wasn't any competition. Anyway, we fished the river fairly high up. One day we were fishing lower down the river than we did normally. We caught one king, then another and another. We gradually worked our way down the river. After that day, we targeted kings. I took a doctor from Port Heiden up there. He wanted to fish for rainbows. I showed him our kings and he went wild. I remember he said, "Jesus Christ, Bob, you've got a gold mine here!"*

*Later, I saw the big salmon from the air. Once I knew they were there, I learned how to catch them. I really tried to keep those kings a secret. I told all the clients to keep it quiet, too. It was amazing. I hired my nephew, Jim Rettig, to help guide. I told him to keep quiet, too. I lied to Eddie King. I thought he'd spot them in the lower river but he never did. We had many clients book more than one hundred fish a day. We cast bait, spoons, and flies. Everything worked. It was my private fishery for several years.*

*I think the first clients on the river, other than mine, were Dean Paddock's. They did a few float trips. By 1974, the word started to spread. Once in a while, I saw Glen VanValen land on the lower river. I knew Kulik fished it occasionally. Bill Sims and Ray Loesche also landed there once in a while, but I lived on the river and fished it every day.*

Van Hartley worked as a fishing guide at Kulik during the 1973 lodge season. He told me that numerous times that year he was flown to the Branch River with several guests and an inflatable raft to fish for kings. Van told me that other than Bob Cusack, he never saw another fisherman on the Alagnak. He also mentioned that Ray Loesche kept a few canoes and a boat not too far from Agnes Estrada's cabin. Bob Cusack told me that one morning he was sitting on the deck of his barge having a cup of coffee with some clients when he noticed a huge plume of smoke coming from the direction of Agnes Estrada's cabin. Quickly, Bob scurried to his Cessna 185. After a quick pre-flight, he departed northbound to find the source of the smoke. Bob explained what he found:

*When I found the source of the smoke, I realized the tundra and low bushes surrounding Ray Loesche's boats were smoldering. In the charred area, I spotted someone curled up by the river. I landed below Ray's boats and taxied onto the smoke-filled beach. As soon as I got out of the airplane, I could tell the guy on the beach was one of Ray's guides. His clothes, arms, and face were charred and he had severe burns on his legs and stomach. He was going into shock but told me how he tried to start a campfire the previous night. He was alone and couldn't find any dry wood to burn. He tried to boost the fire with gasoline from his outboard fuel tank. Naturally, in the process he spilled gas on his clothes and on his camp. He was in a bad way when first the fuel can ignited and then his clothes lit up. He spent the night soaking his burns in the cold river water. He was lucky I came along when I did. I put the guy in my airplane and flew him to the air force base at King Salmon.*

*Later, I saw Ray Loesche in King Salmon and inquired about the guide's health. Ray promptly told me he didn't know how his former guide was doing. He told me he'd fired the guy as soon as he learned what had happened. The guy was damn dumb and deserved to lose his job as a guide.*

According to Bob, the area kept smoldering. Some smokejumpers were flown in to extinguish the fire more than a week after the incident. Evidently, they extended their stay so they could smoke some kings, too.

## Bristol Bay Lodge
## John and Maggie Garry

I believe there must be something about building lodges that affects the minds of rational men, because after helping Bob Curtis erect the main lodge building at Tikchik Narrows Lodge, John Garry started thinking about having his own lodge.

Arriving in Alaska in 1967, John went to work for Bob Curtis. At the close of the season, he returned to Vermont with the determination to build and operate his own fishing lodge. In 1969, he and his wife, Maggie, both worked at Tikchik Narrows Lodge. Maggie told me she worked there to decide for herself if she really wanted to spend her life in the lodge business. I guess she found the life appealing. A few years after working at Tikchik Narrows, John and Maggie not only bought some property and a cabin from George and Elsie Chamrad, they turned their purchase into one of the best-known lodges in Bristol Bay.

After the lodge season of 1969 ended, John and Maggie returned to Anchorage. After months of waiting, the possibility of employment loomed in Dillingham, and the young couple moved back to Bristol Bay. A short time later they met George and Elsie Chamrad. Near retirement, the Chamrads listened to the new Dillingham residents discuss their future lodge plans and aspirations. George explained that they had some property with a nice cabin they had used for personal recreation. Not knowing much about the needs of the lodge business, the Chamrads assumed that their property might be the perfect location to meet the dreams of the younger couple. They offered the land and cabin for sale, but they informed

*The original cabin at the site of Bristol Bay Lodge. Lefty Kreh Photo*

John and Maggie that they had no title to the property. They applied for title when they obtained the cabin from the original builder, Keith Caldwell, but still had nothing to show for their efforts.

To help the aging Chamrads and to get started on their own dream, John and Maggie agreed to make the purchase, but they had to agree to two separate prices. The first price was for just the cabin without the property. The second price was based on the hope that the title would soon clear.

Three weeks before George and Elsie Chamrad were due to leave Dillingham, they received the title to their land. John and Maggie were more than happy to have the title, too. Immediately they started planning for their lodge. They hosted their first clients at Bristol Bay lodge in 1972. When I asked how they arrived at the name, Bristol Bay Lodge, Maggie told me that it was an easy and straightforward decision:

> *Bob Curtis had already used the names of the two big lakes nearby at his Tikchik Narrows Lodge and Wood River Lodge. We knew that few people could spell or pronounce Agulowak or Aleknagik, so we decided that "Bristol Bay Lodge" would be just fine.*

John and Maggie Garry operated Bristol Bay Lodge until 1978, when a divorce ended their relationship. Maggie remained at the lodge and has continued to operate it with her husband, Ron McMillan.

## Rainbow King Lodge
## Ray Loesche

Despite the rumors and threats posed by the land issues, business continued in Alaska. By the late 1960s, Ray Loesche was the dominant hunting guide in Alaska. However, by the early 1970s, he faced monumental challenges to his business life due to the impending land claim issues.

Like many other young men of the time, Ray Loesche came to Alaska as a member of the armed forces during the last great war, World War II. Ray was sent to Dutch Harbor in 1941. Among others, Ray met and befriended Bud Branham during his military career. After the war ended, Ray started flying. He began his guiding career in 1951. During his initial guiding seasons, he based his hunts out of Alf Madsen's camp on the lower Peninsula. A few years later he built his own camp at Ugashik Lake.

I asked Ray to relate the events that prompted him to get into the fishing lodge business and why he choose Iliamna as his building site.

> *Hunting had been good for me. Maybe Denny Thompson had more hunters, but I think I did. Anyway, the way things were going in the land claims, it looked like I could be forced out of the business. I was nervous about the Native claims. I must have tried 10 or 12 Anchorage attorneys to help me with a lawsuit. The act made it clear that in order to claim the land, the Natives had to have lived on it. I knew damn good and well that many of the claims were bogus. I couldn't find an attorney to help me because they felt like the Native business would be their key to the future. Nobody wanted to upset the money cart.*
>
> *About that same time, the Fish and Game agents were really trying to go after me. They'd heard stories about illegal hunting and concentrated on me. I knew it would be just a matter of time before they took my license. I needed something to do. I decided to build a fishing lodge and give up hunting. I chose Iliamna because I thought, and still*

*believe, it is the most central location in Bristol Bay. I made a deal with Iliamna resident Trig Olsen. Trig was a Native and I agreed to buy his claim as soon as it was available. I started to build the lodge on Trig's land in 1972. It wasn't too long after we had some of the lodge construction started that the Bureau of Indian Affairs got involved. They told Trig that it wasn't legal for me to have any buildings on his property and that the buildings I had there would have to be moved as soon as possible.*

*With the Bureau of Indian Affairs bureaucrats breathing over my shoulders, I had no choice but to find another place to put my lodge. Fortunately, I was able to buy some land that was adjacent to Trig's. I obtained that lot from Iliamna's storekeeper, Leonard McMillan. It wasn't as good a lot, but it was the only one I could get. It was on old barrel storage dump over a shallow, swampy lake. I first had to fill the low areas, then clean up, and remove the barrels. Once that was done, I tore down the half-finished lodge on Trig's place and rebuilt it on my own land.*

Once Ray filled me in on some of the details of his lodge, I asked about the lodge name, Rainbow King.

*Well, rainbows and king salmon were the most popular fish as far as my clients were concerned. So I put the names together and it sounded damn good to me.*

Ray completed the building of Rainbow King Lodge. Although he hosted many fishing guests in 1973, he also guided a few hunts. At the close of the guiding season of 1973, Ray Loesche decided to make Rainbow King Lodge a sportfishing operation and surrendered his professional hunting license to the state Fish and Game officials. In what I considered a political statement, Ray told me that he finally obtained Trig Olsen's property, too.

*The BIA lost a lot of money on that one. After they made me move the lodge off Trig's property, Trig built a restaurant. I'm not sure of all the details, but I do know he had a big mortgage and some other financial problems, too. I think the BIA held the papers. In any case, they came to him again and wanted him to get out of the restaurant business for one reason or another. Trig got mad, and as soon as he was able to, he sold me the property and buildings. I don't think he ever paid the BIA.*

Like several other fishing lodge operators of the future, Ken Fanning worked as a hunting guide for Ray Loesche in the early 1970s. He arrived in Alaska in 1967. He came north to work on a six-month fisheries management program in Wrangell. Like so many others before him, it didn't take too long for him to decide to stay. Ken moved to Fairbanks after his initial fisheries job. As he'd had previous guide experience in Colorado, Ken immediately started the five-year process to become a registered guide in Alaska.

Ken applied for a guide job with Ray Loesche. He spent more than two months living and guiding out of Ray's big base camp at Ugashik Lake. When I asked the former state legislator about his experience, he grimaced, and told me the whole story.

*Ray Loesche sent me down to Ugashik for a couple of weeks or at least that's what he told me. I ended up there for more than two and a half months. I took several rolls of film, but the damned weather was so bad that I could only take pictures on one afternoon. It rained like hell, the wind howled beyond belief. When it wasn't pouring down rain, the fog was so thick I couldn't see my feet, let alone see anything to photograph. The weather wasn't the only problem at Ugashik.*

*All the fish we caught had scratches and bite marks. When the wind calmed enough for the hunters to take a shot, the trophies we got were all banged up from fighting. It seemed like most of the hides were useless. No taxidermist could repair them. I learned real fast to hate that part of the world. The clients complained. The weather was horrible. The fish and animals had a heck of a time just surviving. Once that seemingly endless season came to an end and I made it back to civilization, I decided that Bristol Bay was just too tough a place for man and beast. I wanted to stay in the guide business and hoped to have a lodge of my own, but I knew I needed to find a softer place.*

Ken learned some great lessons early in his guiding career. He bought a boat and began guiding fishermen on the Gulkana River. While he fished for most species, king salmon soon became his specialty. Besides his own clients, Ken offered boat rides and fishing information to anyone who asked. Later, he realized his friendly ways were causing problems for his business:

*It seemed like every time I gave somebody a ride up the river, I'd regret it later. The next time I'd go to the river, I'd find the same guys in a cheap raft in my favorite holes. I quit being such a nice guy right away.*

Ken's Gulkana River business flourished. Along with his fishing clients, Ken hosted several television programs, including the now famous American Sportsman series hosted by Curt Gowdy. Then one day he floated down the river and discovered that the infamous Alaska Pipeline had been constructed right across his favorite fishing river.

*Although I don't think it had any effect on the fish, it had an effect on me. I told myself that would be the last time I'd float under the pipeline. I'd already had a horrible experience in Bristol Bay. I decided to head a little south and try Yakutat for a while.*

*It didn't take Ken long to establish himself in the guiding business at Yakutat Lodge, where he and his wife hosted clients starting in 1984. I would also like to point out that Ken Fanning served in the Twelfth Alaska State legislature as a member of the House of Representatives from the Fairbanks area from January 1977 through the close of the session in June, 1982. Duty called again during the Fifteenth Alaska State Legislature. After Senator Don Bennett suddenly passed away, then Governor Steve Cowper appointed Ken to fill the vacancy. Senator Fanning retired from political life at the close of the 1988 session.*

## Todd's Igiugig Lodge
## Larry Todd

In 1973, Larry Todd and his wife Elizabeth purchased their first business license to operate a fishing lodge in Bristol Bay. According to Larry, a chance conversation in an Anchorage bar led him into the lodge business.

*My brother-in-law met a guy in a bar in Anchorage one night. After a few drinks, he learned that the guy's name was Brown, and he had a lodge on the Kvichak River that he wanted to sell. He learned that Mr. Brown had done some midnight requisitioning from the derelict canneries and had a good start on a lodge building, but for one reason or another he didn't want to continue. My brother-in-law called me because he thought I might be interested. He knew I had an airplane, a Piper Pacer, and I wanted to get into a business where I could use the plane. A few days after his call, the two of us flew to Igiugig to look the place over.*

*Although what he called a lodge certainly wasn't, I decided to buy Mr. Brown's T&M Site which was five acres. He already had the title so I didn't have any land problems with the government. My wife and I bought building materials, had them flown to Iliamna, and then barged to Igiugig. We worked that entire season building a new lodge. We hosted our first guests in 1974. We started our operation with a maximum of four guests per week.*

## Sonny Petersen Starts Katmai Air

Even with all the various Congressional debates and local land use arguments, I'm pleased to tell you that sportfishing, lodge development, and the flying business did not stop, nor did it falter during the mid-1970s. Leading the charge into the flying business was Sonny Petersen.

Ray Petersen, Sonny's father, displayed uncanny wisdom in all the decisions he made for his airlines and his lodges. Mainline revenues were up and the company's Grumman Mallards were lodge effective. Ray slowly but steadily reduced his small airplane fleet, terminating with the sale of the last single-engine airplane at the close of the 1973 lodge season. Realizing a need, Sonny borrowed $9,000 to buy a Northern Consolidated Cessna 180, N4992A, on floats. During the winter months, he applied for and was granted approval from the Federal Aviation Administration to receive and operate an Air-Taxi certificate.

Although he had only 350 hours of flying time, Sonny was ready for business by the start of the 1974 lodge season. At the time Sonny started Katmai Air, he had the only float-equipped aircraft available for charter in King Salmon. Even though his total time was low, his flying skills were ready for the challenge. After all, Sonny grew up in an airline family and around great pilots such as his father, John Walatka, Hugh Hartley, and their Anchorage next-door neighbor Bob Reeve. Because he had extensive boating experience in the area, Sonny knew the rivers and currents necessary for successful floatplane operation. After the close of the 1974 season, Sonny knew he needed a bigger airplane. He borrowed $40,000 and purchased an almost new C-206 on floats. When Sonny started Katmai Air, he had the only float-equipped aircraft available for charter in King Salmon. His airplane, N9644G, was the first Cessna 206 used in the fishing lodge business in Bristol Bay.

Hugh Hartley assumed the Kulik managerial duties in 1974 after Mildred Walatka chose not to return. Hugh was eager to have Sonny involved at the lodge. Young Mr. Petersen grew up at the lodges and it seemed natural for him to follow his father into the flying business. After guiding fishermen at the lodges, he had plenty of experience. With Hugh's help, Sonny was soon "booked" with Kulik clients demanding his skill as a pilot and guide.

While reviewing the Angler's Paradise records from 1974, I discovered that world-famous angler Lee Wulff had taken Kulik's largest rainbow of the season. Like most of the Kulik guests that year, Lee Wulff and guide Ed Prestage flew to their fishing destination with Sonny. When he arrived at the Battle River to pick them up later that afternoon, Sonny learned about the big fish. Sonny told me that Lee caught the huge rainbow on a fly that he created the evening before, the Kulik Killer. Lee's record rainbow topped the scales at just a little over 13 pounds.

Sonny did all the support flying for the Angler's Paradise Camps. He also handled all of the fly-out trips at Kulik Lodge. Sonny Petersen and Katmai Air were there to stay.

## Royal Coachman Lodge
## Bill Martin

Bill Martin arrived in Kodiak on April 27, 1964, one month after the famous Good Friday earthquake. Bill Rosenbaum, a friend from his home state of Oregon, had worked for the Commercial Fish Division of the Alaska Department of Fish and Game the previous year. He persuaded Bill to travel to Alaska and work where he did, at the Chignik weir, for supervisor Jack Lechner. As he tells it, Bill bought a "milk run" ticket on Pacific Northern Airlines and suffered through several stops before arriving in Anchorage. From Anchorage, he again boarded a PNA flight to Kodiak.

Not long after arriving in the coastal town, Bill started exploring and immediately discovered the extensive damage caused by the big shaker. While examining the harbor damage, Bill met the local chief of police, who obviously was in need of help. After a short conversation, Bill revealed some of his own background. After the chief learned that Bill had some law enforcement experience in Oregon, he quickly offered him a job. Bill thanked him, but said he would need to meet Mr. Lechner before he could make any employment decisions.

Finding his way to one of the few bars that survived the quake, Bill settled in to wait for word about the Chignik weir. Engaging in small talk with another bar patron, Bill mentioned Chignik. To his surprise, the man on the adjacent bar stool turned out to be the superintendent of the big salmon cannery at Sand Point, some five hundred miles down the Alaska Peninsula. Again, after finding some mechanical experience in Bill's background, the cannery manager offered young Martin a maintenance job at his cannery. After a few more drinks, Bill thanked the man for his offer but told him he needed to find Jack Lechner before making any decisions. Bill retired to his small hotel.

Early the next morning, Bill made his way to the offices of the Alaska Department of Fish and Game. Trying to find the Com-Fish offices, he inadvertently met O. R. (Mac) McKinley. Bill entered Mac's office where he outlined his work history. Like the police chief had done earlier, once Mac found some law enforcement in his background, he immediately led the discussion away from Com-Fish. According to Bill, Mac McKinley made it very clear that he was a law enforcement man and liked that in Bill.

*You don't want to work for that damned Com-fish Division; you should work for Protection!*

After more discussion, Bill was intrigued. He had been in Kodiak less than 24 hours and had already been offered three jobs, yet hadn't found the man for whom he'd come to work. For two more days Bill waited patiently expecting Jack Lechner to arrive and outline his job at the Chignik weir. Bill's routine was the same both days. He waited at the hotel until late morning, then headed to the Alaska Department of Fish and Game to chat with Mac McKinley. By the end of the second day,

Mac became more insistent that Bill accept employment with the Protection division. With Bill sitting in his office, Mac called Anchorage and spoke with the senior Protection Officer, Bill Roberts. After a seemingly quiet conversation, Bill squirmed when Mac raised the volume of his voice and told his listener that he had a young man sitting in his office that should be hired by Protection. Seconds later, Mac handed Bill the telephone. He listened to Don Roberts:

*If Mac McKinley said you should work for us, that's good enough for me. Get a ticket and meet me in Homer as soon as you can!*

As he had done three times already, Bill said he couldn't commit until he met Jack Lechner. Again, he waited, only this time he grew impatient. Finding no one in the Com-Fish offices who could give him any information about the Chignik project nor Jack Lechner, Bill returned to see Mac McKinley. He agreed to fly to Homer to meet Don Roberts. He checked out of the hotel, went back to the airport, bought a ticket, and boarded a flight to Homer. Bill found that Don Roberts was not nearly as hard to find as Jack Lechner had been. He met with Officer Roberts and readily accepted seasonal employment with the Alaska Department of Fish and Game Protection Division. His first job was on the "MV Teal."

At the close of Bill's first summer season in Alaska, Don Roberts called and told him that he wanted to offer full-time employment but budget constraints would restrict the offer until the following spring. Bill told Don Roberts that the offer sounded great.

*Rather than go back to Oregon, I spent my first winter in Alaska at Talkeetna operating a cat. I cleared an area that eventually became the main road into Talkeetna. Besides running the cat, I cut firewood at the job site. I made more money that winter than I ever had in my life. The next spring I went to work for the Protection Division permanently. I worked for them until tax day of 1972.*

Bill Martin was fortunate in that he was able (sometimes required) to travel the state and monitor fish and game populations. Bill started flying in 1965 thanks to the GI Bill. By 1967, he transferred into Anchorage where he completed his commercial ratings and started flying Protection aircraft in the line of duty. It didn't take him too long to discover the great fishing opportunities in the Bristol Bay region. On one of his frequent assignments to the Dillingham region, Carl Branham, a fellow Protection officer, took Bill to the Tikchik Lakes area to fish. Carl kept a boat stashed there for his off-duty time. That location offered some of the best fishing Bill had ever experienced. Every time duty took them to the region, Bill and Carl flew to the Tikchik location to fish. According to Bill:

*The fishing was fantastic. Rainbows in the 30-inch class! I fell in love with the place. Later, I found out that Jay Hammond owned the 5-acre site. Jay had acquired the property through the 1906 Homestead Act. I believe Jay was still a Dillingham-based Predator Control Officer for Fish and Wildlife when he invited a surveyor friend to go up there fishing. I'm sure he only surveyed when his arms hurt from fighting the fish.*

*I first met Jay Hammond in 1967 when I was working in King Salmon. Once I fished at his property, I told him that if he ever wanted to sell, I wanted to buy the place. At that time, I believe Jay was a member of the House of*

*Representatives. Then he went to the Senate. In an unusual turn of circumstances and some political redistricting, Jay found himself unable to run for the Senate from his home district. Late in 1968, Governor Hickel accepted an appointment as the Secretary of the Interior under President Nixon. He immediately appointed Jay Hammond to the Federal Land Use Commission. To make a long story short, I got a call from Jay Hammond. He told me that he was on the Commission and that having the land in the Tikchik region was a conflict of interest. He needed to sell it and asked if I was still interested. He told me he wanted $40,000. I told him that I wanted it so badly that I'd sell my Super Cub to raise the money. He told me not to sell my airplane. He offered me the property at 10 percent down with the remainder at 8 percent over ten years. I eagerly said I'd put a check in the mail. I bought the property during the winter of 1971-72.*

*Once I had the property secured, I discussed the possibilities of starting a lodge with my friend, Bill Duncan. He was a surveyor and gave me the impression he liked the idea. At that same time, however, I joined some other friends and tried to convince Jay Hammond to run for Governor. He did. I worked for his campaign, and he won the election. That's about the time I decided to retire from the Alaska Department of Fish and Game and start a lodge.*

*As soon as the dust settled from the 1974 election, Bill Duncan and I sat down and computed the cost of starting a lodge. He decided the stakes were too high and backed out. Another friend, an orthodontist from Anchorage, Kenny Mears, told me he had some extra money from two practices, one in Anchorage and one in Fairbanks. He went in with me on the lodge. He provided the necessary financial help and helped me with the construction, but was really a silent partner. I ran the lodge business and Kenny continued to run his dental business. I started Alaska Sportfishing Guides, Inc., and then we bought a 1,600-square-foot Pan-Abode cabin for the lodge. It weighed 37,308 pounds when it was unloaded from the barge to the dock, then delivered to the Dillingham airport. Once there, it sat in the rain with the clear plastic tarp flapping in the wind. Many people told me I'd never get it to the site, but Kodiak Western's Albert Ball helped me out when he flew 27 Grumman Goose loads to get the whole thing delivered. I think we were paying $250 per hour for that airplane in those days, and it was a little more than an hour round-trip.*

*We got the building materials up there, finished the foundation, got the floor done, walls up, and the roof on in 1973. Went back out there April 19, 1974, with a crew of five and immediately began the work to finish the job. We were racing the clock, as the first guests were supposed to arrive on June 10.*

*Expecting clients the next morning, we finished the final details such as wiring the generator and hanging the curtains before dinner. We were completely ready for business. An hour later, I received word via our radio that our clients, four guys from Little Rock, had missed some airline connections and wouldn't arrive until the 11th. We all collapsed and had a great, although unexpected, rest. That was the start of Royal Coachman Lodge.*

Bill credits his friend and early financial partner, Kenny Mears, for the name, Royal Coachman Lodge. Bill told me that

Kenny was an excellent fly tier and enthusiastic fisherman. He came up with the name early in the lodge construction. Bill stated,

> *The Royal Coachman is a classic fly pattern, and Kenny knew we'd develop our lodge into a classic.*

## Ole Creek Lodge
## Don Haugen and Ole Wassenkari

*Ole Wassenkari at his cabin. Circa 1972—Jack Holman Photo*

Don Haugen started commercial fishing in Bristol Bay in 1962. Not long after arriving, he met Ole Wassenkari. Ole had been around for many years and had fished for nearly all the canneries. He spent the winters trapping along the Kvichak River. Don told me that he and Ole had had more than one occasion to share a bottle of whiskey. I understand that Ole was no stranger to booze. Not only was he a good drinker, I'm told he put at least one of his daughters through school by selling potato whiskey. Slowly, Don and Ole became good friends. The great commercial fishing season of 1965 gave the two men another opportunity to toast their good luck. Don related that after the 1965 season he learned more about his new friend:

> *We had a record 27 million sockeyes through Igiugig. There were so many fish that the canneries closed early. We took our fishing boats up to Igiugig to watch the fish run into Iliamna Lake. That's when I learned that Ole had a 5-acre recreational site along the Kvichak, right across the river from the village of Igiugig. Ole had his house on Ole Creek, a couple miles down the river.*

Late in the 1960s, Don got the idea to start a fishing lodge. At the close of the commercial fishing season in 1970, Ole and Don got together and cracked a few more bottles of whiskey. Sometime during their discussions, Don asked Ole if he would lease him an acre of ground so that he might start a lodge. He explained that he wanted to build a cabin and that he wanted to keep it simple. Quite to Don's surprise, Ole told him that he, too, wanted to have a lodge but didn't know how to start. Don told me that he didn't know how to start either, but they plowed ahead anyway. The first step was the partnership.

Don and Ole established a value of $12,000 for Ole's five-acre parcel. Don agreed to purchase $12,000 in building materials. With that, Ole and Don became partners in the lodge business. Don promptly ordered the materials necessary to modify the cabin on Ole's property into a lodge. Red Clark had built the cabin for Ole in the late 1960s. Originally planned for Ole's daughter, the cabin was empty in 1970.

The materials were ordered from Seattle and were barged into Alaska and delivered to Bristol Bay. Don contracted Hermie Herrmanns to transport his building supplies from Naknek to the building site. Hermie's barge, the Fajen, was more than one 100 feet long and 35 feet wide. The Fajen was a World War II landing-craft barge. Don told me that if he had known the problems, he would have done something else.

*By the time the Fajen left Naknek with the building materials for Ole Creek Lodge, the former military barge was already worn out. Because it was a landing craft, the bottom had been abused on rocky beaches and was almost gone. Before we loaded the barge, Hermie strengthened some compartments and rigged special pumps in others. To keep it floating, he ran the compressors and pumps continuously. When he wanted to stop for the night, he'd ease into shallow water, then cut the power to the pumps. The barge would settle onto the bottom. When he wanted to move, he'd start the pumps and in an hour, the barge would be floating. It took us thirty days to navigate the Kvichak. We were stuck so many times, I didn't think we'd ever get up the river. Several times the pumps just quit. We were lucky that they never quit in deep water. More than once we had to off-load some of the lumber onto my 32 -foot commercial fishing boat because we were so stuck in the river. It took so long that we had to start shuttling building materials off the Fajen to the site. We were actually under construction with the barge miles away from the final destination.*

*We started having problems right after the Fajen left the dock in Naknek. It seemed like the barge simply fell apart. Everything went wrong. She had three engines but only two rudders. Somehow an anchor line got caught and twisted around the prop shaft. That was the end of that engine. Another engine blew up. Hermie was able to keep one engine running, but that one didn't have a rudder. Finally, we had to have two gillnet boats pushing, and Jackie Drew's barge pulling the barge up the river.*

Originally, Ole and Don planned to have the Fajen beached right in front of the property. As luck would have it, however, they could only get it as far as Red Clark's place, which was a few hundred yards down the river. Once the Fajen was unloaded, it settled further into the beach sand. Don told me that the barge had enough fuel to get back to Naknek.

*Ingdal Bertinussen's cabin along the Kvichak River. Circa 1971—Jack Holman Photo*

When Hermie Herrmanns suggested he could do one more trip to Naknek, everyone told him to stay put. That was the end of the Fajen. It remains adjacent to Red Clark's to this day.

From the time the original materials arrived in 1971, Don and Ole slowly developed the lodge. Each successive summer the lodge grew a little closer to being finished. Don and Ole hosted their first clients in 1974. During that first season, Ole would spend a few days at the lodge and a few days at his home on Ole Creek. Ole's interest waned and Don purchased Ole's half of the business in 1975. Although a few clients have chartered an airplane to take them on a fly-out, Ole Creek Lodge has always been a non-fly-out lodge.

## No See Um Lodge
## Jack Holman

My good friend and former employer, Jack Holman, wasn't worried about land issues when he arrived in Alaska in 1972. After his two-year teaching contract in Guam ended, neither Jack nor his wife had a job. What Jack did have, however, was a strong desire to hunt and fish in Alaska. He and his wife flew directly to Anchorage hoping to find employment.

*I wanted to live in Alaska to hunt and fish. I left Guam and came directly to Alaska to find a job. I was in a bar having a beer. I got into a conversation about teaching with some guy. After a little bar talk, I told him I'd just come from a teaching job in Guam. We finished that beer and had another. By the third beer, I learned that he was a superintendent and needed some teachers. Another beer and I'd finished the impromptu interview. I had a teaching job in Bristol Bay. He liked me so much that he even hired my wife. Once my new employer left the bar, I wanted to celebrate. I had a few more drinks that night and have been drinking ever since.*

Jack taught at the state-run school in Levelock, a Native village about 40 miles from King Salmon. Jack taught grades one through eight in a single classroom from 1972 through 1975. Within the first week of establishing a residence in Levelock, Jack bought a skiff and an outboard motor. It wasn't long before he was exploring the entire Kvichak River. On his first trip up the river, Jack spotted a small cabin about 20 miles up the river. Curiosity got the better of him and he stopped to see who lived in the well-kept but older cabin. That was the day that Jack Holman met Ingdal Bertinussen.

Ingdal had been living by himself along the Kvichak River for 35 years. Jack liked him and his home from their first meeting. It wasn't long before Jack started taking Ingdal's mail up the river on his fishing and hunting excursions. Over the years, Jack became a regular visitor. He helped Ingdal whenever he could. He even bought and delivered groceries and other supplies that he knew Ingdal needed. In short order, the two became good friends. On one of those trips up the river, Jack and his friend Jimmy Woods, the Levelock School janitor, stopped in to see the old trapper. Jack made a comment that eventually changed both his life and lifestyle.

*Ingdal, you're getting old, when are you going to sell this place?*

Within minutes of that comment, Jack learned that Ingdal had already decided that it truly was time to leave the Kvichak. Among other reasons, he had grown tired of his own cooking and the solitary lifestyle. Reluctantly, he told his visitors that he had already agreed to sell his place to a church group. Ingdal mused that the proposed buyers planned to turn the cabin and property into a Bible camp. Trying to restrain his contempt, Jimmy Woods made it perfectly clear that he didn't want any group of "Bible-pushers" moving in along the Kvichak, nor did the rest of the people living along the river. More as a plea than as a question, Jimmy Woods asked Ingdal if the group had put up any money. When Ingdal replied that he hadn't seen any money as yet, Jimmy put Jack Holman on the spot.

*Why don't you sell the place to Jack Holman?*

Jack jumped into the discussion with both feet and a smile. A few moments later, Ingdal agreed to sell, but Jack really didn't know what he was getting into. When Jack inquired about the price, Ingdal told him that he wanted the same amount he paid for the place 35 years earlier, $4,000. Jack agreed and made a deal to pay the total amount over the winter. Wasting no time and not wanting to compete with the Bible camp, Jack made a quick trip down the river to Levelock where he picked up some cash. He returned and made the down payment that same day. He paid the balance over the next few months. Once he had been paid completely, Ingdal packed a few essential possessions and left. He moved into the Pioneer Home in Palmer where he resided until his death in the early 1980s.

Although Ingdal didn't have title to the land, Jack bought the cabin. There was also an old barge parked on the beach in front of the cabin. Jack planned to use the cabin as a base camp for fishing trips. Then a great idea popped into Jack's mind. He could use his newly purchased fishing cabin as a way to write off his boat, motors, maybe even an airplane against his taxes. To make his plan somewhat legitimate, Jack knew he had to appear serious. To that end, he chose to name his lodge after the dreaded, albeit ubiquitous No See Um bugs that plagued the river. Jack smiled as he told me more of his plan.

*I had always wanted a lodge but had no idea about how to get started. I realized that it was a perfect tax dodge. I was a schoolteacher who was looking to writeoff a couple of boats and an airplane. That's why we have such a sophisticated name. Who in their right mind would name a real lodge after a damn bug? I had never been to a lodge. I didn't know what a lodge was supposed to be. I didn't know anyone who had been to a lodge. The whole thing started as a tax scam.*

Jack hosted his first guests at No See Um Lodge in 1975. He had about seven clients that whole season. Jack's lodge featured no running water, no toilets, and no electricity.

*Jack Holman with a king salmon and happy client, Colleen Troxell. Circa 1995—Jack Holman Photo*

*Fortunately, we had a lot of daylight. We used oil lamps. I had a small gas-operated pump on the riverbank. I pumped water right out of the river through a garden hose directly into the old cabin and then into a big garbage can. That was our whole water system. There were no filters of course. A simple system worked. When the garbage can was empty, I'd pump more. I converted the barge into a bunkhouse. It was sparse, too. At least there were some fish.*

It didn't take Jack too long to realize that more was working than his tax plan. His guests liked him and his style of operation. Although a few clients chartered flights that season, Jack didn't have an airplane at the lodge until the next season. During the first years, Jack and his (first) wife hosted no more than six guests at any one time at No See Um Lodge. By the time Jack decided to go full time in the lodge business, he felt it was too late to change the lodge name. After all, he had a small client base and the name was "unforgettable." Jack became a full-time fishing lodge operator in 1979.

Jack didn't have much company on the Kvichak when he started. Red Clark had been hosting clients for nearly ten seasons before Jack hosted one. He knew that Red was a commercial fisherman and believed that trout ate salmon eggs and were, therefore, the enemy. Red and his clients killed every trout they caught. Contrary to Red's expectations for the new lodge on the river, Jack took a more conservative direction with his catch and release policy. While Jack didn't emulate the philosophy of Red Clark, he did aspire to be like another Bristol Bay lodge owner. Ed Seiler became Jack's idol.

*We had this client come to the lodge. He showed me a letter from Enchanted Lake Lodge written by Ed Seiler. Basically, the letter said that Enchanted Lake was completely booked for the next four years. The best Ed could do was to add the guy's name to a waiting list. I wanted to get that kind of reputation. I wanted to be like Ed Seiler.*

Jack Holman told me many stories related to starting his lodge, but one of the best involved another longtime Kvichak River resident, Ole Wassenkari. Like Jack's friend Ingdal, Ole had been in the Bristol Bay area for a long time. Although born in Washington State, Ole was of Finnish descent and about Ingdal's age. Ole arrived in Bristol Bay the same year as Ingdal. Both men worked as commercial fishermen in the summers and trapped in the winters. By 1979, however, age had taken its toll. Ole was legally blind, but bad eyes didn't slow him down. According to Jack, Ole was a true "Alaskan" character, and everyone enjoyed his company.

At the close of the 1980 lodge season, Jack threw a big party in honor of his wedding that was held at the lodge. Naturally, he invited his upriver neighbor, Ole Wassenkari.

On the day of the wedding, Ole diligently prepared his skiff. When he headed down the mighty Kvichak, his only companion was his dog, Ring. When Ole arrived at the lodge, he climbed out of his boat cursing like mad. He kicked at his dog to get him out of the boat and then threw the anchor with disgust. When Jack asked him why he was so mad, Ole told him that Jackie Drew, the local barge operator, had tried to run him down with his barge. He was mad because the big barge changed course on purpose and headed right for him. Ole kept right on swearing. According to Jack, Ole was mad as hell when he said:

*I had to swerve to get out of the way. That son of a bitch tried to kill me!*

A few days later Jack was in King Salmon and ran into Jackie Drew, the barge operator. Jack related Ole's story, then asked if the barge was going too fast for him to see the elderly Wassenkari in the small skiff. Jackie laughed, and then told Jack the rest of the story.

*I saw him all right. He was going like a bat out of hell and coming right at me. I thought he was going to hit the barge. I was standing on the deck yelling and waving, but he's so blind he didn't see me, or the barge. At the last second, he saw the barge and swerved like hell, then kept going down the river. I saw him shake his fist and knew he was yelling but I couldn't hear him. I don't know why he's mad at me, though. The barge was anchored at the time and wasn't even moving!*

## Ed Rice Gets an Idea

By 1975, hundreds of clients were visiting Alaska and the fishing lodges in Bristol Bay. Looking at it in retrospect, however, perhaps none would have as great an influence to the lodges and the fishing lodge industry as Ed Rice.

After making his mark in network television advertising, Ed Rice started both a new career and a new business in 1974, International Sportsmen's Expositions, and never looked back. Realizing the tremendous market in sportfishing, Ed hosted his first exposition in Portland with a show that featured a wide range of water-related activities. There were no Alaska operators at the Portland show, but the "Expo" was a huge success. Numerous paying customers told Ed he should get some Alaskans down for his next show. In an effort to do just that, later that summer Ed bought a ticket and flew to Alaska.

Like most first-time visiting anglers, Ed had his initial Alaskan fishing experience on the Kenai River. Ed fished for salmon as well as for potential exhibitors. By 1975, Ed was exploring Alaska on his own. Through some sport show contacts, whom he later learned knew less than they portrayed, Ed agreed to be taken to the Ugashik Lakes area where his "wanna-be" lodge host assured him great action for char, grayling and huge rainbows. In a trip that he described as questionable at best, Ed found great fishing for grayling and char, but there were no rainbows.

*Ed Rice kissing a trophy rainbow at Talarik Creek. Circa 1980—Sonny Petersen Photo*

*Fortunately, the fishing was good, because that's all we had to eat. The airplane that was supposed to arrive the next morning with the rest of our gear and all the food didn't arrive. We waited and waited, but it didn't come. Naturally, we didn't have a radio. It rained and the wind blew like hell. I finally broke into a nearby cabin and found a very old sack of dehydrated potatoes. I learned a lot that trip. That was also the first time I had been around big bears. I was in Alaska about a week longer than I planned. I should have known better, but I trusted someone who didn't have a clue.*

Ed's extended trips to Alaska in 1974 and 1975 created a business direction in his mind that he had to expand and refine. Professionally, Ed realized that to improve his sport shows, he had to limit the range of activities offered. He needed to specialize. Personally, Ed desired to experience the best fishing in the world. Blending his personal desires into his new business, Ed quickly realized that to be guaranteed the world's best fishing, he needed professional guides. In 1976, Ed Rice became a Kulik guest. Shortly thereafter, Ed's sport shows featured only the world's best fishing lodges and outdoor-related businesses. As Ed's shows grew more popular, they influenced the growth of the best, if not all, the lodges in Bristol Bay.

## Catch and Release

Although there is no doubt that catch and release thrives in Alaska today, it was not necessarily the status quo in earlier days. When Ed Rice arrived at Kulik during the 1976 season, he found a lodge wrought with tradition earned only after many years of continuous successful operation. What was new in 1976, however, was the direction charted by Chuck Petersen. Ray Petersen, Chuck's father, had appointed him director of the entire Angler's Paradise operation after the close of the season in 1971. Deciding the time was right for conservation, Chuck exercised his operational control. He modified the brochures and staffed the Angler's Paradise Camps with the goal of reducing the number of rainbows harvested in Bristol Bay. Chuck Petersen spearheaded the push to "catch and release."

Both Ray Petersen and John Walatka became conservationists during their long association in the fishing lodge industry. They witnessed the devastation of the rainbow fishery during the early military buildup. That experience gave them a thorough understanding for the need to be resource conscious. Unfortunately for John, his wives, Lillian, and later Mildred, believed that fishing clients needed to take home a box of fish. This feeling stemmed from their thoughts that seeing the fish would encourage others to journey to Alaska. While John often gave lip service to "limit the kill," I'm told that he frequently yielded to "bedroom" pressure.

Numerous travel and publicity films made at the Angler's Paradise Camps during the 1950s, 60s, and early 70s emphasized barbless hooks and releasing the majority of the fish caught. Still, it was a difficult concept for some anglers to grasp. Dave Shuster told me that he was one of the first guides to confront a client.

*I had a couple clients way up American Creek one day early in the spring. These guys were real meat hunters. By lunchtime, I'd already killed too many char and suggested we let the rest go. They both looked at me as if I was crazy. Later that afternoon we were fishing the tangled back channels when one of the guys hooked a big but dark, male rainbow. I was quite close to the guy and knew the fish had only recently finished spawning. I helped the guy as much as I could. Once I had the fish in my hands, I asked the angler to release it. He said OK, but I could tell he was pissed. I explained about the spawning cycle but that didn't seem to get through to him. Later, I learned that when he left Kulik heading back to Anchorage, both guys told John Walatka that they wouldn't come back if I was still guiding. Someone told me that John just smiled and puffed his cigar as he loaded their heavy fish boxes onto the airplane.*

While many suggestions were made to fishermen throughout the years, Chuck Petersen made catch and release official at the Angler's Paradise Camps for the fishing season of 1976. The brochures that went out to thousands of prospective clients and travel agents were quite clear. With the exception of one trophy rainbow, clients were to release all other freshwater fish. Chuck was committed to catch and release and knew he needed a strong manager and staff at Kulik, as well as at Brooks and Grosvenor to ease the philosophical transition. By early March, Chuck announced his management team for the 1976 season. Bob Carroll became the manager at Kulik Lodge, Gary Anderson became the Brooks Lodge manager and Van Hartley managed Grosvenor. I asked Chuck about circumstances that brought Bob Carroll to Kulik Lodge.

*Well, you need to understand that I was head of the camps, but there were a few people with a lot more seniority at Northern Consolidated. Early in the going I had one of the airline station managers in mind for the manager's job at Kulik. Although I didn't talk to him about the job, he seemed perfect to me. Following company procedures, I went to his supervisor, the director of operations, and I inquired about my intended manager. To make a long story short, I was sold a bill of goods on a different station manager, Bob Carroll. The director of operations told me that Bob was a "natural" to manage our big lodge. He had run some military officer's clubs and had a good background in the service industry. Then he assured me that Bob had done a great job running the Wien station at Galena. Later that day, I agreed to have Bob manage Kulik.*

*I flew up to Galena to meet my new manager. Once I saw the station, I had some doubts. Galena was a small station that hardly had room for the passengers and their freight. Imagine how I felt when I walked into the station and found a monument to Bob Carroll erected by Bob Carroll in the middle of the small terminal.*

Chuck mentioned that Bob Carroll had completed a newsworthy trek or set some kind of snowmobile record but couldn't remember which. To commemorate his accomplishments, Bob had roped off most of the usable floor space inside the Galena terminal. He placed several tables inside the area and then covered them with white cloth and Christmas decorations so they appeared to be snow-covered. Bob Carroll then created a monument to himself by encasing his snowmobile and a mannequin dressed in his own special outfit. Adjacent to the snow machine, Bob placed a plaque that described his accomplishments. He never gave any thought to the lack of terminal space nor the imposition on the passengers and their freight. According to Chuck Petersen, that was the nature of Kulik manager, Bob Carroll.

Chuck was interested in improving the quality of his guide staff at the lodges, so he consulted with his longtime friend, Kay Mitsuyoshi, to help him find guides who could lead the charge into catch and release. Kay had come to Anchorage in 1958 as an employee of Japan Airlines and quickly became an Angler's Paradise advocate. Once he moved to California, Kay left the airline industry and became heavily involved in a fishing shop. He knew and fished with the top guides on the west coast and was responsible for many clients who came to Alaska. Chuck trusted his judgement.

Van Hartley had long before proven his skill as a guide and became the guide-manager at Grosvenor for the 1976 season. After evaluating numerous applicants, Chuck hired Gary Anderson to manage and guide at Brooks Lodge. Chuck hired another experienced Oregon guide, Al Perryman, to lead the guide corps at Kulik. At the urging of Kay Mitsuyoshi, Chuck hired world casting champion, Steve Rajeffe.

Typical of lodge operations in Alaska, the managers opened the camps. Bob Carroll and Gary Anderson met Chuck in Anchorage early in May. Together, they planned the season and prepared for opening. Other staff members started to assemble a few days before the arrival of the first guests. Getting organized was easy for Van Hartley. He lived in Alaska and had started working at the lodges in 1970. He knew what to expect. Things weren't the same for Steve Rajeffe and Al Perryman. Neither had been to Alaska; neither had any lodge experience. Both young men had spoken to Chuck and Kay, looked at pictures, and talked to former guests. They were excited but didn't admit their apprehension about flying in small airplanes.

After an uneventful flight to Anchorage, the excited lads boarded a Wien flight to King Salmon. At almost the exact time that their flight left Anchorage, Wien Mallard pilot and former Kulik manager, Hugh Hartley, was in the King Salmon office waiting for three Brooks Lodge guests and the new Kulik guides. Hugh was reading the paper when the radioman told him Ed Seiler wanted to talk. The radio crackled as Ed explained his big problem.

Hugh's face contorted as he learned that during a take-off attempt, Ed had flipped his Cessna C-185 at Gibraltar Lake. No one was hurt, but the airplane was completely upside down and floating. Ed had to half-swim and half-walk to the shore. He had no choice but to walk to Kakhonak Village. Ed told Hugh that he had been lucky and found a working radio and had contacted Iliamna-based air-taxi operator Tim LaPorte for a ride home. Tim had flown him back to Enchanted Lake. Once Hugh learned the situation, he helped Ed plan the salvage operation. They agreed to meet at Kulik after Hugh finished the Mallard schedule. When Ed asked if Hugh had anyone around to help, Hugh told him that he had a couple guys in the back of his mind. By the time the neophyte guides walked into the terminal at King Salmon, Hugh was all smiles as he introduced himself, welcomed them to Angler's Paradise, and helped with their bags. They didn't know that Hugh had been eagerly anticipating their muscle power, not Al's guiding knowledge, or Steve's world-championship fly-casting ability.

Neither Al, Steve, nor the Brooks guests sensed any urgency as Hugh Hartley ushered everyone into the Mallard for the quick flight to Brooks. Hugh told the guides to sit tight as he unloaded some freight and the passengers disembarked. Wasting no time, Hugh cranked up the engines, eased the big flying boat back into the water, and departed for Kulik. To their great surprise and relief, the new guides had been in Alaska only six hours and were already starting to lose their "small plane" apprehensions.

Hugh shut down the engines and climbed out of the pilot's chair in one fluid motion. He was pulling the guides' bags off the airplane before they realized the doors were open. Immediately Hugh barked some orders to his new employees.

*Pile your gear over there and get into your*

*waders. We're going up to Gibraltar Lake right away!*

Those words are music to the ears of every new guide. They'd both heard about the fabulous fishing at that lake. Zippers tugged and buckles unsnapped. Both young guides rapidly searched their gear for waders, rods, lines, and leaders. They were too absorbed to notice the man standing beside Hugh.

*You won't need any fishing gear today, boys. By the way, this is Ed Seiler. He runs the lodge down the lake. He has a little problem and we're going to help him for a while. Start putting this pile of equipment in the airplane and don't forget to bring a coat.*

With no more explanation, Al and Steve followed the orders. They loaded ropes and pulleys, several inflatable rafts, and assorted hardware but no fishing gear. After Ed and Hugh had a discussion in the shop, they pulled some flexible pipe out of the rafters and scurried to find some hand pumps. When the big pile of gear had been safely stowed, Hugh told the new guides to buckle their seatbelts. Ed settled into the copilot seat and watched as Hugh cranked the big radial engines. Again, the "new guys" headed skyward. They didn't have a clue.

About fifteen minutes after takeoff, the fear of flying suddenly became an issue for both young men. They spotted an airplane upside down right after Hugh started his first circle only 200 feet above the wreck. Only the bottoms of the floats were visible. Ed casually looked back at the two pale passengers. He yelled over the engine noise,

*That's my airplane. We are going to rescue it today!*

Ed and Hugh knew it, but their helpers weren't aware that the waves were pounding the airplane into the beach and damaging the rudder. Hugh finished another two circles while both pilots evaluated the scene. They needed to get the airplane secured as soon as possible.

Once he had the Mallard parked, Hugh told Steve and Al to place the inflatable raft under the spreader bars of the floats. Although the raft was completely under the water, they were able to inflate it using the flexible pipe and several pumps. They raised the airplane a little at a time. While Al and Steve wrestled with the inflatables, Hugh and Ed used the ropes to secure the aircraft to both banks of the wide river mouth. It was nearly dark when Hugh started the Mallard engines and headed back to Kulik. There was no doubt that Al and Steve really got their feet wet on their first day in Alaska.

Poor weather and heavy wind prevented them from returning for several days. Once the weather cleared, the four returned to Gibraltar with a little more equipment. They untied the aircraft from both banks and pulled the airplane to a steep gravel beach about 300 yards up the lake. As they pulled the airplane toward the beach, Al and Steve placed a mattress under the nose and prop of the C-185. They eased the airplane nose-first into the beach. The mattress cushioned the nose from further damage in the gravel. Hugh attached a line to the tail. They used a big set of blocks and hand-held winches with lots of manpower to pull the aircraft completely over its nose and then eased it down onto the floats. Once the plane was right side up, both pilots checked for damage. Ed changed the oil while Al and Steve pumped the floats. The gas tanks were drained and fresh gas dumped in. By the time all the work was completed, most of the water had drained from the fuselage. Ed climbed in and started the engine. Al and Steve were relieved as they watched Ed fly away. They both told me that they were allowed to take their fishing gear on their next flight.

The remainder of the 1976 season was rather uneventful. Guests gladly accepted the catch-and-release policy despite the Kulik manager's propensity toward self-indulgence. Things were quiet until August 21, when a supposed violation of park regulations brought the land issues back into focus. Frank Norris highlights the events in *Isolated Paradise*:

> *Lake Grosvenor was one of many considered for closure during the wilderness nomination process. The draft plan, issued in August 1971, had left it open, but a revised draft issued the following July concluded that all but the lake's western end would be recommended for wilderness consideration. The NPS did so for two reasons: it wanted to protect the wilderness qualities of the Savonoski Loop canoe route, and wanted to keep open the flight path used by the concessioner using Grosvenor Camp. That path headed west down Coville Lake to American Creek. As a result, the plan kept Coville Lake, as well as the western end of Lake Grosvenor out of the proposed wilderness.*
>
> *Once the revised wilderness plan was approved in 1972, administrative provisions in the 1964 Wilderness Act allowed Superintendent Gil Blinn to apply de facto wilderness management to the area, even though Congress had not acted on the agency's recommendation.*
>
> *The situation heated up in July 1976 when Grosvenor Camp Manager, Van Hartley, brought a jet boat into the monument. At first, he complied with the regulations, and he obtained Blinn's permission before piloting the boat up Savonoski and Grosvenor rivers on his way to Grosvenor Camp. But on August 21, Hartley illegally took a party of fishermen on the jet boat to the east end of Grosvenor Lake. Hartley failed to slow down sufficiently in the shallows and went aground. Blinn, along with his son and freelance writer-photographer Dave Bohn, were canoeing nearby. They witnessed the accident, which resulted in minor injuries to two of Hartley's fishing clients, and they helped extricate the grounded craft. Blinn, in a private conversation with Hartley, reminded him that operating the jet boat at the east end of the lake was in violation of NPS policy; he did not, however, make his feelings public, and did not cite him or otherwise penalize him.*

As every story has at least two sides, I asked Van Hartley to comment on the grounding at Hardscrabble Creek. Van made it perfectly clear to me that he felt that Superintendent Blinn and his guest, Dave Bohn, had no intention of giving assistance. They came no closer than 75 yards from Van's disabled craft. They purposely called Van away from his injured guests and his efforts to free the stuck vessel. Once Van stopped trying to free the boat and made his way to their distant position, Superintendent Blinn spent the next 15 minutes berating him for the presence of a jet boat in the restricted area. Van listened to the dissertation and then pleaded with the men to help him get his boat back into the water so that he might get the guests back for medical attention. One of Van's guests, Morton White, who could not help but hear every word yelled in the heat of the discussion, finally summoned the uniformed NPS employee to his position in the boat and asked if he was on duty or not. When the uniform-clad superintendent told the injured fisherman that he was not on duty, his response was short and to the point. Van repeated the words of Mr. White:

> *If you're not on duty, take off your Goddamned uniform right now. You had no right to act like you were working and chastise Mr. Hartley for having a motorized vehicle in the Park. If you are on duty, I demand to know why you did not immediately inquire about our condition and provide assistance to visitors in your jurisdiction before you gave such a long and drawn-out tirade to our guide?"*

Van also told me that White's utterance was enough to stimulate the good superintendent into a little action, but his guest, Dave Bohn, was less than enthusiastic about helping. I understand that he was conducting research for his book, *Rambles through an Alaska Wild: Katmai and the Valley of the Smokes.* When I read his book, it became perfectly clear why he was reluctant to assist. Dave Bohn was irritated and annoyed that someone else was in his wilderness retreat. In my opinion, Dave would rather no one visited Katmai again. He is also opposed to fishing, which tends to make me think he and I will never be friends.

> *If Katmai is to remain wild, as it is now, then the philosophical carrying capacity—that is, physical visitation—must remain low. The old idiotic yardstick of "visitor use" must be discarded for this wilderness area. Otherwise the uniqueness of the Katmai will be destroyed, and the potential of that gigantic philosophical resource—the knowledge it is there—will also disappear.*
>
> *Sportfishing in the Katmai, and anywhere else for that matter, is an abomination and should be abolished. It is an insult to the intelligence.*

*Ed Scherockman on the Kulik Lodge porch. Ed was a regular visitor to the Angler's Paradise Camps beginning in the early 1960s. As well as being a great fly-fisherman, Ed had an uncanny ability to tell stories. Circa 1990—Ray Petersen Collection*

Continuing again from *Isolated Paradise:*

*Several days after the incident, Blinn (who by now had returned to Brooks Camp) heard rumors that he had treated Hartley unfairly. He responded by visiting Grosvenor Camp and talking to Hartley about the recent incident. Hartley felt that the NPS policies were unfair, but he understood them. But Chuck Petersen, the head of concession operations, claimed he was unaware of the wilderness management policy until he met with Blinn on September 1. He immediately protested the action, both at the meeting and in a September 3 letter to the superintendent. In his defense, he claimed that concessionaires had been operating motorboats on Lake Grosvenor since the 1950s. He also claimed that Blinn was being arbitrary and evasive and that he was enforcing the rules as part of a "personal vendetta" against him. Blinn, as a park superintendent, was in no position to lift the motorboat restriction so on October 7, he replied with a letter, which merely reiterated and explained the regulation. Petersen, however, would not give up. He sought and obtained a meeting with Pacific Northwest Region Director Russell Dickenson on November 30. Dickenson, like Blinn, told the Wien representative that he could not change Servicewide wilderness management rules; he could only suggest that Petersen write NPS Director Gary Everhardt and ask for a waiver of the 1972 regulation which closed lake Grosvenor to motorboat traffic. Petersen did as suggested and wrote a vociferous lengthy protest letter to the NPS director. He also appealed his case to Alaska's Congressional delegation. He then notified several of Grosvenor Camp's longtime guests of the decision, and asked them to lobby the NPS Director in order to overrule the 1972 administrative regulation.*

For the remainder of the 1976 season, Superintendent Blinn remained firm in his position about the use of motorized boats on Grosvenor Lake. Whether this had any influence on Bob Carroll's decision to have the Grosvenor jet boat delivered to Kulik is unknown. More than one person told me that the new Kulik manager wanted the jet boat at Kulik because it was new, and he was a little miffed that he didn't have such a fancy machine at Kulik. According to several people who knew him, Bob always liked to have the biggest and best of everything, regardless of the economics. That rationale notwithstanding, once the last guests of the season left Grosvenor, Bob ordered Van Hartley to Kulik to plan the trip.

The basic plan called for Van to drive the boat from American Creek all the way back to King Salmon and then make the run into Kvichak Bay, up the Alagnak to Nonvianuk Lake, and finally to Kulik. The trip would take two days and there would be a little time to fish the Alagnak. During the initial planning, Bob Carroll suggested that his new friend and longtime Angler's Paradise guest, Ed Scherockman, go along for the experience. Van expressed some concerns and was a little apprehensive. He knew that Ed had been furloughed by Delta Airlines for medical reasons, and he could see that Ed was not in the best physical condition. Van's biggest concern, however, was Ed's lack of experience in jet boat protocol and what that meant on big, muddy rivers.

Ed Scherockman had been a fishing guest at the Angler's Paradise Camps every year since the early 1960s. He fished well and had an uncanny ability to tell stories. It didn't take long for the longtime guest and Bob Carroll, the new Kulik manager, to become great friends. After all, they shared a thriving friendship, more likely a passionate love, for two other well-known lodge regulars, Mr. Schmirnoff and Mr. Jack Daniels. Each evening their mutual admiration society met to discuss and celebrate anything and everything. During one of these nightly sessions, they discussed the upcoming jet boat journey. Ed wanted a chance to fish the lower Alagnak, and Bob thought the ride would be a great experience for his newfound friend. Bob promised that he would convince the Grosvenor manager to take a passenger. The pair exchanged toasts late into the evening.

Throughout the next day, Bob Carroll was relentless, encouraging Van at every opportunity. Given the continued insistence of manager Bob Carroll, Van finally relented and agreed to take the manager's friend. Van returned to his cabin to pack some gear. Ed Scherockman and Bob Carroll celebrated their fortune late into the evening again.

Early the next morning, Sonny Petersen loaded Van Hartley and Ed Scherockman into N9644G for the 15-minute flight to American Creek. A few minutes later, Van had the big jet boat loaded and warming up at a gentle idle. Van gave his passenger a briefing on jet boat rules, including a short dissertation about staying seated when the boat was traveling at full speed. Van waited to ease into the river until Sonny took off in the narrow channel. The weather was great when Van and Ed started on a journey that would turn out to be a long and unforgettable experience for them both.

The trip down Coville and Grosvenor Lakes was beautiful and uneventful. The boat seemed to fly down the Grosvenor River, and in no time, they entered the perilous, muddy Savonoski River. Van negotiated each subtle turn and changed channels as if he could see through the dark brown water. Feeling no danger, Ed stood up to take some pictures. Van pulled him back into his seat and shouted over the engine noise:

> *Ed, don't get out of your seat going this speed. It's way too dangerous! We could hit a sand bar or a submerged log any time.*

Luck was on their side as they eased into Naknek Lake. The wind was calm and the lake was flat. Van pushed the throttles forward and passed Margot Creek on the way to Brooks Lodge. They stopped at Brooks just long enough to refuel and check the latest weather. Brooks Lodge manager, Gary Anderson, told Van what he already knew. The weather was changing, but if they left soon, they would have no problems. Wanting to take full advantage of the calm wind conditions, Van told Ed to take his seat. They were off. The cruise into King Salmon was easy, perhaps too easy, for Ed.

Once they were on the dock in King Salmon, Van busied himself with preparations for the next leg of the journey to Kulik. Completely immersed in his duties, Van didn't notice as Ed wandered off toward the King Salmon Commercial Company store to buy some Jack Daniels. Sitting in that boat just seemed to build a terrible thirst in the former pilot. He didn't want to be thirsty on the long trip ahead. During his absence, Van filled the boat tanks. Then he had the dockhands help him load three 55-gallon fuel drums into the jet boat. Van also learned that the weather forecast predicted a heavy windstorm later that night. By the time Ed returned to the dock, Van was more than ready to get underway. During the short warm-up, Ed noted a change in the high altitude clouds, then told Van that it looked like a storm was on the way. Although Ed had little jet boat experience, Van knew that he had vast experience reading cloud formations thanks to his extensive military and airline career. Corroborating his prediction, Van related the official forecast. Then he explained that they needed to get through the open water of Kvichak Bay and into the Alagnak River before darkness and the heavy wind caught them in the open. The pair donned extra clothing to insulate them from the cold wind. They departed King Salmon about 5:30 p.m. Van figured it would be dark by 10:30. They had only five hours.

Because he had made the trip down the Alagnak from Kulik to King Salmon earlier in the season, Van was reasonably sure he could find the deep-water channel. Once they drove out of the Naknek River and into Kvichak Bay, Van found the going extremely good. They were making great time. So far, they had been lucky, at least there was no wind to create big waves. Looking to the west, Van noted that the sky was changing and nudged the throttles forward. By the time they were close to the Kvichak River, the rapidly increasing cloud cover created a flat light condition that made forward visibility poor. The dull light coupled with a dropping tide made it difficult, if not impossible, to maintain the proper position in the narrow, deep-water channel. Although he had difficulty with the channel, Van pushed his speed as he passed the first of the Diamond canneries.

Unlike the first segment of the trip from Coville Lake to King Salmon when the men sat side by side, the extra weight and space taken by the three fuel drums necessitated a different seating arrangement. Ed sat directly behind Van on the tandem seat. Concentrating on the difficult task of staying in the channel, Van didn't notice when his passenger opened and then lost the cap from the Jack Daniels bottle. Ed really didn't understand Van's previous warnings. The whole bay was flat. There wasn't even a ripple on the surface. All he could see was miles of flat water. Ed was bored, but at least he had his bottle. After consuming half the contents of his potent elixir, nature called. Ed didn't tell the young boat driver that he needed to drain his bladder.

The jet boat was making about 35 knots across the flat water when Ed stood up, tucked the open bottle under his left arm, stepped to the back of the boat, and braced his knees against the inner back railing. Ed fumbled with his zipper. Once the yellow stream started to flow, Ed grabbed the neck of the whiskey bottle with his right hand, raised the bottle to a position in front of his face, and toasted the glorious day. His lips parted and he began a long, carefree drink as the pressure in his bladder eased. At the very instant that the urine stopped flowing and the Jack Daniels started; Van lost the channel. The heavy boat slammed into a submerged sand bar and stopped violently in the shallow water. Re-living a nightmare, Van related the details:

> *We were going like hell one minute, and stopped the next. All three fuel drums broke loose and flew forward out of the boat. Ed wasn't too far behind them. He flew past me completely inverted, one hand on his zipper, the other still holding the whiskey bottle. His head smashed into the front of the boat, but that didn't stop his forward motion. Although his head seemed to slow with the sudden impact with the boat, his body didn't. His body vaulted forward completely out of the boat, then crumpled like a rock. Somehow, during his 25-foot flight, Ed's grip on the Jack Daniels relaxed and the half-empty bottle fell to the floor of the boat. Surprisingly, the*

*bottle landed upright, not a drop lost in the process. Ed wasn't so lucky. He hit the water face first as his body slammed down, collapsing heavily in a big heap. Ed was unconscious and face down in the shallow water.*

*I thought he was dead. I jumped out of the boat and into the water beside the body. Somehow I wrestled Ed back into the boat and tried to revive him. He was groggy as hell, but alive.*

Ed was in and out of consciousness when Van noticed a slight trickle of blood oozing from under the wool that covered his head. Van didn't know it at the time, but he was about to discover that Ed's sudden impact with the metal boat railing had sliced and ripped his scalp completely free of his head. Trying to find the source of the blood, Van gently pulled off the cap. In the process, Ed's head moved just a little. Van was horrified when the bleeding scalp literally dropped over Ed's eyes, covering them like the protective visor of a twelfth-century knight's helmet.

The Kulik guest and former pilot was bleeding heavily. Van knew he had to stop the flow or Ed would bleed to death. Neither man had much time. In one quick motion, Van opened his guide pack and grabbed a roll of gray cloth tape (known in Alaska as Super Cub tape). Then he noticed the bottle of booze. He grabbed the bottle and poured the Jack Daniels liberally over Ed's head in an attempt to sterilize the wound. Then he pushed the bleeding and torn scalp back into place. Holding the scalp in position with one hand, Van used his other hand and his teeth to rip small pieces of tape off the roll. He taped Ed's scalp back into position. Once Ed's scalp was stabilized, Van pulled a clean T-shirt out of his guide pack and wrapped Ed's skull tightly.

Van tried to get Ed as comfortable as he could. He struggled but succeeded in getting Ed into a sleeping bag to keep him warm. Once he had Ed as comfortable as he could be, his attention turned to getting help. Surveying his situation, he noted that it was already 10:15 p.m. He tried the marine VFH radio. He called and called, but couldn't reach anyone. Finally, he noticed that the antenna had snapped during the sudden stop. Van experimented and held the broken antenna directly onto the radio transmitter. Immediately the garbled but recognizable voice of Bill Tolbert broke the silence. Although communication was broken at best, Van gave his position and urgent request for medical help to the King Salmon station manager. Van didn't know it at the time, but his message echoed through many radio receivers in Bristol Bay and started a frantic search.

While transmitting, Van used the designation, *Wien Jet Boat*, and reported that he was "stuck in the bay." The message heard, however, was *Wien Jet* and interpreted as crashed in the bay. Although daylight was rapidly turning into darkness, things started to happen. Bill Tolbert radioed Anchorage and reported that one of their jets had crashed. He notified the Coast Guard, and they immediately dispatched a search and rescue helicopter. Monte Handy, a local Naknek pilot, heard the radio call and promptly jumped in his Piper Cherokee. He departed the Naknek airfield to start the search. It was dark and Monty flew low. He finally spotted the grounded jet boat and circled even lower to get a good look.

Leaving nothing to chance, Van wanted to be sure the pilot spotted the boat. He tore through his guide pack and pulled out a flare gun. As the Cherokee circled overhead, Van fired off a flare. Monte was flying so close that the flare nearly hit the Cherokee. Monte got the message and radioed a positive identification and a location to King Salmon. Unknown to all involved, a local fisherman, who will forever remain anonymous, was secretly engaged in some illegal chum salmon netting not far up the Alagnak River. The poacher heard the commotion of the airplane, turned off his lights, and turned on his radio. Once he heard the radio messages and learned the predicament, he helped as his single crewman quickly pulled in the nets. While the deckhand stashed the illegal catch, the captain headed downriver to see if they could help.

By the time the pseudo rescue boat arrived, Van already had wrestled one of the full fuel drums back into the boat. The fishermen pulled a skiff up to the jet boat. Van helped the boat crew carefully transfer Ed to the larger and free-floating boat. Once Ed was secure, the captain immediately headed for the Diamond J Cannery some ten miles up Kvichak Bay. Originally constructed in 1895-96, the Diamond J was the first cannery built in Bristol Bay. Van told the crew he'd meet them at the cannery as soon as possible. He stayed with the jet boat and waited for the tide to free him. Van's wait lasted about forty-five minutes. During the delay, he kept himself busy by filling the fuel tanks. He was ready when the tide finally floated the jet boat.

Once their course was set, the fishing crew tended to Ed. When they removed Van's T-shirt, all they saw was a bloody mass of ripped tissue. The radio buzzed with vivid reports leading listeners to believe that Ed couldn't possibly survive. By the time the fishing boat turned rescue vessel reached the Diamond J, the cannery first aid team was ready for action. Seeing his desperate condition, they decided not to move Ed until the helicopter arrived. Van arrived at the cannery about an hour after the fishing boat. The hours passed slowly while they waited for the rescue helicopter to arrive.

The helicopter arrived at about 6 a.m. Unable to find a clear landing area at the cannery site, the helicopter hovered over the small dock and dropped a basket. Van helped the cannery first-aid staff load Ed into the basket and watched as he was pulled aboard. The helicopter turned toward Anchorage. They knew Ed had severe scalp wounds, but they didn't know he had also broken his neck.

Once Ed was on his way to the hospital, Van continued his journey to Kulik. Winding his way up the river, he didn't feel the effect of the wind that had finally started to blow. Arriving at Nonvianuk Camp, however, he faced a huge storm and realized he could go no farther. Van was forced to endure another long night. He told me that he drifted in and out of sleep and had some vicious nightmares before daylight and reduced winds greeted him the next morning.

During the following winter, the staff of the Angler's Paradise Camps received a double dose of good news. Although he would never return to a pilot seat, Ed Scherockman would heal and be able to return to Kulik. The second dose of good news came in a letter addressed to Chuck Petersen. The extensive lobbying efforts that he had orchestrated late in the fall had finally worked. NPS Director Everhardt notified Chuck that his agency would allow the use of motorized boat service on Lake Grosvenor, pending action by Congress on wilderness recommendations. Historian Frank Norris points out that the Petersens weren't the only operators concerned with access rights in the monument. Again quoting from *Isolated Paradise*:

*The imposition of wilderness management on Katmai's land and waters brought complaints from other disgruntled users. One of those was Edwin W. Seiler, who was the owner of a nearby fishing lodge, a pilot, and a pioneer businessman in nearby King Salmon. In May 1977, Seiler wrote Governor Jay Hammond and NPS Director Gary Everhardt about the newly imposed floatplane landing restrictions, opining that "this is something I believe Gil Blinn cooked up with prodding from some overzealous environmentalists." Seiler hoped that the NPS might relax the regulation "by issuing revocable licenses to responsible guides and Air-Taxi operators." NPS Director William Whalen, who responded to Seiler in August, didn't directly answer his complaint; he took some pains, however, to put the problem in perspective. He defended Blinn and the wilderness process, noting that the closure of all waters other than Naknek Lake and the Naknek River to aircraft and motorboats was based upon a concept of using the Naknek Lake system for primary access, with the principal developments being located in this zone and within the coastal zone. "A wild lands type of management was to be applied to the remaining positions of the national monument." But he also recognized that "most wilderness areas in Alaska should have some degree of access by floatplane. It appears that the temporary impact of aircraft landings on some wilderness waters should be acceptable."*

## Fishing Unlimited
## Ken and Lorane Owsichek

Ken Owsichek first came to Alaska in 1968. He worked for hunting guide Lee Holen. Ken knew that he wanted to get into the hunting and fishing business but realized that would come only after he learned to fly. Not long after Ken completed his commercial pilot's course in 1969, he started flying for Hank Rust, who had started Rust's Flying Service based out of Anchorage in 1963. A short time later, Ken became Hank Rust's partner. Ken flew most of the trips into the Iliamna Lake area. On one of those trips, Ken flew a real estate agent to Lake Clark to examine a lodge that was for sale. The agent wasn't the only one looking at Chulitna Lodge. As soon as he unloaded his passenger at their Anchorage dock, Ken promptly tried to convince his partner that they should buy the facility. Almost a full year later, they purchased the lodge at the close of the 1972 hunting season.

Like most of the older establishments in Alaska, the Chulitna Lodge had an interesting history. According to National Park Service historian John Branson, the lodge was first built as a homestead by Bill Smith in the mid 1930s. Brothers William and Tom Moore owned it in the late 1930s. The Moores sold it to John Walatka in 1940. It was next owned and operated as a hunting lodge by Glen Andrews during the 1960s. Although it is a popular rumor that the lodge served as the headquarters of a gold-mining operation, John told me that he seriously doubted that use of the facility.

Once the property was purchased, Ken and his wife became the working partners at Chulitna Lodge. They made frequent trips to Lake Clark in preparation for the following season. They repaired and cleaned the facilities. Ken and Lorane hosted their first clients in 1973. Although they started with more hunters than fishermen, gradually the fishing business increased. By the 1975 season, Lorane told me the revenues were equally split between hunting and fishing. At the close of the 1975 season, however, their partnership with Hank Rust ended abruptly. Chulitna Lodge was sold.

Although it was a temporary setback, the sale of Chulitna Lodge provided the Owsicheks enough resources to continue in the lodge business. The land freeze hampered land acquisition throughout the state, but Ken got lucky and found some deeded property to buy. Ken and Lorane purchased half of a 5-acre Trade and Manufacturing site at Port Alsworth, directly across the lake from Chulitna Lodge. Right after they acquired the property, Ken ordered his building supplies.

As Ray Petersen had done 26 years before, Ken decided to have his building materials delivered right to his property. Ken ordered just one airplane to land on the hard winter ice in front of his lodge site. Late in February 1976, the big twin-engine DC-3 cargo airplane touched down right on schedule. Ken assembled a small crew and began the process of building his lodge. Lorane told me that just one load of materials was delivered and that was enough to build the lodge and remodel the cabins that were already on the property. She also told me that the building crew was finishing the installation of the last toilets when their first guests were on final approach. Ken and Lorane hosted guests at their new lodge, Hunting and Fishing Unlimited, during the 1976 season. Although their fishing clients outnumbered their hunters, they maintained the lodge name until the 1978 season, when the name changed to Fishing Unlimited. Ken ceased all hunting operations after the 1980 season.

Slowly but steadily, Fishing Unlimited grew. The other half of the 5-acre trade and manufacturing site was purchased and additional cabins added. Divorce ended Ken's involvement in the business. Lorane has continued in the lodge business.

## Iliaska Lodge
## Ted &Mary Gerken

Showing incredible determination, Ted and Mary Gerken decided to buy a lodge. They hosted their first guests at Iliaska Lodge in 1977. The Gerkens didn't have the luxury of being discriminatory during their first seasons in Iliamna; they catered to anyone and everyone who wanted a place to stay or a meal. Even though they provided food and lodging to all comers, gradually a steady trickle of fishermen started to fill the beds. Ted wrote and published a great book describing the trials and tribulations experienced during their start-up years in the lodge business. I recommend that you read it to get the entire story. From Ted's book, *Gamble at Iliamna*:

*I was 43 that year, a bit over 6 feet tall and 175 pounds. Slim, but no longer a skinny kid, I had managed to stay in pretty good shape despite the numerous desk jobs I'd held in the past.*

*A graduate of the United States Coast Guard Academy, Class of 1955, I had followed the direction and lifestyle of a Coast Guard officer for 20 years, moving from job to job and place to place as my commission and the dictates of the service demanded. I'd served on Ocean Weather Stations and Search and Rescue Cutters in the North Atlantic, spent a year of isolated duty in the Philippine Islands in charge of a Loran*

*Station, set buoys off the coast of Florida, and then, upon transfer to Key West, rescued hundreds of Cuban refugees seeking political asylum from communist Cuba.*

*My last 12 years of commissioned service all involved Civil Engineering duties around the globe, including assignments in Sault St. Marie, Michigan; Bangkok, Thailand; Seattle; and New Orleans; all the while requesting assignment to anything in Alaska, where I'd heard the country was still as wild as it had been during the Gold Rush. I imagined a place where the rivers poured down from the mountains, pure and sweet, and full of fish eager to strike a fly; where the caribou, moose, and bear reigned supreme over millions of uncharted acres of mountain and plain; where a man could still lose himself in the peace and beauty of wilderness untouched by human hands.*

*But duty called and Alaska didn't—it wasn't until I'd served my country in all its other waters that someone finally listened, and I was transferred to Kodiak Island. The U.S. Navy was decommissioning their station at Kodiak, and the Coast Guard decided to take over the entire facility and establish a new base from which to serve all their units in Western Alaska. My lifelong dream had finally come true. My assignment was as the first Public Works officer at the new base, and I was fully prepared and qualified to do the job—but my heart was already in the wilderness. To take full advantage of that small segment of paradise, I bought my first airplane.*

*I had been a pilot for several years, earning my first rating in a J-3 Piper Cub in 1965. A commercial license, my instructor's rating, and an instrument rating followed over the next few years using funds available through the GI Bill. After four months on the job in Kodiak, I took a commercial flight to Seattle, bought a used Cessna 180 on floats (with wheels for winter flying), arranged for instruction, received my float rating in the new plane, and took off solo for Alaska—the next day!*

*Then I felt prepared to "do it all." An indefatigable fly-fisherman from childhood, I could now pit my skills against the salmon, steelhead, char, and trout of Kodiak and the nearby mainland. An enthusiastic hunter, I could now stalk the bear, moose, elk, sheep, caribou, and deer of the region and fill our freezer with the tastiest of wild game. And best of all, I now had an airplane to get there with, an aerial taxi at my own disposal. With a flick of an ignition key, the remotest parts of Alaska were now within my reach.*

*If it wasn't too good to be true, it was, unfortunately, too good to last. After three years, the Coast Guard decided they needed me elsewhere. My first wife was ecstatic–she hated Alaska ever since her first winter and couldn't wait to get back to civilization and into the thick of things again.*

*But elsewhere–I suspected Washington, D.C.–even with a promotion to Captain was a bit thick for me and I put in for a voluntary early retirement instead. Why move on when I was already where I'd always wanted to be? As for the Coast Guard, I would have to learn to live without it–and yes, without my wife, too, if it came to that. It did. She left me for the States for three and four weeks at a time after my retirement officially began on June 30, 1975, leaving our three half-*

*grown sons with me to care for during her prolonged absences.*

*The next day, July 1st, I began a new career as City Manager for the city of Kodiak. If I'd expected the civilian world to be as sure and steady as the Coast Guard, local politics in Kodiak quickly disenchanted me. After one year, I'd already outlasted most of my predecessors. Exactly a year and seven months after taking office, I was fired. Shortly after that, my wife and I divorced.*

*Evidence of progress. Ray Petersen's (upper) Northern Concolidated's hangar at the new Anchorage International Airport. Circa 1955—Ray Petersen Collection*

*By the mid-1960s things had changed significantly. This photo (right) shows not only new jet airplanes, but also large propellor-driven aircraft on the ramp at Anchorage International Airport. Note the lack of development at Lake Hood in the upper right corner of the photograph. Circa 1966—Ray Petersen Collection*

*Within a month I proposed to my ex-secretary from City Hall, Mary, who'd been raised in Alaska since the age of three and loved it more than I did. She cooked like an angel; danced like a dream, worked like a beaver—she'd been brought up on a homestead—she even liked to fish and hunt. When we saw an ad in The Anchorage Times offering this lodge for sale, it didn't take us very long to make up our minds to buy it. So here we were, newlyweds, setting out on a new adventure that promised everything we'd always dreamed of: freedom, wilderness, self-sufficiency–and fish!*

Iliaska Lodge had a grand tradition of operation; it was constructed on the site of Seversen's Roadhouse. When the facility Ted purchased was remodeled and upgraded in 1946, it was one of the largest buildings in the village of Iliamna. In an earlier chapter, I traced the development of Seversen's Roadhouse. After Mary Seversen Clark sold the family business to a missionary group, the roadhouse served as a bible camp and a school. Nearly ten years later, the school was moved to Lake Clark, because Iliamna was just too remote. Jack Vantrease headed a group that purchased the 31–acre site from the missionaries. Once purchased, the property was subdivided, and a portion of it became the site of Iliaska Lodge. I asked Mr. Vantrease to explain how they came up with the lodge name:

*Well, there were five of us, Dave Wilder, Hal Grindle, Paul Carlson, and Chuck Crapuchettes. Once we subdivided the property, we planned to make the roadhouse into a lodge. I believe that Chuck came up with the name. He blended Iliamna with Alaska and said "Iliaska." Once he had the name, the rest of us approved it right away. It sounded right to us. We leased the lodge to members of our group. I can't recall the order, but the Carlsons ran it for a while and so did the Grindles and the Wilders. There were also managers that were hired to take care of the place. When the Gerkens took over from the Wilders, it was still a roadhouse. We never ran it as a fishing lodge. Ted and Mary started that.*

During the 1960s, the roof of the lodge was painted a greenish-blue color and the name Iliaska Lodge was painted in white. Mary Gerken told me that the color of the roof stood out so well, it acted as a beacon for boats and airplanes in bad weather.

It did not take too long for the Gerkins to realize that the roadhouse business wasn't what they perceived. They opened for business within one week of moving in themselves. Slowly, Ted and Mary transformed the roadhouse-hotel they purchased into one of the finest fly-out fishing lodges in Bristol Bay.

As the sun eased over the horizon to end the final Bristol Bay fishing lodge season of the 1970s, darkness spread over more than twice as many lodges as it had found only ten years earlier. The march of progress would not be denied. Despite the fact that some lodges had come and gone, most had improved their facilities and fine-tuned their performance. There was no doubt that sportfishing and the lodges were becoming more popular. Alaska fishing license sales soared. Alaska Department of Fish and Game records indicate that nonresident license sales jumped from 71,711 in 1970 to more than 130,458 in 1979. By the close of the decade, the lodge business had finally grown into an industry. Like fine red wine, the lodge industry was aging, blending, and developing complexity. Competition loomed in the morning light of the coming decade.

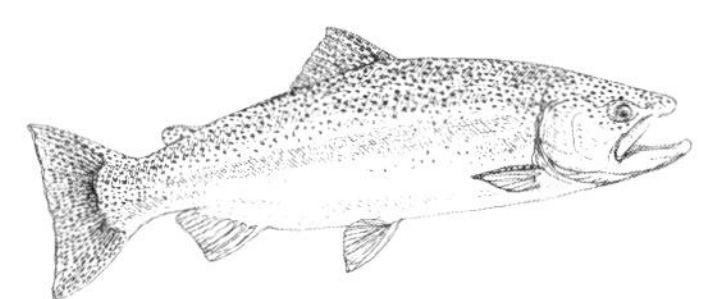

# Chapter 6
# The Decade of the 1980s

"The best history is like the art of Rembrandt; it casts a vivid light on those which were best and greatest; it leaves all the rest in shadow and unseen."
*Walter Bagehot*

Without question, the decade of the 1980s produced the greatest changes in Bristol Bay's fishing lodge industry. According to Alaska Department of Fish and Game records, nonresident license sales more than doubled from 74,699 in 1980 to a staggering 163,098 in 1989. There were just 21 lodges and fish camps operating at the close of the 1970s, and that number more than doubled by the close of the 1980s. The new decade produced a plethora of new players eager to contribute to lodge history. Like a giant game of chess, new lodges–both good and not so good–developed rapidly, while others closed their doors. Even though the earlier decades had been predicated on encouragement, gentlemanly agreements, and cooperation among the players, the decade of the 1980s brought the age of "self-preservation" to the fishing lodges in Bristol Bay.

In chapter 5, I reported that the thought of competition might have prompted John Walatka and Ray Petersen to make changes at the Angler's Paradise Camps. They bought new boats and improved the fishing program. There is no doubt that during the 1980s, competition prompted a proliferation of changes in all the lodges. More than anything else, however, the decade of the 1980s should be called the "Decade of Lodge Expansion." At no other time in Bristol Bay have more lodges zoomed into existence. The 1980s created some great lodges and some greater stories.

## Valhalla Lodge
## Kirk Gay

Ward Gay first came to Alaska in the

mid-1930s from Denver, Colorado. Almost immediately, he became interested and involved in the hunting business. Summers were spent commercial fishing in Bristol Bay with cannery boats equipped with oars. During the spring and fall, Ward spent his time hunting and his winters were spent trapping beaver. He soon realized that airplanes would become a necessity. Without delay, Ward became a licensed airplane mechanic, then traded those skills for flying time. He earned his wings in 1939 along with his territorial Guide License (guides were also issued Deputy Game Warden badges in those early years) and started his flying and guiding service.

During the late 1940s, exploration for oil started gaining interest in the Territory. Several of the early exploratory groups sought out Ward Gay and hired him to do their support flying. By 1944, Ward conceived a business plan to support the oil field exploration. He soon started Sea Airmotive, an air taxi operation based in Anchorage. Despite his quick success in the flying business, Ward never quit hunting. By the 1950s, he'd set up many hunting and fishing camps in Southcentral Alaska, the Kenai Peninsula, and the Alaska Peninsula. Those camps served local fishermen as well as some of Ward's prestigious oil field clients and sportsmen from around the world.

*The original cabin at Six-Mile Lake purchased by Ward Gay. Circa 1955—Kirk Gay Collection*

Realizing a need to have a halfway facility between Anchorage and the Alaska Peninsula camps, Ward purchased a five-acre homestead site on Six-Mile Lake (lower Lake Clark). The property and duplex cabin were part of the estate of Doc Davis, who had come to the area some years earlier.

Dr. Davis had been sent to the area by Indian Affairs to administer medicine to the Natives of the nearby village at Nondalton. According to the record, Doc Davis passed away in 1955. Once purchased, Ward's cabin served as a convenient stopping place in bad weather. It wasn't too long after that he started taking clients there to take advantage of the great Bristol Bay rainbow fishing. Eventually the cabin was referred to as the "Lake Clark Fish Camp," a name it would have until 1980.

By 1959, Ward's son, Kirk, started flying. He was born in 1944 and immersed in the hunting and flying business at the earliest of ages, and it seemed natural to his father to put Kirk in an airplane as soon as possible. While most kids were playing during the summers, Kirk was busy cutting logs and helping his father build "Tsusena Lodge" north of Anchorage along the upper Susitna River. Kirk earned his private pilot's license in 1965. While attending West High School in Anchorage, Kirk missed the first weeks of classes each September because he was guiding clients and flying lodge support with a Super Cub on floats at Tsusena Lodge. By 1966, Kirk had earned his commercial pilot certificate.

After he had his commercial license, Kirk started flying for his father's business, Sea Airmotive. He flew floatplanes and multi-engine amphibs in the summers guiding fishermen, and in the winters, he flew turbine-powered de Havilland Beavers and Twin-Otters on the frigid North Slope oil fields. He also flew passengers and mail out of Bethel on a lucrative contract that

Sea Air handled for Wien Consolidated Airline. Although he enjoyed the flying and claims it was one of the best experiences of his life, flying just wasn't enough. He had guiding in his veins. Kirk guided late spring and fall hunters every year until Uncle Sam intervened and sent Kirk to Vietnam at the height of the war.

Finally back in Alaska, Kirk's mind returned immediately to the hunting and fishing business. He spent the winter of 1968 building the first duplex at the Lake Clark "fish camp" his father had purchased in 1958. By that spring, he was hosting the occasional hunter and guiding fishermen at the camp when he wasn't plying the skies as a Sea Airmotive line pilot. In 1976, Ward Gay sold his interest in Sea Airmotive to his brother Al Gay and then retired. Kirk remained with the company and eventually became its vice-president. By 1979, however, things were getting too big. According to Kirk:

> *At the height of the business, we had 30 airplanes and 15 helicopters, everything from standard Beavers all the way up to the big Convair 580s; from Bell jet rangers all the way through the twin turbine IFR 212 helicopters. We had bases all over Alaska. I felt it was getting too big and not much fun. I resigned and started the groundwork for a major change at the "fish camp." That winter I purchased the cedar logs and materials for the current lodge in Seattle and had them barged to Anchorage. Then I had to have them flown from Anchorage to Six-Mile Lake during the winter. I contracted Sholton-Carlson (now Northern Air Cargo) to haul my supplies in their surplus C-119 flying boxcars. They landed on the ice right in front of the camp. Everything worked out, except the cost. As I recall, the shipping from Seattle to Anchorage, roughly 1,500 miles, cost just about $10,000. The shipping from Anchorage to Six-Mile Lake, a distance of only about 200 miles, cost more than $50,000.*

Despite the heavy shipping costs, the lodge went up as Kirk planned. Kirk hosted his first guests at Valhalla Lodge in 1980. When I asked him how he named the lodge, he told me that while Doc Davis stayed at the site in the 1940s and early 1950s, applying his medical skills to the area, he had a small skiff that he used for fishing. On the side of that skiff, he had a wooden plaque with the name "Valhalla" nicely carved and painted. Kirk told me:

*Kirk spent the winter of 1968 building this duplex at the family "Fish Camp." This photo was taken in 1975. Kirk Gay Collection*

> *Doc Davis was of Norwegian descent and my mother's side of the family was Norwegian. Norse legend tells us that Valhalla was the eternal paradise where the Vikings hoped to go after death, the place reserved for those that lived honorably. I thought that if it was good enough for Doc, it's good enough for me. It was "Valhalla Lodge" from that day on, and I still have the wooden boat plaque hanging above the entrance to the main lodge. I expect it to remain a family tradition for many years to come.*

In my opinion, tradition is one thing that the Gay family embraced. Ward Gay was one of the most respected guides and airplane operators in the state. From his retirement until his death on July 13, 1998, Ward was a regular visitor at Valhalla Lodge. Kirk is cast from the same mold. Kirk's two sons, Chris and John, are on their way to becoming commercially rated pilots. Oldest son Chris is Valhalla's chief guide. Chris has been fly-fishing since he was five years old and, like his father and his grandfather, has an eagle eye for finding those big rainbow trout. Brenda, Kirk's

*"Seattle Post Intelligencer" reporter Burris Enking came to Alaska in 1958 and created a story about Ward Gay. This drawing was featured in the article. Kirk Gay Collection*

daughter, met and fell in love with a young guide, Brad Whitman, who went to work at Valhalla Lodge. They have since married and have given Kirk a grandson, thus another generation to continue the family tradition. Kirk's wife Liza is also a commercial-instrument rated pilot and has owned her yellow PA-12 for 23 years. Liza worked for 17 years as an Assistant Attorney General for Alaska, specializing in natural resource law. Now, she spends her summers at Valhalla Lodge hosting guests. As far as the Gays are concerned, there is no doubt that the lodge business is also a great family business.

## Alaska's Wilderness Lodge
## A Consortium

According to official records, Alaska's Wilderness Lodge, Inc. is owned by 21 shareholders with the largest shareholder owning 7 percent. That same document indicates that the lodge was built in 1980 on fee simple land. It has been operated as a full-service, daily fly-out fishing lodge since it was built.

Mark Lang, who flew for and managed the lodge in the mid-1980s, told me that the land was obtained from Port Alsworth resident Wayne Alsworth, Sr. Once the land was purchased, the owners bought the materials, had them sent through Anchorage and delivered to Port Alsworth. The lodge rapidly took shape and was ready for operation late that season. Owner managers Carl and Pat Bullo have been involved in the management of the lodge since 1981. Prior to 1990, an employee/manager has served as the on-site manager. Since 1991, however, Alaska's Wilderness Lodge became owner operated. This physical and philosophical change serves as the cornerstone of management into the future.

## Katmai Fish Camp
## John Noe and Tony Sarp

Before the start of the 1977 season, Chuck Petersen, then head of the Angler's Paradise Camps, agreed to have outside expert guides do some exploratory fishing in Bristol Bay. When I asked Chuck about the circumstances, he couldn't remember all the details, but he told me he was interested in salmon, specifically king salmon. He sought out the opinions of some of the most respected fishing guides from the Pacific Northwest. John Noe and another guide came to Alaska during the 1977 season and spent a few days at Kulik. During his stay, he fished the Alagnak River for king salmon. When he returned to the Seattle area, he told one of his fishing friends about his adventure and the great fishing.

he has grown and developed Katmai Lodge into the largest freshwater sportfishing lodge in the world. According to Tony, his lodge is also the most successful and makes the most money with the least amount of debt service. Things weren't always that way for Mr. Sarp, especially in 1979. Space prevents me from telling the entire story, but it is one of sacrifice and determination. I should also point out that through his efforts to create his own lodge, Tony created an opportunity for Van

*Alaska's Wilderness Lodge was built in 1980 on fee simple land at Port Alsworth. Evan Swensen Collection*

One season later, Everett-based Air-taxi operator Tony Sarp came to Alaska and fished Bristol Bay for the first time. I believe that more than any other current or previous lodge owner I have been privileged enough to meet, Tony Sarp epitomizes the old Hollywood adage, It doesn't matter what they say about you, just as long as they talk about you. For those who have not had the pleasure to meet Mr. Sarp, let me say I believe him to be just a little flamboyant and perhaps a bit more vociferous than most other lodge operators. He's definitely proud of his lodge business. He started our interview by telling me that from his humble start at Katmai Fish Camp,

Hartley to start Branch River Air Service and is indirectly responsible for the development of two competitive lodges on the Alagnak River: the Alagnak Lodge and Branch River Lodge. From my interview with Tony:

> *I always wanted to go to Alaska, but I couldn't book a trip no matter what I did. I called Alaska Airlines, called Wien Airlines, called everybody. All I ever got was a reservation gal, and all she wanted to do was sell me a seat to Anchorage. She didn't know where Angler's Paradise was, where Bell Island Resort was, or where anything was, so I couldn't get there. Then I realized why*

*nobody went to Bristol Bay to go fishing in the 1970s–they didn't know how to get there. So, I finally decided I was gonna go up there on my own. I was either going to fly my own airplane or fly up commercially, and then I was going to go float some river. I did a bunch of research, found the Alagnak River, and decided that would be a great place to go float. I got a group of my buddies together and we went. We flew on Wien Airlines to King Salmon, and then Penn Air took us out in a Goose and a Widgeon. We landed up at Kukaklek Lake. We didn't float the easy Nonvianuk branch, we floated the tough branch, the Kukaklek. We spent about ten days on the river. We floated clear down to the Diamond J Cannery. We were five miles into Kvichak Bay, all the way into saltwater which is a goofy thing. Penn Air flew us out of that little strip down there with Cherokee 6s. They said they would never go in there again and I don't believe they ever have. Anyway, that was the only thing we could do; but we had a great time, and I fell in love with the river. After our float, I was in King Salmon waiting for the jet to go back home. The captain of the Wien Boeing 737 turned out to be a friend of mine. I had taught him how to fly and got him his job with Wien Airlines years before. We were good friends in those days. By this time, he was a senior captain with Wien Airlines. I hadn't seen him in 10 years. So he ordered me on the airplane and he put me up in the jump seat. Once we were in Anchorage, he took me out that evening. I stayed at his house and he introduced me to Wien Airlines, specifically to a guy named Bob Carroll. Bob Carroll said, wow, you like to float. Do I have a deal for you! One thing led to another. The next thing you know, we put a deal together. I had just sold my business, which was an air charter and flight school operation. I thought it was a great deal and Alaska would be a nice place to spend the summer. Bob Carroll agreed to lease us the Angler's Paradise Camp at Nonvianuk Lake. Bob said they were going to support us with the airplanes and everything else we needed. All we had to do was show up and bring boats for the float trips. They would book the float trips for us and we could do some booking on our own. We put this thing together in the late fall and winter. So, that is how the whole thing started.*

*Come spring, we went to Anchorage on April 1 to sign the agreement. I will never forget that date. John Noe and I went to Anchorage to sign the papers. I wasn't at the office long before things didn't look right. I didn't like the deal. They didn't want to do this, they didn't want to do that, we couldn't do this, and we couldn't do that. Then I found out that Bob Carroll had lied to us. While I was still in Everett gathering gear, Bob Carroll told me that he had 27 people booked for a float trip and had their money. That meant that we had at least 27 guaranteed customers, and they were still booking guys. I spent a lot of money based on his telephone call. Well, then we went to Anchorage and talked with the man in charge. Bruce Jones became the manager over all of the Angler's Paradise Lodges after Chuck Petersen left the company. Mr. Jones told us that Bob Carroll was not only wrong about the bookings, but he was not in any position to make a deal with anyone. In fact, Bruce Jones told us that they didn't have anyone booked and, indeed, had no plans to lease the Nonvianuk Camp. I was stuck about $30,000 in the project at that point. I just said to hell with it, I want to go fishing. So, my captain friend that I taught to fly and got him the job at Wien put me in contact with Hugh Hartley. Hugh knew John*

*Tallekpalek, a Levelock resident who owned a little cabin on the Alagnak River. I leased the Tallekpalek's cabin for the summer. I lost my ass. That was in 1979.*

Bruce Jones told me that while he didn't remember all the details and circumstances, he did recall trying to smooth out a few wrinkles created by Bob Carroll. In fact, Bruce gave me the feeling that Bob Carroll made more than one deal that didn't work out.

Author's Note: Tony Sarp's eagerness to lease a facility spread, too. Four years after Tony was led to believe he could lease the Angler's Paradise facilities located at the outlet of Nonvianuk Lake by Bob Carroll, the facility was leased to Bill Wright, d/b/a Alaska Campout Adventures. Like Tony, Bill bought some equipment, including a large inboard jet boat, went to the Nonvianuk Camp, and started a float trip program similar to that proposed by Tony Sarp and Bob Carroll. Things functioned well until August, when Mr. Wright overstepped the limits of his lease. He changed the name of his operation to Cry of the Loon Lodge and advertised the camp for fishing adventures. On August 24, the terms of the lease were modified. From a letter to Mr. Wright from Raymond I. Petersen, Katmailand, Inc., dated August 24, 1983:

*It was our understanding that your operation at the outlet of Nonvianuk Lake was to be used as a headquarters for float trips on the Alagnak River. We also understood that your jet boat was purchased to run the Alagnak River. It was not and is not our intention to lease the camp as a competitive lodge providing the same type service as Kulik Lodge, either directly or indirectly.*

*Your operation as a condition of the lease must interface not compete with Katmailand's operation. Further, we object to your advertising as a lodge. We have no objection to you calling it something that more properly describes your service. For example, Cry of the Loon River Float Base. We insist that "Lodge" be taken out of the name and your advertising.*

Once Bill realized that he had to stay within the terms of the lease and not compete as a fishing location, he continued his operation through 1986 when escalating financial problems ended his lease arrangement.

From a profit point of view, the first years didn't go well at all for Tony Sarp. Financial troubles notwithstanding, Tony was determined. Besides John Noe, Tony enlisted the help of guides JD Love and Bob Fredhall. Rounding out the group were two Bristol Bay commercial fishermen, Andre Reel and Wilbur Laviguerre, both of whom knew Tony in Everett. For the first couple of seasons, Tony and his partners operated from John and Mary Tallekpalek's winter trapping cabin along the Alagnak River. They hosted few clients, but more importantly, they learned the fishery. Tony certainly learned enough to know that he planned to return the next season. In preparation for the 1981 season, Tony Sarp hired Bob DeVito to be a fishing guide. Bob clarified the circumstances:

*Early in June 1981, I answered an ad in the local Seattle paper for a fishing guide position. I always wanted to go to Alaska. I had fished in the state of Washington for salmon since I was five years old. I decided to give a call, whereupon I had an appointment the next day with Tony Sarp at his home. Following that conversation and meeting, I was handed an airplane ticket. It was interesting, my ticket had Mr. JD*

*Love's name on it, and I was told to use that ticket to travel to King Salmon nine days later. Apparently, JD had decided not to come back and work for Tony in the season of 1981. I was told that they were in the process of building a camp and that Reel's and Laviguerre's commercial fishing boats were going to be loaded with materials and they would be going up the river to start building the first land-based lodge on the Alagnak River. Bob Cusack had a commercial operation on his barge, but it wasn't a land-based lodge and neither was the Anderson barge at Swan Bay. Anyway, as I said, in June of 1981, I met Tony Sarp. I also met Robert Boone Vincent of Darrington, Washington, a very well-known steelhead guide. He was hired as Tony's head guide. I had a job and was off to Alaska for the grand sum total of a guaranteed $500 a month. At least I thought it was guaranteed at the time.*

*I arrived at King Salmon and was met by a floatplane pilot who happened to be Sonny Petersen. Sonny flew me out to the river in the fabled Cessna 206, N9644G. Once we landed on the river, I noted that one building had been put up and another was under construction. That first building happened to be the kitchen and dining area, which was a small little plywood building with no insulation. The construction was minimal, to say the least. The other building was going to turn out to be the bunkhouse at Katmai Fish Camp. It housed all of the guides and all the guests. I was shown to my space, which was an upper bunk with a hook in the rafters for hanging my duffel bag. That was the only room I had for the next four months.*

*Three days after I arrived on the Alagnak River, I was directed down the river. I managed to stumble my way down to tidewater and dropped my hook in a place now known as a slew. I proceeded to catch twenty bright salmon without moving the boat and didn't see another fisherman all day. A career was born as they say. Anyway, I found the fishing during the 1981 season to be fabulous, and we successfully fished a number of people. The operations at Katmai Fish Camp were up and down to say the least, but I had a good time. I decided that I would like to go back and explore this fishery further, if possible. I was offered a raise in salary. I think it was about $1,100 a month after I managed to get my wages in 1981. I decided to go back. I went up there in early June 1982. There were some more accommodations put in, and I actually had a room which I shared with JD Love, who decided to come back for the '82 season. I think that Katmai Fish Camp had a fairly successful season in 1982.*

## Alagnak Lodge
## Vin Roccanova

Researching this book taught me some interesting lessons. For example, I learned that few, if any, lodge players kept journals to record their thoughts and actions. I also learned that two people can share an experience, yet seldom do they explain the circumstances in the same way. When you add some financial wizardry and then add more than fifteen years to muddy the memory, it's not surprising that the picture painted by one of the participants is not necessarily the same as the scene created by the other. Understanding this quirk in the nature of man, I sought out Bob DeVito, who worked at the Katmai Fish Camp as a fishing guide in 1981. He shed some light on the circumstances that led to the creation of the Alagnak Lodge:

*During the '81 season, Vin Roccanova and another guy came to the Katmai Fish Camp. I got the impression they were Tony's friends.*

*Because there wasn't any room in the bunkhouse, they were put up in a tent. I believe that Tony was hoping that Vin Roccanova would give him some capital backing for his operation, but they were apparently put off about being put in a tent for their stay. They weren't really offered a guide and a good boat to go downriver. Their trip was a little less than they expected. Rather than continue to fish at Katmai Fish Camp, they searched out a lease in the lower river in the spring of 1982.*

*Once Vin leased the land from Miss Alma Peterson, a woman from Levelock, they hired a contractor and built a major lodge for that time on the Alagnak River. It was the most complete facility built on the Alagnak River at that time. Its accommodations and construction were further along than Katmai Fish Camp in 1982. Their facility became known as Alagnak Lodge. It was the first real lodge on the Alagnak River. The river was blessed with a really strong run of salmon the whole season of 1982.*

*At Katmai Fish Camp, my job was to be a guide. We probably landed several hundred kings out of my boat alone. Then the silver run came in. It was just a bonanza, still the strongest salmon fishing I have ever seen since, and Alagnak Lodge based its future on that run and a lot of press was written in magazine articles.*

## Branch River Lodge
## Bob DeVito

*My own career changed during the winter of 1982. The usual financial troubles involving Katmai Fish Camp continued, and I didn't get my promised wages. In fact, I had a hard time getting my last month or two of wages during the fall of 1982. I was very disappointed about that because I had worked hard for several months, a young man with a family. I decided I couldn't continue there. I went and searched out my own lease and found a place that Mr. Noe had adjacent to the site of the original Katmai Fish Camp. Evidently, John Noe kept in touch with John and Mary Tallekpalek after his first season with Tony Sarp. He obtained a lease on the land adjacent to Tony's camp. Mr. Noe built a nice little tent camp with one hard building that I believe they constructed in the fall of 1982. They tried to run a fishing business, but Mr. Noe had a problem managing the operation. The moneyman, Carlson, decided to get rid of Mr. Noe and then had problems of his own. He decided to sell the whole operation only a few months after it was built. I was able to pick it up in January 1983.*

*The first problem I encountered was to get the lease transferred into my name, which is an interesting story. I went to Alaska and had a lumber load on the way on a Northland barge from Seattle. I chartered an airplane and went to Levelock to find John Tallekpalek. Once there, I learned he was on a barge headed up the Kvichak. John used to operate barges for the Levelock Native Corporation, and at that time, John was on a fuel barge headed for Igiugig. Anyway, we proceeded up the Kvichak River and saw the barge steaming upstream. I convinced the pilot to buzz them a couple of times. Once they slowed down, we landed and tied up behind the barge. I jumped aboard and I said, "Are you John Tallekpalek?" He said, "Yes." I said, "I want to lease your land." He said, "Good, I want $10,000 a year." Then I said, "Well, we will talk about that." And that was how I got my lease. It was, well, let's just say interesting.*

*I had a few clients that season, but I really just planned to have a peaceful season building the lodge. I was able to build the first four guestrooms at the site of what is now Branch River Lodge. Everyone referred to their places as camps in those days, so, it was called Branch River Camp at that time.*

## The Beginning of Katmai Lodge Tony Sarp

Despite two new lodges entering the business on the Alagnak River, Tony Sarp never wavered from his drive to be the biggest. Tony explained how he started:

*I found a site but had to take the owner out there so that he could identify the property. Sonny Petersen flew us out there in 9644G. Once we landed up the river, I said, "Is this your place?" He said, "Yes." I said, "Good, this is what I want." I signed the deal, gave him 50 dollars in cash to consummate the deal. We signed the lease on a piece of yellow paper. I know that Sonny went back to King Salmon and talked to Lynn Shawback. He laughed, giggled, and said if Sarp even gets out there—let alone builds anything—I'll be a monkey's uncle.*

*I took in some stockholders to make it work. So, we struggled through 1980, '81, '82, and '83. Anyway in 1984, I had a parting of the ways with my stockholders. I had to start over again. We went from 160 clients in 1983 down to about 60, but I got rid of my partners. We were always nip and tuck. We were always about a week from disaster. I remember that a guy had written an article in the Seattle Post Intelligencer in the spring of 1981 about his trip to Alaska. Because of that one article, I booked a whole bunch of guys one morning. I didn't have a lodge, I had a couple of little buildings. I'd have probably ended up in the federal penitentiary because I took these people's money, and I didn't have but just a little-bitty operation. It could only hold about six people, but I had twelve people booked. I had to put the whole thing together in just a short time. In fact, I think I had exactly 17 days to get the materials, put them on the barge, build the lodge, and be ready to take those people fishing when they arrived!*

*Well, besides my own boats, we loaded up two commercial fishing boats designed to haul about 10,000 pounds. We put about 30,000 pounds on each one of them. There were ten of us, a dog, five gallons of fresh water, and five boats full of stuff. We took off from Naknek intending to be at the mouth of the Alagnak River in about six hours. Three days later we entered the Alagnak River. Another three days later, we ended up at the site where Katmai Lodge sits today. When we left Naknek, Lynn Shawback and a bunch of the boys said we would never ever get those boats up to where we were gonna build the lodge. He said that we couldn't get the boats up the river even if they were empty. It was impossible. Everyone laughed, including Sonny Petersen. A week or so later, we were not only at the site, but we had the first two buildings completed.*

## Branch River Air Service Van Hartley

Unlike most of the lodge builders of the 1960s and 1970s, many of the lodge developers of the 1980s were not pilots. The lodges they created, however, were in remote locations that required air support. Van Hartley knew well the lodge business through his work as a guide and manager at the Angler's Paradise Camps. Van explained how he got started in the air taxi business:

*I was sitting at my dad's house in December*

*of 1983. The telephone rang. I soon realized that it was Tony Sarp on the other end of the line. Tony called my dad and asked him to invest a substantial sum of money into his lodge. During their brief conversation, Tony explained his situation but my dad declined any investment. After the conversation ended, I asked my dad what he knew about him and his operation.*

Later, Van called Tony and expressed interest in his lodge operation. They talked about the possibility of Van coming out with an airplane and doing some flying. Tony was exited about the possibilities. Van said:

*I explained that having an airplane was an expensive proposition. Mr. Sarp decided it was a good idea to consult with both the Alagnak Lodge and the Branch River Lodge to see if they were interested in having me come out and do their flying as well. Tony gave me the telephone numbers for both Vin Roccanova and Bob DeVito. I called them and expressed my desire to come out with an airplane and do their flying as an air taxi service. Everyone thought it was a good idea. I commenced to get my commercial license and instrument rating, and I started the process required to form an air taxi service. Once I had my commercial license and instrument rating, I had to get my state air transport approval, my 135 certificate, my airplane, and an FAA Part 135-check ride. I managed to complete everything between January and June 1984, when I showed up on Mr. Sarp's doorstep with an airplane, a certificate, and was ready to go. During the first season, I had a Cessna 206 based out of Katmai Lodge. I leased my dad's Beaver and in 1985 based that airplane at Branch River Lodge. Late in 1986, my dad hurt his knee and had to quit flying. I had to hire another pilot to finish the season. I purchased my dad's Beaver in 1987. Before the season of 1988, Tony Sarp informed me that Mark Air Express would be doing his flying in the future. That year I moved my base of operations from Katmai Lodge to King Salmon.*

## The Unthinkable Robbery and Murder

At the close of the lodge season of 1973, Mildred Walatka retired from her position as Kulik Lodge manager and returned to Anchorage. Since the 1959 season, Mildred had been an integral part of the Angler's Paradise Lodge operation.

Although she didn't return to the lodges after 1973, she kept close contact with her "lodge family" in Bristol Bay. Since her retirement from the lodges in the early 1970s, Mildred lived in the Turnagain area home that she had shared with her late husband, John Walatka. By 1981, her niece lived with her, as well as her son Herbert, who had only recently returned to Anchorage from Juneau. He had developed a sudden and severe case of diabetes that had forced him to retire from the communications business.

Tragedy struck the Walatka family on May 29, 1981. At 4:30 p.m., Mildred Walatka, then 71, walked into the First National Bank of Anchorage on Northern Lights Boulevard. Following closely behind her was an unidentified man. Approaching the teller, Mildred withdrew six-hundred dollars from her account. The two left the bank together and went to a car that matched a description of her car. She and the unidentified man got into the car. That was the last time anyone saw Mildred Walatka alive.

Later that night, the bodies of Mildred and her son, Herbert, were found by a camper. Mildred had been shot six times and Herbert had been shot four times. Their bodies were some 50 yards off the Glenn Highway not far from Palmer, Alaska. The Alaska State Troopers immediately investigated Mildred's home. They surmised that robbery had been the initial motive, as the whole house had been ransacked.

*Mildred Walatka on the radio at Kulik Lodge. Circa 1972—Ray Petersen Collection.*

The police assumed that Mildred and her son had not been surprised by the assailants because they found no evidence of a struggle at the home. Within a few days, police arrested one suspect, and had two others in custody. An article in the *Anchorage Times* (next page) on June 13, 1981, summed up the grisly details.

I spoke with Fred Walatka about the circumstances that led to Mildred's murder. He told me that Mildred always had a big heart and offered help to friends, relatives, and neighbors. She always opened her home to family and neighborhood guests during the holidays. He told me that Mildred had a small ivory collection and numerous artifacts that led one young visitor to speculate that she was rich beyond his wildest dreams. Evidently, this youth passed his "hot information" on to some other less-than-law-abiding young men, and Mildred became an immediate target. Unfortunately for the Walatka family and for justice, intervening circumstances halted legal proceedings. Murder suspect Hopkins copped a plea and in return, was not convicted.

## Cusacks's Alaska Peninsula Lodge
## Bob and Lula Cusack

In chapter 5, I outlined the first commercial guiding operation on the Alagnak River. Bob Cusack started feeling the pressure from the new land-based lodges. He decided to build another lodge in a more remote setting. According to Bob:

*After many years of operating my barge on the Alagnak, my wife, Lula, and I were compelled to seek a more permanent and less populated base of operations. Iliamna resident Dick Sjoden helped me locate some property. After I received some photos of the*

## Man Charged in Walatka Murder

A 20-year old Anchorage man has been charged with first-degree murder in connection with the shooting deaths of Mildred Walatka, 71, and her son, Herbert Oakley, 48. Timothy Hopkins, who listed no permanent address, was charged Friday. Bail was set at $100,000 on the murder charges and Hopkins is to be arraigned in district court at 1:30 p.m. today. A court document filled by the district attorney's office said a bank teller had positively identified Hopkins as the man who accompanied Mrs. Walatka when she withdrew $600 from her bank account the day she and her son were killed.

The document also lists other evidence against Hopkins, including the fact that his palm print was found on Mrs. Walatka's car and that he had blood on his pants at the time he was arrested.

A search of the hotel room where Hopkins was arrested turned up golf gloves that tested positive for blood in a field examination performed at the scene. The test determined that the substance on the gloves was blood, District Attorney Larry Weeks said Friday night.

Blood samples would have to be sent out for analysis.

Hopkins and two other men were arrested at the Kobuk Motel Monday night on outstanding misdemeanor warrants. All three were charged Thursday with possession of stolen property in connection with a May 13 burglary committed in Wasilla. The other two men were identified as Scott A. Walker, 19, and Dale Wilhite, 22. Court documents said in the summer of 1979, Wilhite and Walker had worked for the man whose home had been robbed. Weeks wouldn't say Friday whether Walker and Wilhite were also suspects in the murder investigation. He did say, however, that the investigation is going on "vigorously" and that officials think more than one person was involved in the slayings.

Hopkins was quoted as telling investigators "I can tell you who the shooter is but I'm afraid for my family." State Troopers said he was originally from Kenosha, Wisconsin.

The bodies of Walatka and Oakley were found May 29 by a camper near Palmer. Mrs. Walatka had been shot six times and her son four times with a 9mm pistol.

Hopkins's bail on the murder charges was set at $100,000. He is to be arraigned in Anchorage District Court at 1:30 p.m. today.

Mrs. Walatka was last seen alive when she approached a teller at the First national Bank of Anchorage at Northern Lights and Spenard and withdrew $600 from her account.

When the teller asked how Mrs. Walatka wanted the money, she told authorities, the man identified as Hopkins spoke up and said, "Any way she can get it." The money was given to Mrs. Walatka in the form of four $100 bills and two $50 bills.

The teller said she called her supervisor and another bank employee to watch Mrs. Walatka leave the premises and get into a car that met the description of Mrs. Walatka's car, which later was found in a parking lot at the Boniface Center.

Bank employees said at least two and maybe three other people were in the car when Mrs. Walatka and Hopkins entered it.

The day after the killings, the court document states that Hopkins checked into a hotel and paid for the cost of the room with two $100 bills and two $50 bills. He was identified by the hotel clerk.

The three men were arrested the next day at the Kobuk Hotel. Several guns found in the hotel room were traced to the Wasilla robbery, but none of the guns were the weapons used to kill Mrs. Walatka and Oakley, the document says.

All the guns stolen during the robbery were recovered except for two 9mm firearms; a Colt and a Browning pistol. Ballistics tests showed that Walatka and Oakley were killed with a Browning and a Colt 9mm. The document said a box of 9mm Remington-Peters ammunition was found in a search of a vehicle purchased by the three persons answering the description of Hopkins and his two companions. The vehicle was involved in a hit-and-run accident on May 26 near Boniface and Northern Lights, the court document said.

*property, I gave him a deposit on the land at the east end of Iliamna Lake, near the Copper River. It was the old Denny Moore homestead. The area was known for spectacular rainbow trout fishing. We were so busy during the summer hosting clients at the barge and later hosting hunting clients that we decided to build the new lodge during the winter. To conserve time and labor, I bought a log package from Idaho. It was trucked from Boise to Seattle, barged from Seattle to Anchorage, trucked from Anchorage to Kenai, flown from Kenai to Iliamna, trucked from the Iliamna airport to the lakeshore, and finally barged to the lodge site. Everything else was flown to the site and landed on the hard winter ice. The lodge was completed during the winter of 1982-83. The construction went better than I expected, but we still had problems. One worker received divorce papers and the constant wind nearly drove the others insane.*

*My intention was to have the new facility, Cusacks's Alaska Peninsula Lodge, be a fly-fishing-only lodge. Unfortunately, I was flying back and forth to the Branch River to fish for kings because we had 12 fishermen at the barge and from 8 to 10 at the new lodge. Lula and I found ourselves making jobs instead of money because the operation was so labor intensive. To complicate matters, my Cessna 206 was delayed in the maintenance shop. Dr. Alex Russell and I had to double-trip most of the flights in a C-185 and a Super Cub. By the next year, things started to stabilize. Alex Russell and Bo Bennett flew and guided for me.*
*Lula and I decided to sever ourselves from the Branch River. For more than seven years, I was the only operator on the Branch River. I had constantly concealed the fact there were king salmon in the Branch River from Eddie King, Jack Holman, and everyone else I saw or talked to. We went from complete solitude to seeing as many as five or six float trips pass the barge. The river became cluttered with boats and "boat jockeys." Several lodges sprang up in the late 1970s and early 1980s. Everyone seemed to be fishing the Branch. Several of my old clients had divulged the secrets of the river to their friends in Washington State and Minnesota, and they were moving north and cutting deals with the Native corporations for even more lodges.*

*Bob Hope, then Anchorage Mayor Tony Knowles, Mike Cusack, and Jim Repine on a fishing encounter during the late 1980s. Mike Cusack Photo*

*I sold the barge to Pat Patton, and after two years, he disappeared. I reclaimed it and gave it to my brother, Mike. He housed his own lodge workers on it for a few years. The "old girl" still resides in King Salmon. Looking at it in retrospect, the barge got me started and was a low-overhead, economic son of a gun. The new lodge made life tolerable and a little more relaxing. Our daughter, Nicole, was not going to fall overboard, and the equipment I purchased was not disappearing. We enjoy the seclusion of the new lodge and the convenience of using it as a base for hunting clients. I started guiding when I was twenty-four. After thirty years in the business, I'm sure I'll build another lodge in a few years. I observed Ed Seiler going strong at 70, so I think I'll keep plugging away until I'm 80. Maybe I'll get a real job. I'd like to see how those nine-to-five jobs compare to the twenty-nine-hour days in the lodge business.*

## Mike Cusack's King Salmon Lodge
## Mike and Bonnie Cusack

What started out as a great place to go and a cabin built to accommodate his wife's love for fishing ended up to be one of the most visible lodges of Bristol Bay. It took a few years, but Mike Cusack's King Salmon Lodge evolved from a personal getaway into a great fishing lodge. Mike gave me a quick summary of the details:

*My wife, Bonnie, really loved to fish. I built a cabin in King Salmon for her. Once it was up, I thought, what the hell, I can take a few clients and defray the cost of our own fishing. From then on, it went nuts!*

*Doing what she enjoyed the most. From the left: Bob Hope, Mike and Bonnie Cusack fishing for salmon on one of Bristol Bay's premier rivers. Mike Cusack Photo*

According to Mike, he came to Alaska after finishing his medical studies at the University of Illinois and his residency at the University of Tennessee and UCLA. When I asked him why he chose to come to Alaska, he told me that he was always into golf, hunting, and fishing. Then he said,

*My golf game sucked in those days, so I came to Alaska to take advantage of the great hunting and fishing.*

Once in Alaska, Mike befriended Bill Sims and a few other fishing lodge operators. Late in the 1970s, the tragic death of one of his nephews prompted Mike to invite the boy's father, his brother Jim, to Alaska to cheer him up. Once in Anchorage, they decided to go on a fishing trip at Bill Sims's Lodge in Nondalton. Another of Mike's brothers, Bob, made the trip, too. Not surprisingly, that wasn't the only time

Mike stayed at a fishing lodge. It didn't take Mike too long to realize that he needed to fly. Like many new Alaskans, Mike took up flying. Unlike many Alaskans, once he started his lodge business, he made a decision to leave the flying to professionals.

*I still have my license, but I don't fly anymore. I used to fly a little. I took Bonnie out to Bill Sims's lodge in a Super Cub, but I never flew any of my own clients. When I got into the lodge business, I hired professional pilots. I heard about way too many doctors crashing. I never really had the time to concentrate on a flying career.*

Mike told me that he always considered both his original cabin, and later his lodge, as a family place. Mike explained:

*The original cabin had a kitchen and was a nice place for our family. It started to grow once we started taking a few guests. One thing led to another and we had to expand; but I always made it big enough for our family, and I have a big family. By the time we remodel again, I'll finally have enough room to separate family from our paying guests.*

*Mike Cusack's King Salmon Lodge under construction. Circa 1985—Mike Cusack Photo*

## Alaska Rainbow Lodge
## Ron and Sharon Hayes

By the 1980 season, Ron Hayes was again looking for another lodge site. He had already sold both his fishing lodge, Iliamna River Lodge, and his hunting facility at Wildman Lake Lodge. Ron explained the circumstances:

*I looked myself and told just about everyone that I*

*was in the market for another lodge site but couldn't find anything suitable in Bristol Bay. I heard about a parcel that was located about four miles across Iliamna Lake from Bob Cusack's lodge. Dick Sjoden owned the property and the two of us went up there to look it over. Initially, I thought it would be acceptable, so I started the process of moving my gear, nearly a ton of assorted guiding paraphernalia and some building materials, to Dick's land right away. Well, after I'd flown in there a few times, I realized that the place was too exposed in some wind conditions and had no suitable place to operate an airplane. The waves were just too big, and they'd beat the airplanes to death. I had an uneasy feeling that it just wasn't right for any kind of lodge, let alone a daily fly-out place.*

*Despite my concerns, I continued to move more things to the site. One day I was in King Salmon and a guy asked me if I was still in the market for a site. I asked why and he told me that he knew a lady who might want to sell her allotment on the Kvichak River.*

*To make a long story short, I finally got in touch with Elizabeth Hester, a Levelock resident who worked for the Post Office in Naknek at that time. I told her I was looking for a parcel, and she told me she would be interested in selling when she had complete title to her allotment. Immediately I jumped in my airplane and flew up the Kvichak to see the place. It was great, the perfect place for a lodge in my opinion. I went back to Elizabeth and told her and her husband that I planned to put a lodge on the facility and wanted to let them know I was just a little concerned about building a place before I had a title. They knew I was serious when I looked them right in the eye and said that I planned to spend a couple hundred thousand on a facility and didn't want to have any problems down the road. We shook hands on the deal, and then I spent more than $400,000. It took a while, but I got the title. Governmental red tape caused the slow-down, not Elizabeth. Those were the days when a handshake meant something.*

It didn't take Ron too long to move his gear from Iliamna Lake to his new site on the Kvichak. In fact he told me that he was so excited about the deal, that after he shook hands with Elizabeth Hester and her husband, he flew directly to the Kvichak River property and dropped Sharon at their new site.

*I left her there with just a poncho while I went up to Dick's property to get our camping gear. When I got back she was covered in mosquitoes, but we had a great site.*

Once he had his mound of gear at the site, he ordered more building materials and equipment and had them sent from Seattle to Naknek via Northland Services, the company owned by Jim Haagan, the man who gave Ron his first job in Alaska in 1953.

As soon as the materials were in Naknek, Moody Services delivered them via barge right to the lodge site. Ron and Sharon spent the next season building their new lodge. Ron and Sharon Hayes hosted their first clients at Alaska Rainbow Lodge in 1983. Since then, they have made their facility into one of the best.

When I asked Ron about his lodge and its logistical ease, he told me that he'd had enough trouble during his long lodge career with logistical problems. He mentioned all the remote sites he'd opened and operated. Then told me that he has more time to deal with his guests now that food, fuel, and other necessary items and equipment are delivered to his doorstep. As I said earlier in this book, I believe Ron Hayes has built and operated more lodges than any other player. When he talks, I listen.

## Aleknagik Mission Lodge
## Jim Broady

Jim Broady first saw Alaska in 1965 while he was visiting his uncle. I can just imagine the impact Alaska had on the impressionable high school student from Florida. Things just didn't seem the same in Tallahassee after his military duty ended in Vietnam. He even bought a house and tried to settle down to a "normal" life. Unfortunately, he had seen Alaska. Like several other lodge owners had done, he returned to the Great Land to start a new life.

Jim came to Alaska in 1969. He met and started working part-time for hunting guide Bill Sims. When he couldn't make ends meet flying, he sought other employment. He was a mechanical engineer, but flying was more fun.

During the course of Jim's travels in the hunting business, he discovered a place that he thought would make a great lodge. The Seventh Day Adventist Church had a school and mission on the Wood River, north of Dillingham. The school started in the 1940s when some old cannery buildings were donated and then taken up the river to construct the school. Over the years, numerous improvements were made, and by the time the school closed in 1978, the site and buildings were solid but ready for a facelift. Jim explained why the school and mission closed:

*During the 1970s, many nearby villages built schools. The Alaska Native Claims Settlement Act changed the way many people lived. It just wasn't an accepted practice to send kids away from home. The school just slowly faded away and then closed altogether.*

*I started negotiating with the church in 1979. It took several years to make a deal. A committee ran the church and they weren't in a hurry. One of the problems that the church committee had was the concept of turning over a former mission site to a lodge. They just couldn't accept the fact that lodge goers would be drinking and swearing on the premises. It was really the tradition of the mission that bothered some of the committee. During the negotiations, I mentioned mission lodge in passing, not even thinking about a name for the place. That seemed to break the ice for the church.*

*In order to purchase the place, I needed more money than I had or could sign for. I needed a somewhat silent partner. My longtime friend Dale DePriest decided to help me financially. My wife and I were then able to purchase the facility before the season of 1983. Although we were still working on the upgrades and making it a great facility, we hosted our first guests near the end of the 1983 season. We had our first full year of clients in 1984.*

## Rainbow Bay Resort
## Jerry Pippen

Before 1969, Jerry Pippen had what he considered a great job. He was happy and things looked good in his corporate future. Later that year, his company, the Xerox Corporation, decided that Jerry was the right man to send to Alaska. Jerry explained:

*I was excited when they told me I was going to move to Alaska. I thought about all the hunting and fishing I was going to do. I went right out, bought a brand-new pickup truck, and then drove it to Fairbanks. Once I got there, I learned that there weren't any roads to speak of. I knew right away that if I was going to get a chance to hunt and fish, I needed an airplane. I didn't have a license when I bought my first airplane, a Citabria GCBC. Then I learned to fly. It was great.*

After two years in Alaska, Jerry realized that Xerox was not the life he wanted. Impressed with the grandeur and beauty of the state, he started looking for work in the hunting and fishing industry. It wasn't long before he accepted some part-time work with big game guide Ray Loesche. Among other tasks, Jerry helped Ray build Rainbow King Lodge. Later, Jerry worked with guides Dave Smith and Ken Oldham.

Coupling his love of the outdoors with his business acumen, Jerry accepted the management position at Arctic Circle Hot Springs north of Fairbanks. Despite the fact that his employer was pleased with his work, Jerry wasn't. He still wanted to get into the hunting and fishing business. A few weeks later he saw and answered an advertisement in the Anchorage newspaper. Jerry was excited when he flew to Anchorage, met Sonny Petersen, and interviewed for a management position at the Angler's Paradise Lodges. Jerry felt confident that he'd be in Bristol Bay soon. Unfortunately, a few days later Jerry was notified that his services weren't required at Katmailand.

Jerry made a monumental personal decision based on Sonny's comments. Jerry decided that he would prove to Sonny and everyone else in the world that he could run a fishing lodge. To reach that goal, Jerry decided to build his own lodge.

Immediately the search for property began. Jerry looked himself and had numerous people looking for him, including former Anchorage-based remote real estate agent and future lodge owner Duke Bertke. Fate found Jerry waiting patiently. Early in 1983, Duke called Jerry and told him he'd had a strange call, but thought Jerry might be interested. Jerry explained the circumstances:

*Jerry and Karen Pippen's Rainbow Bay Resort, situated on the shores of Lake Iliamna at Pedro Bay, is a short 20-minute flightseeing trip from Iliamna. Traveling from the lodge to the fishing hole is either by airplane or riverboat. All five species of pacific salmon, char, rainbow trout, arctic grayling, and pacific halibut are available. Evan Swensen Collection*

*Duke called me and said he'd just spoken with the daughter of Sammy Joe Townsend. He was kind of a hermit geologist who had a cabin and some property on Iliamna Lake. About seven years earlier, he turned up missing. They found his boat and never found him. Nobody knows what happened. Anyway, his daughter called Duke and said she wanted to sell the property. Duke suggested I go look at it.*

*My son and daughter-in-law were staying with us when Duke called. Property was so hard to find in those days that I told them to grab their coats. At that time, I had a Cessna 180 on floats. We climbed in and flew down to look over the property. About 15 minutes later, I was so impressed that I unloaded the kids' emergency overnight bag and told them to stay on the property. I jumped right back in my C-185 and flew to Anchorage to give Duke a deposit. I went back to get the kids the next day as the proud owner of five acres.*

When I asked Jerry if he had experienced any problems with the land transfer, he said that Mr. Townsend had homesteaded the five-acre parcel and that recording the sale was uneventful. It wasn't the same getting his lodge materials delivered to the lodge site, however.

Like numerous other lodge builders, Jerry purchased the materials for the lodge and had them barged from Seattle to Naknek. He planned to have the materials simply change vessels at the Naknek docking area and then transported directly to his site from Naknek. Unfortunately, he found the lowest water conditions in years. No materials would make it up the mighty Kvichak that spring, if at all that season. Facing a huge problem, fate found Jerry pacing the floor. He heard through the grapevine that a number of C-130 Hercules aircraft were going to start delivering building materials from Anchorage to Naknek and were scheduled to return empty. Jerry quickly made a deal with the transport company. They agreed to haul his materials from Naknek to the big runway at Iliamna. Jerry told me that those flights were expensive, but he didn't have a choice. Slowly the lodge took shape. During the building process, Jerry learned a few things about his location, and Mother Nature directed him to the perfect name.

*We didn't plan it that way, but when we have rain showers and then the sun comes out, it is very common to see big, huge, brilliant rainbows cover the bay in front of the lodge. It just seemed like every day during the building phase we'd have these fantastic rainbows. Rainbow Bay Resort seemed a natural name to me. I wanted to use the word "rainbow" in the name, but I was thinking about the fish. It's a dual name for us now.*

Jerry Pippen hosted his first guests at Rainbow Bay Resort in 1984. He told me that he had only 15 guests that year because he was delayed so long in getting the lodge finished. His first full season was 1985 when he hosted 65 clients. Then he told me that he charged $1,595 per week including daily fly-outs and round trip airfare from the client's home city. Jerry finished by saying, "Those were the days!"

## Maurice's Floating Lodge
## Maurice Bertini

Like many of corporate America's best young executives, Maurice Bertini was on the way up in the early 1980s. He had it all. New York is a long way from Bristol Bay, however. According to Maurice:

*I was in New York City. I was one of your corporate golden boys. I used to work for Pitney Bowes, and at the time, I was their first major account representative in the United States. I was a very happy young man. Then one day I went to a retirement dinner. There was a very nice fellow whose name was Joe Thompson. He was one of the best men in the Pitney Bowes Corporation. During the dinner, I learned that he had terminal cancer. I really felt bad about that because he was a great guy. I looked up there and I said to myself, 25 years from now I am going to be another Joe Thompson. Do I really want to live and be in the corporate world for another 25 years? Well, fate gave me a little twist and I was transferred to San Francisco, the city by the bay.*

*In the office one day, one of the guys asked me if I'd go fishing in Bristol Bay, Alaska. I said sure. I didn't know he was really serious. I didn't know anything about the place but I agreed to go. Lani Waller had a fly shop in the bay area at the time, and he booked the trip. We flew to Anchorage, then to Brooks Lodge, and then to Grosvenor Lodge. God, we had such a great time! I met Grosvenor managers Kurt Roe and Rachael. They taught me lots about fishing and gave me a real opportunity to feel the power of Alaska. Before that trip was over, I decided that even if I had to beg, borrow or steal the money, I knew I wanted to be involved in the fishing business for the rest of my life.*

*Well, I went back to San Francisco. Lani Waller and I met to discuss the fishing trip. We were at the No Name Bar in Sausalito. After three or four double scotches, Lani got me thinking about going back to Alaska and having my own fishing lodge in the Bristol Bay watershed.*

*I knew the corporate world, so I tried to do it the corporate way. I opened a limited partnership, ran around like a chicken but raised a lot of money. I went back to Alaska with more than one million dollars in my account to buy Bill Martin's Royal Coachmen Lodge. At just the wrong time, one of my partners, naturally the guy who put in the most money, had the audacity to die on me. My limited partnership went right down the drain, and I had to send back all of the money because I happened to be an honest guy. That was that. I had done more than two years of research on Bristol Bay, all the different lodges, and where I wanted to go. I can remember sitting along the Wood River wondering what I was going to do next. I was looking at a fishing tender that was going down the river. The boat had a nice big cabin. I watched it pass me and then the idea hit me. Right then, I decided to build a floating lodge that looked like a big log cabin. A lodge that could be moved at will so I could take fishermen to all the best places.*

*Immediately I went to Homer, Alaska, and took all the money I had and started building a floating lodge. I thought it would take about a year to finish the project, but it actually took more than three and a half. Once finished, I launched the lodge and tried three different times to take the floating lodge into the Shelikof Straits toward False Pass, but each time a huge storm came up and I was blown back into the harbor at Homer. I finally realized that in order to get my new business platform into Bristol Bay in one piece, I had to put it on a huge steel barge and pay to have it delivered to Dillingham. About a month later, I launched the floating lodge near Dillingham.*

*I hosted my first clients in 1986. My first two years were along the Nushagak River. Later, I moved the boat up into the Wood River. I got a permit to operate in the Wood River. I've been there ever since.*

## Fox Bay Lodge
## Mike and Chris Branham

In every sense of the word, Kakhonak Falls Lodge was a family operation. By 1971, however, things started to change. Dennis and his adopted son Chris sold their interest in the Bristol Bay fishing business and promptly built a lodge at Finger Lake, near the Hayes River, about one hundred miles northwest of Anchorage. Hayes River Lodge served as hunting and fishing headquarters for Dennis and Chris. Dennis also established a weather reporting station at Hayes River in 1974.

*Fox Bay Lodge. Circa 1988—Chris Branham Collection*

In the mid-1980s, Bud Branham and his adopted son, Mike, sold Kakhonak Falls Lodge to Sigmund Frolich, a wealthy businessman. Immediately after the sale, Mr. Frolich spent an enormous sum rebuilding the lodge and facilities at Kakhonak. The season after the sale, Mike agreed to serve as manager and hosted his large following of clients at Kakhonak Falls Lodge. Chris told me that Mike just didn't feel the same about the lodge after the remodeling job. The atmosphere wasn't the same. Mike, and more importantly his clients, noted the difference. After that season, Mike canceled his contract to manage Kakhonak Lodge. Soon afterward, the young Branham brothers joined forces and decided to build a fishing lodge in Bristol Bay.

Mike and Chris Branham formed a partnership and purchased some property along the Naknek River between King Salmon and Naknek Lake. At the time they started building Fox Bay Lodge, there were no other lodges in that section of the river made famous by Rapids Camp, the military rest and relaxation established during the military buildup during World War II.

Once the parcel of land had been obtained from Eddie Clark, a local King Salmon resident, Mike and Chris quickly purchased the building materials and got started on the building project. They hosted a few guests during the building season of 1987, but their first full season of operation was in 1988.

### Those Were the Days!

During the 1987 sport show season, the normal entourage of players arrived at the Executive Tower Hotel in Denver to attend Ed Rice's International Sportsmen's Exposition. Alaska was well represented with the usual players gathering for work and play. The 1987 show was a little different from other years as the dates of the ISE show coincided with all-star Wrestlemania showing at one of the local arenas. As luck would have it, the wrestlers, too, checked in at the Executive Tower. As the show progressed as expected, the gathering at the hotel bar was highlighted by the likes of Andre the Giant, Bam Bam, and probably the most famous of all the wrestlers, Hulk Hogan. I can assure you that the fishing gurus, especially the Alaskans, were neither shy nor intimidated by the presence of those giants of the World

Wrestling Federation. Indeed, fishing legend Les Eichorn, who enjoyed his evening elixirs nearly as much as the author, relished the evening bantering with the wrestling showmen. According to Les, he was more than a match for Bam Bam when it came to exchanging comments about anatomy in the men's washroom. Sonny Petersen commented about shaking hands with the Hulkster. Andre the Giant, perhaps the largest man on earth, was calm by comparison to the ISE aficionados. Things were going smoothly until Friday night at about 10:30 p.m.

Hulk Hogan and four of his colleagues were in the bar and had evidently ordered a cab from the lounge telephone. Katmai Lodge owner Tony Sarp and another gentleman gulped down their cocktails, left the bar, proceeded into the lobby, and asked the doorman to get them a cab. As the cab pulled up to the front of the hotel, the doorman, who had no idea that the Hulkster had telephoned ahead, escorted Tony and his friend to the cab. Sarp put his briefcase in the cab and was in the process of getting in when Hulk Hogan ran at the cab yelling "that's my cab you little (expletive deleted)!" Tony Sarp is not one to be easily discouraged, so he turned to see who the hell was trying to take his cab. The driver had already popped the trunk and Tony's friend was already around the cab and had slid into the back seat. With Tony standing at street level, and the Hulkster standing on the curb, Sarp found himself looking at the middle of Hogan's belt buckle. Tony told me that when he looked up, all he could see was the veins bulging in the enraged wrestler's neck. Obviously, Hulk was really pissed. By this time, the trunk was up and even the driver looked scared. Born at night, but not that night, Sarp's pal quickly got out of the cab and fled the scene. The doorman had disappeared and Tony could see he was going to give up the cab in a hurry. Hulk yelled back at the hotel for his friends to come out. The cab driver, who assumed all hell was about to break-out, jumped back into the cab, started then revved the engine, and sped away with the tires screeching, all the doors open, and the trunk flopping.

As the story goes, Hulk started after the cab at a dead run. Witnesses told me that he would have caught it had the driver not gone through a red light. Hulk was furious as he walked toward the front door looking for Mr. Sarp, who had seized the opportunity to seek safer terrain. By this time, most of the bar crowd had come out to watch the fracas. Tony watched from the safety of the lobby as the Hulkster stood in the middle of the road and stopped the next cab by threatening the driver with bodily harm. Once the cab stopped, Hulk placed his hands on the hood and told the driver, "Stay right where you are." One by one, his wrestler pals got in the cab, then Hulk got in. The cab drove off listing to one side from the weight of those five big guys. When he finally returned to the hotel, Hulk started to search for the man who tried to steal his cab! Naturally, Tony wasn't to be found. The Alaska guys are tough, but as in the words of one of Kenny Rogers' biggest hit songs, they "know when to fold'em!"

## The Competitive Edge

Like most of the early lodge players, Ed Scherockman was proud of Kulik and definitely resented the fact that other lodges and lodge airplanes started to use and fly into some of the waters that had previously been fished by Kulik guests alone.

No matter how many times Ed was told that times were changing, he just couldn't accept the fact that other lodge airplanes started to frequent the Kulik River. Ed developed a possessiveness that few could comprehend. After all, he had been a steady customer since the early 1960s when he seldom saw another angler, and no other lodge operator had the audacity to fish around another group of fishermen, let alone right at someone's lodge site. After Ed's jet-boat accident in 1977, he became an employee and worked at Kulik Lodge as a bartender and part-time fishing guide. Once he became a member of the staff, his resentment intensified dramatically.

On one blustery day during the 1986 lodge season, a stout west wind prevented Enchanted Lake Lodge guide Brian King from taking their boat safely back to Enchanted Lake. With no other option, Brian left the boat parked near the outlet of Kulik Lake and flew back to their lodge with the guests. Ed Scherockman, who had been guiding Kulik guests after dinner, saw the boat and grew furious that another lodge was infringing on his territory. Once fishing ended for the evening, Ed returned his guests to the lodge, grabbed an ax, and returned to the river alone. Ed was so incensed that he chopped a hole in the boat. Frustrations somewhat abated, he returned triumphantly to camp. Sonny Petersen was in the lodge when Ed made a dramatic entrance. Sonny highlighted the conversation:

*Ed came into the lodge and started talking to some of the other guys at the bar. I could tell they were getting excited, so I went over to see what was going on. Ed proudly said that he had taken care of the problem.*

*I asked, "What problem?"*

*Ed said, "The problem, you know, the boat! The boat! They're leaving a boat on our river!"*

*I asked what he was talking about.*
*Then Ed blurted out, "I chopped a hole in it."*

*Once Ed told me what he had done, a couple of us went up the river to look at the boat. It was obvious that Ed had taken several good whacks at the bottom of the boat with an ax. There were numerous dents in the bottom but only one ax swing had been strong enough to cut the metal. There was only one big hole in the boat, but it was definitely out of commission. I told Ed and whoever else that was in hearing distance that I didn't care how much they resented the boat being on the river, that kind of behavior couldn't and wouldn't be tolerated again. No matter what!*

*The next morning was clear and calm. I waited until Dick Mathews flew overhead expecting to find his boat where he left it. I took a boat up the river. I was waiting when Dick taxied into the beach. I told him that I had brought him a boat to use for the day. With a curious look on his face, he asked why?*

*I told him there was a little problem with his boat.*

*Dick replied, "Oh yeah, what kind of a problem?"*

*"Well Dick, Let's just say one of my employees tampered with it!"*

*Right away, he knew who it was. He took me aside and told me that Ed had gone down there for dinner just a few days earlier. I told Dick that I really didn't understand why he would do such a thing. Perplexed to say the least, Dick climbed back into his Beaver and departed. Then Brian King took me back to the lodge and then returned to his clients. Later that day, Kulik maintenance man Harry Wehrman repaired the Enchanted Lake Lodge boat. Late in the afternoon, their airplane landed at Kulik to pick up Brian's fishermen. Once his clients were safely aboard Enchanted Lake's Beaver and headed back to their lodge, Brian traded boats with Harry and then returned to Enchanted Lake. That ended the hostilities, but not Ed's animosity.*

*The hatchet-man, Ed Scherockman with a Kulik River rainbow during the 1988 lodge season. Ray Petersen Collection*

As the decade of the 1980s came to a close, so did the age of rapid expansion. The fishing lodge industry had finally become just that, an industry. With that recognition, each of the players had to get serious about running a business. Facing increased levels of bureaucracy and governmental regulations, some of the players started to communicate and cooperate by the end of the decade. I believe that more than anything else, however, the growth experienced during the 1980s forced all the lodges not only to refine their fishing programs, but to realize that each was a part of a much bigger picture. I like to call that picture the fishing lodge industry.

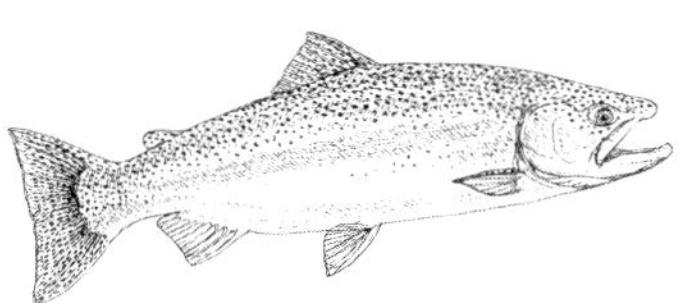

# Chapter 7
# The Decade of the 1990s

"This isn't the end. This isn't even the beginning of the end.
But it is, perhaps, the end of the beginning."
*Anonymous*

Compared to the decade of the 1980s, the '90s brought few new lodges and fewer new players to the Bristol Bay region. As you might expect, however, fishing license sales continued to swell, as more regions of the state grew popular with the Isaac Walton types. The sportfishing season of 1990 ushered in a new trend in state fishing license revenue. For the first time in Alaska, nonresident fishing license sales outnumbered resident purchases. During that year, 182,779 nonresidents and 180,214 residents purchased a fishing license. I asked Alaska Department of Fish and Game fisheries biologist Al Howe about those numbers. He told me that 1990 is often cited as the year of the change. He explained that the Alaska Department of Fish and Game receives a great portion of its funding through license sales, then noted that nonresident fees are higher than those for residents. Considering those facts, he confirmed that his department pays close attention to the overall numbers. By 1998, nonresident sales soared to 254,494 while resident sales dropped to 173,833. No matter what significance those numbers have to anyone, the fact remains that fishing is a huge attraction in Alaska. Television, movies, magazines and newspapers have been spreading the word since 1950, when Ray Petersen opened the first full-time fishing lodges. The owner of the first new facility created during the 1990s heard about Alaska as a young boy.

## Alaska Trophy Adventures
## Charlie Summerville

In 1985, Charlie Summerville came to Alaska to work as a United States Coast Guard licensed river guide on the Naknek River. Charlie came with lots of experience. Since 1982 he had owned and operated his own guide business, Trophy Trout Anglers, in upper New York State. There, he fished the world-famous Salmon River with a drift boat for steelhead, trout, and salmon. His New York off-season, June through September, was a perfect fit for an Alaska adventure.

During his first two seasons in Bristol Bay, Charlie felt that there was a niche unfilled by the numerous businesses offering sportfishing. In 1987, Charlie decided to expand his New York guide business to include Bristol Bay and the Aleutian Islands. He offered guided wilderness float trips and custom overnight trips catering to small groups of serious anglers who wanted an Alaskan experience at a reasonable price.

The following spring, Charlie arrived in King Salmon with $1,000 in his pocket, and his pick-up truck and trailer that carried his custom-made 17-foot aluminum riverboat. Charlie drove that truck and trailer from New York to Anchorage and then had them barged to Naknek. He had 16 clients booked for the season on various trips in and around Bristol Bay.

Although he thought his first season had been a success as far as the clients were concerned, Charlie had to be concerned about his living situation between trips. That first season in King Salmon he squatted in an old abandoned gravel pit and lived in a wall tent all summer. He had to sneak into the local boat yard at night to take a shower and to get water. Things had to get better. Every time he considered giving up, he remembered his parents' lessons about having a positive attitude. Rather than dwelling on the negatives, Charlie became excited about the excellent fishing he found in the Alagnak River. After his third season, Charlie felt he had a good feel for what his guests wanted and expected from a trip to Alaska. Armed with these thoughts, he set off as a privateer in paradise to build on this idea and start his deluxe Alagnak River Outcamp.

After a lot of research, Charlie arranged a short-term lease with a local Native gentleman on a 160-acre allotment located just above the start of the now famous "braids" section of the Alagnak River. Charlie established his presence on the Alagnak River in 1991 when he put in his Weatherport camp. The camp has continued to grow each season with the help of his longtime friend and his first employee, Capt. Troy Creasy. By 1996, Charlie expanded his operation again adding two more camps on the Alaska Peninsula.

Today, Charlie lives in King Salmon full time with his wife Helen and their three daughters. When I asked him to reflect on the business, he smiled and told me that he's simply living the boyhood dreams that he had since his days at Sandy Creek High School in the early 1980s when his schoolmates called him "Fishhead."

## Angler's Alibi Lodge
## Jack Holman and Karl Storath

In my opinion, Karl Storath is one of the finest guides and camp operators in Bristol Bay. After all, he got some great advice from one of his regular lounge customers while working as a bartender in northern New York State. According to Karl, Rod Serling, the creator of the *Twilight Zone*, often waxed eloquent after a few drinks. Now that I'm thinking about it, there are certain similarities that cannot be ignored. Each new lodge season is like another science-fiction episode. From my interview with Karl:

*I first came to Alaska in 1974. Jack Holman invited me up for a visit while he was teaching at Levelock. A year later, he bought Ingdal's place and I came up again to help him get started. I worked with him every summer through the season of 1977. In 1978 and 1979, I worked for the Alaska Department of Fish and Game at their facility in Igiugig, at the head of the Kvichak River. I worked as a maintenance man and single-handedly rebuilt their entire facility. In 1980, I worked as a deckhand on a commercial fishing boat in Bristol Bay. During that long summer, I started thinking about starting a fishing lodge on the upper Kvichak. After considering all the pros and cons, I made a deal with Hermie Hermann to lease his property on the bottom end of Otter Island.*

*To make a long story short, while I was working for Fish and Game in Igiugig, I managed to make a couple of deals for Hermie and he ended up owing me a little money. I inquired about his property on Otter Island and he agreed to lease it to me for a very reasonable price. It was a great place for a lodge. Things were shaping up until I simply changed my mind. I don't remember the exact reason, but I was probably tired of commercial fishing. I just know I didn't go for it. I went back to New York after the close of the fishing season and promptly built a restaurant. I ran that for seven years. I came back and guided for Jack at No See Um Lodge in 1984 and 1985. I also ran my own commercial fishing boat. Jack had a commercial boat and permit that he had purchased from Jimmy Woods. Jack was too busy running the lodge to fish the permit so he sold it to me for one dollar. I fished that season and then sold boat and permit back to Jack for the same dollar bill I had used to buy it with two months earlier.*

*Viewed from the Kvichak River, Karl Storath's Angler's Alibi Lodge. Circa 1997—Karl Storath Photo*

When I asked Karl about the value of the permit, he told me that when he sold the boat and permit back to Jack for the grand total of one dollar, it had a market value of about $175,000. What are friends for?

*In 1993, Jack called and wanted to know if I would come up and manage his tent camp on the Alagnak River. He'd been taking clients to the Alagnak for numerous years and wanted to have a more permanent camp. Indeed, when I first worked for Jack, we put a boat on the Alagnak River in 1976. Anyway, after Jack called, I decided to give it a try. We called the Alagnak camp Angler's Alibi. At the end of that first season, Jack and I sat down with a bottle of Kendall-Jackson's finest wine and worked out a deal that I couldn't refuse. The following year, I put up some more tents and increased the capacity of Angler's Alibi from six to nine guests.*

## Royal Wolf Lodge
## Chris and Linda Branham

As Mike Branham had previously experienced at Kakhonak Falls Lodge after the rebuild by the new owner, the situation at Fox Bay Lodge just didn't feel right for Mike and Chris. Within two years of opening, things just needed to change for the Branham brothers. According to Chris:

*Fox Bay Lodge was an ideal location logistically, but as a fishing lodge, it lacked the wilderness atmosphere and experience we knew the guests wanted and needed.*

In 1990, Mike and Chris sold Fox Bay Lodge to German-born industrialist Klaus Stiegler. As the majority partner, Mike agreed to sign a no-compete clause as a condition of the sale. Once the sale was complete, Mike left Alaska and returned to the family ranch in Utah and his hunting interests in Africa. Chris Branham explained the situation:

*When Mike and I first conceived the plan, I agreed to be at Fox Bay in June and July. I had hunters and my own fishermen in August and September. Dennis and I had Hayes River and the camp at Big River Lakes. Most of our big hunts were based at Hayes River Lodge. We took fishermen various places for different species. For sheefish, we'd go the Sleetmute where I rented some cabins from Nick Mellick. From there, we'd go to Hayes River for grayling and char. We'd take the salmon fishermen and wildlife watchers to Dennis's cabin at Big River Lakes. Big River Lakes, like Hayes River in 1974, became an official state weather-reporting station in 1984. We hired some caretakers to give the weather observations and to take care of our fishermen. Because I agreed to be at Fox Bay for a short time each season, Mike had the controlling interest. Originally, Linda and I agreed to stay full time at Fox Bay. Linda was going to be the head chef and I was going to help with the flying, guiding and help Klaus with the transition. Over the following winter, however, Klaus decided to learn to fly, and his wife, Doris, decided to assume the chef's duties.*

*Once we learned of the Stieglers' decision, Linda and I started searching for a lodge site. I spent hours going over the land use and ownership records at the Anchorage office of the Bureau of Land Management. I was searching for Native allotment land that could be transferred easily. Once I had several sites, I had to track down the owners to see if they were interested in selling their land. Interestingly enough, one site that we examined thoroughly is now the home of Rapids Camp Lodge. In time, I found the perfect place for our lodge. The property was just above the Alagnak River near the outlet of Nonvianuk Lake. Levelock resident Edwin Petersen owned it, so I contacted him and made an offer. The property was transferred to us on August 23, 1993.*

Chris and Linda Branham weren't the only ones who thought Edwin Petersen's property was perfect for a lodge. Bill Sims told me a story about the same property that Chris eventually purchased. According to Bill, sometime during the hunting season of 1970, he and Denny Thompson flew their friend, Edwin Petersen, to the outlet of Nonvianuk Lake, where Edwin wanted to stake his land. He was entitled to a land selection due to the Alaska Native Claims Settlement Act. Bill told me that he and Denny Thompson hunted and fished the area and offered to lease or buy Edwin's claim as soon as it was processed because they thought it was an ideal location for a lodge. Fortunately for Chris and Linda Branham, by the time the claim was processed and transferred to Mr. Petersen, Bill Sims already had another site and a lodge.

From conversations I've had with most of the lodge builders, I can tell you that it is one thing to locate and then obtain a piece of property in Bristol Bay, it is altogether another thing to build and create a successful lodge business. Chris explained the logistical process he had to endure:

> *Over the next eleven months, Linda and I were totally immersed in the building project. I still conducted some fall hunts to keep the cash flowing. I ordered some of my supplies from King Salmon and some came from Anchorage. With the help of Katmai Air, especially Sonny Petersen and Bo Bennett, who changed their own flying schedules to accommodate us, we were able to get all the materials from King Salmon to the lodge. The material that came from Anchorage arrived in the village of Igiugig via Wood's Air DC-6. Like the materials from King Salmon, those materials were flown to our site by Katmai Air's float-equipped DH-3 Otter. The materials started to arrive in June of 1994, and we hustled to get enough of a camp open to host a few clients. That first season, the guests slept in wooden-floored wall tents just like the first guests did at the Angler's Paradise Camps in 1950. By the spring of 1995, we completed all the wooden guest cabins and the lodge itself.*

During the research for this book, I became interested in the names various lodge owners have chosen, and their rationale for doing so. When I asked Chris about Royal Wolf Lodge, he told me that he wanted people to associate the lodge with adventure, excellent fishing, and wild Alaska. He chose the word Wolf because wolves represent the wildest of Alaska's animals. They represent unspoiled wilderness and live in wild country. Then, in a play on words, he told me that even though the spelling is different, he hoped that people would associate the lodge name, Royal Wolf, with the well-known and now famous fishing fly, the Royal Wulff, created by Lee Wulff, hereby casting the fly-fishing image over his business. I believe it has worked for the Branhams very well.

*Chris and Linda Branham at Royal Wolf Lodge. Circa 1995—Chris Branham Collection*

Chris closed his comments by telling

me that this is it as far as lodges go for him. Since coming to the United States as a young lad, he has spent his entire adult life working at Kakhonak Falls Lodge, Hayes River Lodge, Big River and Fox Bay Lodge. Finally, at Royal Wolf Lodge, Chris and Linda have found the perfect location and plan to continue their family tradition at Royal Wolf Lodge until retirement time.

*We finally found the ideal location that can produce the kind of fishing and adventure experience that our clients deserve.*

## Rapids Camp Lodge
## Richard Van Druten

More than a few lodges have opened because of the dreams of a fisherman. I met Richard Van Druten soon after his arrival in Bristol Bay early in the 1990s. Recently, I asked him to explain why he came to Alaska and how he got into the lodge business. According to Richard:

*I started fly-fishing when I was ten. It became the focus of my life and grew into a passion that gave my life both direction and meaning. After a mandatory two years in the South African Army, I attended college in Texas. I excelled in American football, and after graduation I tried the NFL. After a brief two-year stint playing football that stopped with a career-ending injury, I met the world-renowned fly-casting instructor and teacher, Mel Krieger. I attended one of his seminars and we became friends. Shortly thereafter, I invited Mel back to Africa with me, where he gave a series of seminars with me as his assistant. We took some time for ourselves, too. We fished for tigerfish in Botswana, saltwater fish in Mozambique, and trout in South Africa. During our safari, Mel told me that I needed to experience Alaska, a fly-fisherman's dream. He gave me the address of a fishing lodge in Bristol Bay and a contact name. I immediately submitted my resume, hoping to get a job as a guide. I was hired shortly thereafter and began my Alaskan experience during the 1991 season.*

*The impact that Bristol Bay had on me was soul quenching. I decided that Alaska had to be included in my lifestyle forever. For the next five seasons, I guided clients and learned the fishing country. I jumped at every opportunity to see more rivers and fish new water. I learned the geographical terrain like the back of my hand. I learned the politics and respected and enjoyed the local culture. I learned which rivers were fishable and when they peaked. After five years, I knew the names and the places, who was who in the industry, and how the industry functioned. I loved what I was doing.*

*By my third season as a guide at the lodge, my passion for this lifestyle spawned the idea of owning and running my own lodge business. I had run upriver in my boat countless times to fish at the famous rapids on the Naknek River. It was during these excursions that I noticed the sudden erection of a cabin on the north shore of the river opposite the rapids. I remember thinking, Wow, what a great spot for a lodge. I just had to find out who owned that property. I wanted it.*

*Instinctively, I started putting a business plan together. After locating the property owner, I asked if he would sell me the land. He wasn't interested. I persisted in pestering him for the next two and a half years. His answer was still no. Finally, I got him to agree that if he ever wanted to sell, he'd give me the first chance.*

*After the season of 1993, I was in Arizona doing some marketing research, and discussing my plan with a fishing friend. It was here that I first designed the lodge. Fortunately, the design changed a few times after that night.*

*I redesigned the lodge again on a napkin at the KingKo Bar and Grill in King Salmon. The KingKo had just been rebuilt after being destroyed by a fire the season before. I met some of the building contractors who became known in King Salmon as the "dream team" because of the rapid rebuild of the bar. I approached one of the builders and told him what I wanted to do. He put my rough sketch to scale and even went out to the property and measured the site. Not long after that I went to the property with my video camera and made a sales tape. My idea was solid by this time!*

*A small portion of Alaska's Sportsman's Lodge building materials and equipment that were delivered in the two boats on the right. Brian Kraft Photo*

*By the summer of 1994, I had told a few select people about my idea. Even though I still hadn't convinced the owner of the perfect property to sell, I pursued my dream. After the season of 1994, I went back to Dallas and started playing rugby for my old team, the Dallas Harlequins. I networked my ideas about a lodge with a few players. Optimistically, I started mailing out a business proposal to anyone I knew who could possibly help my venture. Not long after that, the property owner contacted me. He said that he had decided to sell and had already received some offers. I had no money at the time. I needed an investor. As luck would have it, I was able to locate a guy with some money. He thought the idea sounded good.*

*After overcoming the logistics and the rigors of building a lodge from the ground up in a remote part of the world, I felt like I had paid my dues. Rapids Camp Lodge opened for guests during the season of 1996. My dream had come true.*

## Alaska Sportsman's Lodge
## Brian Kraft
### He shoots—He scores!

Brian Kraft first came to Anchorage to play hockey for the University of Alaska Anchorage Seawolves. The young right-winger from Chicago lived in Anchorage and played hockey from 1988 through the season of 1992. Between hockey seasons and school schedules, Brian worked a two-week-on, two-week-off schedule for Doyon Drilling on Alaska's North Slope. Brian told me that the work was hard, but his schedule allowed him to start fishing in a very serious manner.

By his senior year, Brian was an accomplished fisherman and decided to take the entire hockey team on a Kenai River float trip before their grueling season started. The only problem was that he couldn't find anyone to rent him some rafts. As a marketing major, Brian stepped up to the challenge. If he couldn't find a raft, he felt sure that neither could anyone else. As his senior year marketing project, Brian researched the rafting business as well as the air taxi business in Anchorage. His research led him to believe that a company offering raft rentals might be successful.

*By mid-July, the lodge was starting to take shape. Brian Kraft Photo*

Shortly after graduation, Brian received a contract to play professional hockey in Europe. He went to Rome in December, 1991. He played for and lived in Bolzono, Italy during the 1992 hockey season. At the close of that season, Brian returned to Anchorage, took the money he made playing hockey and started a raft rental company that he called Kraft Adventures. Brian told me that he couldn't afford any advertising other than word of mouth, but that worked so well that he had trouble keeping up with the demand. His business became so popular that he soon faced increased pressure to start guiding float trips himself. It didn't take him too long to start offering daylong trips in the upper Cook Inlet area. Brian said:

*Once I started doing the guided day floats in the Anchorage area, it was a natural progression to go to Bristol Bay. I did some guided floats on the Alagnak River. In 1995, I read an article about a guy who got indicted for running drugs in Alaska. The paper listed one of his assets as the Big Mountain Lodge. Because I knew the area, I did a little research and found out that the government had seized the property but hadn't taken possession because they didn't yet have a conviction. The property was on a Bureau of Indian Affairs land lease. I talked to the BIA, the United States attorney, and the guy who had been arrested. I worked out a deal to run the lodge for a year. Then I entered into a second yearly contract. At the end of that year, I was supposed to get an option to purchase the place. Well, the defendant's lawyer stepped in and he got possession of the property. He got the place and I got the shaft.*

*I looked around for a place to buy but wasn't too successful. I kept going back to the Kvichak because I loved the place. I finally found a parcel of land along the Kvichak*

*River. I put together a prospectus and mailed it to everyone I thought might be interested in a lodge project. That's how I found my partner, David Sandlin. He was a guest at Big Mountain when I managed the place. He had been trying to put together a lodge up at Lake Creek, near Anchorage, but that didn't work out. He was interested in this type of business. He had a perfect attitude. He said, whatever it takes, let's just do it. He knew the lodge business was risky and meant long hours. I was naive enough to say let's just build a lodge. The building of the lodge is actually a story in itself. I designed the facility based on my experience at Big Mountain Lodge as well as observing the layout of other lodges I'd been fortunate to visit, including Mike Cusack's King Salmon Lodge, Ole Creek Lodge, Brooks Lodge, and most of the other lodges on the Kvichak River. We bought the materials in Seattle and had them barged to Anchorage. From Anchorage they were flown to Igiugig. That's where the fun started. We had to take each piece down to the river, load it into my 18 -foot skiffs for the 4-mile boat ride to the lodge site. Then each single piece had to be unloaded and then carried up a steep hill to the building site. When you consider that we had about 500,000 pounds to move, it was quite a feat!*

Brian made it very clear that he had lots of help during the building stage. As well as a grand thank you to all the residents of the village of Igiugig, he gave credit to Kevin Diliston and Brent Lineberger, who were friends of his partner's daughter. They came to Alaska just for the experience. Then Brian told me that some of his professional hockey-playing teammates provided a big help. Anchorage Aces players Hayden O'Rear, Dave Ducette, Paul Williams, Jim Mayes and Dean Larson made a big impact. He told me all the guys worked numerous 18-hour days. Brian also made it clear that Lee Nieman, a contractor from Palmer, was the project leader. Brian stressed the point that Lee really knew what he was doing, and he did it right.

*We started with bare ground on June 23, and we opened the lodge to guests on August 17, 1997. It was quite an interesting project.*

## The First and the Last Kulik Lodge

Earlier in this volume you learned that the Angler's Paradise Lodges, Brooks, Grosvenor, Nonvianuk, Battle and Kulik were the first true fishing lodges in Bristol Bay and the first in Alaska. During the first 49 seasons of operation, Kulik has become the center of the Angler's Paradise system as well as Alaska's premier fishing lodge. Kulik is the place against which all other lodges are judged.

Throughout this book, I've tried to highlight and chronicle the development of an industry. From the 1950s through the 1990s, the growth was no less than phenomenal. Prior to the 50th season of continuous fishing lodge operation, the Alaska State legislature honored Ray Petersen not for his huge contribution to Alaska's flying community, but for his lodge development. The legislature named him the "Father of Alaska's Sportfishing Lodges" in recognition of his efforts in starting the first fishing lodges in Alaska. I think it is safe to speculate that the great fishing lodges in Alaska are here to stay. Considering all the growth, somehow, I think it is not only fitting but also ironic to close this chapter with the first major Bristol Bay lodge rebuilding project. The entire lodge story starts and ends with the crown jewel of the Angler's Paradise system, Kulik Lodge.

Over the years, age had taken its toll on the main lodge building. Although I don't believe that Sonny Petersen had any other plan in mind when he decided to restore and add to the lodge building, his decision allowed the decade to close on the lodge business as it had opened fifty seasons before, with a major building project at Kulik.

During the 1998 season, Sonny made the decision to not only repair the lodge building, but to modernize the lodge by increasing the size of the kitchen and adding a new lounge to the log lodge. Once that decision was made, the logistical problems loomed over Katmailand as they had for each and every lodge builder since Bud Branham started the first lodge building in 1949. Sonny's problem, however, was compounded by the fact that he had no summer months to complete the project. Sonny just couldn't cancel any part of an already booked season. The Kulik project had to be completed between October and the end of May, quite unlike any other lodge building project in Bristol Bay.

Late in the season, premier log-home builder Lee Raymond of Eagle River made the first of several visits to Kulik to evaluate the lodge building. Almost immediately, he

*October at Kulik Lodge in 1998. Once the last guests departed, the work began. Sonny Petersen Photo*

*Kulik Lodge under construction. The lodge walls are up, but the roof structure is still missing. Lee Raymond and his crew worked in sub-zero temperatures and bitter winds to get the lodge ready. Sonny Petersen Photo*

told Sonny that before he could begin the new construction, he would have to repair and replace numerous logs in the building. Naturally, the logs that needed replacement were the ones on the bottom of the walls. Over the next few weeks, Lee traveled to Kulik measuring this and that, while getting a feel for the lodge business. By early September, he had a huge log order ready for shipment.

*Bristol Bay usually has some great warm weather in early April and May. Not the year Sonny chose to do some construction. Snowdrifts exceeded 10 feet in many places, including the back of the lodge. The extremely cold weather and deep snow only added to the excitement of the project. Sonny Petersen Collection.*

Once the last guests departed Kulik in early October, the construction blitz commenced with a fury that only impending winter could bring. At the time the original lodge logs were cut, aged, and milled at Kulik, Lee had a sawmill near Chitna machine the logs to his specifications. After the logs were cut, they were taken to the Palmer airport where Lee had a crew of "aggressive" log peelers. Once peeled, the logs and other building materials were assembled at Warren Wood's hangar for shipment to Kulik. Fortunately, Warren's DC-6 could haul about 28,000 pounds. Everyone felt an urgency to get the materials to Kulik before the snow started to fly. Load by load, the DC-6s landed and the materials were taken from the Kulik runway and placed in a systematic pile

*Once the roof was completed, the crew moved inside. Sonny Petersen Photo*

adjacent to the lodge. It took several days for the big airplanes to finish their work. When the crew wasn't unloading the airplanes, they were busy jacking up the entire lodge building so that Lee could replace the aging and rotten logs. Once the old logs were replaced, Lee prepared the foundation for the new construction. The crew left in early November, before the full onslaught of winter. Katmailand employees Harry Wehrman and Jim Brock joined Lee and his crew when they re-

Almost done. Once the outside walls and the roof went up, the crew turned their attention to the lodge floor, which also had to be redone. On May 4, Chef Jim Albert went to the lodge to approve and set up his new kitchen. Despite the weather conditions, the entire project was completed before the first guests arrived for the 1999 fishing season. Sonny Petersen Photo

turned to the lodge in early March. They knew they had to be done by mid-May.

Luck was with the project, even if the weather wasn't. In one of Alaska's coldest winters in recent history, the building crew arrived at Kulik greeted by a huge snow pack and sub-zero temperatures. By late April, the project was right on schedule despite the fact that Nonvianuk Lake still had more than 30 inches of ice. Sonny Petersen landed for the last time on the hard Nonvianuk Lake ice on May 20. The Kulik runway replaced the deteriorating lake ice for the remaining support flights. Although the work continued into mid-May and the rapidly approaching summer season, by the time the first guests arrived, the first major renovation at Kulik Lodge had been completed.

## There Aren't Any Secrets Anymore!

When I made my first foray into Bristol Bay more than thirty years ago, there were secrets; secrets about locations, secrets about how to fish, secrets about how to land and park an airplane in the special places, and secrets about the people who fished and those who flew. The whole damned country was full of secrets. The fact is that you could count the number of truly knowledgeable players on one hand. There was a camaraderie among the earliest lodge operators and guides, yet each and every one of them had "secrets." I heard that from many of the people with whom I spoke. They all made an effort to keep their secrets secret, too!

Over the course of time, the knowledge spread. As hard as some owners and operators tried to keep their secrets, other owners and operators tried equally hard to discover them. I know for a fact that more than one owner financed a trip to a competitive lodge to learn some of their fishing techniques and special places. Others have tried to follow airplanes and boats with surprising luck. An accidental sighting of an airplane or a group of fishermen at a location previously unknown to the observer has betrayed many secret places. I can remember flying for a lodge in the early 1980s and spotting an airplane in a small creek. Before that day, I didn't think the area was landable, let alone fishable. When I went back to the lodge that afternoon and told the owner what I had seen, he got really excited and sent me right back up there to check it out. Fishing was great. From that day on, it became a regular stop for me and the lodge at which I worked. I also know that luck was with me that day because I have since discovered that the lodge whose airplane I spotted that day made it a point to keep the place a secret. Evidently a new pilot-guide hadn't been told their policy of stealth, or maybe he didn't care.

Ed Seiler told me that he made it a ritual to tell his clients not to say anything to anyone at any time about some of the places he fished, but he also said that it rarely worked, especially if the fisherman was partial to a fine glass of wine or a glass or two of beer. I'd hate to tell you how many competitive guides have divulged secret information to me while booze controlled their tongues. Hell, the best crooks can't keep a secret; sooner or later they have to tell someone. One thing leads to another and within a short time, the word is out.

As more and more guests try more and more lodges, information is client-carried from one lodge to another. Guides and pilots make it their business to acquire as much fishing knowledge as they can from other guides and pilots. When these key employees switch lodges and change employers, the knowledge gained at one lodge is transferred directly to the next. And so it goes. But does it matter?

In my opinion, there has been a definite change in the fishing patterns in Bristol Bay since the season of 1990 and many owners and operators blame me for the change. When I first went to Bristol Bay in 1966, no one was concerned about getting up early in the morning to go fishing. It just wasn't necessary. When I worked for both Bob Cusack and Jack Holman in the early 1980s, breakfast was a planning time for the day and there was certainly no urgency to get started at the crack of dawn. If you went to a river and found someone else already there, another destination was quickly substituted. By 1990, however, that had changed.

When I took over the management duties at Kulik Lodge in 1990, I told Sonny Petersen that I was going to make some changes in the breakfast program. Prior to that time, all guests at the lodge came to breakfast around 7 a.m. and the fly-outs left about an hour later. I felt that starting so late in the morning caused problems for the lodge, the staff, and the clients. With that late morning schedule, it was too easy for everyone concerned to stay up exceedingly late and consume a little too much of Mr. Seagram's best. Being the competitive person that I am, I altered our breakfast and fly-out schedule to put our fishermen on the rivers earlier in the day. Accordingly, our clients left the rivers earlier, too. A few years later, people started to follow my lead. Prior to that, our clients would often have two to three hours on the most popular fishing streams before anyone else arrived. My goal was to run our fishing program and lodge more efficiently.

A few years ago, I dropped a few clients at one of the more popular fishing streams early in the morning. As I climbed back into the airplane for departure, I noticed another airplane landing. As maneuvering room was limited, I waited for the other airplane to land and drop his clients. I was standing by my airplane when the other pilot walked over and thanked me for the courtesy. I had never seen him before. When I responded by telling him my name and that I came from Kulik, he gave me a funny look and said, "I know about you. You're the one who is responsible for me getting out of bed so early every morning, but I'll be here earlier tomorrow!" I nodded, smiled, and departed for Kulik.

Several times throughout this book, I have discussed the way it was and the way it is. Unfortunately, we will never be able to get back to the good old days, if indeed there ever were "good old days." Because the Angler's Paradise Lodges were the first and have no peers in terms of years of continuous operation, I can assure you that the database of fishing knowledge accumulated since 1950 is beyond belief. Interestingly enough, though, our clients are catching not only more fish, but bigger fish. Personally, I do not believe there are any places that have not been explored in Bristol Bay. The level of competition started to increase in the late 1970s and exploded in the 1980s. As I said, there are no secrets anymore, but I don't think it matters in the least. What does matter, however, is the desire to provide a quality experience for every client who comes to Bristol Bay. In my opinion, that is the essence of Bristol Bay's great fishing lodges.

## The Essence of Belonging

In the Introduction of this book, I stated the lodge family is my family. Now that you know some lodge history, I'll try to explain my lodge family concept. Throughout my life, I have traveled and fished on five continents. I have not, however, had the intense feeling of belonging at any other location that I have at Bristol Bay. I admit that I like exploring new fishing areas, but I return to Bristol Bay year after year. During those seasons that I didn't work in Alaska and Bristol Bay, I wasn't content until I returned. I have spoken with numerous lodge owners, managers, fishing guides, lodge pilots, several lodge chefs, and numerous clients who share my feelings. What is it that makes people come to Bristol Bay season after season and year after year?

To begin with, coming to Alaska is an adventure where each and every day is different. When you factor in Alaska's magnificent scenery, the thrill of flying, the chance encounters with bears, the remoteness, and the weather, it's easy to understand the challenge that Alaska presents and why other destinations don't offer nearly as much to the visiting sportsman.

I've extolled the virtues of our fishery, yet that really isn't necessary. There has been so much said, written, and filmed about the angling in Bristol Bay that it's almost a foregone conclusion that the fishing will be phenomenal. Although that's true about the expectations, fishing is good, if not great, in other locations on the globe. Quite honestly, for most of us, fishing is a small part of the draw.

From a client's point of view, the experience is beyond belief. Despite the fact that the trips have previously been considered expensive, today there are options for nearly all budgets. I know one couple who saved for at least five years before they came on a "once-in-a-lifetime trip." They made it clear to me before they arrived in Alaska that they could never save enough again. Not surprisingly, they enjoyed themselves so much that they have returned several times, and I expect them to return again.

As a lodge employee, I can assure you there is no great fortune to be made at any lodge as a pilot or as a fishing guide. A good day-trader will make more in his spare time than the highest-paid lodge worker in a season, yet guides, pilots, and chefs pride themselves on their longevity and consecutive season numbers.

Compared to the numbers posted by the majority of businesses listed on Wall Street, the lodge owners are not raking in the cash, either. Without a doubt, the lodge owners of today are bombarded with more red tape than at any time in the past. At the Angler's Paradise Lodges, for example, we are constantly facing changing FAA regulations and new methods of enforcing the old; changing National Park Service codes and regulations; boat and guide licensing by the Coast Guard as well as the State of Alaska; Federal Fish and Wildlife management dictums; compliance with federal drug testing regulations; new health standards, building codes that are designed for city dwellers yet apply at remote lodge locations; Lake and Peninsula Borough bed taxes, worker's compensation insurance scams; the Environmental Protection Agency and their fuel storage regulations; Naknek River dock permits issued by the Army Corps of Engineers, etc., etc., etc. If that's not enough to cloud your mind, it's not only the various state and federal agencies that add to the headaches, it's finding suitable employees, making sure the food orders arrive on time, and hopefully, making the books balance at the end of the season so that the IRS doesn't padlock the doors! Why would anyone build, buy, or remain in the lodge business? I know it's not the cash, nor the cost, nor the lifestyle. I believe the greatest reason that clients, employees and owners alike return to Bristol Bay's fishing lodges is the sense of belonging to a special family.

At Kulik, I've watched as longtime employees and repeat guests greet each other like close relatives after an extended separation year after year. Bristol Bay is nothing more than a geological entity by itself, but when you add the vast array of clients, lodge owners, operators, and their employees, Bristol Bay becomes a concept, not a place. Once you've been there, you soon realize that Bristol Bay is more than a geographic location. For most of us, Bristol Bay is a family, and belonging to the family is what makes it special. This should come as no surprise, considering that nearly all the lodges–new and old–are family operated.

One aspect of lodge operation that is often overlooked is the force of nature and its influence on those who work and play in Bristol Bay. I've already stated that working at one of the great fishing lodges has a lifelong effect. Indeed, I can think of at least four marriages that were ruined by a season or two at a fishing lodge, and those were just my own. I can also name numerous marriages directly attributable to a lodge season. Many lodge owners told me that at one time or another the concept of love has infiltrated each of their lodges.

Alaska's remote sportfishing lodges certainly bring people together. Staffs are assembled before the first guests arrive and work in close proximity to each other for about 16 weeks each season. It should come as no big surprise that every now and then Cupid's arrows fly, romantic energies increase, and romances develop. More often than not, the budding romances don't last more than a few erotic nights. Once in a while, the romance lasts until the end of the season when the reality of going home to a previous lover, husband, or wife ends the fling. I remember a few such situations, but not nearly as fondly as do those couples whose season of love survived. I cannot possibly tell the story of each couple whose summer of love at a fishing lodge turned into marriage any more than I can recant the gruesome details of the numerous divorces that have occurred from similar romantic trysts. There have been way too many.

*Ray Petersen and his long-time friend Bud Seltenreich at Kulik Lodge during the 1999 fishing season. These two men have more than 100 years of combined airplane operation and maintenance experience in Alaska. Bud, born in McCarthy in 1915, was one of the few aviation pioneers actually born in Alaska. Jim Albert Photo*

Although I can't claim to have researched lodge marriages thoroughly, I believe that Brooks Lodge has been the site of more lodge weddings than any other lodge in Bristol Bay. At last count, Brooks has been the site of eight marriages, including the wedding of the granddaughter of one of the earliest lodge developers, John Walatka. The biggest ceremony, however, was held in 1995 when then Brooks Lodge manager Perry Mollan married the love of his life and former employee, Angela Jones. Naturally, they had met during a previous lodge season. Other marriages have been held on the lodge porch, at the bear-viewing platform, and in the Valley of Ten Thousand Smokes. Perry and Angela were the first to be married inside the main lodge building. It was a lodge wedding all the way. Kulik fishing guide Pete Raynor conducted the ceremony attended by family, friends, and lodge staff. None of the attending pilots could toast the bride with champagne, however. We had to fly all the guests back to King Salmon and other fishing lodges in the area. The Mollans' wedding gives testimony to the fact that the lodges become special places in the hearts and minds of all who come to Bristol Bay. As I stated earlier, it is a feeling of belonging.

Fishing is the catalyst that brings people to Bristol Bay, but once there, it is the family aspect of the lodges that makes them return. My dad took me fishing long before I could handle a rod by myself. Ray and Toni Petersen raised four kids at the Angler's Paradise Lodges. Bud and Dennis Branham both brought sons into their lodge world as did Bob Curtis,

Ron Hayes, Bill Sims, Jack Holman, and the list goes on and on. It is the family that makes the lodge business special. All the lodges are about people.

At Kulik, and I'm sure at all the great lodges, it's as if the lodge comes alive each season and every employee becomes a son or daughter of the lodge itself. Stories about previous guests and staff members are shared at the same time that new employees and guests are introduced to the family, and when each one departs, their presence stays forever. This special atmosphere and camaraderie is not based on the catch of the day, but rather on the concept of belonging. Like a drug that leads the mind into paradise, the sense of belonging is the connection to Bristol Bay that everyone who works and plays at our great lodges craves during the long months between Alaska seasons. Believe me, there is absolutely no way to compare any other place in the fishing world to Bristol Bay. No other area in the world has the rich lodge history nor the great personalities that characterize Bristol Bay's best fishing lodges. That's a fact.

*The first Bristol Bay lodge family with a third generation lodge pilot. From the right, Sonny Petersen, Sonny's father and the Father of Alaska's Sportfishing Lodges, Ray Petersen, and his grandson, Sean Petersen on the porch at Kulik Lodge in 1998. Sean became a full-fledged FAA Part-135 lodge pilot in 1999. Jim Albert Photo*

The decade of the 1990s, like each preceding decade, closed in anticipation of the future. During the research for this volume, I spoke with a varied sample of lodge employees, clients, and owners about the future. Although some have told me that there are too many lodges and that some form of limits will need to be established, others told me that the industry is self-regulating and only the market can dictate future expansion or demise. After all my research, all I know is that those who developed lodges did so because they felt the draw of Bristol Bay, and there will be others who cannot resist those same feelings. One of the earliest lodge developers summed up his feelings and in doing so spoke for the entire industry when he said: "Starting a fishing lodge in Bristol Bay and being involved in the lodge industry was the best experience of my life, I only wish I had done it earlier."

# Chapter 8
# Bears Are Where They Find You

"If bears wanted to eat people, part of me was readily available that night."
*Bo Bennett*

The angler peered into the river. His attention focused on the sight of more rainbows than he had ever seen. He didn't notice that he had walked away from his companions, nor did he care. Spawning salmon covered the bottom of the river like a plush red carpet. Carcasses littered the banks. Had he been looking, he would have seen the signs. The fisherman didn't see the freshly caught, yet still bleeding, half-eaten salmon lying in the huge tracks. Engrossed in casting to a great rainbow, the unwary angler didn't sense the angry bear crouching like a leopard in the thick alders just inches from his rod tip during his last back cast.

The noise that broke the angler's concentration was the sickening sound of his own skull being crushed. He didn't have time to cry out. Huge canine teeth ripped through flesh and bone without resistance. The gigantic bruin swatted the man with such force that all the air was forced from his lungs. The massive, razor-sharp claws shredded both the fisherman's clothing and his flesh. Blood and intestines slipped from his body as the bear intensified the death grip. Terrified and trying to scream, the man woke from his nightmare scared and short of breath. Slowly, his breathing returned to normal, but each time he closed his eyes and tried to relax, the sight of the giant bear waiting in the darkness kept him frightened and awake.

Finding it impossible to go back to sleep, he rolled out of bed, turned on his light, and returned to the journal he had been reading. No wonder he'd had a nightmare. He was reading Larry Kaniut's scary book, Alaska Bear Tales. This book is a collection of stories that puts goose bumps on everyone who reads it. This isn't the only collection of stories that leads us to believe that bears are ferocious animals that we need to fear, but have the bears earned this reputation or, like wolves, have they been wrongly accused?

Bristol Bay's great fishing lodges expose hundreds, if not thousands, of guests to bears each season. Katmai National Park in general, and Brooks Lodge in particular, host a staggering number of bear-watchers and their numbers grow each year. Because bears have become commonplace at the fishing sites in and around the Katmai region, I decided to present an entire chapter on bears rather than provide the information helter-skelter throughout this book. To help you accept and understand some of the stories, I think it best to relate some human-bear history and theory. Canadian bear expert James Gary Shelton published a great book called the *Bear Encounter Survival Guide*. In it, he gives a quick history of human and bear interaction:

> *Human-bear conflict probably started 100,000 years ago when our primitive ancestors fanned out across the Northern Hemispheres. At that time there were many large predators that humans had to deal with in order to survive. By about 13,000 years ago, the last glacial period had ended, and many predators and other types of animals had suffered extinction. In most northern regimes, this left humans competing primarily with bears and wolves.*
>
> *Human conflict with animals took on new meaning approximately 9,000 years ago when we took up farming and animal husbandry as our main means of survival. As human populations started increasing and expanding throughout Eurasia, bear populations started a long continuous decline, and were eventually eliminated from vast areas of that continent. During the European exploration and settlement of North America, there was considerable conflict between people and wild animals, and of course major conflict between Europeans and Native Americans. At that time in history, the conquest of new lands and peoples was the priority, and nature was an enemy to be subdued. Both of these competing human cultures impacted the land, but European technology and weaponry was a thousand years more advanced, and by the middle of the 19th century, the North American continent had already been significantly altered.*

Since the days of the Lewis and Clark expedition, grizzly bears have been a source of fears and nightmares. The exploits of adventurers and hunters alike added to the mystique of the largest bears. Stories originally told over campfires ended up in newspapers, magazines, and books. These tales both fascinated and terrorized readers with gruesome and gory facts. In his book *Backcountry Bear Basics*, Dave Smith sheds a little light on our treatment of bears during the great move to the west:

> *We slaughtered grizzlies with the fervor of a Hitler and the perversity of a Marquis de Sade. Let's not forget that shortly after the Lewis and Clark expedition killed 37 grizzly bears on their journey to the Pacific, we slaughtered millions of buffalo and began trapping and shooting bears to protect dull-witted domestic livestock. As civilization advanced, ranchers introduced bears to the perils of strychnine, 1080, and other deadly poisons. In the 1960s, Alaska State employees–at the request of cattle ranchers on Kodiak*

*Island– gunned down the biggest bears on earth from planes. During Alaska's pipeline days, construction workers fed bears dynamite sandwiches and blew their heads off. In less than 200 years, we reduced the grizzly population in the continental United States from at least 50,000 bears to less than 1,000. Little wonder the few surviving grizzlies have a tendency to avoid us.*

*Outdoor Life* editor Jim Zumbo told me that his readers are both intrigued and fascinated with bear stories and more so with bear attacks. Jim said that factual and fictional stories seem to get equal press. Gruesome stories not only make headlines, they create fear. Unfortunately, the stories of maulings and killings followed the footsteps of the exploration of North America. By the time American exploration started in Alaska, those fears were real and affected human behavior. Robert F. Griggs and his party brought some of those fears into the Katmai region during the National Geographic Society's first exploratory expedition in 1915. Griggs and his party did not see a bear during their first two seasons in Katmai, yet passages from his book, *The Valley of Ten Thousand Smokes,* yield clues about the anticipated ferocity of the Katmai bruins:

*The Katmai coast and six brown bears in 1996. I'm sure this is what National Geographic explorer Robert Griggs and his associates expected to find behind every turn in the trail. Tom Smith Photo*

*Wherever we traveled through the devastated country, except under the very shadow of the volcano, we found tracks of these great bears very numerous. Everywhere we went we apprehensively kept a sharp lookout, for these tracks were so thick that it seemed as though there must be a bear crouching behind every rock. At first we were much concerned lest we should come upon one suddenly, supposing that in such country they must be ravenously hungry. When we were first landed, one member of our party would not go for 50 yards from the tent without carrying his rifle. Yet we never caught a glimpse of one the first year. As the days wore on without sight of the animals, we gradually became as indifferent to danger from an encounter with them as at first we had been apprehensive. When we came to start up into the interior for the first time, our packs were so heavy we could not well add a rifle, and we finally went out into the wilderness armed with only a couple of pistols. Long before we were through with the country, the man who at first would not venture away from the campfire without a gun became so disgusted that he refused to lug his rifle even on long tramps through country in which bears were certainly plentiful.*

Despite the efforts of Walt Disney and the Discovery Channel, deep-rooted anxiety about bears cannot be ignored. Two Grosvenor Lodge guests learned the hard way that their own fears were more dangerous than the bears they imagined. Grosvenor Lodge manager, Dave Saurman, explained the unusual happenings during the late night hours of July 22, 1992:

*Bob Smith and his adult son, Brad, arrived at Grosvenor Lodge late in the afternoon. They had been guests at Brooks Lodge before starting their fishing trip at Grosvenor. While at Brooks Lodge, they attended the required bear briefing and had seen many bears. Seeing the bears in their natural surroundings and at close range made Brad realize that he wasn't in a zoo; the bears could appear anytime and anywhere, especially when they weren't expected.*

*After getting settled at the lodge, the pair met the other guests. They enjoyed a great dinner, some late evening fishing, and retired looking forward to another great day. Sometime late in the night, the senior Smith felt nature calling and decided he could not wait. He slipped from his bed and made a definite effort to be quiet so that he didn't disturb his sleeping son. Quietly, he opened the cabin door and made the short walk to the nearby washroom. He noted that it was nearly three o'clock in the morning.*

*Walking back to the cabin in the near dark, he stumbled slightly on the porch steps. As he opened the door with one hand, he reached his other up and inside the doorway in an effort to pull himself into the cabin. Unfortunately, his stumbling startled his sleeping son. The son must have been dreaming about bears, because, according to him, he heard a bear on the porch. Somehow, the bear opened the door. In the dark cabin, he saw the bear's paw reach into the cabin. Panic shook him out of his near-sleep state. Trying to protect his father, Brad bolted from his bed, grabbed for the handle and slammed the door crushing the bear's claws against the solid doorjamb.*

Dave told me that when he heard the yelling, he also thought there must be a bear in camp. The sleepy camp manager quickly found the elder Smith writhing in pain and bleeding profusely from having his fingers smashed by the door. Other guests were shaking their heads in disbelief. The sudden realization that the claws he saw were actually his father's fingers devastated the younger Smith.

After moving the elder Mr. Smith to the main lodge, Dave did his best to administer immediate first aid. He knew the injured man would need professional help, and that meant a medivac flight. Before he radioed Kulik, Dave went outside and tried to get an idea about the weather. It was dark and raining. Returning to the lodge, Dave told the Smith family that the weather wasn't very good and it might be a long time before they could be taken to the hospital. Tensions and anxiety were high.

By about 5:15 a.m. Kulik guide Pete Raynor was in the office getting ready to wake his clients. Pete responded to Dave's radio distress call, then ran to my cabin, pounded on my door, and told me that he had just taken an emergency call from Grosvenor Lodge. The reception was so bad that he couldn't make out the details, but he got enough to know that someone had to get to the hospital. As I grabbed for my pants, I told Pete to go back to the radio, call Grosvenor, and tell them I'd try to get there. I also told Pete to get a weather report from Grosvenor, then alert the Piper Navajo pilot of a potential medivac flight to Anchorage.

I pulled on my hip boots, grabbed a flashlight and ran to the airplanes. I thought about fuel. The first C-206 I checked was nearly empty. Moving rapidly to the next one in line, I got lucky; it had plenty. I did a quick preflight and untied the airplane. I started the engine and taxied out of the parking area and into the river. Rain and low clouds seemed to hold back the daylight. I hoped that by the time the engine temperature needle moved into takeoff range, I'd be able to see enough to go. Once I was airborne, daylight brightened both the sky and my apprehension about the weather. Although I had to go via the American Canyon, I made great time. I made it to Grosvenor about 28 minutes after Pete took the initial radio call.

Dave and the Smiths were in front of the lodge waiting for me. I still didn't know what had happened, but when I climbed out of the airplane, at least everyone was smiling. I have been unfortunate enough to pilot several serious medivac flights. They all had one thing in common; no one was smiling when I arrived at the scene. Dave explained that once Brad's initial panic and his father's pain had been replaced with sympathy and some first aid treatments, the more humorous aspects of the night started to prevail.

The Smith family was still very concerned about the weather and any possible delays in getting Bob to the hospital. Everyone agreed that he needed immediate professional medical help. He had extensive damage to his fingers. I assured them that our airplane would be ready and waiting. By the time we got back to Kulik and transferred both father and son to our Piper Navajo for the flight to Anchorage, most of their tensions eased. They also agreed that Brad's fear of bears caused the serious and permanent damage to his father's fingers.

Unlike other grizzlies and large brown bears around the world, the bruins in the Katmai region today seem to behave differently with respect to people. They are not as aggressive as other large brown grizzly bears. The Griggs expedition realized it during their first summer in 1918. Since then, tourists, employees, and even some bear researchers have determined that the bears that frequent the Brooks River and surrounding areas are not the vicious creatures of which stories are told. In fact, there is considerable evidence to indicate that, even though grizzly bears in the Katmai region may have been highly aggressive thousands of years ago, they don't have the proverbial "chip on the shoulder" that most of their geographically different cousins display regularly.

The Brooks River has been home to both people and bears since at least the mid-1400s. Archaeologists confirm and fossil evidence indicates that bears and people shared life at the Brooks River. National Park Service historians told me that from 1450 to 1912, the Brooks River was the wintertime seasonal home of an estimated 60 to 100 residents. Research teams have found fossil evidence of bears with the excavations of the pit-homes created by the earliest modern human residents at the Brooks River. Since 1950, the summertime population at the Brooks Lodge and campground has hovered between 60 to 100 residents. There has been interaction between bears and humans in the Brooks River area dating back to the beginning of human life, as we know it, in Bristol Bay.

The local Native population wintered at the Brooks River. Researchers told me that the people left their summer camps nearer to the sea and arrived at Brooks during the fall. At their winter camps along the Brooks River, they caught and preserved salmon. After spending the winter at Brooks, they traveled down the lake and spent the summers fishing and collecting food near the river mouths and saltwater, returning again to Brooks in the fall to continue the cycle. It is realistic to assume that the bears, too, arrived at Brooks with the salmon just as they do today. I'm sure the Natives developed methods for keeping their dried and drying fish from the bears. It is also my opinion that over hundreds of years, the bears became genetically cooperative. The residents had no choice but to selectively kill any and every bear that threatened their food supply and their lives. The local residents had no reason to bother those bears that were not aggressive. Eventually, mother bears taught their young cubs cooperative living skills. It is my opinion that the bears that frequent the Brooks River area today are direct descendants of bears that learned the rules established by people. The bears at Brooks have been habituated through centuries of human contact.

Although I have heard it said by numerous people and in various ways since, Sonny Petersen was the first person I heard vocalizing the cooperation theory. Of all the people who have lived and worked in Bristol Bay, I believe Sonny is the most qualified to express his thoughts about bears. Although he has no university degree in bear research, he has more personal knowledge of bears than any Ph.D. Sonny has spent every summer and fall of his life living in close proximity to the bears of Katmai. Growing up in bear country and being around bears gave him experiences that researchers cannot get. Since being at Grosvenor Lodge at the tender age of six months, Sonny watched, feared, played with, studied, threatened, harassed, pushed, teased, admired and tormented bears in ways only a teenager can understand. His skills as a pilot enabled him to monitor bear life styles and patterns of travel better than any other researcher. Indeed, he has facilitated nearly all the bear studies with airplane support. Sonny has flown tranquilized bears, saved their lives, and killed bears. More than anyone else, Sonny Petersen has both respect for and economic interest in bears. Quite simply, bears are Sonny's business.

Sonny's theory of cooperation makes sense to me when you realize that the people living at Brooks hundreds of years ago simply couldn't afford to have the bears eat their winter food supply. Sonny theorizes that when a bear became a problem, the men of the village would get together and eliminate that particular bear, not all the bears. Each time a bear became a threat, the problem bear was eliminated. The people and the bears had to coexist; both needed the salmon to survive. The hostility and aggressiveness of bears toward people was modified over time, and those behaviors have been nearly eliminated through selective human intervention.

I spoke with Dr. Tom Smith, wildlife biologist with the U.S. Geological Survey. Tom is a recognized brown bear expert and has worked on numerous research projects in Bristol Bay. He conducted a major study of the bears on the Kulik River, which he completed in 1997. I asked Dr. Smith to explain the differences between the Katmai bears and all the other large brown bears.

Dr. Smith told me that the first scientist to classify North America's largest bears was C. Hart Merriam. In 1918, his article *Review of Grizzly and Big Brown Bears of North America* appeared in the *Journal of North American Fauna*. This work established the existence of 87 different species of large bears in North America alone. By 1953, however, the scientific community accepted new conclusions by Raush when he determined there were only three subspecies of a single race of brown bears. By 1963, he completed an exhaustive project and reached the conclusion that there were just two subspecies, Kodiak Island bears and all other brown-grizzly bears. He felt that because all the bears were so genetically similar, it was more a difference in habitat that created the largest bears. He speculated that if an interior grizzly was introduced into the population of the Kodiaks, that bear would grow larger than other interior bears.

After that explanation, I asked about fatal attacks. Dr. Smith confirmed that despite the fact that there have been numerous fatal bear attacks in other parts of Alaska, North America, Europe and Russia, there has never been a fatal attack in Katmai Park. When I asked him if he could explain why, he told me that it was highly likely that the brown

*A noted brown bear expert, Dr. Tom Smith is shown here with a small bear during a research project in Katmai National Park. The bear was tranquilized to prevent injuries to the bear and to the research team. Tom Smith Photo*

bear population has lived for so long near people, that man has altered their genetic make-up. Tom cited research conducted by H. U. Roth and his paper, "Status of the Last Brown Bears of the Alps in Trentino, Italy." According to Mr. Roth:

> *Less than 1,000 years ago, brown bears (Ursus arctos) were found throughout most of continental Europe, but today only a few remnant populations occur in small and isolated areas. Although mountainous regions typically form a last stronghold for the bears, they were exterminated from the greater part of the Alps during the 1800s. Only two small populations survived by 1900, one in the French Alps and one in the Italian Alps. Those of the French Alps disappeared before World War II, whereas, in Italy, one small group still remains in the Alpine province of Trentino. These bears are extremely shy and nocturnal.*

Dr. Smith then stated that other researchers speculate that park bear-human encounter incidents are amazingly few in number because Katmai is so resource abundant that bears don't need to aggressively defend food resources. This means that when people get too close, accidentally or otherwise, the bear can move off without really giving up anything. In short, nearly any direction a bear moves in Katmai is toward a food resource. After I read and studied the remainder of Mr. Roth's work, Tom still needed to explain some of the finer and subtler points to me.

> *Roth and a few other researchers now believe that hunting, selectively removing bears displaying certain behaviors, has shaped the behavior of the entire bear population. People have made them act differently. Bears, which were naturally diurnal, are now nocturnal. Bears that were naturally inquisitive are now ultra shy and avoid people.*

From Dave Smith's *Backcountry Bear Basics*:

> *Brown bears in the Pyrenee Mountains of Spain are the same species as North America's fabled grizzlies, yet centuries of human domination and selective killing that eliminated the boldest bears have turned them into ghosts that are rarely seen.*

Dr. Smith asked me if I thought the bears of Katmai were extremely shy. I said no. Then he asked if they were exclusively nocturnal. Slowly, I started to understand the point he was trying to establish. Then Tom told me that most hard-core animal research experts are overwhelmed when they first visit the Brooks River. He said:

> *When they get to Brooks and see the number of bears and the number of people, they simply can't believe that there haven't been a few people mauled and killed. Without any doubt, the largest population density of brown bears occurs in Katmai Park, and without a doubt the greatest number of people who come in close contact with bears occurs near the Brooks River. The bears of Katmai show behaviors that are not consistent with other bear populations.*

Dr. Smith told me that numerous scientists and researchers chronicled the lack of aggression, but there has never been a scientific study to determine any differences between the Katmai bears and the other large bears of North America with respect to aggressive behavior and the ability to live in harmony with any human population. Then Tom reiterated his opinion about bear-human interactions in the

Katmai region. He said that some researchers have speculated that:

> *1) aggressive levels are genetically controlled–that some populations are composed of mean, grouchy bears whereas others aren't. The shy bears of the Italian Alps suggest that this might be true to a degree and in extreme situations;*
> *2) bear aggressive levels are related to how familiar bears are with people–hence bears at Brooks and McNeil River are thought, by some, to be less aggressive due to their familiarity with people who neither reward them nor hurt them. Bear-to-people habituation would be the phenomenon. We know this phenomenon does exist or Bart the Bear would have eaten Doug Seuss the Trainer a long while back;*
> *3) bear aggression is a function of food availability. In areas where food resources are rich, bears are unaggressive as they have not only full bellies but also because even when a person displaces them, bears are always moving toward food, never away from a lone food source. This is true to a degree. The NPS used to erect bleachers at dumps in many western parks and tourists filled them watching bears frolicking in banana peels and coffee grounds.*

> *My theory is this—in areas where food resources are varied (many different things to eat), abundant (great quantities of food), high quality (e.g., protein rich, such as intertidal sedge meadows and spawning salmon), and stable through time, bears will be present in great numbers and being in great numbers is possible only through bear-to-bear habituation. However, bears normally avoid other bears. A bunch of angry, cantankerous bears would be a dangerous lot to hang with so somehow (subconsciously, but it occurs nonetheless) they forego their normally large personal space, shrink it, lower their aggressive levels and jointly benefit from the bounteous food, whatever it is that they have found. Hence, the normally solitary animals congregated in great numbers at Yellowstone's Trout Creek dump for decades until it was abolished in the 1960s.*

*According to Dr. Smith, bear aggression is a function of food availability. U.S. Fish and Wildlife Service Photo*

> *When a whale carcass washes up on some beach, many bears will jointly have a blubber-fest. I've heard of as many as 18 on one whale down at Puale Bay a few years back. Many bears share a single bison carcass in Yellowstone. Brooks Camp is, of course, famous for bears, as is McNeil, and to a lesser extent, Kulik. The common thread then I feel is that the primary phenomenon occurring at Brooks, McNeil and so forth is that of*

*bear-to-bear habitation, not bear-to-human habituation as thought by many. Consequently, these bears are docile, have small personal spaces and are less "jumpy" all around. When people arrive, the stage is already set for a nonaggressive situation because layered over the bear-to-human habituation is the fact that individual bears generally have little experience with people and demonstrate a natural deference to us. My belief is that most bears at Brooks act the way they do because of the quieting influence of bear-bear habituation, not just bear-human habituation. Were it otherwise, how would you account for the total lack of injurious incidents there in spite of the fact that many bears who have never been seen there before and have no experience there, pass through and cause no trouble at all with the thronging masses of people? Also, I've been to many places in the park and in most all of the places bears simply could not have had much experience with Homo sapiens and yet they act nearly identically to those at Brooks–most barely glance at us as they go on their way.*

*The implications are not trivial either. For instance, some researchers have found that a small number of bears avoid Brooks in the summer and they have ascribed that to their fear of humans. But I can show you from other studies that large congregations of bears have been observed to exclude less dominant, more shy bears because those bears feared being in the company of so many potential backstabbers. So, if we base the way we manage that area on the assumption that bears are being excluded because of human activity when in fact they simply would avoid the area with or without people, then we've based a management decision on something other than fact. Of course, there may be some bears that are displaced by people; however, I believe that the greater part are being displaced by bears, not people. So, I think what is happening at Brooks may well be a bear-to-bear phenomenon, not a bear-person thing. Do bears habituate to people at Brooks? Of course, I am not saying that they do not. I am simply trying to put that phenomenon in its correct position on the list of things affecting bear behavior in and around the Katmai National Park and Preserve.*

Although it is almost impossible to fish in some of Katmai's rivers and streams and not see bears today, it is hard to believe that the population of bears was quite different when Ray Petersen chose the Brooks River as one of his primary fishing lodge sites. There is no way of knowing how many bears lived at or near the Brooks River before the early 1950s. Robert F. Grigg's comments give the feeling of a vast bear population, although he didn't see even one bear during his first summer in Katmai. Fishermen and other visitors to the Angler's Paradise Camps seldom saw bears during the initial years of operation. Early Brooks Camp Register notations indicate that bears were plentiful along the Savonoski River and rangers had to take reporters there by boat to film bears. It's hard for me to imagine the Brooks River without bears. Looking through the early lodge registers, however, I was amazed to find that each time a bear made an appearance or left tracks, written reports followed in the guest registers. From the *Brooks Guest Register*, July, 1953:

*July 21: ... the ranger reports numerous bear signs ... .*

*July 23: ... bear tracks on the beach ...*

*July 27: ... bears have raided the camp established by the NPS in Mortuary Cove. They scattered the canned food and bit holes in the cans, but so far have not attacked the tent. The NPS plans to relocate the camp ...*

*Aug. 2: ... bear tracks on the beach ...*

I found some interesting information in a book written by Victor Calahane, *A Biological Survey of Katmai National Monument*. Quite unlike the modern research fanatics and some ranger types who may never have seen a bear, yet claim to be experts, at least Calahane sought out the opinions of local residents to help him form his conclusions. The opinions forged by Calahane about bears and their numbers became the framework upon which all early National Park Service bear management decisions were made. Calahane notes that:

> *It was my impression that bears were less abundant in the summers of 1953-54 than at the time of my first visit to Katmai in the fall of 1940. This impression was strengthened by the fact that they should appear more numerous in the summer season when the animals are concentrated along the salmon waters. Two local observers, John Walatka, manager of the public camp at Brooks River, and Jay Hammond, formerly warden of the Alaska Game Commission at Naknek, expressed the view that bears had indeed declined somewhat in numbers prior to 1953.*

In an earlier chapter, I pointed out the lack of conservation and control during the military buildup during and immediately following World War II. Certainly many bears were killed in the name of sport. Several longtime residents inferred that once the locals discovered guns, most of the bears were eliminated from the area. Both circumstances may have accounted for a decline in the bear population. It is also possible that the decline was normal and a natural cycle of bear life. The big problem was that no accurate census had been taken. Calahane continues his dissertation on the population of brown bears:

> *The haphazard tallies of bears that have been made in the Monument are interesting, although they are not very significant in forming an estimate of the total populations. The largest count that I made was 23 bears along ten miles of the Savonoski River, west of Rainbow River, on August 19, 1953. Ten bears were seen August 24, 1953, on the mud flats of the north side of the valley back of Hallo Bay. These counts are dwarfed, however, by one that was described to me on September 7, 1954, by a bush pilot, George R. Tibbetts of Naknek. While flying down the valley of Savonoski River about a week previously, he saw a total of 60 bears. If this count is reliable, it is possible that the total number of brown bears in the monument approaches or even exceeds 200.*

I asked George Tibbetts about the numbers he gave to Mr. Calahane. George had been a pilot in the area since 1948. He told me that he didn't recall Mr. Calahane, although he did say, "that was a long time ago." The more we talked, the more I realized he didn't like bears too much. George verified that between 1948 and 1952, there were many bears on the Savonoski, but few at Brooks. George figured the bears moved back to Brooks because of the fishing camp: George said, "Those bears weren't dumb. Once old Petersen moved in and put in his fishing camp along the Brooks River, the bears moved back in. Ray's fishermen didn't shoot bears."

In addition to the establishment of the Angler's Paradise Camp in 1950, the Brooks River weir and the extensive salmon research projects organized by the Fish and Wildlife Service also brought workers to the Brooks River area. Jim Adams, who worked on the weir in the early 1950s, told me that bears simply weren't a problem because there were so few in the area. He thought illegal hunting was to blame.

Of course there were a few bears, but they certainly weren't found in the numbers we have today. One of the first written reports of bear problems comes from the *Midnight Sun*, September 1958:

> Slim Beck, camp manager at Kulik in Angler's Paradise hasn't been getting much sleep for the past couple of weeks. The reason, those darn bears. The three Musky Bears, as they have been tabbed by Slim, are regular visitors at Kulik Lodge, not only in the evening, but also during the day. Apparently attracted by food, they wander right up to the lodge proper, and it was not an unusual sight to see the guests, along with Slim and Charlie Blue, chef, get outside throwing rocks at them to scare them away from the camp. It was an unusual sight to see Slim chasing them up the beach at Nonvianuk Lake about 10 miles an hour to scare them away. However, they are persistent cusses, apparently knowing that the bear season down there doesn't open until November.

Another reason that the bears weren't so conspicuous in those days was alluded to in the *Midnight Sun,* article, their was legal and legitimate hunting. Several guides worked the Katmai area adjacent to the monument. One of the more famous, although less scrupulous, of those guides actually brought a client to the site of the Kulik garbage dump to dispatch a mighty beast. As the story goes, hunting had been particularly poor on the lower Alaska Peninsula. Guide and hunter had nothing to show for their combined time and the hunter's money. Returning to Kenai, the not-so-professional guide chose to fly over Kulik. Naturally, he spotted a bear near the garbage dump. Figuring it wouldn't take long, he swooped down for a landing. Although it wasn't exactly a fair chase hunt, his enthusiastic client promptly stepped from the airplane, stealthily approached the garbage dump where the bear was happily eating a snack Mildred Walatka had supplied earlier in the day. As you will read later in this chapter, the small bear was one of Mildred's favorites and a camp pet. The guide and his hunter waited for the perfect moment. The hunter faced the beast and dispatched it with one shot. Mildred and Toni Petersen were in the office at Kulik when they heard the unmistakable blast. The two women ran out of the office. Heading toward the sound of the shot, they discovered the brave hunter and his cunning guide with the dead bear. Immediately they asked if shooting the camp pet took all that much skill.

Wounded in ego if not in conscience, both guide and hunter hung their heads in shame. The guide skinned the small bear, escorted his client back to the airplane, and vowed never to return. The wrath of Mildred was too great. After all, she fed those vicious bears by hand!

## Would the Real Charlie Brown Please Stand Up?

John Walatka and his wife, Mildred, managed Kulik Lodge for nearly twenty years. John was a proud Alaskan and often wrote stories and took photos to promote the Angler's Paradise camps. He was a regular contributor to *Alaska Sportsman* magazine. I believe it is appropriate that you read his story about Charlie Brown. I think you will get a feeling about how John felt about bears, and more importantly, how he understood that a certain amount of discipline was necessary. John's story *Charlie Brown* was published in *Alaska Sportsman* in August, 1966, and is presented courtesy of Alaska Magazine:

*On a windy Alaska Peninsula day in June of 1959, at Northern Consolidated Airlines' Angler's Paradise Camp, Kulik Lodge, three one-year-old brown bear cubs started coming to the camp area to investigate the possibilities of handouts.*

*At no time did these three cubs show any indication of fear of people at the camp. They were extremely playful, but inclined to be a little rough. Two cubs were females, and the third a boar. The boar, while the largest and prettiest of the three, from the very beginning developed a real affinity for the kitchen. Scraps the cook normally tossed into the garbage can helped to fill the inside of bears with something more than the normal food bears get in the completely wild stage.*

*During the time the three cubs were making themselves a nuisance, as well as pets, their mother, a huge sow, would sit on the hill in the brush behind camp and make certain that no harm came to her offspring. On several occasions, when the bears became too rough,*

*Mildred Walatka and Charlie Brown playing Charlie's favorite game, feed the bear, during the 1960 fishing season. Ray Petersen Collection. John Walatka and Charlie (inset) earlier in the season. Alaska Magazine Photo*

*it would be necessary for us to switch them, which would invariably produce a loud squall. At such time, the sow would immediately rear up on her hind feet and call the cubs to her.*

*In the spring of 1960, when we opened the camp, our growing young boar came to camp within the first week we started working. He would stay behind the kitchen a good many hours each day and frequently was fed scraps from the kitchen. The two sow cubs in the second year seldom put in an appearance, but would occasionally accompany their larger brother on these forays. The entire season of 1960 the boar became practically a guest.*

*With the opening of camp in 1961, we had a cook by the name of Charlie Blue. Charlie Blue lived in a tenthouse at the end of camp, close to the alder brush and also fairly close to the kitchen. He became an immediate pal of the big bear and the bear would sleep outside Charlie's tenthouse at night, sometimes with his big paws right up on the porch, and many times accompanied Charlie to the kitchen when he went to work in the morning at about 5:30 a.m. This bear became so attached to Charlie Blue we then hung the nickname of "Charlie Brown." From that day until the day of his demise, he went by the name of Charlie Brown and, in fact, got to the point where he would recognize his name when called.*

*It was not unusual to see the guests lined up taking pictures of Charlie, and Charlie Blue, or one of the camp employees who knew the bear, would feed him. Charlie Brown this summer developed the habit of going down to the lake to take a bath before coming up to the kitchen for his daily hors d'oeuvres, and after eating would go back down to the lake and take another bath. Charlie's baths reminded a person of a playful pup or seal. He would get into the water, splash and throw sticks into the air–or–rocks or anything he could get ahold of, and catch them in his mouth, and dive and play with them by the hour. That bear furnished us many hours of entertainment, not only for ourselves, but also for our guests at Kulik. The same summer Charlie got his name, he also discovered that the fishermen catching fish were putting them on a stringer or hanging them in a nearby bush until ready to go back to camp. Charlie would naturally devour some of the fishermen's prize catches, much to their dismay and disgust. One of Charlie's prize tricks was to get out in the middle of the stream and chase a trout or salmon down the center of the stream, causing a great commotion while people on the shore howled their disgust. He didn't improve fishing. Charlie became a real ham. He would know about what time the fishermen were going upstream on their daily excursions, and would oftentimes be on hand before many of them arrived at their favorite fishing spot. If not there ahead of them, he could time it so that, without fail, he would be there within a few minutes after they started. Some people got a bit disgusted with Charlie. Not only did he make fishing difficult, but he kept timid souls from fishing at all. It was this particular season that Charlie also discovered that when the airplanes landed, he could invariably get another handout, such as a leftover sandwich from a fisherman returning from a trip, a lake trout, or the cleanings from some of the fishermen's catches, which he would devour with great gusto.*

*Charlie also enjoyed watching the mechanics work. He had discovered that mechanics kept grease and oil around, for which he had developed an affinity. Charlie also seemed to like gaskets, miscellaneous other aircraft or automotive parts, or anything that could be masticated in his powerful jaws. Some of the less brave mechanics often insisted they have firecrackers or a shotgun around.*

*On one occasion, we were having trouble starting our camp tractor. One of our Eskimo boys, Kupon (Raphael Kupanoak), had been standing behind me to help me, and unknown to me, had left to go into the shop. As I continued to work on the machine, I was conscious of him behind me, apparently peering over my shoulder. All at once, it dawned on me that Kupon was too short to look over my shoulder, and about the time I turned around, the tractor kicked over with a roar and Charlie Brown let out a "Woof!" Instead of Kupon looking over my shoulder, it was Charlie, standing there checking over the proceedings. Where he had come from, or how he had gotten there next to me without anyone seeing him was a mystery. About that same time Kupon came out of the shop and was greatly surprised to see the bear standing right behind me intently watching the process of starting the tractor. As the tractor chugged away, Charlie got down on all fours and sauntered away. It was a noisy machine.*

*Many times during his career, he startled people in approximately the same manner at odd times of the day or night. He often would sit by the sawmill and watch the boys cutting lumber. One time, Pete Valka, another of my good Eskimo boys, was peeling logs by himself about a hundred yards from camp, when he suddenly became conscious of having company. He took a fast look behind him and discovered that Charlie was as much engrossed in the peeling process as Pete was. Pete let out a scream, threw his draw knife straight in the air, and bolted for the safety of the camp. He wouldn't go back to peeling logs until somebody came along to keep an eye on Charlie.*

*Charlie, however, always recognized authority. On several occasions when he became too obstreperous with cameramen and other people, it was necessary for me to administer a load of 12 gauge No. 8 birdshot to his rear extremities to convince him he wasn't boss of the camp. After several such treatments, when I would shout his name and threaten him, he would get up and walk away, or trot away, depending on how much foul language was used in the chasing process.*

*It was also common for Charlie to be lying in the brush somewhere out of sight and when either Charlie Blue, me or my wife called him by name, he would come running for his handout.*

*In the opening of the 1962 season, Charlie continued to put in his daily appearances, with baths before and after each meal, exhibiting a fondness for us that could only have been excelled by a lap dog. However, he had grown to fairly good-sized proportions. In 1962 Charlie would stand seven and one-half feet at the minimum, with silver-tipped ears and beautiful fur in the early spring and late fall. In the fall of the year, Charlie would turn a beautiful chocolate brown. With his silver-tipped ears, and on a windy day when there were whitecaps on the rainbarrel, Charlie's fur would ripple and glisten like silk in the sunlight. However, during summer, his hair would fall out and he would look like a piece of sole leather wrapped around a bear. His sole leather hide was shiny, indicating he was in prime condition.*

*The following year, 1963, Charlie had in-*

*creased his size still further, but had apparently fallen in love. He would take extended visiting trips, often leaving camp for a week to ten days. Between forays, he would come running back to camp during the middle of the day, exhausted and tired. He would lie behind the kitchen, such as a dog would lie by his house, until someone fed him. He would normally stay around camp for four or five days to a week before taking off on his next rendezvous.*

*In 1964, Charlie had grown to what we estimated to be a 9-foot beautiful Alaska brown bear, weighing approximately 800 to 900 pounds. That year Charlie did not show up at the camp until four weeks after we had opened and was much more skittish about becoming too closely associated with people, perhaps partially because his friend, Charlie Blue, the cook, was unable to return to camp. The Fish and Wildlife Service had established a camp on American River in May. American River is approximately 35 miles from Kulik, and biologists reported a large, beautiful bear stayed at their camp. They fed him and watched him while in camp and told us they thought it was Charlie, which would have accounted for his late arrival this year.*

*Thousands of feet of movie film and hundreds of slides of Charlie exist all over the world. We always were hoping that sooner or later one of Charlie's offspring (what else explains his frequent absences from Kulik!) might happen to have as good a nature as Charlie and would favor us with a return to Angler's Paradise.*

*About the first of August 1964, Charlie left camp for three weeks, and he returned as his usual old, worn-out, tired self and he stayed long enough to get fattened up and back in prime condition.*

*When we closed the camp in October 1964, he was there to see us off for the season. Near the end of October, when a group of us returned to Kulik after a day's goose hunting at the Ugashik Flats, Charlie greeted us with great gusto and even accompanied us from the airplane to the cabin where we remained overnight. During this time he consumed several loaves of bread, as well as all the other delicacies that a group of three men on a hunting trip might have left over. This was the last time, to our knowledge, that Charlie was seen by any of us, and we believe that a certain so-called "guide" added Charlie to his collection of bears from our camp area. We have had, on several occasions, other eager "guides" come to our Kulik camp. One even shot another of our pets in the garbage pit, accompanied by a pseudo-big-time sportsman from the States. I sure would like to hear what the big-time hunter told his friends about how he killed Charlie when Charlie ran up to the airplane looking for his usual handout.*

Despite some legal and illegal hunting, the bear population was building. More and more people were visiting Brooks to see and photograph bears. Things went well between bears and people until July 21, 1966, when Katmai National Park had its first and only (knock on wood) visitor injured by a bear. Brooks River campground guest, John Huckabee, filed this Bear Incident report with the senior ranger at Brooks:

*I set up camp at midday and explored around until late evening. The weather was very good, clear and warm. For this reason, I slept out in the open, rather than in my lean-to. This was the second most important contributing factor in the attack, as will be seen below. The other camper had not been bothered in his tent.*

*That time of year there were a few hours of semidarkness and an hour or so of darkness. Before dark, I caught a lake trout for dinner. It was too large for one, so quite a bit was left over. I simply placed the remains on a rock. I did not wash the skillet, but left it by the fire ready for breakfast. All food was left on the ground in the vicinity.*

*Then I went to sleep about 10 meters from the fireplace. I was awakened, during complete darkness, by the sounds of the bear rummaging about, knocking over dishes and equipment. I looked at it for a moment, and it did not appear to see me. I decided it was too close to run, so I elected to lie low. After a few minutes, it walked over to where I lay. I remember the audible soft thud of its footsteps. I was on my abdomen, and the bear began to sniff my sleeping bag. It rather delicately hooked under my hip with foreclaws and rolled me over. I decided a bite on the backside was better than a bite in the abdomen, so I rolled back over and forthwith received a bite on the backside. I yelled as loud as I could, and my impression was that the animal was startled. I do not recall—never did—any details while I was in the thing's teeth. It dropped me about three to four meters away. I remained motionless and quiet, and it did not bother me any more, but continued ransacking my camp. Sometime later the other camper walked up, properly making lots of racket. The bear left like a shadow, not making a sound. I called out to the camper to help and beware. He satisfied himself that the animal was gone (he never saw it) and then assisted me to the HQ area.*

*A physician from Alabama was vacationing at the lodge. They awoke him and he administered first aid. I have always wished I could thank him, but of course I didn't remember his name. I was not in shock, and was not badly bleeding. He gave me a sedative and splinted my dislocated right index finger (I have no idea how it was dislocated). The one bite and the finger were my only injuries.*

*I was admitted to the hospital—this was a couple of hours after midnight—where I stayed for nine days in a ward with Aleuts and Eskimos hospitalized with alcohol-related injuries and illness, and a couple others. The experience was so negative that I threatened to walk out if they didn't discharge me. One of the physicians, who was sympathetic, arranged for me to become an outpatient of a colleague of his in Anchorage. By far the worst post-attack phenomenon was the nightmares, which deprived me of sleep for two or three weeks, but which did not disappear entirely for almost ten years.*

Before continuing with my discussion of bears, I think it important to discuss people and their agenda while in bear country. Because I am a fisherman and have spent many years fishing the bear-infested streams of Alaska and northern Canada, I don't think that fishermen are perceived to be much of a threat by bears. For the most part, bear-fishermen encounters are accidental as both the bears and the people are looking for fish. Seldom, if ever, do fishermen challenge any bear for space on a river or stream. People usually back off when bears are encountered. As a result, I believe bears acknowledge and accept fishermen as they do other animals that share their food resource.

I have quite a different philosophy when it comes to photographers, however. People carrying cameras are much more likely to push the rules of safe conduct in bear country to get a better photograph. Camera-toting people seldom stand in the rivers giving the bears the sense they are fishing. Shutterbugs quite often try to get too close, wait too long before yielding ground, and may give bears the impression that they are being stalked.

In his book, *Backcountry Bear Basics*, Dave Smith makes a similar case about a photographer who was trying to film a grizzly sow from about 70 feet. Dave quotes the photographer's article that was published in *Field & Stream:*

*I watched intently for an indication that she was unhappy with my presence in her territory, but there was none. The hair on her neck was not raised in alarm, and she made no noise other than the guttural sounds that come from a bear gathering a berry breakfast. Suddenly, without warning, she charged!*

Dave Smith quite clearly highlights the stupidity of this photographer:

*I'm not sure what sort of warning the author expected—maybe he thought the bear was going to pick up a megaphone and say, "Back off, chump," but any wild animal that frequently stops feeding or other activity to watch you is a bit uneasy. Whether you're watching bears or porcupines, you have an ethical obligation to stop bothering the animal, and it's just plain stupid to keep pressing a grizzly bear.*

Personally, I don't like guiding picture-takers too much. Their interest in getting a better photo blurs their judgement. Master Guide Clark Engle had extensive experience with bears, hunters, and photographers. *Alaska Bear Tales* author Larry Kaniut quotes Clark:

*God and Nikon made long lenses so people didn't have to get too close to bears.*

Rather than invest the money in big lenses, the photogs seem to keep inching closer and closer. I truly believe that the bears view fishermen as nonthreatening competitors. I also think they look at and feel differently about photographers. Indeed, they may actually view photographers as a potential threat, and then maybe an easy meal. In either case, I've always wondered if people, whether they are fishing or taking pictures, are as fascinating to bears as bears are to us.

During the same time that Brooks Camp experienced its only bear attack, things were quite different at the Angler's Paradise Kulik camp. John and Mildred had their hopes of Charlie Brown's offspring visiting Kulik come true three times more than anyone expected. John Walatka's story, "Charlie Brown's Kids," appeared in *Alaska Sportsman* in June of 1967. This story is important because it clearly indicates John's respect for, and knowledge of, bears. It is presented with the courtesy of *Alaska Magazine*.

*On a bright morning about the first of July 1966, as everyone at NCA's Kulik camp began to stir about, we saw what appeared to be a three-year-old brown bear cub sitting in a trail near the camp office. A closer look showed the bear to be a silver tip brown female. She rose when we got close and slowly walked down the trail. When my wife, Mildred, called to her and tossed some meat scraps, the bear turned around and came back to take the food as though she hadn't eaten for a month. From that time on she became as tame or tamer than the original Charlie Brown and would sit outside the office door waiting for Mildred to feed her. We promptly dubbed her "Charlene."*

*About a week after Charlene became acquainted with us she would stand up and wave for food. She came in one morning with another bear the same size and markings as herself and plenty tame. This one turned out to be a boar and we named him "Charlie Jr." He was a nut and delighted in getting on your heels and following you around, which can be slightly nerve racking, especially to newcomers. It does keep a person on the alert.*

*Several days later–lo and behold!—another bear—same markings, same size. So now we have three bears and boy, can they do away the food!*

*The latest addition turned out to be another female, and the shyest of the three. She would sit or stand much of the time behind Charlie Jr. and Charlene and watch the proceedings but, on occasions, she would join the others in playing and wrestling all over Mildred's flower beds and young trees. This third bear we named "Charlette." She loved to dig a big hole in the ground and lie cool in it by the hour.*

*Charlene and Charlie Jr. would sit up or stand to wave and beg to be fed. Even when we were inside we could often look out the windows and see the pair standing on the porch begging with no one in sight. What a sight it was to see these beautiful animals acting like kids.*

*Susie Petersen with one of Charlie's many daughters, Charlene, the bear at Kulik Lodge. Ray Petersen Collection*

*These three goofballs also will go to the lake and play and romp in the water like a bunch of kids in a swimming pool. In August when the salmon run was at its peak, all three of them were at the river fishing and would oftentimes let the river current take them several hundred yards out into the lake where they would dive and fish by the hour. They had to be kidding. They weren't really fishing. They were just plain clowns.*

*Charlie Jr. liked to follow Bill Jefford around, and this grated on Bill's nerves, so Bill doubled the electric fence around his cabin. He claimed the cabin was too small for him and Charlie Jr. both.*

*Charlene took a liking to Raphael Kupanoak, a Pikmikralik Eskimo, who has now worked for NCA's camps for 11 years. He could talk to her for 15 to 30 minutes at a time. Charlie Jr. would sit and listen to "Kupon's" bear talk, too. This was really a sight to see, as the bears would watch Raphael intently, their ears up and their heads cocked as if to hear better.*

*Charlie Jr., besides following Bill Jefford, would often follow Mildred, and on several occasions she had to slam the kitchen door on his nose. One time we came around the corner of the lodge with the jeep and Junior was sitting in the road refusing to move. I slowed down and actually pushed him off the road. Since that time he has had more respect for the camp vehicles. After being around bears for many years, a person gets to know and understand quite a bit about them and must learn to know that every bear will act differently under different circumstances. They are never to be fully trusted as they are wild animals.*

*When they come into camp, they want and expect food and after eating they will normally leave. They seem to be happy to pose for the shutterbug and will play and show off as long as they get an occasional candy bar or slice of bread or some other snack. At times all three of our new bear friends line up outside the fish house while we are cleaning fish and they get the leavings. The problem here is when you run out of fish guts, how do you get out of the fish house? It usually takes a bit of can rattling, shouting and commotion to get them away.*

*Naturally, we hope they'll come to see us again this summer. If they do they'll be as usual–hungry bears.*

## Everyone Has a Bear Story

When people get together and talk about Alaska and fishing, nearly everyone has a great bear story. They might not have a story personally, but they know someone who has. Bears just seem to bring out the stories. It is no secret that the Angler's Paradise Lodges are in the center of the bear country. No other lodges can compare with the bear activity at Brooks, Kulik, and Grosvenor. For the same reason Ray chose the campsites for fishermen, the bears choose the sites to gorge themselves on salmon. The employees of the Angler's Paradise Lodges have more bear contact than any other lodge employees. That's not bragging, just a fact.

A few early camp visitors have told me that John Walatka always had a tale or two about bears. You've already read two of his great stories. Maybe John is part of the reason that so many bear stories are mixed with the fishing tales. Not long ago, I asked Ray Petersen if he and his wife, Toni, had any concerns or fears about raising their kids in the heart of bear country. Ray told me that there really weren't enough bears around to be overly concerned. According to Ray, they never had any incidents that were anything but a little humorous around Kulik and Grosvenor Camps.

*One summer we had the Reeve kids, Richard, Roberta, and Janice staying with us. Well, you know how kids are. They were always trying to scare each other with stories about bears and trying to convince each other of the presence of a big bear. In fact, they did it so many times that it was just like the boy calling "wolf." Well, we were all sitting near the cookhouse one day and we heard Roberta yell, "Bear! Bear!" No one paid any attention. She kept yelling, and finally her brother recognized something extra in her voice. We all went around to the other side of the building. There was Roberta, running toward the cabin, and a small two-year-old bear was loping along following her down the beach. That was the only time I remember a bear scaring anyone at Grosvenor.*

*A couple seasons in a row we arrived at the lodge to find that a bear had broken into the cabins and done some damage, but that was part of bush living. One year we arrived at Grosvenor and found a dead bear on the beach. I don't know who had killed it. I always suspected Roy Fure. He had a way of ending bear problems like that. I don't know for sure, but he was the likely culprit.*

Toni had a pet wolf that frightened more people than the bears ever did. Like kids everywhere, the Petersens had their share of pets. At first they had a black Labrador named Toxibuck, the Eskimo name for "black man." Next, they had a pair of dachshunds, Hans and Fritz, and finally, Ami, a medium-sized poodle straight from France that Ray obtained from an Air Force colonel. Ray continued:

*Susie the wolf, Sonny and Susie Petersen at Grosvenor Camp in 1967. According to Ray Petersen, the two wolves that frequented Grosvenor Camp seemed to like being around people. Ray Petersen Collection*

*One year we had a wolf near the lodge several times. Every time the wolf came by, Ami would bark like hell and tear out of the cabins and scare the wolf off. One day Toni told me that she'd have that wolf eating out of her hand if we didn't have Ami chasing it away every time it came by.*

The next year there was no dog when the Petersen family arrived at Grosvenor Camp. As Toni expected, the wolf started to frequent the vicinity of the lodge; this year though, the wolf had a pup. It wasn't too long after their initial sighting that the wolves were regular visitors, and like all pets, had names. The larger wolf was named Honey Pup, and the smaller of the two was named Suzie. Sonny's good friend, Craig Otto, named the wolves during one of his numerous visits to the lodges. Craig told me that he did remember coming up with the name "Suzie" because he always liked Sonny's sister Suzie, but he thought Honey Pup was more likely a name given to the older wolf by Sonny's grandmother Schodde. Feeding the wolves seemed to be the thing to do. Craig and Sonny both told me that the wolves would take a piece of meat off the end of a short stick, and they fed them lots. When I asked Ray how tame the wolves became, he said:

*They would often sit on the porch with their noses pushed up against the screen door. You couldn't touch them, but I could easily see how dogs evolved. The wolves actually seemed to like being around people.*

*Once we had Jeanie Lawrence's niece visiting from Alsace-Lorraine in Europe. You know, in Europe so many stories were told about wolves chasing and eating people that she was scared to death of wolves. Anyway, this young girl was sitting outside the cookhouse talking and eating a sandwich. She didn't notice that one of the wolves had come up behind her. As she was talking, she raised her arm to the side. Very gently, the wolf took the sandwich from her hand. She just wet her pants when she realized what had happened.*

*The Fish and Wildlife Service set up a research station on the west shore across the river from the camp at Grosvenor in the early 1960s. University students manned the station and Toni would let them come over and use the shower. They said it sure seemed funny to be walking through the camp having a wolf trotting along at their heels.*

*On another day, I was taking some movies of the camp, the kids, and the wolves. Sonny was there, he was about 12. I put the camera down and told Sonny to watch the camera so the wolf doesn't get it. The wolves were just like pack rats, they'd take anything. Anyway, I told Sonny to watch it, but he goofed off someplace and didn't pay attention. Pretty soon I saw the wolf running off with my camera. I hollered, "Damn it Sonny, I told you to watch my camera." Sonny looked at me and said, "Don't worry dad. I know where the cache is!"*

*I remember one time I stepped out of the back of the cabin to take a leak, I didn't want to walk to the bathhouse. All of a sudden I felt this presence behind me. Here was this wolf standing by my heels. I looked down and said, "Damn it Honey Pup, at least let me know you're there, you scared the hell out of me."*

*Finally they moved the research station up the American Creek; by then the wolves were so tame they would go into the cabin. The following year the wolves moved from their den above our camp. I remember one wolf coming through. It looked like someone had shot her in the face with a shotgun. She looked awful.*

*I was at Kulik one day. I walked out of the lodge and saw a wolf trotting up the beach. It looked like one of the tame wolves. I called out, "Honey Pup is that you?" but the wolf just kept walking. That was the last time I saw a wolf in the Katmai country.*

Even though bears didn't bother Ray and his family, they were becoming more important in the scheme of things in our parks. From Gary Shelton's capsular history of bears and humans in *Bear Encounter Survival Guide:*

*In the late 1800s after considerable destruction of the animal populations, a system of protecting wildlife species slowly evolved. Between 1900 and about 1958 our culture, to a degree, still embraced a belief system about nature that was based on our right to exploit it as we saw fit. But during that period wildlife conservation became a sophisticated system of game management that was mainly designed and financed by hunters. Many parks and wilderness areas were established to protect wildlife and to create recreational areas for future generations. During the 1960s, a new nature philosophy evolved which expounded the principle that we must reduce our impact on the environment. This much-needed principle was mainly pushed forward by newly formed environmental groups.*

Management of bears at Brooks Camp evolved along the lines of history that Shelton delineates. Between 1962 and 1983, Katmai National Park Service records reveal that nine bears were destroyed either by accident or on purpose. Three bears were destroyed while they were in the process of breaking into cabins. One researcher told me that of the bears destroyed, the majority were accidentally killed while being drugged for transport. One example is explained in Will Troyer's *Brown Bear Studies–Katmai 1976:*

*Bear #978 never fully recovered from the drugs. She was seen the first and second day after the drugging and was moving abnormally. At one point she fell down a riverbank, was submerged in the water but recovered sufficiently to climb back out on the bank. The dosage of 6ccs of Sernylan was probably excessive but it should not have had such long-term adverse effects. She was found dead, near Brooks Falls, three days after capturing.*

I found the following account of transporting problem bears away from Brooks Lodge in 1982 in a letter to the Superintendent of Katmai National Park from wildlife biologist Frank Singer during a review of bear incident reports:

*Records indicated that 18 bears were relocated in Brooks Camp, 1965-81. In at least two additional cases unsuccessful attempts were made to drug problem bears, but the bears got away. A major problem in Katmai is the inability to get bears far enough away to guarantee no return. Two bears were relocated to the coast, at least one outside of the park to Big Mountain (near Iliamna Lake). There has been a high rate of return for those bears relocated close by such as along Naknek Lake, but the overall return rate was not analyzable from the records.*

I guess it is safe to say that even though the transporting may not have been a highly successful method of management, it did provide some great experiences that led to some greater stories.

In 1975 Katmai National Park Superintendent, Gil Blinn, finally decided that one particular bear family group had to be moved over the mountains to Kukak Bay on the Katmai coast. The sow, Momma, and three cubs were fearless of humans and often came in close contact with people. On several occasions they destroyed campers' tents. On June 20, 1975, Alaska Department of Fish and Game representative Jim Faro and Park Ranger Mike Tollifson drugged the entire family of bears. The Park Service chartered Katmai Air and pilot Sonny Petersen to transport the bears to Kukak Bay. Sonny Petersen stated:

> *I remember that the bears were lined up on the beach in front of the lodge. No one quite knew how to get the bears into the airplane. I came up with the idea of using a tarp and using it like a stretcher. I guess about six to eight of us lifted the bear into the airplane. We slid the sow bear–ass end first–toward the front of the airplane on the co-pilot's side. The cubs were small enough that one man could easily put them into the airplane. We threw the three cubs into the back. We didn't tie any of them down.*
>
> *I hooked up the seat belts so that Jim Faro could sit on the bear's ass. The seat belts attached to the floor and went up around the sow bear. I made Jim take a full syringe of the knockout juice they used to tranquilize the bears and a loaded pistol. I told him that if the bear moves, stick the needle in and if that doesn't work, blast her. Jim said, "Don't worry."*
>
> *We flew over to Kukak Bay; the weather was beautiful and clear. I remember on final approach to landing that I looked back to make sure everything was ready. The cubs were sitting on their haunches looking out the window. They were coming to.*
>
> *Once we pulled ashore, I turned the airplane around. One guy could take a cub and put 'em on the beach. It looked like the tide was coming in. I either read the tide book wrong or the correction was off or something, anyway we made a point of hauling the bears above the high tide mark on the beach. Of course the sow bear was sitting on the tarp. Well, six or eight of us put her in, but there's only two of us to get her out.*

Sonny and Jim Faro grabbed the tarp and finally pulled the bear to the back of the Cessna 206.

> *We grabbed the tarp and pulled like hell. The sow bear slammed down the steps and into the water. We were huffin' and puffin' trying to get her above the tide line. For some reason I looked at the airplane, the tide was actually going out, the airplane was going high and dry, and the bear was starting to come alive. We quit pushing on the bear and started pushing on the airplane; trying to get it into deeper water. Neither of us wanted to be on the beach with that bear when she fully recovered.*

According to Will Troyer, Supervising Biologist, the sow bear was back at Brooks within about twenty days. She lost one cub during her journey directly back to Brooks through the Valley of Ten Thousand Smokes. That particular sow bear raised three more sets of triplets over the next several seasons at Brooks. Several of her male cubs grew up, wandered out of the Park and were shot in Naknek. One of the cubs that returned from Kukak Bay with the sow grew up to be the most notorious of all Brooks bears, "Sister." Sister had learned way too many nasty little tricks and had to be destroyed at Brooks early in her adult life.

Another famous Alaskan had some fun flying the large furry creatures we call brown bears. Jay Hammond tells the following story about a young bear he transported from Brooks Camp. From his book, *Tales of Alaska's Bush Rat Governor*:

> *Of all my various passengers, few have conducted themselves better than the several tranquilized brown bears I have hauled. One exception involved the redecoration of my aircraft interior by a young bear suffering from a gastro-intestinal disturbance. It seemed he recently consumed a cathartic concoction of vegetation used by brown bears to purge their systems after hibernation.*

Jay also had a close call with another irate passenger.

> *Thirty-knot gusts from the southeast bucked over the ridges and clawed at my Cessna 185 floatplane. The turbulence bounced us like a mouse batted by a cat. My concentration oscillated from a rock-strewn streambed 50 feet below, to canyon walls just off my wing tips, to the gray curtain ahead.*
>
> *Suddenly, from just behind me came a drunken moan followed by frantic thrashing. My fingers sought the comfort of a .44 Magnum revolver stashed under my seat. I glanced at my huge passenger. Mouth frothing, he floundered on the cabin floor. Fixed on me were his evil, red-rimmed eyes–discom-*

*This bear is similar to the one transported by Jay Hammond and Jim Faro in the late 1960s. Perry Mollan Photo*

*forting as twin barrels of a shotgun.*
*"Please Lord," I breathed in silent supplication, "please let those ropes hold."*

*I winged the Cessna around and headed back downstream. The last thing I wanted was to try placing a bullet between those pig-like eyes if my passenger freed himself and attacked. The cabin of a Cessna 185 seems mighty small when a crazed passenger goes berserk. How could I get my aircraft safely out of that troubled sky–and myself unscathed with it? I had agreed to haul my passenger, not kill the both of us. After he had terrorized a number of people, the authorities had chartered my plane. Although he was sedated, it took several men to truss him in a straight jacket and load him aboard the aircraft.*

*"You have at least two hours before he recovers," the arresting officers had declared. Since my destination was less than two hundred miles away and the floatplane cruised at 125 miles per hour, it appeared I had ample time. But I was unaware of bad weather sneaking into my flight path. After an uneventful hour and a half, fog, snow squalls, and scud had enveloped us, forcing a change in course. And now, my passenger was aroused from his stupor.*

*While his bonds were strong enough so long as he was tranquilized, I doubted they would hold once he fully recovered. And I did not care to find out. Locating a suitable lake, I landed and taxied toward the beach. Once around, revolver in hand, I leaped out and slogged around to the passenger door. Though his protests were increasing, I was able to cut some of his lashings. I grabbed his legs and hauled his bulk through the aircraft door. He flopped onto the floats like a sack of potatoes, then rolled into the water.*
*Reluctantly rejecting the inclination to let him slip beneath the surface, I grabbed a handful of hair, held his head above the water, and cut the remaining bindings of his canvas straitjacket. When he recovered enough to keep his head above water, I backed off and waited while he hauled his 600-pound carcass to shore. With tooth-popping coughs, my passenger–an Alaskan brown bear–wobbled up the beach and out of sight into the alders.*

Former Governor Hammond told me that he flew five or six problem bears away from Brooks Camp in the late 1960s and early 70s, but the above-mentioned bear was the most fun. Incidentally, Jim Faro, who sat on the sow bear that Sonny Petersen flew to Kukak Bay, was also aboard the flight that was so much fun for Jay Hammond. Through a mutual friend, Jim told me that he was in the cabin with the massive bear that was coming to life. He let me know in no uncertain terms that it was he who convinced Jay to land in a hurry, even though they were short of their final destination.

Speaking of fun, the next several stories shouldn't keep you in constant nightmare mode, but might give you a little different perspective of our Katmai bears. Just like Paul Harvey's *The Rest of the Story*, these stories, too, are true.

## Why Don't They Like Martinis?

The Brooks Lodge crew closed the camp in 1975 as they had every year before. What food inventory was left was either flown to Anchorage or sent over to Kulik. A few soft drinks and the entire alcohol inventory went into the root cellar. The root cellars at Kulik and Brooks were and still are great storage facilities for drinks of all kinds. During the coldest winter weather, the root cellars do not freeze.

At the close of the 1975 season, the root cellar contained a few cases of bottled booze such as rum, scotch and vodka. There were also about 15 to 20 cases of canned pre-mixed drinks waiting for the following spring opening.

Gary Anderson, the newly hired Brooks Lodge manager and a small crew arrived early in May to open the camp and start the process of getting ready for clients. Once at Brooks, Gary and the guys started finding empty bear-crushed rum-and-coke cans all over the lodge complex. On closer examination, Gary discovered that the root cellar had been dug up and opened from the top by bears.

When Gary asked the local biologists why and when the break-in occurred, he was told that they knew a family of ground squirrels had burrowed into the ground directly above the root cellar. Sometime during the winter a bear woke from his long nap and was hungry. He probably smelled the squirrels and started digging. As the bear went deeper looking for a meal of squirrel, he ended up digging right into the booze cache. Once in the cellar, he wasted no time in opening all the cases and exploring their contents. The bear systematically opened and ripped up every case and box in the room. He must have liked what he found because the bear crushed, opened and consumed about 15 cases of 48 drinks each, more than enough to keep a big bear looped for a long time. For some reason, however, he didn't seem to like the canned martinis, only one can from the five cases of martinis had been tried. No one knows for sure how the bear knew what each can held. The cans were all the same size and weight. The only difference was the color. One thing for sure, you can bet he didn't read the labels.

Besides drinking all the pre-mixed cocktails, the booze-hungry bears also licked the labels, government seals, and certificates completely off all the bottles stored in the root cellar. Gary told me that after the rangers evaluated the situation and the damage, they would not allow him to sell any of the booze without labels, and certainly not any of the bottles missing the all-important government seals. He was not allowed to use the alcohol in drinks mixed and sold at the bar. Being the enterprising manager that he was, Gary decided to use the booze as a treat for good work by his staff. I spoke with numerous previous employees who had some of the bear-be-gotten elixir and they were all appreciative that the bears didn't have a taste for martinis. Even though they don't necessarily mean to be, bears can be destructive animals. Just check the claw marks on any of the cabins at Brooks or Kulik Lodge.

## I Knew Bears Were Smart

Many people have commented on the relative intelligence of bears. According to Dave Smith's *Backcountry Bear Basics:*

> *Animal trainers like Doug Seuss, who works with TV and movie star Bart the Kodiak Bear, point out that you only have to show bears how to do something one time, maybe twice, and they've got it. In Yosemite, that kind of intelligence has given us bears who specialize at breaking into a particular make, model and year of car. Once a bear figures how to rip open the door of a 1987 Toyota Corolla, you're out of luck if you park yours at a trailhead.*

Over the years I had heard similar statements. I never connected wild bears with the large brown bears that perform amazing tricks in the Russian version of the Ringling Brothers Circus. I've seen film clips of bears dancing, riding bicycles, and tossing beach balls into the air like the best jugglers of the world.

I have worked for several lodges in Bristol Bay as a pilot and guide. I have been a bear hunter and guide. I can honestly tell you I didn't learn too much about bears until I started living at Kulik Lodge. That first year was quite a learning experience for me. I knew bears were smart, but had no idea how smart. It took some airplane damage and a clever cub to teach me a lesson.

Bears seem to be inquisitive animals. Bears can also be destructive animals. They are large, powerful, and extremely intelligent. Everyone has heard stories that bears have taken fish from fishing lines, lunches, camera bags, and once in a while they have damaged boats and rafts. They've also broken into and damaged cabins and ruined and destroyed their contents, broken lodge windows, bitten into and flattened tires, and generally made a mess of anything left unprotected.

On numerous occasions, bears have done significant damage to airplanes left unattended in bear country. In defense of the bears, more often than not, the operators of those airplanes left tempting morsels of food and, every now and then, a freshly caught fish in the airplane. I learned my lesson the hard way in 1989.

As a pilot-guide, I often took a six-pack of Coke or 7-Up for my clients to drink at lunch or after a long hike. While I knew I should never leave any food in the airplane, I really didn't see the harm in leaving cans of pop or fruit juice in the float compartments of the airplanes overnight. There was no way a bear could smell what is inside a can, and the cans are odorless. Guess again!

One morning I was on my way to the river to get an airplane ready when I started finding crushed and punctured soft drink cans littering the path. The closer I got to the airplane, the more I found. Bear tracks led to and from my assigned aircraft. Harry Wehrman, the Kulik manager in 1989, was ahead of me on the trail. When I walked up to the airplane he was glaring at me in disgust.

"Didn't I warn you about leaving food in the airplanes?" His question was more of a statement.

"Not me, Harry. I didn't leave any food in the airplane. Wow, look at this!"

Closer examination revealed that a sow bear had simply pulled up the left side float hatch-cover. I knew it was a sow bear because there were both adult and cub tracks on the beach and on the floats of the airplane. Naturally, she didn't use the pop-out latches; she just bent up the hatch cover, ruining it in the process. Only the left float compartment hatch was bent and broken, the right side was open but not damaged. There were also numerous scratches and claw gouges around the cargo door of the Cessna-206; fortunately, the bear did not rip out the side of the plane nor did she get into the airplane.

The interesting thing to me, of course, was that there was no food of any kind in either the airplane or the damaged float compartment, only the cans of pop. How did the bear know that stuff was in there? Besides that, I knew I hadn't left the right cover open and up, but who had?

Thinking about the previous day's fishing yielded the answer to the question of how she knew. I had kept those 2 six-packs in the floats for at least a week. The day before the bear got into the floats, I had been guiding for salmon. I remembered I was cleaning a fish when one of my clients asked for some pop. I opened the hatch, grabbed a six pack and put it on the float. After lunch I returned the remaining four cans to the float compartment. It didn't take a rocket scientist to establish the fact that I had the smell of fish on my hands when I grabbed the cans. The bear merely smelled fish and went looking for it. Under Harry's direction, I spent the next few hours washing out the airplane, especially the float compartments with Pine-Sol and hot water. The mechanics let me know in no uncertain terms how unhappy they were at having to replace the hinges and float hatch.

I didn't see either of those bears drink a can of pop, but I have seen several do it since. I watched one bear pick up a can in his teeth, lift his head back and bite into the can allowing him to consume the contents without spilling too much. Once a bear learns how to do it, they can drink'em really fast, too.

When I made my way to the boat-slip the next morning, I learned who left the float-hatch cover open. There were cub tracks all over both floats. It became very obvious that the small bear watched his mother rip up the hatch and get a reward. That little bear pried and tapped on the cover until it had released the locking mechanism. The cub learned to open the hatch by accident. Every day for the next few weeks I found cub tracks on the floats and the hatch locks open. Without finding anything else to eat or drink, I guess the little guy finally gave up on float compartments.

## Don't Let the Guide Out of Sight!

A few weeks later that season, I had to do some late flying and didn't get back to Kulik until most of the guests had retired for the evening. The chief guide, Phil Rynerson, assigned me to guide a group of three Irish fishermen for rainbows for the following day. He left me a note and suggested I go to one of the nearby streams, as the three guys were still a little worn out from their long flight from Europe.

I met my clients at breakfast the next morning. I explained that I'd be taking them for rainbow trout and checked their gear, then loaded them into a Cessna 206, 88Z, for the short flight to my favorite fishing site, Nunucktuk Creek.

Light wisps of early morning fog and a little rain kept me from my normal routine of flying down the creek to check on the salmon activity and to see how many bears were already fishing. I looked back at my clients and the three were seeing leprechauns, not rainbows, as they were all sound asleep. I landed in the big lake and taxied into the lagoon. Once they woke up a little, they seemed excited about fishing. I secured the airplane, helped them with their rods, and we started up the creek.

We hadn't gone very far when one of the three spotted a set of bear tracks in the sand. I told them it was a small bear. All three were trying to get out their cameras. I suggested we start fishing where we were, at the top of the first big pool. Rather than fish, the trio set up tripods and continued to photograph the tracks. I told them that they just might be able to photograph a real bear and should not to use up all their film on mere tracks. I guess the sudden realization that they were in Alaska and a live, wild bear made those tracks finally hit them.

Fear seemed to swell in their minds and made it to their throats.

"Do you have a gun?"

I tried my best to calm their nerves and explained to them that I hadn't seen any bears on the trip there. I didn't tell them I wasn't looking, however. I told them that the salmon run was just getting started and that they really had nothing to fear, and as long as they were making a little noise, they probably wouldn't see a bear anyway. I reassured them by taking my short-barreled Ruger .41 Magnum out of my daypack. I told them we'd stay together and warned them not to walk off alone. I didn't have to worry about that. Every time I tried to walk ahead to check the next pool, all three of them were right on my heels.

Eventually I got them fishing. The morning fog burned off and the sun came out. The day was going well. They were excellent casters and were catching on to the Alaska techniques. Lunch was uneventful. Once the sun came out and warmed up, the only problem I could see was keeping them awake.

For those of you who have not fished Nunucktuk Creek, it is a small creek with thick vegetation, but it is also a great fishing stream. Later in the afternoon, my Irish guests were getting tired and were making some hints at returning to the lodge. Their fine sterling flasks had long since been drained of that lovely Irish whiskey. Patrick, the youngest and least brave of the bunch, was already taking his rod apart when I spotted a really large rainbow against the far shore. Geoff was standing beside me when I saw the great fish. I told him to make a few casts to the trout while I went down the creek to tell the others not to get too far ahead. I guess the thought of that big fish concealed his fears of being alone as he didn't seem too concerned as I disappeared from his sight behind some alders. I hurried toward the airplane and the two wanderers. Once around the corner, I motioned to the two tired and thirsty guys to wait a few seconds so I could brief them about their companion who just might hook a great fish. I hurried back up the creek. I guess I might have been about a hundred yards down the creek when I spotted a small bear on the shore directly across the creek from Geoff.

Rather than follow the creek path, I made a diagonal cut through the alders to try to get to Geoff. I eased out of the alders just in time to see Geoff look up and see the bear. I remember seeing the following series of events in that slow-motion madness the mind creates when you are trying so hard to get something done and cannot.

Geoff's eyes looked like two pie plates as the terror in his mind drained the blood from his head. I was about 10 yards downriver from the bear on the opposite bank from Geoff. His two Irish comrades were still trying to weasel their way through the alders to see Geoff land the big fish. Unfortunately that's not what they saw. They saw me pull my .41 magnum out of the holster and fire one shot into the air. I guess they thought I was trying to get Geoff's attention or something because they couldn't see the bear. I saw the bear bolt back into the alders and head upriver and away from us. As I turned back toward Geoff, his eyes closed and he passed out. He fell face first in the water, just like he'd been hit by a solid Mike Tyson left hook.

Within seconds I was across the stream and helped Geoff out of the water. He was choking, spitting water, and still trying to run from the bear as I helped him up and onto the bank. His two friends were rolling on the bank in disbelief and laughter. They hadn't seen the bear; they had only seen Geoff keel over and land in the water. I had to take the other two guys up the creek and show them some tracks before they would believe Geoff's story.

Once all of us calmed down and the story had been told several times, we made our way back to the airplane. I was glad I had a beer or two to give to Geoff. He'd really been terrified by the bear and somewhat humiliated by his cohorts. Once Geoff had his beer, we taxied out of the lagoon and headed for Kulik. Needless to say, Geoff became the target of lots of abuse for the remainder of his stay, and he didn't let any guide get out of his sight again.

## Watch That Fence, It's Hot

Every once in a while, some efforts to discourage bears don't work out as planned. One of the more infamous lodge owners, who will forever remain unnamed, told me this story about a troublesome bear and a more arrogant client. He suggested I not mention his name for fear of judicial reprisal.

*Early in 1983, we started having a bear problem. A large male bear started hanging around the lodge and was becoming more and more aggressive. Rather than shoot the bear, I decided to put up an electric bear fence. I called on the radio and ordered the strongest, most powerful fence I could get. This sucker was guaranteed to knock the biggest bear right on his ass! A few days later the unit arrived. By the time it arrived, the bear was getting into everything. The bear was smart, too, it only came around at night, usually after midnight.*

*I put up the fence, tied orange surveyor's tape to it and warned everyone at the lodge that it was up and really hot. During those years we always turned off the generators by about 11 p.m. I was so concerned about the bear coming in around midnight that I forgot to tell the guests that the generator would be on all night.*

*Well, we had this one guy who really felt macho and rather than using the bathroom in the building he was staying in, he would get up in the night, walk out of his cabin stark naked, and urinate off the porch. Needless to say, he had been warned. He had been at the lodge numerous times before and knew the generator would go off at 11:00 p.m. or so, or at least that is what he assumed when he stepped out of his cabin at about 12:30 a.m. Half asleep and not hearing the telltale noise, he prepared for his nightly duty.*

*I was waiting for the bear in another part of the camp. When his yellow stream hit the hot wire all hell broke loose. I heard the guy scream and knew immediately what had happened. I rushed to the guy and thought he was dead. He was lying on the ground totally naked, all the hair on his eyebrows singed and his head smoking. He had been thrown about 20 feet from where he had been standing by the force of the bear fence.*

*For the next few days the guy was pretty low key. We were lucky that he didn't have a heart attack or brain failure. One thing for sure though, that guy always used the restroom after that night.*

## If Bears Wanted to Eat People

I've lived the past ten years in bear-infested country and have had many close encounters. None of my experiences before or after caught me so completely off guard as did a one-time, midnight thriller I had in September of 1992.

The Kulik River is loaded with spawning salmon in September. As a result about 30 to 40 bears reside near the lodge at that time of the year. I have always maintained that the bears in the Katmai region are well fed and not aggressive toward fishermen; during the late night hours, however, I knew their temperaments could change. Besides that, all the creatures of the night, be they imagined or real, take advantage of the darkness.

For those of you who have not been to Kulik Lodge, imagine that the lodge, guest and employee cabins are separated from the river by about 300 yards of alders and dense bush. A narrow trail through the alders connects our boat-slip and the outer employee cabins. During my first years as lodge manager, I lived as far from the office as possible. My cabin was the dividing line between wilderness and civilization. Between my cabin and the lodge were two others. One housed a pilot, Buster Patin, and the other, directly across a small patch of alders, was the home of the two single girls working for the lodge that year.

One night I had been swapping stories and drinking a beer or two with Buster in his cabin. It was about midnight when I decided to head home and go to bed. My cabin had the only porch light at that end of camp. Rather than going all the way to the men's bathhouse in the middle of the camp, I decided to empty my bladder in the bushes close to my cabin door. I turned off my porch light so I would not be seen, just in case one of the young ladies decided to open her door and head to the employees' wash room.

Vividly I remember how dark it was after the light went out. I stepped about three feet from my porch and began my mission. As my eyes started to adjust, I glanced up at the stars on the clear, cold night. The eerie sound of two bears growling and fighting and the very distinctive sound of at least one of them running toward me shattered the calm. The bear was galloping up the narrow trail right in front of my cabin. I, too, was standing on that narrow trail.

Anxiety raced into my veins much faster than the yellow fluid drained my kidneys. I tried to stop. I was committed to doing one thing, tried to do another, and in the process, didn't do anything right. In what seemed to last an hour but took less than a few seconds, I sprayed the wall and my porch. As the bear raced past within a foot of my position, I sprayed the bear, too. Clawing at the door to get into my cabin, I got myself and the floor of my cabin. What a night!

Fortunately for me, it started raining later that night and at least the outside of the cabin was washed by nature. I can personally assure you that if the bears at Kulik wanted to eat people, at least part of me was readily available that night.

## The Strangest of All

Perhaps the strangest close-as-they-get encounter of the bear kind happened during the season of 1992. A true classic, this is one of the stories that is told and retold when bears are discussed. Late in the afternoon of July 16, I flew to Brooks Lodge and picked up some Kulik guests and longtime Angler's Paradise guide, Pete Raynor. I first heard this story from Pete and his guests as I was flying them back to Kulik. This experience had such an impact on Pat Melcic that she wrote the following article describing her experience. Rather than re-telling the story for the millionth time, the Melcics sent me a copy of the Bear Incident Report and Pat's story, which was published in the 1994 edition of *Travel Age West*:

> *We arrived in Katmai in midafternoon. As we landed in the lake, gliding toward the shore, I looked out the window to see a huge grizzly swimming next to the plane. Two smaller bears wrestled with each other on shore. We already were closer to bears than I ever thought we would be.*
>
> *At the ranger station we attended Bear School, a mandatory education for all visitors to Katmai. Here we learned the basics; keep your distance if you encounter a bear, stay calm and never run; in the woods, talk loudly to let the bears know you are in the area. Our lessons concluded with learning the simple chant, "Hey bear, hey bear, hey bear."*
>
> *That night in the campground, our sleep was occasionally interrupted by the banging of pots and pans by fellow campers calling, "Hey bear, hey bear," as bears walking along the beach took a shortcut through the campground.*
>
> *The next morning we rose early to begin the tour to the Land of Ten Thousand Smokes. Here we learned that the myriad puffs of smoke ceased to exist when the volcanoes became dormant. After a day of hiking, we were dropped off at the trail to Brooks Falls, where we encountered many people on the trail, but no bears. Then we arrived at the elevated platform above the falls and discovered a truly spectacular sight. Flocks of birds circled in the air above us as eight bears splashed in the water, above, below and on the edge of the falls. They were busily fishing for salmon, catching their prey with their paws and jaws as the fish leaped up the falls. I glanced down and noticed just below me a mother bear with two cubs. They were so close I could have touched them with my foot.*
>
> *Feeling we had experienced enough for one day, Tom and I decided to leave. Tom was ahead of me on the narrow trail, and I was about ten feet behind. Suddenly, ahead and on my right–a midsize golden brown grizzly bear was coming onto the trail immediately in front of me. I forced myself not to run, trying to calm my racing heart, which was beating so loudly I thought the bear could hear it. I began to move backwards slowly, saying as steadily as I could, "Hey bear, hey bear, hey bear." Each time I stepped backwards, the bear moved closer to me. I remembered one of the lessons in bear school: move off the trail, let the bear pass by. I stepped off the trail, but the bear followed, moving toward me. I moved behind a tree and the bear came over and stuck his head around one side of the tree, then the other, sniffing me. To my relief, it lost interest and sat down directly in front of the tree facing me.*
>
> *My husband, keeping his distance to avoid antagonizing the bear, yelled for the ranger while managing to take a few photos. I crouched down, hoping the bear would wander away. As soon as I had done this, the bear was up, walking around to my side of the tree. He came to within five feet of me, sat down, stretched out and took a nap. I could feel its heavy breathing on my face and the thin grass around my feet swayed with each breath. Several black flies that had been swirling around its long snout landed on me and began to bite. From the corner of my eye I saw my husband Tom with a huge tree limb, preparing to strike the bear if it woke and attacked.*

*Finally the ranger arrived, accompanied by a group of people who were yelling and shouting to distract the sleeping bear. The bear woke, sat up and walked sleepily back onto the trail away from me and the shouting onlookers. Despite my stiff and aching knees, I moved quickly away from the bear, who was still sitting on the trail.*

*We were circling around that bear by cutting through the woods when we came on another bear. This one was sitting near a tree, so we had no choice but to return to where the first bear was still blocking the trail. We waited patiently until it got up and left the trail. Back at the ranger's office we completed a Bear Incident Report. Not surprisingly, I had no appetite for dinner that evening.*

*We returned home without a wild fish tale to tell our friends, but our close encounter with the bears is one story where we were glad we were the ones that got away.*

## Some Agents Just Can't Take a Joke

On more than one occasion, complacency has been the reason I have ended up too close to a bear. Like most other fishing guides and lodge workers, I know that I should keep a good vigil in bear country, but sometimes circumstances overshadow good judgement. Encounters of the bear kind just happen.

A few years ago, I had the opportunity, duty, and pleasure to escort an eager European travel agent to Brooks Lodge to tour our lodge facilities. This well-traveled agent wanted to see a bear more than a cabin but had little time. He arrived in King Salmon in the early afternoon and planned to depart on the late jet. I had only a couple hours to view the lodge, try to find a bear, and then return the young man to King Salmon in time to catch the jet for his next whirlwind tour to see another lodge facility in Manitoba and hopefully a polar bear.

The lodge tour went well, but when we walked up the road toward the falls a ranger met us at the trailhead and insisted we wait until there was room for us at the platform. She told us the delay might be as long as an hour. I didn't have an hour. I just needed to find a bear. Politely, I told the lady ranger that we'd walk up to Brooks Lake and would return to check in with her later. The travel agent looked sad and thought he would see no bears. That was a bit of a mistake, to say the least.

We walked a few hundred yards up the road. I told the eager man that we were going to the falls by a route that none of his future clients would ever see. He smiled and made some comment about having visited the lions in Africa and was ready for any adventure I could give him. He didn't look like the adventurous and outdoor type to me, but who was I to judge? After all, he was wearing the latest in safari clothing and had all the appropriate stickers on his shiny new daypack. I didn't think too much about it when he asked if bears were dangerous. I recall making some remark like the bears only eat travel agents, never their clients or some such thing. He wasn't too impressed. I started telling him they really weren't too dangerous, but in case one jumped out and killed me, he should try to get away when they stopped eating me up and were flossing their teeth with my belt. I took off toward the falls with the suspicious agent trying to keep up.

We were about 50 yards from the top of the hill above the platform and almost to the trail. I was feeling quite proud of myself for outwitting the rangers and being such a grand guide when I damned near stepped on the outstretched leg of a sleeping whopper of a bear. I was literally within inches of his leg when he raised his oil-drum-sized head and whoofed in a way only a big bear could.

I jumped back as the bear snapped his head around to see what was going on. I looked at the bear–the bear looked at me, his stare not in anger but one which said "Can't I ever get away from you humans?" The European agent was about two feet to my left and about even with me on the trail, maybe three feet from the bear. I didn't know it at the time but the guy wet his pants when he realized how close he was to a real, live, wild bear. Slowly I put my arm up and grabbed the back of his jacket. I started backing away from the bear pulling him with me and saying nice, sweet things to the bear. The bear stared at us but didn't get up. I guess the bear liked what I said because the disturbed monster relaxed and put his head back down.

Once we were a safe distance from the bruin and knew he had returned to rest, I told the guy we'd go around a different way so that he could get a few pictures. He had long since forgotten about getting any photos. He told me that I must be completely out of my (expletive deleted) mind wandering around the (expletive deleted) bush with big (expletive deleted) animals on the (expletive deleted) loose. It was about then that I noticed his wet pants and the strange look on his face. He made some utterance about the time. I realized that he had certainly had enough fun for one day. When we got out to the road, he stopped and took a sweater out of his pack. He wrapped it low around his waist to prevent anyone from seeing the outward signs of his internal fear.

Once we were in the airplane he asked why the bear didn't attack when it woke up. I told him that bears were really smart and had keen senses. Trying to uplift his spirits, I explained to him that I doubted that the bear was asleep at all; he was only playing "possum," letting us get closer so he didn't have to tire himself out trying to catch us. After all, it takes lots of energy to rip humans into bite size pieces. Now that I'm thinking about it, I don't believe that agent has ever sent us a client. (Expletive deleted.)

This story, along with some of the others presented, should give you the feeling that the bears of Katmai don't really seem to be all that aggressive, at least not yet.

## That Bear Killed You, I Saw It!

Earlier in this chapter, I stated that Sonny Petersen has had more bear experience and encounters than anyone living, working, or playing in Bristol Bay. In the summer of 1971, Sonny was working as a guide at Brooks Lodge. In their infinite wisdom, the rangers closed the Brooks River to boat traffic during the summer of 1969. While the reasons were certainly unclear to Sonny, he had to accept their rule. He could only remember and talk about the "good old days" of boat operation. Typical of the young Petersen, one day he was bragging to a new guide, Don Borjick, about how he and a few other highly skilled guides used to run prop boats up the Brooks River all the way to the bottom of the rapids just below the falls. Don was skeptical and told Sonny that there was no way it could be done without wrecking the motor and tearing up the propeller. Sonny bet him twenty bucks that he could do it without damaging either. Don immediately accepted the bet. Sonny told Don he'd have to prove it to him later that night after dark. He wanted to wait until everyone was either at the lodge or in their cabins so that no one would hear them. Sonny certainly didn't want the rangers, or anyone else, to catch them up the river in a boat.

Later that evening, Sonny eased the boat into the river. Don jumped in as Sonny started the 20-horsepower Chrysler outboard. Off they went. Sonny knew that the first trick was to get the boat planing and then keep up the speed over the shallow water using the tiller handle to adjust the depth of the propeller. This was a skill learned only through practice and experience. While I'm sure several outboards and numerous props were damaged during the learning process, Sonny didn't elaborate.

There was just enough moonlight so that Sonny could see the river, but not much more. Soon they were approaching the rapids in water about 8 inches deep. Don was amazed that anyone could run the shallow water with a prop. In the darkness Sonny didn't see the bear that was standing on the beach below the falls. As he veered the boat toward the beach to successfully complete the upriver trip and win the bet, the bear either jumped into the boat, was hit and thrown into the boat, or was so scared he jumped up and literally fell into the boat. Sonny totally misjudged his distance; he had way too much speed and the boat slammed into the beach.

*Can you imagine being just a few inches from this large bear? Daniel Gutierrez Photo*

Hitting the shore at full speed, the impact threw Sonny backward out of the boat and into the water. The driver-less boat continued ahead and slid up the rocky beach completely out of the water. As Sonny splashed in the water and finally righted himself, he saw Don sitting upright, straddling the seat, with the big bear's front paws between Don's knees. Don and the massive bruin were literally nose to nose.

The bear lifted his right paw and took a swipe at Don. In the darkness, Sonny saw the bear hit Don, driving him back and crushing his skull. In reality, Don had seen the bear start to swing and threw himself back to avoid the blow, knocking himself out cold on the rail of the boat. The bear then stepped closer and had his chest right over Don, giving Sonny the impression that the bear was ripping out Don's throat and eating it.

Sonny grabbed the gas can from the boat, hollered at the bear and hit the boat seat, making as much noise as he possibly could. The bear was so startled that it jumped out of the boat and ran up the bank a few steps. Sonny could see Don lying in the bottom of the boat unconscious. In the darkness he couldn't see any blood, but he knew Don was dead. The bear's courage returned and it stepped toward the boat. In one of those rare moments driven by fear that give people superhuman strength, Sonny grabbed the boat and not only pulled it back into the water but spun it around and had it headed downstream. The bear was charging. Sonny jumped into the boat and pulled the starter cord rapidly. The bear kept coming. Sonny went to full power in very shallow water. Luckily, nothing broke as the boat rapidly accelerated until planing above the shallow gravel bottom. When clear of the bear and in deep water, Sonny stopped the boat so he could take a look at Don's mangled and ripped body. As Sonny stepped to the center of the boat, Don suddenly sat up, waking from his unconsciousness.

"It was like a dead man popping out of a coffin in a Boris Karloff movie," Sonny said.

Fortunately, Don had been out cold while the bear stood over his chest.

"What the hell happened back there?" asked Don.

"That bear killed you. I saw it!" Was Sonny's reply.

Don had been face to face with the bear. While still on the river, the teenagers agreed not to tell a soul of their experience. They put the boat away and ambled into the bar. Don was white with fear and Sonny was soaking wet. The pair also looked pretty excited as someone asked what the hell had happened to them. Obviously, the next few hours were spent describing the gory details of Don's death during the last boat ride ever made to the falls on the Brooks River.

## Are the Inmates Running the Asylum?

During the past few years, the National Park Service has been trying to advance the theory that people are displacing bears on the Brooks River, as well as on some other rivers in Katmai National Park. Visitors to the park have been told that the population of bears will decrease if significant changes are not made promptly. Their thoughts are based on limited field research and the opinions of the university-based research leaders. We are supposed to believe that all the bears are threatened and will soon disappear if we don't stop visiting Brooks Lodge and Katmai National Park and Preserve. Fishermen and sightseers are stressing the bears. Since the rangers started keeping visitor statistics in 1970, official Katmai National Park records indicate that more than 207,803 visitor days have been recorded.

Ted Birkedal presented his paper *Ancient Hunters in the Alaskan Wilderness: Human Predators and Their Role and*

*Effect on Wildlife Populations and the Implications for Resource Management* at the "Cultural Perspectives on Wilderness" session at the Seventh George Wright Society Meeting in 1992. Mr. Birkedal comments on the Brooks River:

> *During the summer and early fall, thousands of salmon pass through the river on their annual spawning cycle and its constricted width and shallow bottom structure makes it one of Alaska's premier salmon streams. At the height of the runs up to 40 brown bear may be attracted to the easy pickings offered by the enormous population of fish that concentrate in the river. For the past two decades the National Park Service has downplayed Brooks River's importance as a sports fishery and placed management emphasis on providing brown bears with unhampered access to the river's rich supply of salmon. At first glance, it would seem that these huge, awe-inspiring bears, which according to the park brochure "symbolize the wildness of Katmai today," have been restored to their rightful place in the scheme of things. To the multitude of visitors that crowd the bear-viewing platform each year, nothing appears more natural than the sight of dozens of satiated bears feeding and cavorting in the waters of Brooks River. Yet, from a historical vantage point, nothing could be further from the truth–this "bear heaven" is not a creation of Mother Nature; rather, it is a cultural artifact of National Park Service management.*
>
> *Even as late as the 1960s, Professor Don Dumond, the primary archeological investigator at Brooks River, seldom saw more than eight individual bears in the course of a single summer field season. Thus, the large numbers of brown bear now seen at Brooks River most likely have no parallel in the history of the river; it is an entirely new phenomenon, not the restoration of an older, more natural regime.*

In my opinion, the volunteers, the inexperienced rangers, and most of the bear researchers don't have a clue. The bear population is strong and growing annually. In 1954, Calahane estimated the bear population to be more than 200 in Katmai National Monument. Since then, Katmai National Park was created and expanded, the adjacent McNeil River Bear Sanctuary was formed, and the surrounding preserves established. The last semi-official bear census was conducted in the 1980s. That study indicated that more than 2,500 bears inhabit the Katmai region. Alaska Department of Fish and Game bear biologist, Dick Sellers, that he believes the bear population is expanding.

In his book, *Bear Encounter Survival Guide*, Gary Shelton states:

> *During the last five years I have seen considerable misinformation about bears spread out on the table of public debate, and most of it orchestrated by people with a burning cause and an agenda to ram forward. The most damaging types of misinformation I have seen are the beautifully presented TV documentaries about bears being endangered. The researchers for these projects have followed a prescribed and biased story line by picking and choosing studies or biologists that will project the agenda. People who are unfamiliar with it all, and who do not know that scientific inquiry is an oscillating process of challenge and debate, can easily be misled.*

One of the most respected of all bear

experts, Dr. Dale McCullough, wrote a paper, *Behavior, Bears, and Humans,* that addresses a seldom mentioned but often abused concept:

> *With each new report of a human injured or killed by a bear we question where management went wrong. We fail to recall that most problems with bears in parks stem not from human malevolence but from too much benevolence.*

Do personal agendas muddy the waters? Consider, if you will, the research opinions that helped lead and redirect the bear management plans of Katmai Park. Dr. Barrie Gilbert and a graduate assistant spent a few seasons at Brooks. I'm sure many of my readers will remember his presence. Barrie's face is not one you would easily forget; he was nearly mauled to death by a grizzly bear. While few mortal humans can read the report due to its highly scientific and statistical analyses, I believe Barrie's personal bias is highly evident, and in my opinion, most of the report is misleading. To support my position consider this statement from *Brown Bear Behavior and Human Activity at Salmon Streams in Katmai National Park, Alaska*, which by the way, was one of the principal research documents from which the national planners and other government types garnered their facts to substantiate their plans to move the Brooks Lodge facilities:

> *The stability of Katmai National Park's brown bear population is closely tied to the food sources upon which bears depend, particularly to the salmon concentrations such as in the Brooks River. Because Brooks has the earliest run of salmon in the season and late accumulations of spawned-out salmon in October it has salmon available longer than any other river in the park.*

Quite frankly, the statement implies that the Brooks River plays a great role in maintaining all the brown bears of the park. Given the statistical information that is readily available, it is very safe to say that the bears that inhabit the Brooks River represent less than 3 percent of the park's population. All the bears at Brooks could be wiped out with Hitler-like precision and the total population would not be significantly impacted. The rest of this course-setting paper is riddled with such generalities. I am a great advocate of preserving bears, but I also think that Gary Shelton is on the right track. Again from his book, *Bear Encounter Survival Guide*, published in 1990:

> *Between 1960 and 1980, most park services introduced a more lenient approach to killing aggressive bears than they had in the 1950s. This trend continued until about eight years ago. There have now been successful lawsuits against National Parks pertaining to bear attacks, and most parks have slowly returned to a more vigorous policy for dealing with dangerous bears. From 1980 to the present, bear attacks on people have continued to increase.*
>
> *Reducing bear/human conflict is a double-edged sword; we must teach people how to try to avoid bear encounters and how to reduce their impact on bears, but we must also manage bear populations and individual bears in a manner that will reduce the danger and impact on people. We are presently preserving and protecting bears in such a way that there are going to be more of them. People have long ago accepted the risk of*

*driving a car, riding an ATV, or riding a horse, but nobody ever gets used to the idea of having a bear take them down and remove half their face, no matter what level of risk is involved.*

*Many biologists and politicians have been operating as if there is no connection between the way we manage bears and the frequency of bear attacks on people. There is a direct relationship between the two, and the time has come for North Americans to reconsider the unnecessary and dangerous drift toward preservationism. We must manage bears for human safety first, and bear safety second.*

Bear expert Gary Shelton believes we should protect the bear at the species level and protect human life at the individual level. Like Shelton, I believe that removing a problem bear from the population does not threaten the survival of all bears. This is exactly what native residents did for more than 500 years along the Brooks River and other rivers in the area. By not following Shelton's advice and the lead of the early Brooks area residents who killed problem bears, we may soon create a new, more aggressive strain of bear.

There is no shortage of data to indicate that bears are smart, and the mother bear's job is certainly not complete until she has passed her wisdom to her cubs. I believe there is a great similarity to the way human children and bear babies are raised. Our human mothers taught us many lessons to which I'd like to believe I listened and about which I didn't complain. Today, however, our older children and teenagers would file child-abuse lawsuits if their mothers treated them with the stern lessons of life that bear mothers use. From a December 1963 *Alaska Sportsman* article by Frank DuFresne:

*Once I observed a family in the act of crossing a glacial torrent in Alaska's Valley of Ten Thousand Smokes. While the cubs fretted anxiously, the mother picked each one up by the scruff of the neck and ferried it to the other shore. But when they balked at the mere rill a few moments later, the mother spanked her whimpering brats soundly on their rumps and sent them bawling through the shallows. She knew where to draw the line on pampering.*

The cubs of that mother bear and probably every other bear cub ever born or yet to be born, are raised to realize that a swat in the ass means they did something wrong, and if they continue to do it, there might be a far greater penalty. There is absolutely no doubt in my mind, nor in the minds of anyone who has been around bears for any length of time, that a good swat on the backside with a few pellets from a shotgun does nothing more to a bear than make it remember the teachings of its mother. It usually doesn't take too many reminders to change the behavior of any bear. Dr. Dale McCullough says: "Some bears will learn bad habits just like some humans refuse to learn good ones."

You will remember that John Walatka used to demonstrate his authority by giving Charlie Brown a 12-gauge reminder when he felt it was necessary. This lesson wasn't done to inflict pain or injury to their pet, but to remind the large bruin which rules were enforced. Like human beings, bears can and do live by a set of rules. Bear society uses harsher techniques than a swat on the ass with a little birdshot. While the sob sisters of the world may whimper and whine at the thought, I believe a quick and deliberate round or two of birdshot is still the single most effective behavior modification tool available. If the whiners would only watch mother bears swat their cubs, they would realize that a blast in the ass is just an extension of the bear's own discipline style, and bears do understand it.

According to the studies of Will Troyer, supervising biologist of Katmai National Park during the 1970s, park personnel embarked on a "peppering" mission to negatively influence the bears. The occasional crack of a shotgun started in October 1973, long after any guests were still at Brooks. Indeed, the damage caused by bears exceeded $43,000 from the seasons of 1965 to 1981. No wonder there was an effort to modify the behavior of some bears. Unfortunately, the effort to change certain destructive bear behaviors stopped quite a long time ago. The misplaced efforts of the let-the-bears-be, they-were-here-first preaching sob sisters took over. Believe me, some of the ranger types watch way too much Walt Disney, especially Bambi.

Gary Shelton's *Bear Encounter Survival Guide* sums it up much better than most:

> *There are literally thousands of people who live in bear country who know that if a bold bear is killed, it doesn't come back. They know that bears who are dosed with shotgun pellets become fearful of people. It always amazes me when I meet people who cannot accept that this kind of behavior modification exists. It is now unacceptable to shoot bears with shotgun pellets, but until the late 1970s, this was the most common and effective way of modifying bear behavior.*

I cannot explain the feelings of the many fishermen who have commented to me that seeing, being around, and fishing with the bears made their experience in Katmai special and complete. Guides, lodge owners, and clients alike have said that Alaska would be just another place without the bears. In his book, *The Grizzly Bear Family Book*, Michio Hoshino sums up the feeling of most who have experienced our Alaska bears:

> *If there wasn't a single bear in all of Alaska, I could hike through the mountains with complete peace of mind. I could camp without worry. But what a dull place Alaska would be. Here people share the land with bears. There is a certain wariness between people and bears. And that wariness forces upon us a valuable sense of humility. People continue to subjugate nature. But when we visit the few remaining scraps of wilderness where bears roam free, we can still feel an instinctive fear. And how precious these places, and these bears, are.*

Tragedy struck hard in August 1996, when Michio Hoshino was savagely attacked and killed by a bear on the Kamchatka Peninsula of Russia. One of Alaska's most famous photographers, he was in Russia acting as a consultant on a Japanese film production about bears. From the November issue of *International Bear News*:

> *Michio Hoshino was fatally mauled by a 7-year-old male brown bear on August 7, 1996, as he slept alone in a tent on Russia's Kamchatka peninsula. Hoshino was working as an advisor on a nature documentary for Tokyo Broadcasting System. Members of the documentary crew urged him to sleep in a lodge with them, but he refused, believing the nearby bears would ignore him because they were feeding on salmon. Crew members heard Hoshino's screams as the bear attacked*

*him early in the morning, but were unable to prevent the animal from dragging Hoshino into the forest. Hoshino's body was found several hours later by Russian rescuers. The bear believed to be responsible for the attack was shot and killed.*

Will these Brooks River cubs become problem bears simply because they live in a National Park? Perry Mollan Photo

On October 13, 1996, the Anchorage Daily News Magazine, *We Alaskans*, featured a firsthand account of Michio's death by Anchorage photographer Curtis Hight. Hight had much in common with Michio. Both were avid photographers and both had visited the Brooks River to film and study bears. While Hight had been to the Russian bear zone numerous times, Hoshino was on his first visit. They shared a campsite in the heart of Russian bear country. In his account of the events leading up to and immediately after the death of Michio, Hight made the following observations:

*There are remarkable similarities between Brooks Camp in Katmai National Park in Alaska and Kurilskoya Lake in Kamchatka in Russia. Both have volcanic origins and they share similar scenery. Both have shorelines that are inundated by brown bears when the fish arrive. But the likeness ends there. Brooks Camp is a thriving resort with thousands of visitors a year. Kurilskoya is virtually unpopulated. Brooks is carefully monitored by biologists and rangers with government funding. Kurilskoya has virtually no staff or budget. To me, Kurilskoya is what Brooks probably was 60 years ago.*

*The most glaring disparity was menacing Kurilskoya at that very moment in the form of a dangerous bear. Gun solutions weren't authorized at Grassy Cape. Darting, netting and helicopter-transport techniques weren't available. So the big boar continued to hound the camp, night after night.*

Considering the comparison, I already outlined the fact that there were very few, if any, bears around the Brooks River 60 years ago. Katmai Park's bear management regime has changed significantly since the days of problem bear behavior modification, drugging, transporting, and destruction. I can only hope that the powers that be in Katmai National Park are still receptive to realistic management. Frankly, I'm not so sure that there is a logical conclusion to the problems that faced the bear photographers in Russia. I'm concerned that if such an event happened inside Katmai Park, fishing as we know it would certainly be different, if allowed at all.

One of the most respected bear research types, Dr. Dale R. McCullough of the University of California, states it best in this paper, *Behavior, Bears and Humans:*

> *In recent years the U.S. National Park Service has launched an education program to convince visitors that bears are dangerous and unpredictable. Equally required in parks where habituated bears have become a hazard to humans is a program to reinforce fear of humans in bears. A relationship based on fear and respect in both bear and human populations will favor mutual avoidance and, I suggest, a more hopeful prospect of long-term coexistence in parks with a minimum of bloodshed on both sides.*

Throughout this book, I have tried to explain why fishing is special in Alaska, and particularly in Bristol Bay. On many days, bears are constant riverside companion to the fisherman. Over the past ten years I have had the opportunity to fly fishermen and other park visitors to some of the most bear-infested rivers and streams in Katmai Park and Preserve. During those flights, I have seen and shown hundreds of bears to thrilled and excited clients. Seldom have I seen a sow bear with only one cub, most have two or three. Scientists claim that in times of stress and poor nutrition the animals either do not mate or have reduced litters. Perhaps those who predict doom and dismay for the bears of Katmai based on the stress induced by fishermen should spend a little more time fishing. By doing so they, too, would see that the bear population is growing and prospering. I believe that as long as there are salmon in the rivers, there will be no shortage of bears. By managing the bear population properly and consistently, future generations will always be able to see and interact with these magnificent beasts. Continuing the current lack of standard procedures is a mistake that may not be correctable if we wait too long.

The great lodges of Alaska have come a long way since 1950. Staying at one of them is like being in a fancy hotel in the middle of the bush. Naturally, part of the lure is the fishing, part must be the remoteness, and for many others, the wildlife that Alaska offers is the primary attraction. The first 50 years of lodge history is rich in personalities and in stories, but what will the future hold? The following chapter may provide the answers!

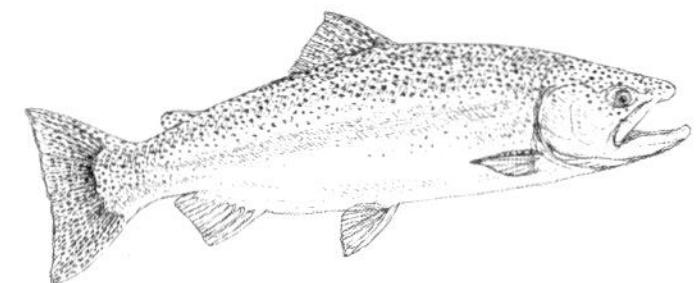

# Chapter 9
# The Hustle and The Future

During the 50-year period since Ray Petersen hosted his first fishing clients at the Angler's Paradise Lodges, hundreds of wannabe's have come to Alaska to find their niche in fly-fishing and the lodge industry. Today, employment opportunities extend to gourmet chefs in France, flytiers in Sri Lanka, travel writers in Florida, fly line manufacturers in England, and college students looking for summer work from every state in the union. Fly shops flourish and more than a few offer full-time travel agents to direct and arrange fishing excursions around the world. Fishing consultants, wader manufacturers, rod makers, reel builders, outdoor clothing stores, boat builders and numerous other fishing-related businesses continue to expand in today's market. There is no doubt about it; fishing lodges are big business. Although the last official state economic studies were done more than a decade ago and no new studies are scheduled, one state economist who did not want his name in print told me that Alaska's sportfishing industry generated more than $150 million in 1997. The great Bristol Bay fishing lodges account for a great portion of that sum. Considering the constant publicity our industry receives, I believe that the future of the lodge business looks great.

Every Saturday morning, television networks feature outdoor programs about fishing and fishing destinations. Hollywood hasn't hurt the growth of our industry either. Movies like *Gone Fishin'* and *A River Runs through It* encourage more and more people to try our sport. Community colleges offer classes in fly-casting and fly tying to eager students. I've seen public fishing ponds and lakes in our largest metropolitan centers. Sportsmen's shows cover every population center and feature not only the opportunity to meet lodge owners and guides, but also the industry's gurus. These shows provide clinics to educate and expose beginners and experts alike to the newest fishing equipment and technologies. Fishing magazines and industry newspaper advertisements offer readers a multitude of deluxe fly-out lodges, non-fly-out lodges, floating lodges, rustic cabins with boats to rent, individual guide services and tent camps all over the world with most catering to every budget. It is important to remember, however, that sportfishing is an extremely popular personal pastime, it's also a business, a big business.

## The Hustle

***There's a sucker born every minute.***
***Phineas T. Barnum***

Bristol Bay's fishing lodges have come a long way since Ray Petersen first vocalized the concept to John Walatka in 1948. At last count, there were more than 230 lodges in the state, and more than 70 sportfishing businesses in Bristol Bay. More than 280,000 nonresident anglers are expected to arrive in Alaska for the fishing season of 2000. In addition to the bona fide lodges, those visitors will find a myriad of individual guide services and entrepreneurs eager to serve all their fishing needs.

One major problem facing all the lodges, old and new, is to find and sell enough business to make ends meet. The hustle is overwhelming to clients and industry workers alike. Operating a fishing business in Alaska, and particularly in Bristol Bay, is an expensive proposition. Considering that the fishing season barely lasts sixteen weeks, lodge owners and operators have just 110 to 120 days to generate enough income to pay all the bills and hopefully, make a modest living. It should come as no surprise that this business, like nearly all others, has its share of bandits.

On one of the first pages of this book, I stated that the lodge family was my family. The branches of our family tree are laden with honest and productive lodge owners and managers. I'm sorry to admit, however, that we have a few bad seeds clinging to our lowest limbs. In my opinion, these used-car salesmen take advantage of the rest of the family. Unfortunate as it may be for all families, the bad are seldom exposed for what they are. Earlier, I introduced the concept of stretching the truth. At no time is that concept more visible than when there are big mortgages to pay and so many Bristol Bay lodge beds to fill. Ed Dearwent, one of the best lodge pilots in Bristol Bay, once related a story to me about a guy he knew who would rather climb to the top of a large tree and lie, than stand on the ground and tell the truth. When it comes to stretching reality, I know a few lodge promoters who exemplify the term, forked-tongue devil. Take it from me, there really are some lying sonsabitches in the lodge family.

Not long ago I set up the Angler's Paradise booth at a well-advertised sportsmen's show at one of our largest cities. At this particular show, more than one hundred Alaska lodges were in direct competition for potential clients. The aisles were jammed to the point of overcrowding when I noticed one memorable couple standing in front of our booth. They were obviously waiting for me to start the hustle, yet nervous about hearing it again. They looked confused and completely shell-shocked. I asked if they needed a place to sit down, and more importantly, calm down. Once they realized

I wasn't going to attack them like a carnival barker, they told that me that they had planned to choose a Bristol Bay fishing lodge and make a deposit before they drove home that night. Once they got to the show, however, they had been told so many contradictory stories that they hardly knew which way to turn. After a few moments, they asked me the $64,000 question.

> *There are more than one hundred lodges represented in this show. They can't all be the best. How in the hell can anyone make a logical choice in selecting a lodge?*

I tried to help them and in doing so I realized the problem all lodge owners face in this age of competition. Alaska fishing is expensive, and over the years, our less than scrupulous cousins haven't done us any favors. Rather than attempting to convince them that our lodges were best, I decided to give the confused couple the tools necessary to make their choice.

*The way it is in Bristol Bay. This great Kvichak River rainbow was caught and released during the 1998 season by Wendy Gunn while visiting Jack Holman's No See Um Lodge. Despite the fact that Wendy is a fantastic angler and guide, this fish is proof that fishing is better in Bristol Bay today than ever before. Terry Gunn Photo*

I attempted to delineate the differences between fly-out lodges and the non-fly-out lodges that use boats for transportation rather than airplanes. I presented the pros and cons of both. I agreed with them that choosing a fishing lodge is a difficult task. I thought I should reiterate to them the key elements they should consider when selecting the best lodge from the many that developed in Alaska since Ray Petersen opened Kulik, Brooks, Battle, and Grosvenor in 1950.

I suggested to them that perhaps the most critical aspect of Alaska fishing for them to consider is the availability and quality of fishing at the lodge site. How many hours a day are devoted to fishing? Does the lodge provide guided fishing after dinner? At a fly-out lodge, it is important to consider the distance from the lodge to the great fly-out destinations that make Bristol Bay famous. On those rare days that the weather prevents flying, where and what kind of fishing options, if any, are available?

I tried to make them realize that when comparing prices at various lodges, they should ask what is included for the advertised price. Decide if they need to purchase fishing equipment like rods, reels, and waders or does the lodge provide it? Does the price include the required licenses? Are there extra costs getting to the lodge site? Then I suggested they find out how many guides are employed and how many seasons they have worked at the lodge, and how many years the lodge has been in operation.

Most lodge owners and nearly everyone else in business agree that the best and least expensive form of advertising comes from happy clients. As a result, it is important to check with several people who have paid to fish at the lodge being considered. Finally, I tried to reinforce the idea that by doing their research thoroughly and carefully, they would not end up in P.T. Barnum's favorite category. The couple disappeared into the crowd. I don't know if they booked a trip or not.

## The Future

**... and now the real game begins.**
**The Riddler**

In an earlier chapter I discussed "the way it used to be." I suggested that the idea was fascinating, even romantic. "The way it is," in my opinion, is significantly better than the way it was. Since I started managing Kulik Lodge in 1990, we've had clients catch and set new all-time, all-camps records for rainbow, lake trout, and arctic char. Along with those record setters, we have taken near-record fish in every other category. Numerous guides, lodge managers, and owners have told me that they, too, believe fishing is better in Bristol Bay now than it has ever been.

Unfortunate as it may be for Alaska and for Bristol Bay, competition for the fishing dollar is stronger than ever. New resorts and fancy lodges have opened around the world. These new destinations offer exotic species, warm weather, and lower prices.

What does the future hold for Bristol Bay's sportfishing lodges? If I knew the answer to that question and could actually look into the future, I'm sure my life would be unbelievable. One thing for sure, I wouldn't be allowed to show my face in Las Vegas again!

Just like reading the disclaimers at the end of late-night advertisements for the *Psychic HotLine,* this chapter is for entertainment purposes only. With the exception of the soothsayer who told Caesar not to go to the Senate on that fateful day in March, and Microsoft CEO Bill Gates, who has enough money to buy the future, no one knows what the hell is going to happen in the next five minutes, let alone the next decade.

In trying to help you form your own opinion concerning the fate of the lodges, I challenged a few top industry leaders, some of the more vociferous experts, and numerous silver-tongued gurus to read their tea leaves, throw the bones, and pluck the entrails from as many chickens as they needed to focus their crystal balls. Then I asked them put their hard-earned integrity on the line and commit themselves for all to see. For lack of a better system and from fear of prosecution, their responses appear in alphabetical order with only three exceptions. I asked each one a simple question. I was stunned at some of their responses. I trust you will be, too.

*What do you see in the future for fishing lodges in Alaska, and specifically in Bristol Bay?*

You've already read that Bud Branham and Ray Petersen were the first two players in the Alaska fishing lodge business. Bud Branham died in 1992, three years before I began the research for this book. I'm sorry to admit that I never had the opportunity to meet him, but I am pleased to inform you that his words created my desire to present this chapter. I believe it is only appropriate that I begin the "Future" with comments from Bud's commentary in his book, *Sourdough and Swahili:*

*Alaska is changing. The population in Anchorage when I went there in 1934 was about 2,000. Today it is more than a quarter of a million. There are half a million people in the State of Alaska, and its uses have changed so drastically that it is difficult to paint a word picture of what has happened.*

*When I first started in Rainy Pass Lodge in 1935, there was not another hunting lodge in Alaska. When I started on Iliamna Lake in 1949, there was not another fishing lodge in Alaska. Today there are more than a hundred. Although our clients have remained staunch and our repeat business is as high as ever, the ability to make a profit in our kind of business becomes more difficult every year.*

*The discovery of oil, the increase in the very great number of planes and resultant accidents, and the addition of numerous hunting and fishing lodges all around us—have all contributed to the increased ratio of costs versus income, and today Mike (Branham) has great difficulty in showing any profit at all. When I first started, I got $80 per day for a hunting client, and the average trip lasted thirty days. I was lucky to get one or two clients in a fall. In the fishing business it was about the same. Today, the cost of the average hunting or fishing day in Alaska is many times higher, and the ratio between them narrows each year. I can see the time coming when my son will have to pull himself away from the hunting and fishing business in Alaska, for there will no longer be the possibility of making a living at it.*

**Steve Abel**

According to Steve, he has always been a fly-fisherman. In the early 1980s, he owned a machine shop and manufactured airplane parts and medical supplies. One day he received an order for heart pacemaker parts. Immediately, he had to go to see the design engineer because there was a problem in his blueprint. When Steve stepped into the engineer's office, it looked like his own. There were fly rods and mounted fish on the walls. They hit it off right away. His name was Bill Stutz and he had been designing a fly reel for eight years. At Bill's request, Steve made a few hundred reels, but they just didn't work out because the drag was wrong. Then Steve decided to design his own reel. He studied all the good reels from around the world and incorporated the best of each. He produced the prototype in 1986. Today, Steve Abel is the world's largest producer of big game fly-fishing reels.

*I've been to Alaska quite a few times. I look at the industry as a worldwide picture. Leisure time activities are very important. People work harder than they ever did. We used to think that by the year 2000 we'd only work three days a week. We're working more than ever before. Now our leisure time means more to us, so we don't mind spending more money to go places. It amazes me to know that an Alaskan lodge can get up to $10,000 per week for a hotel room. The only way they can do that is to get two crazy fly-fishermen to spend $5,000 each.*

*The future of flyfishing worldwide is going to grow. This might be a radical thought, but, when you sit down at a restaurant today and order fish, probably half of it is farm-raised fish; salmon, catfish, shrimp, scallops and other species. The way that the fisheries around the world are being depleted, eventually every sport fisherman will be required to catch and release his fish. It may be 20 or 50 years from now, but if you want to fish, it will be barbless hooks and catch and release. Now, that is hard to do with multi-hooked lures. Therefore, I think the future of fishing is fly-fishing. All fishing will be fly-fishing, except for some limited commercial operations. Specific to Alaska, if they maintain the fishery, which I know the Alaska Department of Fish and Game officials monitor closely, Alaska has a long and prosperous future. Of course, I think Bristol Bay is getting more crowded and the lodge numbers are increasing. The state might need to limit access and shorten some fishing seasons. I think that sooner or later there will be some method of limiting access. They should "grandfather" the established lodges and limit any new growth.*

**Chris Branham**

Chris has been in the lodge business his entire adult life. He currently owns and operates Royal Wolf Lodge.

*Like any business, I think our business will grow and there will be more lodges, which will increase the pressure on all the good streams. I'm hoping that at some time there will be limitations put on the number of fishermen allowed on some of the better rivers. I don't like the thought, but I am starting to believe it will be necessary to maintain the quality that we have in Bristol Bay.*

*My opinion about fly-fishing in Southwest Alaska and Katmai Park is that more people are going to develop an interest in fishing. My philosophy is that a lot of places around the world are getting overpopulated and Alaska is still underpopulated. It's getting harder and harder to find places that are remote and unique, and people want to feel secure and comfortable seeing them and experiencing the fishing they offer. The better Alaska lodges certainly qualify as safe and comfortable. My outlook is optimistic for the Alaska lodges and their fly-fishing opportunities.*

**Gary Borger**

I think it goes without saying that Gary is this country's best-known fly-fisher. He is a professor of biology at the University of Wisconsin Center, Wausau, and has been a fly-fisher since 1955. Gary has also written five best-selling books on fly-fishing and pioneered fly-fishing video instruction with the release of "Nymphing" in 1982. Among other distinctions, Gary was a consultant on the movie "A River Runs Through It." He is a design consultant to Thomas and Thomas Rod Company, and the designer of the Weinbrenner Ultimate Wading Shoe, the Gary Borger Fly Vest, the Gary Borger Fly Lines by McKenzie Flies, the Gary Borger Reel by STH, and many other innovative angling products and fly designs.

*Alaska has long held a special place in my heart because of the wilderness experience that it offers.*

*But wilderness, like gold, diamonds, or rare wine, is in short supply, and therefore highly coveted. And this puts incredible pressure on such wondrous places as the Bristol Bay region. That pressure has led to continued development of its resources; in my opinion to overdevelopment. It's not wilderness when 20 to 30 floatplanes land in the same pothole lake in one morning, loaded with eager anglers all wanting to fish the same two-mile stretch of water. Very careful and pragmatic thinking is needed to assure that this area remains a true wilderness. Limiting the number and distribution of lodges and the number of people who can use the wilderness sounds too restrictive for many people, but it's the wilderness we must be concerned with, not the self-serving wishes of the masses. As long as the resource is conserved and preserved, it will be there for all time. When we simply allow the wholesale trampling of the area without consideration of the consequences, the wilderness is soon destroyed not only for ourselves but for all creatures. We have some tough decisions to make.*

### Jason Borger

Jason is a contributor to a variety of international fly-fishing publications, both print-based and electronic. He is also the editor and designer of the Federation of Fly Fishers' Certified Casting Instructor program. In addition, Jason is the fly-casting columnist for the Federation's E-mail publication, the "Club Wire." Presently Jason is working on a new series of fly-designing videos, a new fly-casting video, and a book on fly-casting. Based in Wisconsin, Jason lectures, writes, produces videos, creates artwork and designs products centered around the fly-fishing industry as well as being a screen writer and actor. In 1991 Jason was selected to work on Robert Redford's silver screen adaptation of Norman Maclean's *A River Runs Through It*. Jason created and performed the film version of the shadow cast as well as doubling for three different actors in the casting and fishing scenes. The image of Jason shadow casting was ultimately used as the movie poster. Jason has fished most of the world's fabled waters, and has made several visits to Bristol Bay.

*Alaska is a land of extremes. A land of fire and ice. A land of vast tundra and intimate forests. A land of utter starkness and incomprehensible riches. It can also be a land where anglers, in the pre-dawn hours, rush each other for the best water and pass "words" when perceived territorial boundaries are crossed. It can be a land that smacks of the very things we try to leave behind by escaping the cities. Alaska's Bristol Bay is one of the places that is both blessed and cursed with all of it.*

*Without trying to conjure up the spirit of elitism, one must realize that even in Alaska it is all too easy to give to many access to what is really so little. A resource is only truly valuable if it still exists in a recognizable form. If it gets used or worn out, it becomes only "the good old days." The sport fishery of Bristol Bay is not yet used up, but the use it is getting is pushing the limits of what the resources can provide—while still being the resource that everyone desires it to be.*

*In Bristol Bay I've spent days fishing in solitude; I've also spent days playing musical pools. In Bristol Bay I've landed on empty, quiet lakes; I've also had to circle above the hills awaiting a spot amidst the Beavers and 206's. Alaska is a land of extremes but those are the kind of extremes I don't want or need to see there.*

*We must have intelligent management, and a realization that areas of Bristol Bay are nearing, or have already reached, their sportfishing saturation points. Such a sentiment may not be popular with some, but I would much rather see*

*Alaska's Bristol Bay remain as a land of extremes rather than a land of the "good old days."*

**Trey Combs**

Trey made his first fishing trip to Alaska in the early 1970s. His articles and photos have appeared in nearly every fishing magazine. Trey has also written many of the steelhead and saltwater fly-fishing books found in your local bookstores. Trey is considered by many to be a bluewater fly-fishing expert. I consider him one of the most knowledgeable fishermen in the country.

*I'm basing my comments on the fly-out lodges that made Alaska famous. I think that the big fly-out lodges will survive until the end of time. Everyone who goes to Alaska goes up there to have the "Alaska" experience. The fly-out lodges most dramatically synthesize the adventure for guys from the Lower 48. You get the whole treatment. You get the fly-out, you get the lodge ambiance, you get the big fish, and you get the salmon all wrapped up in six days of total immersion. I don't think any other state or locality in North America offers quite such a dramatic experience. You come back from the Alaskan experience completely fortified. A handful of top fly-out lodges take the Alaskan experience and condense it down to a few days. It's an incredible experience. I don't think it will matter how many different lodges and venues open up around the world, that Alaskan experience is something that anglers will continue to want a hundred years from now. I don't think it can be provided any other way but at one of the big fly-out lodges. Going to Alaska and doing a float wouldn't come close because you only see part of one watershed, as opposed to the immersion offered at a fly-out lodge.*

**Tim Cudney**

Tim has more than 20 years of experience in Alaska as a hunting and fishing guide. Tim worked for and managed several Bristol Bay lodges, including Aleknagik Mission Lodge, Denali Wilderness Lodge, Fox Bay Lodge, Cusack's King Salmon Lodge and Alaska's Wilderness Lodge.

*The steady influx of new lodges is coming to a saturation point. The resource can only stand so much pressure. Every time you turn around there is a new lodge starting operation and the next time you go to your favorite fishing spot there are eight guys there instead of two. We already have crowding and some overpopulated fishing areas. The fight to get to the best spots is already evident.*

*Unfortunately, it's a sign of the times, but there's going to come a time when people are going to say this isn't how it used to be. I believe the established and financially sound lodges will dominate the business while the lodges of lesser quality and inferior fishing programs will slowly disappear.*

**Ted Gerken**

Ted purchased Iliaska Lodge in 1977, and has developed the facility into one of the most respected lodges in Alaska.

*As far as the industry goes, I don't think the rivers can stand any more pressure without showing signs of deterioration. I believe the rivers have too much pressure. For the last few years, I've seen one or more lodges open. Now I'm seeing lodges close. Just last summer two lodges just didn't open in Iliamna. The constant pressure on the rivers is starting to show in the condition of the fish. We're seeing fish with scars and "ripped lips" on a regular basis. I think this is attributable to the use of beads. They're very effective but very damaging on the fish, especially if they're used improperly. If you're going to fly-fish, use a fly, not a bead. Of more significance than fishing pressure is the presence of sockeye salmon. If we don't get enough sockeye salmon, none of us will have any fish left. It is incumbent on the board of fisheries and the managers to make sure the escapements meet their desired quotas so that the protein from the backs of all those sockeye salmon regenerate the ecosystems. That is much more important than the fishing pressure from anglers. As long as the fish have enough food to eat, there will be plenty of rainbows and char. They'll stay in good shape. In my twenty-five years in Alaska, I've seen three cycles when the escapements have dropped way below the desired levels. When they drop down that far, the condition of the rainbows is abysmal.*

**Harry Gualco**

Harry owns and operates Rod & Reel Adventures, a booking service in Copperopolis, California.

*I have been fishing the Alaska fresh- and saltwater ways for more than 15 years. My business has taken me in and out of some the finest fishing lodges that the state has to offer. Of course, anyone who has fished Alaska knows the prime destination for a multitude of freshwater species (salmon, rainbow trout, Dolly Varden, char, grayling, pike, etc.) is the Bristol Bay drainage. If there is a blight on the scene currently it is overabundance of fishing lodges. Many of us can attest to the fact that on many days it is a floatplant race between lodges to get to certain "beats" on the rivers. This can get pretty depressing for the angler looking to "get away from it all."*

*However, with this comment I don't wish to throw a damp towel over one of the finest fisheries on the planet. It is still just that. What do I see as the solution over time? I believe that there will be a natural attrition of lodges that are opening up and are under-capitalized. I see the same fate for some of the older lodges that can't keep up, too.*

**Wayne "Sierra" Hansen**

Wayne started his Bristol Bay guiding career at Kulik Lodge in 1987. He became the senior guide in 1990.

*I have seen the fishing for rainbow trout improve significantly over the past 10 years, but I also have seen the king salmon fishery decline. I've only been watching the runs for 13, but the last few years have not been as good as they were when I started. It may be that all the fish are cyclic in nature and we're just in a down side of the king salmon cycle. I'd like to see the fisheries people get accurate fish counts in all the rivers so we know the real story. We've learned plenty from the rainbow-tagging programs and maybe we need more information about the kings, too.*

*As far as the lodge business is concerned, I'm just a guide, but somebody must think the future of the lodge industry is great in Bristol Bay because there are a lot more guides around now than there were when I started. Bristol Bay has been really good to me, and I think it will be good for anyone who comes up to try it.*

**Jack Holman**

Jack moved to Alaska in 1972 and taught grades 1 through 8 in Levelock. Jack started No See Um Lodge during the summer of 1975. He quit teaching and entered the lodge business full-time in 1979.

*I don't know. I suspect that it depends on the economy as much as anything, and if I knew that, I'd already be filthy rich. The numbers of clients will continue to increase, but there are some limiting factors. A major problem in the world could cause fuel costs to skyrocket, making our prices go up. The government entities may decide on some method of taxing fishing and fishermen. The upper end fly-out lodges may already be near or at the maximum price that people are willing to pay. The number of lodges will be self-limiting based on price. At the moment the future looks great for lower price lodges offering less service and fewer amenities. People may be willing to do more nonguided trips to lower their cost of fishing.*

*Because there are few, if any, secrets in the fishing business, there are many people fishing in the traditionally known best places. Alaska is not like England in offering private waters. If our system was more like theirs, only the very wealthy would ever fish in Bristol Bay, and that wouldn't be good.*

**Lance Kaufman**

Lance has been fishing and sending fishermen around the world for more years than he wants to admit. He has made numerous trips to Bristol Bay in his pursuit for the best for his fly-fishing store as well as his major mail order business.

*I see a very bright future for Bristol Bay lodges. Compared to the Lower 48 fishing, Alaska has everything to offer. The lodges really understand taking care of guests, and have nearly all of their logistical problems solved. Indeed, all lodges worldwide are compared to the full-service lodges of Bristol Bay. Barring any collapse in the salmon runs, Bristol Bay lodges will remain at the absolute top of the fishing industry worldwide.*

**Bob Marriott**

Bob visited all the reputable lodges and according to him, a few strays. Bob was in the commercial real estate business when the bottom dropped out of the market during the early 1980s. Interest rates went to hell. Bob bought a small fishing tackle retail store with the plan to set up a residential real estate business in the back room. Two years later he surrendered his real estate license. Today, Bob operates the world's largest fly-fishing-only store.

*I went to Alaska to fish in 1978 and there weren't all that many lodges. There has been a huge proliferation of lodges since then. Not only that, but fly-fishing was not a big item on the scene. The only reels we had that would work on the salmon were the Pfleuger line, the Seamaster and the Finnor.*

*I think what happened is a proliferation of lodges and a lack of regulation by the State to stop or limit the expansion. In my opinion, this is more of a downfall than a blessing. The other problem that may start facing the lodges is the price. Today, the income level has risen so that a four- to five-thousand dollar trip is not so outrageous as it was a few years ago. As long as the lodges don't price themselves out of the market, I think the future looks good.*

**Mike Michelak**

Mike started the Fly Shop in Redding, California in 1978. Mike has considerable knowledge about Alaska as he operated Rainbow River Lodge in 1983.

*The day of the full-fledged fly-out lodge is slowly coming to an end. The high cost and a perceived loss of quality experiences are slowly eroding the credibility of the Alaska lodges. Only those places that can offer good local fishing will survive. For those lodges that offer great fishing at the lodge site, of which there are only a handful, the future is great. I believe there will be significant economical problems for the vast majority of lodges in Alaska. Those who survive will still offer the best fishing that North America has to offer. Fish and Wildlife will start greater regulatory functions and will consider the overcrowding issue. Overcrowding is an issue that must be faced by all the lodges Bristol Bay. The day of selective waters is coming to Alaska. It is the only way for certain lodges to survive.*

**Howard McKinny**

Howard made his first trip to Alaska in 1972. He owns and operates Fish-about, a travel agency devoted to fishermen, with his partner, Kay Mitsyoshi.

*We've been booking Alaska fishing and travel for the last 20 years. What were seeing as travel wholesalers is that a lot of the guys who have been going to Alaska steadily have started to venture out and are trying different destinations like saltwater fly-fishing and fishing in the Amazon. The newcomers joining the sport are just as excited about going to Alaska today as those who traveled north 20 years ago. Although some say that the fishing may not be what it was 30 years ago, it is still the best fishing in the world. I believe that the Alaska lodges have a great future. If the Alaska Department of Fish and Game manages the salmon runs properly, we'll have fishermen traveling to Alaska's lodges well into the twenty-first century.*

**Kay Mitsuyoshi**

Kay worked for Japan Airlines from 1958 until he retired from the airline in 1971. During his career at JAL, Kay lived in Alaska and frequented the Angler's Paradise Lodges during the late 1950s, 1960s and 1970s. Besides working closely with Ray Petersen, John Walatka, and Chuck Petersen during the early years, Kay moved to San Francisco and assisted several lodge owners and operators, including John Pearson and Bob Curtis with marketing plans and Lower 48 operational assistance. A keen fisherman, he started Fish-About with Howard McKinney in 1989. As a booking agent, Kay told me that he is vitally concerned about the escalating prices of the major Bristol Bay lodges.

*The average guy is simply being priced out of the pool. The lodges need to take a hard look at their price structure. Many of my clients are choosing to go to Alaskan lodges that will make them a deal. I personally think there are too many lodges. The other problem is that the lodges are getting too big. People are looking for smaller lodges with great service. Clients are also looking toward saltwater much more than ever before.*

**Jim Murphy**

Jim owned and operated several very successful bookstores in Massachusets. After he sold his businesses, he managed the operations of Thomas and Thomas, the rod builders. Jim started the Reddington Company in 1983. His innovative equipment designs and revolutionary marketing programs have rocketed him to the pinnacle of the fly-fishing equipment business.

*I believe the future looks good for the lodges of Alaska. I believe that the tendency of baby boomers to buy experiences, particularly outdoor experiences, will be a continued force in the growth. Communication through the Internet will allow more and more people to learn what kind of fishing experiences are available. The Internet allows people to look at all the adventure travel destinations from the security of their home or office. People can compare the prices and see what the lodges are like right from home. They can buy equipment. I think the Internet will increase the number of fishermen in general. More fishermen need more places to go, and lodges to accommodate them.*

**Brian OKeefe**

Brian is and has been in the fishing business since the late 1970s. He is currently a sales rep for Scientific Angler, Scott Rods, Frontier Flies and Ronny Waders. His photographs appear regularly in many of the fly-fishing catalogs and magazines including *Field & Stream, Outside* and *USA Today*. Early in his career, he worked as a fishing guide in Bristol Bay. Brian is one of the world's best fly casters and is noted for his exploratory exploits finding exotic saltwater hotspots.

*What's good for the fish is good for the fisherman. If the rainbow, king, and silver salmon fishery stays in good health, there will always be a high quality lodge industry. Certain rivers may need additional management like barbless single hooks, no bait restrictions, mandatory catch and release, and possibly access limitations. I believe most anglers would prefer to see fewer people, have quality rather than quantity, and share the streams with eagles, moose, and bears. If the Alaska experience is as good as the pictures on those glossy brochures, then I'll be back for many years to come.*

**Ed Rice**

Ed Rice was a television executive before he started his International Sportsmen's Expositions. Although currently semi-retired, Ed's influence on the fishing industry is unparalleled. Through his shows, Ed exposed millions of people to quality fishing adventures. He has fished at most of the world's great destinations and has extensive experience in Alaska. He is also one of the very best fly casters with whom I've had the pleasure to fish.

*I believe the quality of sportfishing at the lodges will go down in the future. Kulik, as an example, used to have places they could go where no one else would be. Now people are everywhere. Lodges will find certain areas where fisheries can be maintained, but it won't be possible for everyone to access as many different areas on one trip. The wilderness seems to be dwindling as every lake seems to have a lodge on it. I also believe that catch and release is crucial.*

*The real push in Alaska lodges started in 1980. For example, my shows had as many as 75 to 80 Alaska lodges apply for space. I had to cut back, I accepted only the best. In the 1950s, 1960s, and 1970s, people went to the same destination year after year. Things are different today. More clients are trying more lodges. I've got to tell you that bonefishing or permit fishing in warm water and exotic destinations is great. Go once and your appetite is whetted for different places. I believe that some people have started to alternate destinations, and add new ones. They go back to the same place maybe every three years. The travel habits of sportfishermen are very different today than they were 10 to 15 years ago. More people are fishing. More people travel constantly because more people are talking about more places, whether it is Africa, Alaska, or Russia.*

*There are more publications and more people writing about more places. As long as someone can maintain a fishery, it is a viable industry. More fishing in different places leads to more tackle development. Specifically, in the western trout rivers, trout fishing used to be six- to eight-weight rods with dry flies, now it is three-, four-, and five-weights with heavy flies. Six-to eight-weight rods are considered medium. Talking about trout fishing in Alaska with four- and five-weights—good luck, it's six and eights. It's a different type of fishery, bigger fish, and more fish. Alaska-style fishing is very influential in the industry. Alaska has more fly-fishermen than anywhere else in the world, more even than Florida in the short season. It's like fishing a fishing paradise. You haven't reached the big time in fishing until you've fished Alaska. Alaska has the best rainbow fishery in the world for numbers and size. For numbers and size, there's no place like Alaska.*

**Bill Sims**

Bill has been flying and guiding clients in and around Bristol Bay since 1959. A professional hunter and commercial fisherman, Bill hosted his first fishing guests at Newhalen Lodge in 1971. Only the Angler's Paradise Lodges can claim more years of continuous operation by the same family.

*While I haven't given it much thought, I think that the catch and release policy has stabilized the fishing. I believe that some of our trout fishing is better now than it was 20 years ago, and I think there are two reasons why. First, almost all the lodges have adopted catch and release, and I think that the numbers of new lodges has peaked. Mind you, I said the same thing years ago and quite a few new places opened up. I was wrong on that. I expect some of the older operators to sell, but the numbers should stay about the same. Changes in regulations may cause us some problems in the future, but I'm sure there will be fishing lodges in Bristol Bay for many years to come.*

**Karl Storath**

Karl made his first visit to Bristol Bay in 1974. He commercial fished in Bristol Bay and guided sportfishermen at No See Um Lodge beginning in 1975. Karl opened his Angler's Alibi Lodge on the Alagnak River in 1994.

*The fact of the matter is that more and more lodges are opening. Everyone seems to want to get into the act. The biggest problem I see today is overcrowding on the popular rivers. While most lodge people won't agree with me, I believe that within a few years the Alaska Department of Fish and Game and or the National Park Service will find a way to open up the area to helicopters. This will allow more people to fish and lessen the crowds. We need to have easier access to the fishing. There are numerous rivers and tributaries where I know there are fish. I just can't get to them easily. I think the quality of fishing is holding steady, except for silver salmon. I don't know if it's high seas fishing, or a problem in the river (Alagnak), I just know it isn't as good as it was 20 years ago. As long as clients want to fish, I'll be here to take them.*

**Evan Swensen**

Evan, who came to live in Alaska in 1957, has been writing, publishing, and making TV shows and videos about fishing, and other Alaska outdoor recreation, for more than 20 years.

*I cast my first fly in a Bristol Bay drainage stream over three decades ago and it forever changed the way I fished. There are two Alaskas: one the resident sees, and the one visitors come to, and these two Alaskas are entirely different. Residents, by and large, fish for food along the road system—combat fishing it's called—filling the freezer their primary goal for going afield. Visitors, for the most part, take rod in hand for the fishing experience—catch and release is a pleasant part of the that experience. For the past 20 years and more, I've fished Alaska like a nonresident—fishing for the pleasure of the sport, seldom killing a fish.*

*With that bit of background I'll throw in my two-bits worth of speculation of what the future holds for fishing lodges in Alaska, and specifically in Bristol Bay drainage streams and lakes.*

*My response to Bo's question answered from both the visitor and resident perspective.*

*My first response, speaking as a resident of Anchorage, is simply, it doesn't matter what the fishing lodge business does in Bristol Bay as it hardly impacts my life in any degree. I suspect that most urban Alaska residents feel that the road system—freezer-filling opportunities—will continue to decline as more and more watersheds are fished out and salmon runs are managed to support only commercial fishing. I don't think I'd want to be in the sportfishing business along any of Alaska's roads.*

*But for the rest of Alaska, some call it the real Alaska, the Alaska visitors pay big bucks to enjoy, the future is bright with increased opportunity. I see more government interference and threats to access by Native groups, but the honest and persistent will get by the regulations and work with Native organizations to make the fishing lodge business more business than fishing. Even today, the most successful lodges are those whose owners have learned to adapt to change and regulation.*

*I've fished with nearly all of the Bristol Bay fishing lodge owners or their guides, some many times. I have learned that, like most successful businesses, those who render quality service and keep their promises continue year after year. The others are short-timers, going bust in the lodge business, and moving on, making excuses for their failure, never accepting their poor service for their demise from perhaps the most fun and exciting business in Alaska.*

*I, however, think those who maintain a business-as-usual attitude will soon fade from the Alaska fishing lodge scene. The next decade will see dramatic changes in the way lodges use the land and resources, buy goods and services, and treat all aspects of running a lodge. Lodges of the future will form coops for marketing, purchasing, fighting government intrusion and crippling regulation, and for finding ways to work with Alaska Natives. The new millennium lodge may even be an international lodge group with lodges in Alaska and other worldwide locations, either owned by a hotel or motel chain or other like business—an alien or absent owner business.*

*I'm not entirely sure what the future holds for the Bristol Bay lodge business, but the 2000 and beyond lodge business will look as different from today's lodge business as Petersen's Kulik Lodge is different from Bud Branham's first cabin at Kakhonak Falls.*

*I'm thankful my lot fell where I've been able to fish Alaska for the last 40 years. I trust that the lodges will be there for the next 40 years. I hope I can fish them all—again!*

**Richard Van Druten**

Richard worked five years as a guide in Bristol Bay before starting his own business, Rapids Camp Lodge.

*Making a living at what you love is essentially defined as success. To experience what you love, even for a brief spell, is fortunate. Considering the world population, there are only a few of us who have been fortunate enough to experience the richness of Bristol Bay. My first impression of the Bristol Bay ecosystem instilled in me a passion unlike any other and which does not seem to dissipate. I believed I could help make a difference by throwing my influence behind conservation and preservation of the great Bristol Bay fish resource–even if that meant confronting another person downriver who was mishandling his catch or doing something that broke the code of ethics that a few of us uphold, stand by and understand.*

*There are those in the lodge family that have been in Bristol Bay for many years, and there are those that are new to the area. There is a certain code of ethics and understanding that is recognized by a few people in this game of ours. They gel together; it is a cohesiveness that only a few really share. There is a tone and an atmosphere that these individuals exude. You can meet these folks on a river, in a bar, almost anywhere in the world and you just know. These are the good guys.*

*Unfortunately, there are others in the lodge business. There are many players in our business. Some belong and some do not. Some of us are here for reasons that go far beyond a job. Lately it just seems like anyone with a few bucks to throw around is able to start a lodge. I believe that different ethics and values are being introduced which scare me as to the future of Bristol Bay. I think that there seems to be a lot of folks in the business for the wrong reasons. They are trying to capitalize on the tourism market and the money they think it will yield. There is a great opportunity in the fishing lodge business, or perhaps I should say there was. Somehow, there doesn't seem to be as much heart in the lodge business as there used to be.*

*For anyone pondering a step into the business, I offer the following advice: Research the code of ethics before you enter this game or you will screw it up for all of us. Learn the etiquette if you don't possess it, and make sure you enter into this wilderness with surgical precision, maneuvering around any local or political controversy with minimal impact.*

**Lani Waller**

Lani owns and operates Worldwide Anglers, a booking service in Novato, California. Lani has written numerous fishing books and his articles appear in nearly every fishing magazine. Lani has been a prominent advocate of the Alaska fishery since his first trip north in 1977.

*I fished at the Angler's Paradise lodges at Kulik, Brooks and Grosvenor steadily for 15 years. I started traveling to Alaska in 1977. Some of my best fishing memories are of those locations. It was a great fishery then, and it is a great fishery now. I think the future for Alaska fishing lodges will continue to see more pressure on the key watersheds. There might be some crowding, at least as I would define it after having first fished there in 1977. I believe there will be more competition and more people will be traveling to fish in Alaska, perhaps even more people coming from different parts of the world than we have now.*

*I'd like to see the State of Alaska give some consideration to restricting guide permits and leases, but that might take a long time. Other than that, I think it will be business as usual for the lodges in Alaska. I think the fishing will stay good. Alaska is a great destination and offers the angler a wide choice of fish and fishing lodges.*

**Sonny Petersen**

Born into the fishing lodge industry, Sonny started his career as an infant. Growing up at Grosvenor Lodge and entering the guiding arena as early as he did makes Sonny Petersen the most experienced lodge operator in Alaska, bar none. He is currently the president of Katmailand, Inc. In my opinion, Sonny is also the best airplane driver with whom I've ever had the privilege to work.

*I sort of cheated because I had the opportunity to read "Rods and Wings" before writing this, including others' comments about the future. In fact, after I read it, I actually asked Bo to let me change my comments. I've always been very optimistic about the future of the lodge business in Southwest Alaska, but I don't think I ever really knew why until after I read the book.*

*What I find interesting is that the guys newest to the area seem more optimistic then those who first arrived back in the 70s and 80s. That is not hard to understand because after all, you would have to be either insane or optimistic about the future of the business to have recently invested so much of your time and money into it.*

*Some of those who came on the scene in the 70s and 80s, whether they are lodge guys, agents, or legend types mention overcrowding and too many lodges. What they can't possibly know or understand is that that's what I thought back when they showed up. But I don't feel that way anymore, and as you will see by his comments, neither does my dad. I don't think he ever did. Now I believe I know why.*

*First, as it has turned out, the arrival of new players in the 70s and 80s didn't ruin the country or the business after all. Sure it was different and in some ways not as good, but not ruined. I guess now I'm more used to change than those guys are. Second, if the really new guys are optimistic, I should be more so because our lodges have better locations. And these new operators may be more qualified than the oldtimers are to assess the future marketability of the area. They see the area much as others did before them, as a land of wilderness, opportunity and great fishing. If it looks like that to them, that's probably what it looks like to first-time fishermen. It doesn't matter what I think. What future clients think is what will matter. And finally, it's true, the fishing is every bit as good as ever. We have caught several all-time camp record fish in the 90s. If you think its gone to hell you need to come to Kulik or Grosvenor and let me take you up the river in the evening after the fly-out boys have gone home. Its just like it was in the 50s.*

*What worries me more is the increase in government oversight, regulations, and meddling. About the only agency we don't have to deal with today is the Atomic Energy Commission. Those asking for government regulation and use limits in hopes of holding onto the past better be careful, they just might get what they're asking for.*

*I remember,for example, when we had the only boat on American Creek. Eventually Ed Seiler put a boat there and then Ted Gerkin. A few years later, after Seiler sold his lodge to Dick Mathews several others got into the act. The three of us who were there first cried for limits and the Park Service implemented a permit system. Well, guess who didn't get permits? Yup, you guessed it, the three of us who were there first were aced out. Government feels no loyalty or obligation toward pioneers. In fact, they seem to resent anyone who knows more or has been around longer. We finally got an American Creek permit attached to our park concession contract but Mathews and Gerkin never did get one. Nope, I'll take the competition over the government any old day.*

*I believe that the lodge business by nature has been somewhat self-regulating. Furthermore, I believe the fishing will stay good for a long time to come, and I certainly believe our lodge system will continue to lead the industry well into the next century.*

*Look at my dad's comments about the future. There's no pessimism there. He seems to be just as much a visionary as he was back in the fifties. He was the Thomas Edison and Henry Ford of our industry. Maybe I'll be the Bill Gates. If I were to make a bet on whose prophecies will come true, it would be Ray Petersen's*

### Raymond I. Petersen

The father of the sportfishing lodge industry in Alaska. Throughout his long and distinguished career in the airline and lodge business, Ray had an uncanny ability to gauge the future. Ray told me that he couldn't speak for the industry in general, but made clear and specific comments pertaining to the Angler's Paradise Camps he started.

*As far as the lodges go, I don't see any difference at Kulik in the next 10 years, but I do see change in the next 50 years, assuming it is still in private ownership. The Park Service may want to take over, but based on private ownership, I can see a 30- or 40-room hotel and a paved runway. I see bikers and other outdoor enthusiasts utilizing Hammersly Lake and the surrounding area. Kulik will switch from being primarily a fishing lodge to multiple-use facility. There may be fly-outs like we have today, but God only knows what kind of flying machines you'll have in 50 years, considering the progress we've already had.*

*Ten years from now it appears that Brooks will see major changes. I'd like to see more capacity at Brooks Lodge. There should be more accommodations for overnight guests at Brooks Lodge. In the early days, we planned to have accommodations for 100 people at Brooks. They cut us back to 64 in the early 1960s but there is no reason not to expand the facility.*

### Bo Bennett

I made my first trip to Bristol Bay in 1966. I worked as a pilot-guide for several lodges in Bristol Bay before becoming the manager at Kulik Lodge in 1990.

*In my not so humble opinion, as long as there are fish to catch and fishermen to catch them, Alaska will remain the primary freshwater hotspot. Like many others, I believe that Bristol Bay is the best freshwater fishing destination in the world, and it will stay the best.*

*There is no doubt that there will be changes in the lodge industry based on lifestyle changes in the population. There has already been a tremendous change in ecological attitude and this has helped the fishing industry. Based on the philosophical changes I have seen and heard, I can see a day when all sportfishing is catch-and-release fishing, and this too, will be good for the fishing lodge industry. I can also see a time when Eco-tourists may outnumber fishing guests in Bristol Bay. I'm not certain that the shift from fishing to Eco-tourism will occur before I retire from the lodge business, but I believe it will happen.*

*During the past few years, I've been impressed with the number of parents who have been bringing their youngsters to the Angler's Paradise lodges. There is no doubt that the lodge industry that has developed over the past 50 seasons will continue to mature, evolve, and change. There is also no doubt that the next century will produce a new set of players eager for the challenge, and that, too, will be good for the lodges. More than anything else, I believe that the great lodges of Bristol Bay will continue to host and thrill visitors far into the future. The area is huge and can certainly support any multi-use program that may develop.*

*If you have experienced fishing in the Bristol Bay watershed, you owe it to yourself to return often and return with your children. If you have not fished our fabled waters, I trust you will book a trip soon, so that you, too, can experience the trip of a lifetime.*

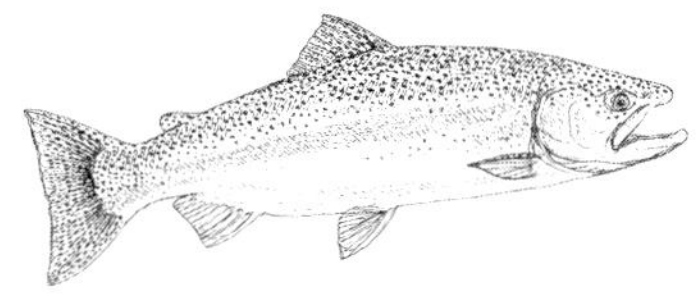

# Chapter 10
# The Ten Important Firsts in Bristol Bay Lodge History

"A fact is like a sack—it won't stand up if it's empty. To make it stand up, first you have to put in it all the reasons and feelings that caused it in the first place."
*Luigi Pirandello*

Compiling the "top ten" has not been an easy task. Because there were no other fishing businesses in Bristol Bay that were in direct competition with the Angler's Paradise Lodges until 1965, it is not surprising to discover that many firsts occurred at Ray Petersen's facilities. Obviously, the Angler's Paradise Lodges hired the first lodge employees and they hired the first fishing guides. As far as airplanes go, Angler's Paradise Lodges were the first to use most of the different types of airplanes that have seen lodge service such as the Noordyn Norseman, the military surplus converted PBY, the de Havilland Beaver, the Pilatus Porter, the Beechcraft T-50, and the Cessna 206. The Angler's Paradise Lodge at Kulik was the first to have an airstrip, and the first to have scheduled airline service directly to the lodge.

In making my selection of the prominent firsts, I selected those firsts that were most important to the development of the lodge industry. In my opinion, the ten most important events in the history of the lodge business in Bristol Bay are listed on the following pages.

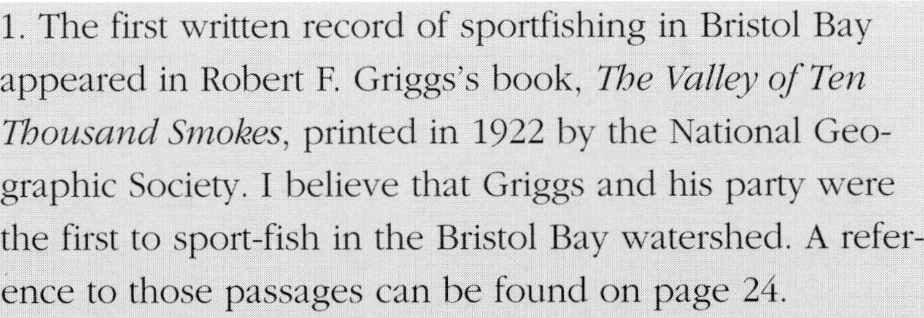

1. The first written record of sportfishing in Bristol Bay appeared in Robert F. Griggs's book, *The Valley of Ten Thousand Smokes*, printed in 1922 by the National Geographic Society. I believe that Griggs and his party were the first to sport-fish in the Bristol Bay watershed. A reference to those passages can be found on page 24.

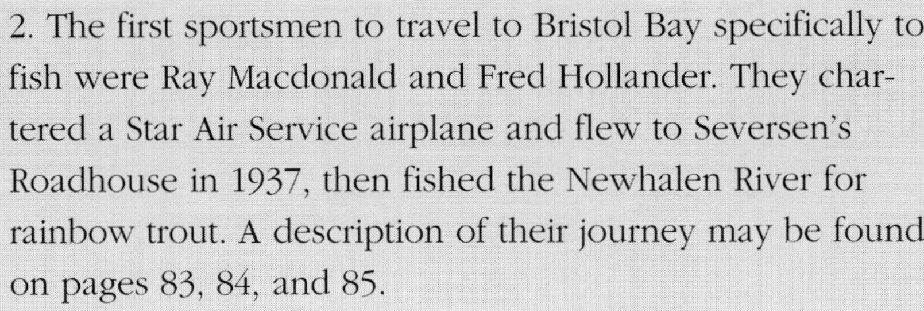

2. The first sportsmen to travel to Bristol Bay specifically to fish were Ray Macdonald and Fred Hollander. They chartered a Star Air Service airplane and flew to Seversen's Roadhouse in 1937, then fished the Newhalen River for rainbow trout. A description of their journey may be found on pages 83, 84, and 85.

3. The first building erected in Bristol Bay specifically to be a sportsman's lodge facility was started in 1949 by Bud Branham at the site of Kakhonak Falls on Iliamna Lake. Bud's own description may be found on page 93.

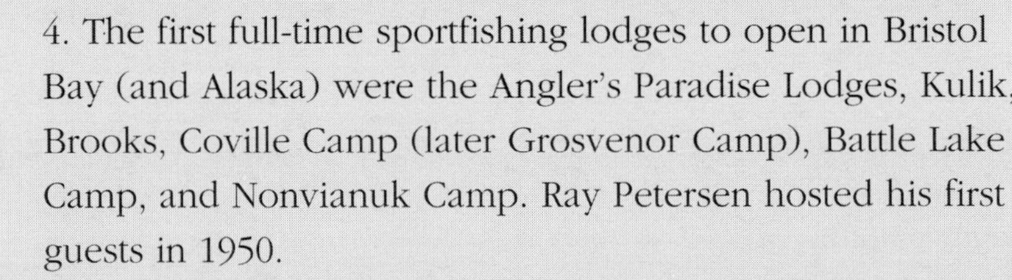

4. The first full-time sportfishing lodges to open in Bristol Bay (and Alaska) were the Angler's Paradise Lodges, Kulik, Brooks, Coville Camp (later Grosvenor Camp), Battle Lake Camp, and Nonvianuk Camp. Ray Petersen hosted his first guests in 1950.

5. First Alaska lodge business to have a booth at a Lower-48 sport show was the Angler's Paradise Camps in 1951. The historical account may be found on pages 107 and 108.

6. The first full-length fishing movie made in Bristol Bay was completed in 1950 and was shown at the first sportsman's shows and on major television stations during the sport show tour of 1951. Don Horter and Chief Needahbeh made the 16-mm movie at the Angler's Paradise Lodges. A July 12, 1950 article in the *Anchorage Times* references the film. The article may be found on page 106.

7. The first fishing rod manufacturer to make fishing rods and other equipment specifically for Alaska fishing was the Shakespeare Corporation. Their fishing tackle catalog of 1952 featured equipment designed for Alaska after the visit of company President Henry Shakespeare and C.W. "Opie" Davis. A reprint from the catalog is presented on page 113.

8. Other than owner-operators Ray Petersen and Bud and Dennis Branham, Ed Seiler became the first man to pilot-guide at a fishing lodge. Operating his float-equipped Cessna 180 out of King Salmon, Ed contracted with the Angler's Paradise manager John Walatka to do numerous pilot guiding assignments between the early 1950s and the early 1960s. Unlike pilot-guides in the 1990s who live at the lodge sites, Ed never stayed at Kulik Lodge. He picked up his clients at the lodge in the morning and then went back to King Salmon at the end of each guiding mission. References to Ed Seiler may be found in chapter 4.

9. Northern Consolidated Vacations became the dealer for Alaska and then brought the first jet boats to the state in 1960. The boats brought to Alaska were 16-feet in length and featured V-hulls and 6-cylinder Ford engines and they were manufactured by Buehler Turbocraft Boats. Besides the boats taken to Brooks, Kulik and Grosvenor, two others were deployed as demonstrators at Bethel and Dillingham. Former Kulik guide Dave Shuster was one of the first to use this new technology. A story about Dave and these boats begins on page 161.

10. Ray Petersen's Angler's Paradise Lodges at Brooks, Grosvenor and Kulik became the first lodges to reach 50 seasons of continuous operation during the fishing season of 1999.

# Chapter 11
# Names of Interest in the Bristol Bay Watershed and Alaska

The following place names and their origins are found in and presented from *The Dictionary of Alaska Place Names,* by Donald J. Orth, Geological Survey Professional Paper 567, United States Government Printing Office, Washington, DC, 1967. In a few instances, I have included a note or two presenting both local and traditional use.

**Alaska**: The name "Alaska" seems to have been gradually established by local use; vaguely applied at first to a supposed island, later found to be the southwestern end of the Alaska Peninsula. The application of the name gradually developed from this beginning to include the whole area. The Russians officially designated it "Russian America" prior to its 1867 purchase by the United States. The name "Alaska" was proposed in 1867 for official acceptance by W. H. Seward, U.S. Secretary of State, the Honorable Charles Sumner, Senator and Chairman of the Committee on Foreign Relations, and by Maj. General W.H. Halleck, Commander of the Military Division of the Pacific. The name and its application to the state and the peninsula were well established in the late 1880s when W. H. Dall wrote:

> *This name, now applied to the whole of our territory, is a corruption, very far removed from the original word ... called by the natives Al-ak-shak or Al-ay-ek-sa. From Alayeksa the name became Alaksa, Alashka, Aliaska and finally Alaska ... .*

**American Creek**: Named in 1950 by Bill Hammersly of King Salmon. (Bill Hammersly lived for many years at the Nonvianuk River and worked for NCA and Ray Petersen as a promoter for the Angler's Paradise Camps.) Vestiges of Bill's cabin can still be seen at the outlet of Nonvianuk Lake.

**Agulowak River**: Eskimo name, "Ahguhlerok" said to mean "many rapids," reported in 1910 by H.C. Fassett and published in 1929 as Agulowak River by the USBF.

**Aleknagik Lake**: Eskimo name published by Lt. Sarachev as "Alyaknagik." The present spelling of the name is a transliteration from Capt. Tebenkov. Jackson (1866) stated that the name Alaknakik means "well studded with beautiful pine-covered islands" which seems a bit fanciful but may carry the general meaning. From a trader named Mittendorf, J.E. Spurr and W.S. Post, USGS, recorded the name as "Agoulouikatuk," meaning "testicle."

**Alagnak River**: Eskimo name shown as "Alagnak" by Capt. Tebenkov, IRN, on an 1852 map. It is said by R.H Geoghegan to mean "wild raspberry."

**Anchorage:** Alaska's largest city, established in 1913 as the construction camp and headquarters of the Alaska railroad to be built from Seward to Fairbanks. A post office was established in 1914. It was early referred to as "Ship Creek" and "Woodrow", but with the establishment of the post office in 1914-15, the present name soon became firmly established. The name was derived from that of Knik anchorage immediately offshore from the new camp. Its population was estimated to be 6,000 in 1917, but in 1920 it was officially 1,856. In 1930 it was 2,277; 3,495 in 1939 and 11,254 in 1950. The 1998 estimate was 244,500.

**Battle Lake**: Local translation of an Eskimo name was reported by K.F. Mather, USGS, 1925.

**Becharof Lake**: Named in 1868 by W. H. Dall USC&GS, for the navigator "Bocherov" IRN, who was at Kodiak in 1788. The Russian Hydrology Dept. published the name "Oz Ugashek" on a map in 1852.

**Bristol Bay**: Named in 1778 by Capt. Cook, RN, "in honor of the Earl of Bristol."

**Brooks Lake**: Named in 1919 by R.F. Griggs of the National Geographic Society for Alfred Hulse Brooks. The Eskimo name was Ketivik, to which R.H. Sargent, USGS, in 1923 gives the long meaning "beavers broke their houses a long time ago."

**Copper River**: A local name reported in 1954 by the USGS.

**Coville lake**: Named in 1919 by R.F. Griggs of the National Geographic Society for Frederick V. Coville, chairman of the committee on research for the National Geographic Society.

**Contact Creek**: Descriptive name given by R.H. Sargent, USGS, in 1923 "because it flows along a fault in the rock."

**Egegik**: Eskimo name published in 1835 by Adm. A.J. von Krusenstern, IRN, as "Ougagouck." It was shown in 1888 as "Ugaguk River" by USBF and reported in 1915 as "Egigek River" by mineral surveyor G.A. Parks.

**Enchanted Lake**: Named by Ed Seiler in 1963 because the small, beautiful lake reminded him of one of his favorite places in Maine, Enchanted Pond.

**Elmendorf Air Force Base**: Named in honor of Captain Hugh M. Elmendorf. The captain was one of several Air Corps officers between the great wars destined for greatness. He was noted for his aerial gunnery skills. Unfortunately for the Captain, he crashed on Friday the 13th, 1933 during a series of acrobatic flying. When construction first started on the air base in Anchorage, it was called Elmendorf Field.

**Funnel Creek**: Named by R.H. Sargent of the USGS in 1923 because of the strong winds encountered in the stream valley.

**Grosvenor Lake**: Named in 1921 by R.F. Griggs, National Geographic Society. Both lakes Coville and Grosvenor lakes were called the Savonoski Lakes by the National Geographic Society in 1919; in 1923 both lakes were called "Alinak Lake" by the American Geographic Society, after a former Native village near Lake Grosvenor's outlet. R. H. Sargent, USGS, reported the Indian name "Kalhvit" in 1923.

**Grosvenor Camp**: Name reported in 1957 by the AMS. Previously called Coville Camp, the name was changed after a visit to the camp by Gilbert Hovey Grosvenor, 1875-1966, National Geographic Society.

**Hammersly Lake**: Reported in 1951 by USGS.

**Homer**: This town appears to have been established on or near the Homer Spit in November 1895. Both the town and the spit were named for Homer Pennock, a prospector who worked in the Cook Inlet area. A post office was established in the town in 1896.

**Igiugig**: Name of a fishing village where a post office was established in 1934.

**Iliamna Lake**: Native name reported as "Oz Bol Ilyamna" meaning "Big Ilyamna Lake" on a Russian chart in 1852. The lake was earlier called "Oz Shelekhovo" meaning "Lake Shelekov" on an 1802 Russian map. According to G.C. Martin, USGS, Iliamna is said to be the name of a mythical black fish, supposed to inhabit this lake, which bites holes in the bidarkas of bad Natives.

**Iliuk Arm, Naknek Lake**: Eskimo name published in 1922 by R.F. Griggs, National Geographic Society, for this very deep lake. On some Russian maps "Iliuk" is applied to Naknek Lake. In 1923, R.H. Sargent, USGS, reports another Native name as "Nanva-Nelhook," meaning "very bad lake."

**JoJo Lake**: Local name reported in early Angler's Paradise guest registers. This lake, named for Johanna Walatka, is a prime location for large rainbow trout.

**Kamishak River**: Native name published by Lt. Sarichev, (1826 Map) IRN, as "Kamyshak River"

**Katmai National Monument**: Named for Mt. Katmai. It was established on September 24, 1918, and enlarged in 1931, then again in 1942. Katmai National Park was signed into existence by President Jimmy Carter in 1984.

**King Salmon**: The King Salmon post office was established in 1949 at the King Salmon Air Force base.

**Kukaklik Lake**: Native name published by Capt. Tebenkov, IRN, on an 1849 map as "Kukaklek Oz" or "Kukaklek Lake."

**Kulik Lake**: Local name reported in 1923 as Coolic Lake by R.H. Sargent, USGS, and edited to Kulik in 1927. Literally translated from the Native language to mean "upper lake."

**Kvichak River**: Eskimo name reported by Lt. Zagoskin, IRN, in 1842-44 as "Reka Kvinchagak." It is shown, however, as flowing directly into the Bering Sea at about Hazen Bay and thus may refer to another stream. E. W. Nelson, U.S. Signal Service, traveled along the stream in 1879, and gave the Eskimo name as "Kivvichavak" from which the present spelling is derived.

**Lake Clark**: Named after John W. Clark, a leader of one of the first exploratory expeditions to the lake in 1891. Mr. Clark became one of the first settlers in the Lake Clark area. He also ran the trading post at Nushagak in the late 1800s.

**Moraine Creek**: Named in 1923 by K.F. Mather, USGS.

**Mortuary Cove (Naknek Lake)**: Local name applied after the Audubon Society scientists harvested and dissected hundreds of local bird specimens in this cove near the Angler's Paradise Brooks Camp. They chose to do their work in this cove rather than at the camp so that no guests would happen by and be disturbed by the vast number of specimens harvested in the name of research.

**Murray Lake**: Local name published in 1951 by the USGS.

**Naknek**: *Variations are:* Fort Souworoff, Fort Suvaroff, Fort Suworof, Kinghiak, Kingiak, Kiniaak, Kinuiak, Naugvik, Pawik, Suvarov, Suwarof, Suworof. Originally an Eskimo village reported about 1821 by Capt. Vasiliav, IRN, who gave its name as "Naugiek," 1826. Lt. Sarichev, IRN, reported it as "Naugvik." Spelled "Naknek" by Capt. Tebenkov, IRN, in 1852. The Russians built a post called "Fort Surarov" at or near the village, named after the nearby point of land. The 1880 census lists the name as "Kinghiak." Its population in 1880 was 51. The Naknek post office was established in 1907.

**Newhalen River**: Eskimo name reported in 1891 as "Noghelin Painga" meaning mouth of the Noghelin" by A. B. Schanz in the 1890 Census. A.G. Maddren, USGS, and represents pronunciation of the Eskimo name reported the present spelling in 1900 by English-speaking prospectors.

**Nonvianuk Lake**: Eskimo name "Nanwheyenuk" published in 1951 by USGS. Local Native usage implies the literal translation "cry of the loon."

**Nushagak River**: Named about 1809 by the Russian navigator, Ivan Vasiliev, published as Reka Nushegak by Lt. Sarachev, IRN, in 1826. Capt. James Cook called this feature "Bristol River" in 1778.

**Nuyakuk Lake**: The Eskimo name "Tikchik River" was published in 1898 by USC&GS; recorded as Nu-ya-kok or [Tikchik]" on a 1910 manuscript map by H.C. Fassett, USBF.

**Ole Creek**: Local name published in 1956 by USGS. Several longtime residents of the area tell me that Ole Wassenkari is the "Ole" of Ole Creek.

**Pile Bay**: Name shown as Spile Bay in 1906 by J.W. Walker on a manuscript map but shortened by local usage to Pile Bay. Name published by Martin and Kantz (1912), USGS.

**Rainbow River**: Named in 1923 by R.H. Sargent's USGS party because six rainbows were seen there.

**Savonoski River**: named in 1919 as "Savonoski" by R.F. Griggs, National Geographic Society, after the abandoned Eskimo village at its mouth.

**Strike Creek**: So named by R.H. Sargent's USGS field party in 1923 because the stream followed the strike of the underlying rock. Published by K.F. Mather, 1925.

**Takayofo Creek**: Native name said to mean "king salmon" reported in 1923 by R. H. Sargent, USGS

**Talarik Creek**: Name published as Talarik Creek by C.G. Martin in 1912. Local usage added the adjective "upper" to differentiate it from lower Talarik Creek to the west.

**Tikchik Lake**: Eskimo name reported in 1891 as "Tikshik" variously written as "Tikchik" and "Tukshik." Ivan Petroff in the 1880 census recorded the name Lake Nushagak but it may also apply to Lake Beverly. The Eskimo name "Nu-yu-kok" and "Nuyukuk" appear on a 1910 manuscript map by H. C. Fassett, USBF. The name "Tikchik Lake" was adopted because of long local usage.

**Ugashik River**: Eskimo name transcribed in French as "Ougatchik Riviere" in 1828 by Capt. Lutke, IRN. At the same time Capt. M.N. Staniukovich of the corvette Moller, called it "Soulima" in his journal and for many years there was considerable confusion concerning the name of the stream or streams. W.H. Dall gave the present spelling in 1868.

*Abbreviations:*
*IRN = Imperial Russian Navy*
*USGS = U.S. Geological Survey*
*USBF = U.S. Bureau of Fisheries*
*USFS = U.S. Forest Service*

# Afterthoughts
## by Ray Petersen

On my arrival in Alaska in 1934, sportfishing was the last conceivable activity that entered my mind. I was more concerned about my career as an aviator. My fishing experience had been confined to angling with worms and grasshoppers on Owl Creek at my home on a Wyoming ranch.

My first Alaskan fishing experience occurred during my prospecting season in the Fairview Hills at the base of Mt. McKinley in 1934. Lake Creek and Sunflower Creek were teeming with grayling, rainbow and Dolly Varden. The fish were caught with fly-fishing gear that was quite primitive. The favorite lure for grayling was the fly tied to imitate the mosquito and the black gnat. The purpose of the catch was to eat them. The thought of fishing as a sport didn't even enter my mind, or that of the prospectors. Further fishing experience was gained during my flying on the Kuskokwim and Good News Bay regions.

My most disappointing fishing trip occurred during a prospecting trip to Columbia Creek, a tributary of the Kuskokwim River. Big Fritz Wolters, an old sourdough who had hit all the mining camps from Dawson City to Nome and then the platinum discovery at Goodnews Bay, was my companion. Our Eskimo guide, Willie Kysali, resided at Akiak on the Kuskokwim River.

As we progressed up the small Columbia Creek, the stream was alive with grayling. Our diet of bacon, eggs and sourdough pancakes became monotonous. The clouds of mosquitoes were so great that the grayling showed no interest in our lures. It goes without saying that we were not feasting on fish; a net would have been handy.

which operated from Anchorage into Bristol Bay.

By this time, fishing became an integral part of my life. The cannery operations before

*In my opinion Ray Petersen has been the guiding force in the development of the fishing lodge business we have today. Ray is shown here at various times during the first fifty years of lodge operations. Ray has earned the title, "Father of Alaska's Sportfishing Lodges." Ray Petersen Collection*

Later in 1943, at the time of the hostilities with the Third Reich, my company, Ray Petersen Flying Service with its grandfathered certificate to serve the Kuskokwim River and the platinum mine at Goodnews Bay, purchased Bristol Bay Air Service,

Pearl Harbor were conducted by cannery ships that brought cannery workers, fishermen, and all the paraphernalia for canning fish into Bristol Bay. When the war with Japan started, it was no longer prudent to conduct that operation due to the threat of

Japanese submarines. Therefore, cannery workers were brought into Anchorage and flown to Bristol Bay.

During the periodic closure of commercial fishing to permit escapement to the spawning grounds, we would fly the cannery superintendents on a busman's holiday to the trout streams. The fishing gear was mostly Colorado spinners with big hooks and gobs of salmon eggs. The catch was taken back to the cannery where the resident chef prepared the feast. One exception was Nick Bez, the owner of Columbia River Packers. When I suggested a trout-fishing trip, he remarked, "The only way to catch a fish is with a net."

This description might shock the sportsmen of this day, but you must keep in mind that we were only a few years from the time when a bounty was put on trout tails in Bristol Bay to protect the salmon runs. Fortunately, the salmon biologists and commercial fishermen finally concluded this was not the problem and that practice was abandoned.

This experience made us aware of the great potential for sportfishing in Bristol Bay. The problem was, with this charter type of operation, it was inconvenient to fly from what is now King Salmon into the area and then fly back every day. It was decided to create camps in the area.

By the time our camps were established in 1950, sportfishing in Alaska was pretty much confined to adventurers and purists. As my old friend, Cot Hayes, put it, a dedicated fisherman will sleep on a rock if the fish are there. Our primitive camps, therefore, were quite luxurious by that standard.

As news of the fabulous fishing in Bristol Bay became increasingly well known throughout the world, the attraction was such that a less hardy type of fisherman began to take advantage of our facilities. Their ladies liked a little more comfortable accommodation. Therefore, we transitioned from tent camps to log cabins. One old gentleman who had become a perennial remarked, "when the flush toilets come–the fishing goes." We never saw him again.

Our 9-by-9-foot cabins were configured with four bunks and our 16-by-16-foot cabins were configured with eight. There were no complaints from their party when Baron and Nicky Hilton arrived with a group of eight and checked into one cabin, which they promptly dubbed the Kulik Hilton.

Those were exciting and fun-filled days. I am proud that we have evolved during the last 50 years into what we have today. The ability to provide luxurious accommodations by wilderness standards relying completely on air support is gratifying to me, and I hope has guaranteed the satisfaction of all who visit the lodges that have developed over the years.

A chronology of this period and its development by the myriad of lodges is, I think, of importance to anyone who has fished at or plans to visit one of the great lodges in Bristol Bay. For this, I thank Bo Bennett for the prodigious effort he expended producing the foregoing chapters.

# Bibliography


Anderson, Ralph W. & Larssen, A.K., *Fish & Ships,* Bonanza Books, New York, New York 1959

Annabel, Russell, *Hunting and Fishing in Alaska,* Knoppf Co., New York, New York 1948

Bancroft, Hubert Howe, *History of Alaska,* Antiquarian Press Ltd., New York, New York 1886

Banfield, Norman C., *History of Taku Lodge,* Juneau Empire, Juneau, Alaska July 6, 1966

Bodeau, Jean, *Katmai National Park and Preserve,* Alaska Natural History Association and Greatland Graphics, Anchorage, Alaska 1992

Bohn, Dave, *Rambles Through an Alaskan Wild: Katmai and the Valley of the Smokes,* Capra Press, Santa Barbara, California 1979

Bower, Ward T., *Alaska Fishery and Fur Seal Industries: 1940,* U.S. Dept. of the Interior, Fish and Wildlife Service, U.S. Printing Office, Washington DC 1942

Branham, Bud, *Sourdough and Swahili,* Amwell Press, Clinton, New Jersey 1989

Calahane, Victor H., *A Biological Study of Katmai National Monument,* The Smithsonian Institute, Washington DC 1959

Colby, Merle, *A Guide to Alaska,* McMillan Co., New York, New York 1939

Dall, W. H. Essay; *The Harriman Alaska Expedition 1899,* Doubleday, Page & Co., New York, New York 1901-1914

Fedorova, Svetlana G., *The Russian Population in Alaska and California Late 18th Century-1867,* Limestone Press, Kingston, Ontario 1973

Ford, Corey, *Where the Sea Breaks Its Back,* Alaska Northwest Publishing Company 1992

Gerkin, Ted, *Gamble at Iliamna,* Anchor Publishing, Homer, Alaska, 1988

Greenbank, John, *Love & Stuff,* World Press, Denver, Colorado, 1958

*Griggs, Robert F., The Valley of Ten Thousand Smokes,* National Geographic Society, Washington DC 1922

Kaniut, Larry, *Alaska Bear Tales,* Alaska Northwest Publishing Company, Anchorage, Alaska 1983

Lawing, Nellie, *Alaska Nellie*, the author, Seattle, Washington 1940

McDonald, Ray E., *"Giants of the Newhalen",* Alaska Sportsman Magazine, Anchorage, Alaska September, 1938

Norris, Frank B., Fisheries in Alaska's Past, a Symposium, *Sport Fishing in Early Alaska,* Alaska Historical Commission, Anchorage, Alaska 1986

Norris, Frank B., *Tourism in Katmai Country,* National Park Service, Anchorage, Alaska 1992

Orth, Donald, *Dictionary of Alaska Place Names,* U.S. Government Printing Office, Washington DC 1967

Place, Marion T., *New York to Rome,* Macmillan Co., New York, New York 1972

Reeve, Robert "Bob", *Our Alaska Business and People,* Meed Title, Anchorage, Alaska, February 1975

Repine, Jim, *Alaska Angling Adventures,* the author, Anchorage, Alaska 1983

Tewkesbury, David & William, *Who's Who in Alaska,* Tewkesbury Co., Juneau, Alaska 1947

Tewkesbury, David & William, *Alaska Business Index,* Tewkesbury Co., Juneau, Alaska 1947


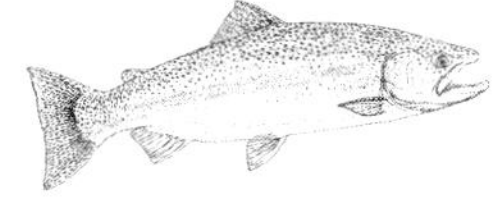

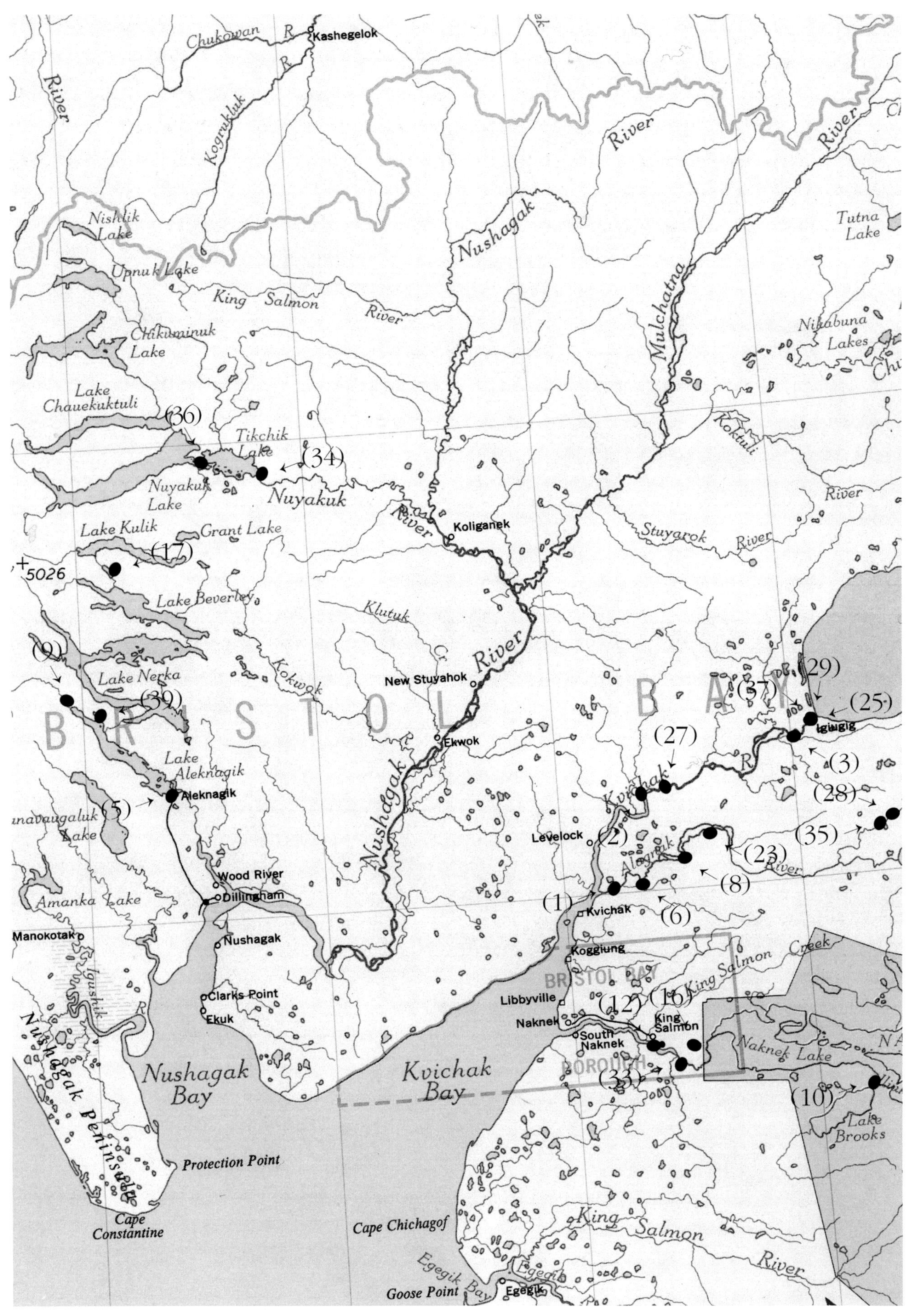

Kashegelok
Chukowan R
Koguktuk R
River
Nishlik Lake
Upnuk Lake
King Salmon River
Chikuminuk Lake
Lake Chauekuktuli
Nushagak River
Mulchatna River
Tutna Lake
Nikabuna Lakes
Koktuli River
Tikchik Lake
Nuyakuk Lake
Nuyakuk River
Koliganek
Stuyarok River
Lake Kulik
Grant Lake
Lake Beverley
5026
Klutuk Cr
Kokwok
Lake Nerka
New Stuyahok
BRISTOL BAY
Ekwok
Lake Aleknagik
Aleknagik
Kvichak R
Levelock
Alagnak River
Iguigig
Wood River
Dillingham
Amanka Lake
Manokotak
Kvichak
Nushagak
Koggiung
King Salmon Creek
BRISTOL BAY BOROUGH
Libbyville
Clarks Point
Ekuk
Naknek
South Naknek
King Salmon
Naknek Lake
Lake Brooks
Igushik R
Nushagak Bay
Kvichak Bay
Nushagak Peninsula
Protection Point
Cape Constantine
Cape Chichagof
King Salmon River
Egegik Bay
Egegik
Goose Point
(1)
(2)
(3)
(5)
(6)
(8)
(9)
(10)
(12)
(16)
(17)
(23)
(25)
(27)
(28)
(29)
(33)
(34)
(35)
(36)
(37)
(39)

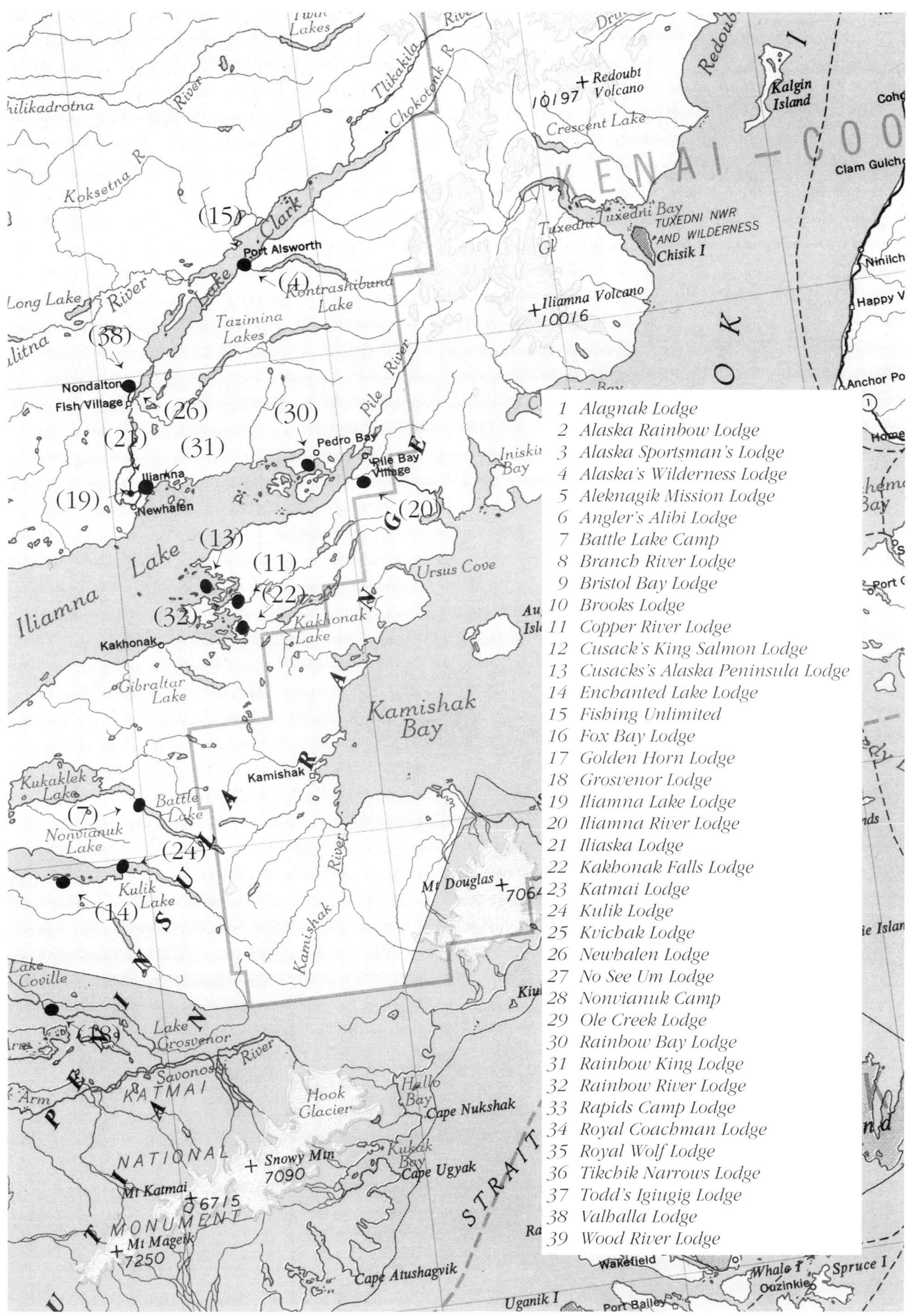
1 Alagnak Lodge
2 Alaska Rainbow Lodge
3 Alaska Sportsman's Lodge
4 Alaska's Wilderness Lodge
5 Aleknagik Mission Lodge
6 Angler's Alibi Lodge
7 Battle Lake Camp
8 Branch River Lodge
9 Bristol Bay Lodge
10 Brooks Lodge
11 Copper River Lodge
12 Cusack's King Salmon Lodge
13 Cusacks's Alaska Peninsula Lodge
14 Enchanted Lake Lodge
15 Fishing Unlimited
16 Fox Bay Lodge
17 Golden Horn Lodge
18 Grosvenor Lodge
19 Iliamna Lake Lodge
20 Iliamna River Lodge
21 Iliaska Lodge
22 Kakhonak Falls Lodge
23 Katmai Lodge
24 Kulik Lodge
25 Kvichak Lodge
26 Newhalen Lodge
27 No See Um Lodge
28 Nonvianuk Camp
29 Ole Creek Lodge
30 Rainbow Bay Lodge
31 Rainbow King Lodge
32 Rainbow River Lodge
33 Rapids Camp Lodge
34 Royal Coachman Lodge
35 Royal Wolf Lodge
36 Tikchik Narrows Lodge
37 Todd's Igiugig Lodge
38 Valhalla Lodge
39 Wood River Lodge
Port Alsworth
Nondalton
Fish Village
Iliamna
Newhalen
Pedro Bay
Pile Bay Village
Kakhonak
Kamishak
Iliamna Lake
Lake Clark
Kamishak Bay
Redoubt Volcano 10197
Iliamna Volcano 10016
Kalgin Island
Chisik I
TUXEDNI NWR AND WILDERNESS
Mt Douglas
Snowy Mtn 7090
Mt Katmai
Mt Mageik 7250
KATMAI NATIONAL MONUMENT
Cape Nukshak
Cape Ugyak
Cape Atushagvik
Uganik I
Kukaklek Lake
Nonvianuk Lake
Kulik Lake
Battle Lake
Lake Coville
Lake Grosvenor
Hook Glacier
Ursus Cove
Tazimina Lakes
Gibraltar Lake
Kakhonak Lake

# Index